Taxing Agricultural Land
in Developing Countries
Richard M. Bird

Agriculture is the largest economic sector in most countries
of Latin America, Africa, and Asia, and the taxation of
agricultural land is a potentially important instrument in the
development policies of such nations. But there is a large
gap between theory and practice, a gap that needs explaining.
In addition, there have been interesting changes in thought on
the role of such taxation in development.

Richard M. Bird covers all this in a complete rethinking
of the whole subject. His book is a distinguished successor to
Haskell P. Wald's classic study, *Taxation of Agricultural
Land in Underdeveloped Economies,* published by Harvard
University Press in 1959 and now out of print.

With abundant evidence Mr. Bird argues that the tax system
of each country, in order to be effective as part of development
policy, must be tailored carefully to the peculiar circumstances and objectives of that country.

Richard M. Bird is a professor in the Department of Political
Economy at the University of Toronto. He is presently
on leave, serving as Chief of the Tax Policy Division, Fiscal
Affairs Department, International Monetary Fund.

TAXING AGRICULTURAL LAND IN DEVELOPING COUNTRIES

HARVARD LAW SCHOOL INTERNATIONAL TAX PROGRAM

Taxing Agricultural Land in Developing Countries

RICHARD M. BIRD

HARVARD UNIVERSITY PRESS
CAMBRIDGE, MASSACHUSETTS
1974

FOR P, M, AND A

FOREWORD

This book carries forward the continuing interest of the International Tax Program in the tax systems of the less developed countries of the world, particularly the program's long concern with the problems associated with agricultural taxation. The program's 1954 conference and volume on *Agricultural Taxation and Economic Development* led to publication in 1959 of Haskell P. Wald's *Taxation of Agricultural Land in Underdeveloped Economies*, now out of print. Subsequent program publications dealing in whole or in part with agricultural tax problems, in addition to the general analyses of the tax laws of particular countries in the volumes of the World Tax Series, include Jonathan V. Levin, *The Export Economies* (1960), Ved P. Gandhi, *Tax Burden on Indian Agriculture* (1966), and Harley H. Hinrichs, *A General Theory of Tax Structure Change During Economic Development* (1966).

Professor Bird, educated in Canada until he entered Columbia University as a graduate student, came to the International Tax Program in 1961 on the recommendation of Columbia's Professor Carl S. Shoup. Since that time, he has been almost continuously associated with the International Tax Program either as a resident member of its staff (1961–1963, 1966–1968), as a collaborator on research, or through cooperative arrangements with the Harvard Development Advisory Service. During this period he has been in continuous touch with the developing countries through his students at Harvard and at the University of Toronto, his periods of residence abroad in Mexico and Colombia, his travels, especially in Latin America, and his prolific research and writing. He is currently on leave from the University of Toronto to serve as Chief of the Tax Policy Division of the International Monetary Fund's Department of Fiscal Affairs.

On the basis of both experience and theoretical analysis, Professor Bird's first recommendation in this book is that the poor countries and their advisers "concentrate on establishing a solidly based simple property tax with meaningful rates, rather than attempting to achieve primarily nonfiscal purposes . . ." (Chapter 13). The book provides a complete rethinking of the role of agricultural land taxation in the developing countries and a careful appraisal of the techniques for taxing agricultural land. Policy makers are given a comprehensive view of policy instruments and goals in the light of political forces and the limitations imposed by administrative capabilities. The book recognizes that the policy process itself is "incremental, sequential, and piecemeal" and that it is more important to identify and pay attention to the factual situation in each country than to give homage to abstract theory. The analytical chapters continually relate theory to the conditions prevailing in the developing countries. Repeated emphasis is given to the advantages of special assessments or betterment levies as an integral part of an agricultural land tax system. Both the analysis and the conclusions reflect Professor Bird's own considerable experience as brought to bear on the existing literature and the available experience of developed and developing countries. The book is essential reading for doers in this field as well as for teachers, students, and researchers.

With this book the Harvard Law School International Tax Program will enter its third decade of research and training. Major areas of research include the relation between economic development and taxation, taxation of international trade and investment, and comparative analysis of foreign tax systems. Specialized training for groups of about twenty officials and teachers from developing countries continues each year with a nine-month program of study. The activities focusing on the developing countries draw upon grants of the Ford Foundation.

OLIVER OLDMAN
Professor of Law and Director, International Tax Program
Harvard Law School
Cambridge, Massachusetts
August 1973

PREFACE

Agricultural taxation is an important instrument of development policy simply because agriculture is important. As the largest economic sector in most developing countries, agriculture inevitably plays a key role in their economic and social development, either as an obstacle to be overcome or as a foundation upon which to build. The sheer size of the agricultural sector in most countries makes its fiscal support to the government significant. Furthermore, the tax system provides a major means of transferring resources out of agriculture—a task often considered essential to effective development policy, especially since some of the ways in which agriculture may be taxed may also have a desirable effect on the volume, composition, and disposition of agricultural production.

In stark contrast to these apparently strong reasons for heavy taxation of agriculture (and the correspondingly vast literature urging such a policy), the agricultural sector is in fact taxed relatively lightly in most countries. Indeed, the inadequacy of the prevailing level of agricultural taxation is a recurrent theme in the literature on economic development and development finance. Similarly, recommendations to increase taxes on agriculture, particularly taxes on agricultural land, appear almost ritualistically in reports on the appropriate role of the fiscal system in this or that developing country. It is, indeed, hard to find a tax expert who has not at some time in his career made such a recommendation; it is perhaps even harder to find one whose recommendation for heavier agricultural taxation has been accepted.

The present book attempts to explain and reconcile differences between the theory and practice of agricultural taxation. This task is approached in several ways. One is by means of a critical survey of agricultural taxation in both theory and practice. Following a summary of the conventional wisdom on the role of agricultural taxation in developing countries in Chapter 1, the recent shift in emphasis in development thought to the task of generating agricultural surpluses instead of mobilizing preexisting surpluses is developed in Chapter 2. The implications of this new view for tax policy strengthen the general argument made in Part One concerning the inadequacy of general theorizing as a guide to appropriate agricultural tax policy in any particular country.

This theme is developed more extensively in Part Two, which surveys the state of agricultural taxation in the world today. Chapter 3 contains a quantitative overview of the revenue importance of agricultural taxation in different countries. Chapter 4 then surveys the major forms of direct agricultural taxation and makes clear the wide range of physical, historical, economic, social, and political conditions affecting agricultural tax systems. A principal theme in this book is that to be effective as part of development policy the tax system of each country must be tailored carefully to the peculiar circumstances and objectives of that country. Chapters 5 and 6 therefore examine in more detail the nature and role of land taxes in a number of countries in Latin America and Asia. Despite the inevitable deficiencies of these case studies, they have been included here for reasons well put by Doreen Warriner in her recent study *Land Reform in Principle and Practice* (Oxford, Eng.: Clarendon Press, 1969): "Since monographic treatment provides no basis for comparison, while abstract analysis leads to false generalization, it is necessary to combine both methods of treatment, using the experience of individual countries to illustrate generalization, and generalizing from the individual cases" (p. xviii).

Part Three of the book then takes another approach—a more systematic and detailed appraisal of the structure, administration, and economic effects of the variety of ways man has evolved to tax agricultural land. Following a taxonomic chapter on types of land taxes, the economic aspects of taxing agricultural land are developed at some length in Chapters 8 and 9. Chapter 10 then brings together a number of considerations affecting the equitableness of land taxes in the rural areas of poor countries. The final chapter of Part Three takes up the extremely important question of land tax administration, focusing particularly on the need to have a tax structure which will not be too badly distorted by poor administration and on possible simplifications in administrative structure to better fit the conditions of many developing countries.

Finally, Part Four sets forth those guides to policy which emerge from the previous discussion. The general outline of objectives and instruments in Part One, the survey and case histories of Part Two, and the analysis of Part Three are brought together in two concluding chapters to suggest appropriate patterns of agricultural land taxation for countries in different circumstances and with different policy objectives.

There are at least two basic problems with this study. The first is the weakness of the factual information on which much of the discussion depends. This book does not pretend to be a completely up-to-date or accurate catalogue of land tax practice throughout the world. Some of the information which it contains is inevitably out of date; some is doubtless partly misleading because it is out of context; some refers to situations (or even countries) which no longer exist. Since the role of this descriptive material is primarily illustrative, however, none of these defects affect the central arguments of the book. They do suggest, however, that caution should be exercised in citing data appearing here as authoritative.

A more serious problem is the artificial nature of the focus of this study on direct taxes on agriculture and on the land tax in particular. A good many interesting ways in which investible resources have been secured from agriculture in different countries, some of them quite successful in particular circumstances, are simply not discussed here or are mentioned only in passing. The principal justification for the scope of the present study lies less in logic than in the existence of an already substantial literature urging more use of agricultural land taxation in developing countries and the need to keep the study within bounds. Within the narrow range of vision imposed by the subject of this book, however, I have tried to be as thorough and as attuned to the complexity of the real world as possible.

This book was originally conceived as a revision of the well-known study by Haskell P. Wald, *The Taxation of Agricultural Land in Underdeveloped Economies* (Cambridge, Mass.: Harvard University Press, 1959). My debt to Wald's pioneering work remains large, despite the greatly expanded and altered form of the present study.

In particular, the classification of land taxes and much of the analysis of their structure and effects in Part Three are adapted directly from Wald's study, with only minor changes.

On the other hand, not only is most of the book almost completely new, but it will soon become clear to the careful reader that I am in fundamental disagreement with the tenor and emphasis of some of Wald's original discussion. This disagreement ranges from such minor points as my more favorable appraisal of special assessments and site value taxes to our apparently different conclusions on the nature of the steps that need to be taken in most developing countries in order to strengthen agricultural land taxation *right now*. The divergent views I have formed, perhaps largely on the basis of yet another decade of frustrating experience at attempted land tax reforms, together with the substantial new material I have introduced, including both detailed studies of the workings of land taxes in selected countries and a considerably expanded appraisal of the appropriate role of agricultural taxation in the process of economic development, make this book quite different from its predecessor.

In addition to this primary intellectual debt, my considerable dependence on the work of many other researchers is obvious. Although relatively little original field research is incorporated in this book, I hope that the emphasis throughout on practicality and on the diversity of the real world in part saves my suggestions for more effective land taxation from the fate which so many fiscal proposals by outside experts, however firmly based in the economics of the closet, have justly suffered in the past.

My association over a period of years with the International Tax Program of the Harvard Law School and especially with its Director, Professor Oliver Oldman, has been of particular value both in teaching me the importance of practical detail and in providing me with many documents, both published and unpublished, which have greatly enriched this work. Many other scholars and practitioners have also helped in this respect: Albert Berry, Anthony Churchill, John Due, Edward Foster, Frederick Jasperson, Hiroshi Kaneko, Milton Taylor, John Strasma, Rudolph Penner, Gerald Helleiner, Daniel Holland, Harley Hinrichs, Edmundo Flores, Jonathan Levin, Werner Baer, George Lent, Stanley Please, Jose M. Gimeno S., and Gerald W. Sazama have all been most generous in directing me to relevant material, in commenting on earlier drafts, and in giving me permission in some cases to use their own unpublished work. Two research assistants, J. C. Parel and P. Manga, helped in the preparation of Chapter 6. My secretary at the University of Toronto, Miss Jessie Leger, has again patiently and promptly produced numerous drafts of a long manuscript. Earlier versions of some of the material in this book were prepared for the United Nations Department of Economic and Social Affairs in 1970 and for a 1971 Conference on Fiscal Policy for Industrialization in Latin America at the University of Florida.

R.M.B.

CONTENTS

PART FOUR. TAXING AGRICULTURAL LAND: AN APPRAISAL

TABLES

FIGURE

PART ONE

AGRICULTURE, DEVELOPMENT, AND TAXES

1

THE CASE FOR TAXING AGRICULTURE

Agriculture is now the largest economic sector in most developing economies. History suggests, however, that it will shrink in importance as development proceeds.[1] The expansion of the nonagricultural sector which characterizes the process of economic development requires an increase in the marketed supply of food, an increase in the nonagricultural labor force, and an increase in capital formation outside of agriculture. A "squeeze" on agriculture is thus, it seems, an essential element of development in most countries.[2]

One obvious way to exert the necessary pressure on the agricultural sector is to tax it heavily:

Unless the agricultural sector is taxed in order to expand the "agricultural surplus," the growth of the non-agricultural sector may be retarded. As development proceeds, the proportion of the working population engaged in non-food production increases; to make this possible, the marketable surplus from agriculture must also rise— that is, the proportion of food produced in the agricultural sector which is not consumed by the food producers must increase and be transferred to the non-agricultural sector. To accomplish this requires either taxes in money which impel greater deliveries to market, taxes in kind or compulsory sales to the government or a deterioration in the terms of trade of the agricultural sector vis-a-vis the non-agricultural sector.

3

Taxation of the agricultural sector may also serve as an important policy instrument in the underdeveloped countries: the incentive and distributional use of taxation may be utilized to redirect agricultural production, encourage the more efficient use of the land, accomplish changes in land tenure, promote new productive investment in agriculture, and stimulate movement of redundant labor from agriculture to non-agriculture employment.[3]

Agricultural taxation is thus the chosen instrument charged with the vital task of transferring surplus food, labor, and capital to the nonagricultural sector, as well as with reallocating resources within agriculture to increase the transferable surplus.[4] Taxes on agriculture are also needed to restrain a rise in rural food consumption which would increase urban food prices and hence the rate of inflation.[5]

The conventional textbook argument is thus that heavy agricultural taxation is needed in order to increase in a noninflationary manner government revenues, savings, and capital formation—all of which are generally assumed to be necessary for economic growth. Heavier taxes on agriculture are needed even more than heavier taxes in general, both because of the sheer size of the agricultural sector and because of the desire not to reduce the rate of development by taxing the nonagricultural sector—presumably the "progressive" sector—disproportionately. Or, as W. Arthur Lewis put it in an influential treatise: "If it is desired to accelerate capital formation at a time when profits are still a small proportion of national income there is in practice no other way of doing this than to levy substantially upon agriculture, both because agriculture constitutes 50 to 60 percent or more of the national income, and also because levying upon other sectors is handicapped by the fact that it is desirable to have these other sectors expand as part of the process of economic growth."[6]

Other authorities on development economics and taxation have echoed the emphasis in these quotations on the triple function which only agricultural taxation can fulfill: to add to total savings, to increase the marketed surplus, and simultaneously to induce more efficient use of resources within the agricultural sector. There is similar near-unanimity that taxes on agricultural land are, if properly designed, the best way to achieve these goals, since only through their use can the agricultural surplus be simultaneously increased and tapped for developmental revenues.[7]

Furthermore, quite apart from its merits or demerits from the point of view of economic objectives, inadequate taxation of the agricultural sector has also often been attacked as violating the traditional fiscal criterion of equity. Wald, for example, has argued vigorously in the Latin American context that much heavier taxation of well-to-do landowners is needed both to prevent the undermining of public confidence in the fairness of the tax system and also to help enforce desired land redistribution and better land use in general.[8]

Many development and fiscal specialists alike seem to agree that the only way to cure many of the ills of the present system and to secure the resources needed for development is by increasing taxes on the agricultural sector. Although the appropriate design of agricultural land taxes can to a large extent be analyzed independently of the resolution of these grand issues, the issues themselves are so important, and their analysis is generally so entangled with that of the tax instruments which are supposed to achieve them, that a preliminary clearing of the ground is warranted. The conventional case for heavy agricultural taxation follows, and the utility of this model as a guide to those concerned with the design of tax policy is then criticized first in general terms and, later (in Chapter 2), in more detail in light of an alternative perspective on agriculture's role in economic development that has emerged in recent years.

THE RELATION BETWEEN TAXATION AND GROWTH

A crucial assumption underlying the conventional case for heavy agricultural taxes is that the process of economic development is everywhere inherently similar in important respects. There are, therefore, universally desirable characteristics of the tax system when considered as an instrument of developmental policy. The economic rationale behind this view appears to derive from two simple propositions: first, that economic growth requires increased capital investment, more investment requires more saving, and higher taxes are needed to provide the saving; second, the expansion of the industrial sector (taken to be identical with economic growth) requires the transfer of substantial resources out of the agricultural sector. The general applicability of both arguments is questionable, however.

The developing world is, for example, ill described by the simple Harrod-Domar growth model which underlies the usual fiscal prescription for higher taxes to raise savings and hence growth rates.

Indeed, every link in the traditional chain of reasoning—that growth requires investment, investment requires saving, and taxes are needed to provide the saving—is weak. Increased investment, it appears, is neither sufficient nor, in some cases, necessary for growth. Imports, which may be an additional requisite to permit investment, may also, by permitting full operation of existing capacity, allow substantial economic expansion without additional investment. Similarly, increased saving alone may, in countries where such an import constraint is significant, as it seems to be in much of Latin America and perhaps in India and Pakistan as well, lead not to an increase in the growth rate but to unemployment and underutilized capacity. Finally, higher taxes may reduce rather than increase total saving depending on the source of the taxes and, equally important, the pattern of government expenditures. It cannot be simply assumed that the circumstances of every country are so similar that the same medicine—higher taxes—can be prescribed without individual diagnosis based on the particular circumstances of each case.[9]

The argument for heavier agricultural taxation on the grounds that higher taxes are needed in most developing countries and that, as agriculture is the largest sector of the economy, it will have to provide much of the needed tax revenue thus requires careful study in order to determine whether it is applicable in any particular country. The same is true of the special arguments for agricultural taxation already alluded to, which are for the most part derived from the principal advance so far made on the Harrod-Domar growth model, namely, the dualistic or two-sector model of the development process.

THE DUALISTIC MODEL OF DEVELOPMENT

Economic development is in this approach viewed as a structural transformation of the economy from a "traditional" one, where economic activity is dominated by subsistence agriculture, to a "modern" one, in which the nonagricultural sector is most important. This view clearly receives much support from the historical experience of the now-developed countries. But many influential writers on economic development have gone much farther than this, and, as Johnston writes, have really taken "the position that structural transformation should be viewed not merely as a consequence of development but as *a process that should be deliberately fostered by policy measures* to accelerate development and to ensure that low-income, pre-industrial societies will succeed in realizing their goals of achieving self-sustained growth."[10] The influential early works by Lewis and Nurkse, for example, stress the key role of this economic transformation.[11] The best-known formal development of this line of thought, however, is the work of Fei and Ranis.[12]

The approach taken in this formal analysis divides the less developed countries into two groups: the agrarian and the dualistic. The agrarian economy—much of present-day Africa, for example—is characterized by the overwhelming preponderance of traditional agricultural pursuits, with the nonagricultural sector largely restricted to artisan and service activities. The developmental problem in such societies is to generate and utilize effectively what Fei and Ranis label "slacks" in the dominant agricultural sector, especially in the form of agricultural produce not required for the maintenance of traditional consumption patterns. Whether such agricultural surpluses will lead in agrarian economies to increased per capita consumption by farmers in general, to more luxurious living by the wealthy, to expansion of nonproductive activities outside of agriculture, or to some other result depends of course on such variable institutional factors as the existing class structure, tenure arrangements, and the prevailing structure of public revenues and expenditures.

The distinguishing feature of the dualistic economy in this analysis is the existence of a commercialized industrial sector that provides an alternative outlet for the agricultural surplus. The development problem is then how to increase real fixed capital in the industrial sector, while at the same time increasing the productivity of agricultural labor in order to free the manpower needed by expanding industry. A crucial assumption in the Fei-Ranis analysis is thus that "physical capital plays a relatively less important role in agriculture; the labor-intensive adoption of new techniques, the application of fertilizer, and the like are considerably more important. *Thus the net flow of capital resources* (as well as labor resources) *in the course of dualistic growth is out of agriculture and into industry."*[13]

The influence of this analysis in the agricultural tax discussion even outside the limited range of "surplus labor" Asian countries for which it was originally designed is clear in remarks such as the following by Stephen Lewis, author of one of the most balanced appraisals of agricultural taxation: "Since agriculture is the predominant sector and since the non-agricultural sectors will grow relative to agriculture, there is at least an *a priori* case that investment resources for the non-agricultural sectors must come in the first instance from agriculture. In other words, the agricultural sector must make *some* net contribution to the rest of the economy."[14]

The conventional wisdom is thus that the principal role of agricultural taxation is to transfer resources from agriculture to industry.[15] The amount of agricultural production is taken as given, and the task of the tax system is, in simple terms, to transfer as much as possible (the "surplus") to more productive employment elsewhere in the economy.

THE IMPORTANCE OF "SLACK"

This prescribed transfer of resources out of agriculture will not, it is usually argued, hamper increases in agricultural productivity. On the contrary, it may even stimulate productivity, at least if it is clear to agricultural decision makers that the proceeds from such increases can be used to acquire ownership of industry or of desired consumer goods. Turning the intersectoral terms of trade against agriculture through such means as heavy agricultural taxes may, in this argument, paradoxically increase agricultural productivity owing to the ensuing increased attractiveness of industry as a result of the presumed investment of the transferred surplus there. The main reason for this paradoxical conclusion lies in the assumption that there exists "slack" (or unutilized potential) in the agricultural sector, which can be mobilized through the combined stick-carrot approach of heavier taxes and more attractive uses of funds outside of agriculture. The experience of Japan in the nineteenth century is the usual example offered to support this proposition.[16] Exactly this reasoning underlies the usual economic case for heavier agricultural taxes, where, again, Japan is the conventional example.

Even more important in the conventional model than an increase in the agricultural surplus produced is an increase in the amount of the surplus marketed, as it is this which really constitutes the supply of savings for economic development. Because farmers have a fixed need for money income, they are, it is usually argued, likely to adjust their sales of produce to price changes so as to produce this requisite amount of money and no more. Higher taxes (to be paid in money) ought therefore to increase, rather than reduce, the marketed surplus. Indeed, as Kaldor put it, "it is *only* the imposition of compulsory levies on the agricultural sector itself which enlarges the supply of 'savings,' in the required sense for economic development"—that is, by increasing the marketed surplus.[17]

Those who stress that limited domestic resources (that is, inadequate saving) are the main obstacle to growth tend to assume that, once the capital is made available, the correct development-generating decisions will automatically be forthcoming. This is the traditional view of the role of tax policy in development. The same attitude is readily detectible in the discussion on agricultural taxation, where it is almost always simply assumed that causation flows from adequate resource availability to correct resource utilization, so that higher agricultural taxes will automatically bring about the desired structural transformation of the economy. In both instances, however, experience suggests that the tax system may at best facilitate desirable real resource transfers; it cannot, by itself, command them.

This caution has been ignored, and the conventional dual sector analysis has often been employed to support two particular policy recommendations, almost without regard for the circumstances of the country in question. The first, already noted, is that there can and should be a flow of capital from agriculture to industry in the earlier stages of development, a transfer preferably effectuated through heavy land taxes because of their desirable incentive effects. The second is that the preoccupation with mobilizing and transferring this "agricultural surplus" (capital, food, labor) has led many to assume, usually implicitly, that in almost all cases a surplus can be extracted from agriculture without paying much attention to the needs of the agricultural sector itself. This neglect has been justified by the belief that the agricultural production function is such that output can be expanded without additional inputs of resources from the nonagricultural sector. Indeed, it is usually argued that there exist substantial unutilized (or underutilized) resources—in Asia mainly labor, in Latin America perhaps land—in the agricultural sector and that such resources will readily be brought into use as a result of increased tax pressure.

Heavy land taxes will not only perform the necessary task of transferring resources out of agriculture, but they will, miraculously, do so without imposing any real long-term burden on the agricultural sector itself: "The increased tax burden will make the farmer work hard and recover the slack by making better use of presently under-utilized resources, including his own labor and other investible resources, government-provided technical knowledge, irrigation facilities, and fertilizers."[18] In a modern version of what Seligman long ago termed the "transformation"[19] of taxation into more efficient production[19] it is thus argued that, where there is "slack" in the agricultural sector, taxation may not only mobilize surplus food, it may actually induce its creation. As Gandhi put this case with respect to India:

> The average farmer in India will have to be made aware of these potentialities (and taxation may act as a lever) so that he picks up the slack and enriches his own life as well as the life of the nation. . . . Providing that slack exists, increasing the tax burden on the average farmer would force him to increase production. In the initial years there may be some element of real burden involved, but in due course, the additional taxation will be paid out of increased productivity resulting from the utilization of slack.[20]

In the Latin American context these views are usually expressed more in relation to the underutilized land resources held by the wealthy than with respect to the work effort of the average farmer, but the underlying reasoning would appear to be the same. Even the most careful writers on agricultural taxation have thus generally accepted, albeit usually after expressing some doubts, that the simple dual-sector model sets forth the correct developmental guidelines within which to design agricultural tax policy for all countries.

THE EQUITY ARGUMENT

In addition to developmental virtues—producing revenues, increasing the marketed surplus, increasing effort and output through penalizing the underemployment or inefficient utilization of resources within agriculture, and moving farmers into the commercialized monetary sector—a strong equity case is often put forward in support of heavy taxes on agricultural land.[21]

Heavy land taxes will, it is argued, not only force many large landowners to sell off some of their land, but they will also, by reducing land prices, permit lower-income peasants to acquire them. Land taxes have therefore often been suggested for use as a redistributive instrument to complement or replace land reform efforts. Besides this potential direct redistributive effect, only through heavy direct taxes (which in the circumstances of most developing countries usually means land or land-related taxes) can rich landowners be made to pay their fair share of taxes—and without some such contribution to the fisc the necessary social cement of "fair shares" may prove too weak to hold the elements of society together. As noted later, this last problem has become especially acute recently in those regions affected by the "Green Revolution" in agricultural technology.

In addition, ingenious attempts have recently been made to justify increased agricultural taxation by measuring the "tax-paying capacity" and the "fair tax burden" of the agricultural sector.[22] These studies may eventually provide useful information for the formulation of tax policy, but it is hard to see how they can provide an objective guide to appropriate tax policy in any country, a point which is pursued further in Chapter 10.

THE DANGERS OF OVERGENERALITY

From the literature on agricultural taxation summarized to this point, one might not suspect that there is considerable ferment at present amongst development theorists concerning the relationship of agricultural development and economic growth. Some of these issues are discussed in the next chapter. First, however, it is worth noting more generally that all "growth stage" models such as those implicit in the conventional argument may be criticized for their lack of analytical power and operational relevance.[23]

Such severely limited conceptual frameworks have proved useful, even necessary, in delimiting, through generalized approximations of reality, the crucial variables relevant for developmental policy. Unfortunately a wide range of the relevant characteristics can be found in different countries—indeed, even within the same country, where, for example, a primitive subsistence group of mountain farmers may be only a few miles away from a group of capital-intensive commercial dairy farmers serving a well-developed urban market. The policy recommendations emerging from any general model of the interconnections between agricultural and industrial development will thus either be so empty as to be useless ("both are good") or else in fact a special case applicable to, at most, a limited group of countries ("tax agriculture heavily").

Whether the flow of resources should be to or from the agricultural sector—the most crucial question in designing agricultural tax policy —depends entirely upon the particular circumstances of the country in question: its social and institutional structure, its technological and market prospects and possibilities, the relative size and productivity of the agricultural and industrial sectors, and so on. No general policy prescription can or should be expected to fit all circumstances.

Paradigms such as the dualistic model serve an essential function in helping to sort out our thinking on such complex analytical questions as the role of agricultural taxation in development, but, when applied uncritically to yield policy recommendations in concrete cases, they are more likely to hinder than to guide correct action. Not only are crucial differences subsumed within their broad categories, but too often the "policy implications" which appear to emerge inexorably from the formal model turn out to have been arbitrarily and unrealistically built into its assumptions. The relevant question for the policy analyst should always be: what combination of policies is needed to obtain our objectives in this particular situation? This elementary and obvious caution needs restatement here precisely because it is so often overlooked by "practical" tax reformers, who, to paraphrase Lord Keynes, are usually the unconscious slaves of some defunct economic model.[24]

One reason for this common oversight is that it is easy to fall into the trap of advocating either agricultural or industrial fundamentalism when considering the appropriate role of agriculture in the development of a particular country. It has been said that intellectuals are perhaps more subject to the whims of fashion than any other group. If so, development economists must indeed be intellectuals, despite the doubts of some, for no group seems more subject to the swings of fad and fashion. For fifteen years after World War II, agriculture was "out," and industry was "in." Few fiscal recommendations even today appear to be based on general development theory of much more recent vintage than 1960. The "industry first" school dominant among general development economists appears for long to have overlooked the crucial importance of changes within the agricultural sector. It is for this reason that the inherent inadequacy as a policy guide of the conception of agriculture's role as simply a supplier of "surplus"—a conception that has influenced most writers on agricultural tax policy to this day—has been stressed here.

Further experience in various parts of the world, together with some general rethinking of the problem, has cast so much doubt on the soundness of what has been labeled here conventional wisdom that some development economists have reversed the old emphasis. The alternative view—that agricultural development in its own right and as an essential component of economic development is much more important than the older view makes it appear—has substantial general merit, although some of its advocates seem also to have gone too far and unnecessarily damaged their case by falling into the trap of agrarian fundamentalism.

Rather than stressing the inherent virtues of one or the other sector, the most productive approach would appear to be to focus on the mutual interdependence of agricultural and industrial development. Most analysts would agree, for example, that the labor force will eventually decline in agriculture as per capita income levels rise and that industrial development will become increasingly important. The direction of causality in this relation is most confused, however. Furthermore, in view of our well-known condition in the long run ("we're all dead"), this information provides absolutely no guide to appropriate short-term (that is, five to ten years) policies in any particular country at any particular stage of its history, and it is these shorter-run issues which dominate most situations. Any general argument stressing the primacy of either agriculture or industry usually has some validity, but in practice everything depends upon how much validity, which can be determined only by careful quantitative analysis. The present, very imperfect state of our knowledge, therefore, seems to require that fiscal economists analyze the effects of each possible tax instrument on all policy objectives without prejudging the desired direction of such effects.

The appropriate fiscal treatment of agriculture is not a subject about which one can make very useful recommendations apart from particular real-world situations, especially since, in addition to the difficulties of determining the appropriate theoretical framework to apply, the nature of agricultural policy, even more than other aspects of development policy, is such that it must always be closely geared to local conditions. Countries differ in many respects: the share of agriculture in output, in exports, in the labor force, and in the provision of public revenues, as well as in income distribution, crop diversification, the state of public education, the capability of administration, and others. The appropriate agricultural tax policy must take all these differences and many other factors into account. The only useful position for a fiscal economist who, like most of us, cannot know everything appears to be one of agnostic pragmatism on the great issues and eclectic piecemeal theorizing on the small, which is the procedure followed for the most part in the present book.

2

THE ROLE OF AGRICULTURAL TAXATION
IN DEVELOPING COUNTRIES

In recent years an alternative view of agriculture's appropriate role in development has emerged, based in part on economic analysis and in part on postwar experience in different areas of the world. This new view puts less stress on the need to transfer the agricultural surplus through taxation and more on the need to develop the agricultural sector itself, for both its intrinsic and its instrumental value. Although this newer approach has as yet had relatively little impact in fiscal reports, its implications for agricultural tax policy could be extremely important.

THE SUPPLY OF LABOR

One of agriculture's main developmental functions in the conventional model is to supply labor to the industrial sector. Tax policy may affect the flow of labor out of agriculture in several ways. The most basic is by affecting the rate of population growth. Heavier taxes may discourage families from having more children (even if offset in part by some "personalization" of the tax to allow for family circumstances.)[1] Also, taxes specific to the agricultural sector may make migration to urban areas marginally more attractive, and it is generally expected that birth rates in urban areas will be lower.

Both of these arguments may of course be countered. If, for example, the tax proceeds are spent in the rural areas, say, on health centers, death rates may fall even more than birth rates so that the rate of population growth increases. Further, even if the surplus is extracted completely from the agricultural sector by taxes, the increased tax pressure may lead families to have more rather than fewer children, insofar as children in poor rural areas are an investment rather than a consumption good. The effect of urbanization on birth rates, even over a generation, is also questionable.[2] Any effects on birth rates would take years to affect the labor force, of course, and the whole question of the relation between taxes and population is too remote and uncertain to warrant further comment.

Looking more specifically at the more important question of migration, it appears that the rate of migration of rural people to the cities can be explained largely by the probability of obtaining employment and the magnitude of the rural-urban wage differential.[3] The effect of heavy agricultural taxes on this magnitude depends on their incidence and hence is not clear. If, on the one hand, the principal result of these taxes is to lower the price of food eaten by urban consumers, as was reportedly the case with the Thai rice tax,[4] migration will presumably be stimulated. If, on the other hand, the ultimate result is to lower the price of wage goods for rural workers, the effect may be the opposite.

In general, any tax measures which make rural life less attractive than urban life, as most sectorally discriminating taxes are likely to do especially when, as is usually envisioned, the proceeds are spent mainly in urban areas, will tend to induce more migration. For this reason, some authors have recently suggested that taxes on rural land are not particularly desirable in East Africa.[5] In contrast, an increased outflow of migrants would apparently be contemplated with equanimity by those who adhere to the crude labor-transfer model sketched earlier,[6] or who, more plausibly, believe migration from agricultural regions must, owing to the labor-saving nature of most new technology, be accelerated in order to increase agricultural productivity.[7]

The explosive social and political problems arising in many countries as a result of increasing open unemployment in congested urban slums, to which the annual influx of rural migrants adds, are well known. One may perhaps therefore doubt whether a tax push to further migration is really needed in many developing countries at the present time. Even if the long-run objective (or at least expectation) remains the restructuring of the economy to reduce the role of agriculture, its immediate importance as employer and sponge containing social unrest is such that fiscal measures driving people off the land are now probably viewed with much less enthusiasm than a few years ago, even by some dedicated proponents of heavy agricultural taxes.[8] Indeed, as noted in Chapter 9, there has come to be increasing interest, in the face of the faster growth of the population over nonagricultural employment opportunities, in using the fiscal system to encourage the employment of more than rather than less labor in agricultural pursuits.[9]

THE SUPPLY OF FOOD

Apart from the problem of finding jobs for those now engaged in agriculture, the other side of the labor transfer argument has also been questioned: will the increase in agricultural productivity, which all agree is needed for development, require more or less labor than is presently employed in this sector? The accepted view, until recently, has been that an increase in agricultural productivity will in all likelihood be accomplished largely by reducing labor inputs. To quote the authoritative statement of Johnston and Mellor: "Reduction of the farm labor force is a necessary condition for establishing factor proportions that yield returns to labor in agriculture that are more or less in accord with returns to labor in other sectors. More concretely, insufficient movement out of agriculture will perpetuate, or lead to, excessively small farms and serious underemployment of labor as the proximate causes of substandard farm incomes."[10] Underlying this view in some instances is the assumption that the marginal product of labor in agriculture is zero or very close to zero in many less developed countries.

Few authorities on the subject now accept this, although one might never suspect as much from reading the taxation literature alone. The general and more plausible view is instead that the marginal product of agricultural labor is positive and that little if any redundant labor exists in agriculture.[11] As Johnston recently summed up the present status of the discussion, in a strikingly different fashion from his own views of ten years earlier: "Although economists commonly stress a trade-off between output and employment objectives, there do not appear to be inherent reasons for serious conflict between those objectives within agriculture."[12]

Going one step further, Myrdal and others have argued that, at least in South Asia, the key to increased agricultural production is not *less* labor per unit of land but *more*: "If by a miracle the cultivators in South Asia could be induced to work diligently, production would rise dramatically."[13] This approach agrees with the conventional argument noted earlier that little if any extra capital is needed to increase output in agriculture because there is a good deal of "slack." The difference between the Myrdal view and conventional views is that the former argues that the aspirations of peasants are limited—a sociological explanation of slack—while the latter suggest that some response to economic incentives can be expected and are therefore extremely optimistic as to the potential effects of heavier taxation in eliciting favorable behavior from a developmental point of view.[14] The sociological approach, as the quotation suggests, requires a "miracle" to achieve the desired result: hard as tax changes are to bring about in most countries, they would appear easier to incorporate into a development plan than miracles.

The view that the people engaged in agriculture, like people everywhere, tend to respond in broadly predictable ("rational") ways to the economic incentives created by their physical and institutional environment has gained increasing acceptance.[15] Instances where normal economic incentives seem not to work can usually, it appears, be explained by the constraints imposed by the environment. It has, for example, been argued that, where the marketed surplus is observed not to rise in response to price increases, the explanation may lie not in economic irrationality on the part of peasants but rather in the tastes of the rural economy for the products of the manufacturing sector.[16] Improvements in the variety, quality, and price of manufactured goods to suit rural needs may be what is needed to transfer the surplus. Rather than heavier taxes on agricultural output, lighter taxes on the uses of income might therefore, in some circumstances at least, be the way to increase the flow of food to urban consumers.

This argument again suggests strongly that the analysis of agricultural taxes cannot be conducted in abstraction from the uses to be made of the proceeds. If, for example, the corresponding expenditures either facilitate marketing (farm-to-market roads) or increase the choice or reduce the price of incentive goods, the net effects on marketed surplus may be quite different from the effects when the proceeds go to raise urban wages, especially those of high-cost civil servants, and the price of manufactured goods purchased by the agricultural sector.

A curious fact is that many of the "revisionist" writers on agriculture's appropriate role in development appear to be as enamored of the potentially positive incentive effects of land taxes as are those who adhere to the older industrialization strategy.[17] As pointed out in Part Three of this book, most tax proposals by development experts substantially overestimate the potential of taxation to solve the many and varied problems underlying low agricultural productivity. If heavy taxes led more or less automatically to increased productivity, life would indeed be simple for the development economist. It is not.

THE SUPPLY OF CAPITAL

The traditional conception of taxes as transferring capital out of the agricultural sector was discussed in Chapter 1. Analysis and experience on this crucial matter now suggests that, while there may be a net inflow or a net outflow from agriculture, a gross inflow to finance certain key projects is usually crucial to agricultural development.[18] Even if the capital is used for the development of the agricultural sector itself, the role of tax policy in mobilizing savings in that sector may of course be vital. Heavy agricultural taxation to finance mainly agricultural investment would seem much more feasible in these circumstances than if agriculture were taxed simply to provide capital to other sectors. Increased investment from rural sources in the agricultural sector and in the health and education of farmers themselves may even subsequently result in substantial indirect transfers of capital when migration occurs (some of the locally provided capital now being embodied in the migrants) or, even more indirectly, in the sense that the farm sector continues to absorb most of the costs of supporting redundant labor.[19]

Whatever the long-run effects, it is clear that recent analysis has directed increasing attention to the need in many countries to increase agricultural production, employment, and productivity simply in order to achieve the distributional and allocative objectives usually meant by "development." Because most people in poor countries are farmers, agricultural development has intrinsic as well as instrumental importance in this emerging view of the developmental process.

No longer, for example, is it clear that "agriculture, as the dominant sector of an underdeveloped economy can and should make a net contribution to the capital required for overhead investment and expansion of secondary industry."[20] Instead, it is now argued by some that the principal immediate task of agricultural development in many, perhaps even most, developing countries is to raise the income and consumption level of the large farm population itself.[21] The earlier argument about the need for more employment in the agricultural sector is of course a closely related point since employment is the main mechanism by which income and consumption are distributed in most societies.

President Nyereye of Tanzania recently expressed this view as follows: "Tanzania will continue to have a predominantly rural economy for a long time to come. As it is in the rural areas that people live and work, so it is in the rural areas that life must be improved. We have some industries now and they will continue to expand; but it would be grossly unrealistic to imagine that in the near future more than a small proportion of our people will live in towns and work in modern industrial enterprises."[22] Most people in most poor countries live in rural areas and will continue to do so for some years. Developmental policies cannot treat the well-being of most of the population as an instrument rather than an objective of policy.

Implementing this view of agriculture's role in development obviously requires quite different tax policies than the more usual conception of agriculture as a sector to be mulcted of both men and money for the good of "the nation" (apparently defined as something different from most of its present population). Tanzania, for instance, has recently deliberately reduced the taxes levied on its rural population. To some extent, a similar concern with social justice, equity, and the distribution of income also underlies the case for land reform in many countries: "land must be viewed as a vehicle for human development as well as a resource for food production."[23] Only through secure tenure can most people have access to the social and economic life of their country. It may also be argued in certain circumstances that the reform of tenurial institutions is needed in order to increase agricultural productivity above traditional norms.[24] This point is discussed further in Chapter 13.

The trend away from the "tax agriculture at all costs" view has been reinforced by the realization that extensive capital investment in agriculture may be needed in order to make technological innovations possible in traditional agriculture and, hence, to accelerate the growth of the agricultural surplus. It seems unlikely that agricultural productivity can grow rapidly enough to meet the food and raw material demands accompanying industrial and urban expansion and also finance most social capital expenditures outside of agriculture, as was thought earlier. Indeed, in view of the rapid growth of the demand for food as incomes rise from an initially low level, a net flow of resources into agriculture may be necessary at early stages in some countries.[25]

Even if this extreme position is not reached, the scope of the immediate increases in agricultural productivity potentially realizable in many countries from labor-intensive, capital-saving techniques now appears to be smaller than it did only a few years ago. If the needed agricultural investment is not carried out, there may be a shift in the internal terms of trade against industry, thus impeding industrialization directly, or else a considerable drain on foreign exchange resources and, hence, an indirect impediment to structural transformation. In either case, the short-run importance of generating sufficient agricultural output has come in many countries to dominate the long-run desire to reduce the weight of agriculture in the national economy.

The need to create institutional infrastructure (in transport and education, for instance), to invest in land development, to foster technical and organizational innovation, and to devote much of industrial and importing capacity to the task of maintaining and improving the rate of growth of agricultural productivity means, in effect, the closure of "the low cost route to agricultural development that seemed to be opened up by the dual economy models which have dominated much of the theoretical discussion of agricultural development during the last decade."[26] The possibility of a net flow of resources from agriculture to help the overall development effort thus turns out to depend very much, even in the long run, upon judicious and perhaps substantial investment in agriculture to maintain and increase the growth of agricultural productivity. The potential of agriculture to supply savings for purposes of nonagricultural development is thus reduced considerably.

These considerations become particularly important if one considers the present state of public administration in many developing countries, which makes it appear that much of the outflow will be wasted from a developmental point of view, by being absorbed by high industrial or service wages or developmentally useless current governmental expenditure, while the taxes will generally hamper agricultural productivity. Once again, the importance of considering both sides of the budget even when one's main concern is with taxation is clear.

AGRICULTURE AS MARKET AND EXPORTER

Increased productive employment in agriculture was earlier emphasized as often both necessary to absorb the growing labor force and desirable to restrain the growth of social unrest in the burgeoning urban centers of developing countries. Furthermore, increased food consumption in the rural sector itself is, it was argued, often necessary to ensure a fairer distribution of the gains from economic progress (and may itself, through improving nutrition, lead to some productivity gains).[27] In addition, without rising incomes in the agricultural sector the expansion of industry may in some countries be severely limited by the size of the domestic market. It has recently been argued that this is the case in Nigeria, for example.[28] A somewhat similar situation may prevail in the very different circumstances of Colombia.[29]

This question is entangled in both theory and practice, but it is certainly arguable that in at least some countries a good case can be made that measures to expand rural markets for simple consumer and producer goods, rather than to contract them through heavy agricultural taxes, will foster growth most.[30] Industrial structure must, of course, be capable of responding to any such increase in rural demand for this point to have merit, but, if it does, the importance of increased agricultural output and of avoiding taxes which deter it unduly is again clear.

These arguments are strengthened when agricultural exports are essential to provide the foreign exchange needed for developmental investment. Heavy agricultural taxation may, by restraining agricultural output and marketing, actually reduce the availability of foreign exchange and hence lead to the early imposition of a foreign exchange constraint on development. In evaluating this argument, too much attention has been paid in the past to the allegedly gloomy long-run prospects for most agricultural exports and too little attention to their immediate, essential role in providing foreign exchange.[31] Even a temporary setback in agricultural exports under these circumstances, for example, through the adverse incentive effects of heavy agricultural taxation, may thus have long-lasting adverse effects on the economy.[32] The amount of evidence on the sensitive response of cash export crops to price changes indicates that this danger is a real one.[33] Since, as seen in Part Two, export taxes have proved in many countries to be the most efficient way to obtain large revenues from the agricultural sector, the policy choice here is a particularly important one.

THE CHANGING ECONOMIC SETTING OF TAX POLICY

In the last year or two, the confused picture outlined to this point has been further confused by what is known as the "Green Revolution."[34] Recent scientific breakthroughs in the development of new seed varieties of wheat and rice potentially mean the food supply problems in many developing countries can be resolved if the new seeds can be properly combined with fertilizer, irrigation, and other complementary investments. These conditions will not be easy to satisfy, and in many countries they may require substantial reorientation of both tax and expenditure policy. Furthermore, changing to more "modern" (that is, standardized, homogeneous) farming practices increases the dangers of disastrous plagues of pests and diseases. Still more research is needed, especially since the methods —chemical fertilizers, herbicides, pesticides, and so forth—used both to launch the revolution and control its side effects are themselves increasingly being questioned on ecological grounds. Even as old problems are resolved, new ones arise. Much the same is true with tax policy, which must be constantly adapted to cope with changing economic conditions.

It is already clear, for example, that gains from these innovations are very unevenly distributed within the agricultural sector. Better-off farmers have both more capability and more opportunity to utilize the new technology, and some of it is geared more to large than to small units. The immediate impact of the Green Revolution, therefore, often accentuates inequality within the agricultural sector. The problem of tapping the presumably increased taxable capacity of agriculture may also have been changed in kind as well as degree. Not only may equity issues have gained importance in countries undergoing this revolution, owing to the resulting increased disparities, but the problem of how to tax increased incomes without dampening incentive for increased productivity has become even more difficult.[35] On the other hand, some writers believe that small farmers, properly supported by public policies, are perfectly capable of adopting and developing the new agricultural technology.[36] Drastic land redistribution policies, whether by fiscal or other means, may well become more rather than less feasible and necessary.

Simultaneously with these revenue problems, full utilization of the technological advances embodied in the new seeds requires substantial new investment in the agricultural sector. The problem of whether there can be a net outflow of resources from agriculture is thus accentuated by the new developments, rather than resolved by them, as one might perhaps have predicted some years ago.

The new techniques may also, because of their nature as well as their distributional impact, encourage the use of more capital-intensive production methods, which will further accentuate employment and income distribution problems. "The new rice technology has added to the displacement of farm labourers [in South Asia]. The widespread use of one-man machines produced in Japan is driving unemployed peasants to the slum fringes of the cities. . . . The rice revolution could contain the seeds of a revolution of another kind."[37] Since it seems that the innovations in question can in theory create rather than destroy employment, the fact that their net impact has apparently been to displace labor once again points to their uneven distributional impact (as well as the distorted prices of capital and labor) as the point calling for policy action.[38]

The argument made by some that the new technology is necessarily labor saving,[39] although it may be true in the long run, ignores the important influence of government policies in many countries on distorting factor prices in such a way as to encourage the use of capital while discouraging the development of technologies adapted to indigenous factor endowments. In many instances, an alternative labor-intensive technology already exists but is not employed because small farmers do not have access to the requisite information and capital resources while the large farmers use capital-intensive mechanical technologies that appear profitable in part because the exchange rate is overvalued.[40] Where adequate technology does not exist, proper development priorities would appear to demand the investment in agricultural science needed to produce it—a policy which would imitate what some scholars consider the true lesson of U.S. and Japanese agricultural development.[41]

In general, then, the Green Revolution has created still more pressures on those who must design agricultural tax policy and has resolved none of the many earlier problems.[42] Necessity, it has been said, is the mother of invention; so also can it be said that invention is the mother of necessity. The impact of the Green Revolution on agricultural problems and policies, including tax policies, suggests the truth of this dictum.

OBJECTIVES AND INITIAL CONDITIONS

The level and form of agricultural taxation appropriate for any particular country depends upon the initial conditions in that country and its developmental objectives and possibilities. The conventional argument that heavy agricultural taxes are always an essential ingredient of development policy is derived from an oversimple model of agriculture's role in development and an unrealistic view of the feasible structure of agricultural taxation. It cannot, therefore, be lightly applied to any particular country without close examination of individual circumstances.

In countries where most of the population is engaged in agriculture, where export earnings depend heavily on agricultural commodities, where internal markets are being exploited for consumer goods, and where the government is responsive to the current well-being of the mass of the population, there is less desire to tax agriculture heavily than in those countries which can better afford, economically and politically, to discourage agricultural productivity and to encourage migration to urban areas. Even where heavy agricultural taxes are imposed, it appears that much of the surplus thus generated has to be reinvested in agriculture itself (even in cases where there is "slack" in one form or another which may potentially be utilized) if the rate of growth of agricultural productivity is to be maintained. The more refined effects of various tax measures must take second place to these basic decisions on the appropriate tax level.

Much the same factors as determine the appropriate level of sectoral taxation also govern its form. If the main function of the tax system is to produce large monetary revenues, then export taxes, as suggested in Part Two, are often the politically and administratively most efficient way to accomplish this. If export production is not very important or is particularly sensitive to the disincentive effects of taxation, taxes in kind or money on production or marketings may be employed to produce the needed revenues. These too exert undesired disincentive effects, however. Some form of taxation of agricultural land is usually to be preferred if political and administrative conditions permit. Even if, as the previous discussion suggests may be the case in some countries, the principal immediate aim of tax policy is to rechannel resources (labor and capital) within agriculture rather than to facilitate their transfer to nonagricultural pursuits, land often turns out to be the best, if not always the most feasible, base for taxation.

One aim of this book is to appraise various possible forms of land taxation in light of many potential objectives outlined above and the widely varying initial conditions in different countries at different times. The assumption underlying this exercise is that since, in any given country at any time, the variety of tax instruments constituting the fiscal system will in any case affect in one way or another the extent to which various policy objectives are attained, such effects should be beneficial.

In short, this work sets forth a policy matrix in which different agricultural taxes and particular structural features of these taxes are arrayed against various conceivable objectives of developmental tax policy. Figure 1 is a preliminary depiction of such a matrix: it does not pretend to be complete. The cells of this matrix may, in theory, be filled in for each tax variant so that the political decision maker may calculate the appropriately optimal agricultural tax system for his peculiar circumstances by applying weights derived from his welfare function to the entries in the different cells.

Life is never so simple as this, of course. It is, for example, usually impossible to enter any quantitative magnitudes, or even directional

Initial conditions \ Objectives	Subsistence agriculture		Commercial export agriculture		Commercial domestic agriculture		Unutilized land	State of technology	Distribution of land	Size of farms
	Owner culti-vator	Land-lord tenant	Food	Nonfood	Food	Nonfood				
Revenue										
Production										
Marketed surplus										
Capital transfer										
Labor transfer										
Choice of technology										
Size of domestic market										
Exports										
Size of farm										
Land redistribution										
Income redistribution										
Population growth										
Agricultural employment										
Food self-sufficiency										

signs, in a matrix of this sort simply because of the lack of the necessary empirical knowledge on the relation between financial instruments and the real variables in which we are primarily interested. In addition, there are often very different agricultural conditions in different regions of a single country, so that it is unlikely any single tax form will be optimal. The relevant initial conditions include the production, marketing, and tenure structure, the technology employed, and the underlying natural endowment, the political power of the landlord, peasant, and urban groups respectively, and the state of various elements of the economic infrastructure. Furthermore, the framework of this entire analysis is, on the whole, inevitably partial and static despite occasional attempts to lighten the darkness thus cast on policy choices.

In real life economies, replete with many existing distortions and with complex and changing interdependencies between different objectives as well as between ends and means, the direct applicability of the present analysis, despite the attempt to present it in a form conceivably applicable to any situation, is inevitably limited. It is, nevertheless, less constrained by blind adherence to a crude development model than most writing in this field.

The discussion in the present chapter has been conducted for the most part with reference to agricultural taxes in general. The rest of the book is devoted almost entirely to a detailed analysis of one particular class of agricultural taxes, those based in some way on land. The emphasis is appropriate for two main reasons. First, agricultural land taxes in one form or another are, as Part Two shows, ubiquitous and, hence, call for careful analysis. Second, most previous analyses of agricultural taxation in general or in particular countries suggest strongly that, at least potentially, taxing agricultural land is the best way to tax agriculture. On the whole, this statement still stands although, as subsequent discussion shows, it is less the conclusion than the beginning of an analysis that is presented in detail here not for its penetrating originality—there is little enough room for that with respect to man's oldest tax—but as a synthesis intended to be useful to all students of development finance.

PART TWO

TAXING AGRICULTURE: A SURVEY

3

A QUANTITATIVE OVERVIEW

The practice of agricultural taxation differs markedly from the theory. The usual theoretical prescription is, as we have seen, that heavy taxes be levied on agricultural land. Even revisionist development theorists who stress the intrinsic and instrumental importance of agricultural development favor land taxes, particularly those based in some fashion on the potential yield of agricultural land. Yet relatively few countries tax agriculture heavily, and almost never are land taxes the principal instrument used by those which do. Furthermore, contrary to the apparent theoretical prescription for countries wishing to make the transition from static traditionalism to dynamic modernity, it appears that land taxes have almost everywhere declined in importance in recent years and that, where their decline is slowest, so is the pace of development. This chapter considers in more detail the present quantitative importance of different agricultural tax instruments and trends in the revenue yield of land taxes. The next chapter reviews the major ways in which agriculture is taxed in different parts of the world.

TABLE 1. THE PATTERN OF AGRICULTURAL TAXATION

Share of total tax receipts produced by agricultural taxes	Number of countries having a given type of tax				Total direct agricultural taxes
	Personal	Export	Land	Other	
Less than 4 percent	9	27	26	3	15
5 to 9 percent	4	13	18	0	20
10 to 20 percent	4	16	4	0	23
Over 20 percent	2	2	0	0	11
Number of countries in sample	19	58	48	3	69

Source: See Appendix.

PATTERNS OF AGRICULTURAL TAXATION

Tables 1 and 2 (and the Appendix) bring together from a wide variety of sources the available information on the revenue importance of different agricultural taxes in different parts of the world. The primary purpose of these tables is simply to illustrate the apparent patterns and trends in agricultural taxation. They do not pretend to do more than provide a rough picture of the situation. There are substantial problems in putting together tables such as these: the available statistical sources for many individual countries, for example, are incomplete, vary in their coverage and definitions, and present incompatible figures. When the data for different countries are brought together, these problems are multiplied. The resulting tables are consequently not strictly comparable either in coverage or time, so that the precise figures in the tables must not be taken as definitive in any sense.[1]

Furthermore, the discussion in this chapter is entirely in terms of the share of tax revenues provided by agricultural taxes—a figure which is clearly inadequate to measure changes in the "burden" of these taxes in relation to agricultural income or output, since it also reflects the relative growth of tax revenues from other sources. What few data are available on the weight of agricultural taxation in relation to income in various countries, however, generally support the conclusions suggested here on the basis of the revenue data; some specific instances are noted in the course of the next few chapters. There is no reason to believe, therefore, that the general picture suggested by these figures is grossly incorrect: on the contrary, all the available evidence tends to support the implications which can be drawn from them.

Several important points are suggested by these tables. First, by far the most widespread and usually the most significant way of taxing agriculture in the less developed world at the present time is by means of export taxes. For the years covered in Table 1, export taxes (which in most of the cases shown are levied primarily on agricultural exports) produced over 20 percent of central government revenues in 2 countries, over 10 percent in 18, and over 5 percent in 31 out of the 58 countries for which some information is available. No other form of agricultural taxation comes even close in importance.

There is no marked regional pattern in reliance on export taxes: on every continent some countries rely heavily on export taxes for revenue, and some do not (see Appendix). More important than geographic location is the nature of the export crop and the size of the country, with, as one would suspect, relatively small countries (Ivory Coast, Uganda, Ceylon, Haiti) with significant cash export crops (coffee, cocoa, tea, rubber, cotton, bananas) being those which tend to rely most heavily on export taxes. In large part, but not entirely, the fiscal importance of export taxes is related to the importance of the export sector in the economy.[2]

Although the revenue importance of these taxes in different countries varies sharply from year to year, the conclusion that export taxes are currently the most important taxes affecting agriculture in the less developed world seems inescapable. In recent years there has probably been a decline in the fiscal importance of export taxes: Pakistan abolished them in 1969; the share of tax revenues provided by the Thai rice "premium" fell from 12 percent in 1968 to 2 percent in 1971; export taxes provided only 3 percent of revenues in Ecuador in 1970 as against 10 percent in 1968. Similar data could be reported for many other countries. Nevertheless, their position as the preeminent technique for taxing agriculture heavily has not been usurped by any of the alternative means of taxing agriculture directly, as Table 2 makes clear.

A second important point suggested by Table 1 is that land taxes are significant revenue sources in very few countries. Only in Nepal do they account for close to one-fifth of revenues; they produce more than 10 percent of revenues in only 3 other countries, and

TABLE 2. THE DECLINE OF TRADITIONAL DIRECT AGRICULTURAL TAXES

Country	Type of tax[a]	Pre-World War I	Pre-World War II[b]	Post-World War II[c]	Recent[d]
Latin America			(percentage of total tax receipts)		
Bolivia	Land	55	—	1	0
Brazil	Land	—	2	1	1
Chile	Land	—	5	4	6
Costa Rica	Land	—	—	4	6
El Salvador	Land	—	3	2	2
Guatemala	Land	—	4	9	6
Jamaica	Land	—	—	15	8
Mexico	Land	—	7	5	0
Nicaragua	Land	—	—	4	7
Panama	Land	—	3	8	4
Paraguay	Land	—	12	12	6
Peru	Land	4	—	0	0
Uruguay	Land	—	—	6	7
Africa					
Ethiopia	Land	—	—	22	8
Kenya	Personal	—	14	5	2
Malawi	Personal	—	25	10	12
Niger	Personal	—	—	47	34
Nigeria	Personal	—	—	14	6
Tanzania	Personal	—	32	15	3
Uganda	Personal	—	31	—	14
Zaire	Personal	46	—	—	3
Zambia	Personal	—	8	1	—

more than 5 percent in a total of only 22. Even these figures are undoubtedly an overstatement since in most cases it has not been possible to separate out the portion of the land or property tax that affects agriculture. In fact, at the present time it would probably not be wrong to say that only in Nepal do taxes on agricultural land maintain anything like the fiscal importance ascribed to them in some development models—and, since taxes amount to only around 4 percent of Gross Domestic Product in Nepal, even there land taxes account for less than 1 percent of total output.

The countries in which land taxes produce significant revenues may be arbitrarily divided into several groups. First, Ethiopia and in particular Nepal represent the traditional low-income country with few alternative revenue sources. Paraguay to some extent also provides an example of the relative revenue productivity in some poor

TABLE 2 (*continued*).

Country	Type of tax[a]	Pre-World War I	Pre-World War II[b]	Post-World War II[c]	Recent[d]
Asia					
Burma	Land	—	30	5	3
China, People's Republic of	Land	—	35	39	16
China, Republic of	Land	—	—	13	11
India	Land	36	19	10	5
Korea	Land	—	—	24	8
Pakistan	Land	36	19	8	6
Philippines	Land	—	—	12	8
Nepal	Land	—	—	. 55	18
Middle East					
Egypt	Land	—	23	14	8
Iraq	Product	—	18	24	—
Morocco	Land	—	—	10	6
Syria	Product	—	33	21	—
Tunisia	Land	—	—	6	4
Turkey	Product	25	10	2	—
Turkey	Land	—	4	—	0

Sources: See note to Appendix. In addition to the sources mentioned there, most of the figures for earlier years are taken from Haskell P. Wald and Joseph N. Froomkin, eds., *Papers and Proceedings of the Conference on Agricultural Taxation and Economic Development* (Cambridge, Mass.: Harvard Law School International Program in Taxation, 1954), pp. 301–302; Haskell P. Wald, *The Taxation of Agricultural Land in Underdeveloped Countries* (Cambridge, Mass.: Harvard University Press, 1959), pp. 62–63; and Walter Elkan, "Central and Local Taxes on Africans in Uganda," *Public Finance/Finances Publiques*, XIII (1958), 312–320.

[a] Arbitrarily classified.
[b] Usually for 1939 or 1940.
[c] Usually for 1950 or 1953.
[d] As in Table 1.

countries of crude, more or less area-based, land taxes.

Second, the two Chinas and Korea represent the efficacy of the traditional land income tax of China, levied originally in kind on the basis of gross produce (or the similar, more modern compulsory procurement policies). Although in both Taiwan and Korea substantial efforts have been devoted to improving and updating these land-based taxes, they have, as Table 2 shows, declined in revenue importance in recent years.

Third, India and Pakistan still show the effects of the great British-inspired reforms of the nineteenth century, which established in principle a land revenue system based on annual rental value, although in fact (as outlined in Chapter 6 below) this tax, too, now often amounts to little more than a tax on land area. A different historical tradition accounts for the continued importance of property taxes in a few countries in North Africa.

Finally, in a number of Latin American countries, all of which tax the capital value of land—Chile, Costa Rica, Nicaragua—the revenue figures show in part the results of more recent attempts at reviving land taxes. The proportion of the yield of these taxes produced by agricultural land, however, appears to be small as a rule, as is noted in Chapter 5, below.

In virtually every instance, however, as Table 2 shows for a number of selected countries, the figures in Table 1, even for the high land-tax countries, represent a marked decline from the relative importance reached in earlier years. A similar decline is also evident with respect to two other traditional agricultural taxes—the African personal tax and the marketing tax of the Middle East, both of which at least in part serve as substitutes for land taxes in those areas.

Indeed, a third inference which can be drawn from the data presented in the Appendix is that, apart from the prevalence of export taxes, there are sharply different patterns of agricultural taxation in different parts of the world. In sub-Saharan Africa, for example, only Ethiopia levies an important land tax, but at least ten other countries tax low-income rural residents significantly through various forms of "personal" taxes, which are really poll taxes of varying degrees of sophistication. This form of taxation is significant nowhere outside of sub-Saharan Africa, although many other countries attempt to levy direct "income" taxes on individuals engaged in agriculture. To take another instance, in Latin America and the Caribbean, all but two or three countries levy taxes on the capital value of land, a form of tax found in few other countries (for example, the Philippines).

Within the broad tax classifications shown in the tables, there are other similar identifiable patterns: for example, the Asian countries which levy significant land taxes appear generally to follow some variant of the Indian (for example, Nepal, Burma) or Chinese (for example, Korea, Taiwan) systems. Similarly, some influence of their particular colonial heritage is discernible in those former British colonies which levy land taxes, as noted in the next chapter. Finally, in Syria and some other countries in the Middle East (see Table 2) the most important taxes on agriculture are levied on domestically marketed produce. While not unknown elsewhere (Nigeria, Tanzania, Mexico), taxes of this type are not significant revenue producers anywhere else in the world.

This brief and inherently limited quantitative overview of the state of agricultural tax practice in the less developed world makes it plain that, apart from a very few small low-income countries, those countries which obtain one-fifth or even one-tenth of their tax revenues from taxes which may be considered to come from agriculture rely mainly on taxing exports.[3] Furthermore, most of the countries which tax agriculture relatively heavily are in sub-Saharan Africa, and many of them are small countries in which most of the population is engaged in subsistence agriculture and the receipts from exporting one or two agricultural crops constitute a relatively large proportion of monetary national income.[4]

The 34 countries which, according to Table 1, appear to obtain more than 10 percent of their tax revenues from taxes which may in large part come from agriculture may thus be divided into three groups: (1) Those with an important export agricultural sector—and a good year! This is by far the largest group, and one with representatives on every continent: Uganda, Nigeria, Sudan, Colombia, Haiti, El Salvador, Afghanistan, and Ceylon. Cotton, coffee, and cocoa appear to be the major products tapped for tax revenues by this group of countries. (2) Relatively traditional societies, mostly in Africa, in which relatively crude and traditional direct taxes on agriculture continue to be important: Niger, Nepal, Mali, Chad, Ethiopia, and Upper Volta. (3) Less stagnant societies in which direct agricultural taxes have, for one reason or another, not yet lost all fiscal importance: the two Chinas, Pakistan, India, Colombia, and Chile, for example. With respect to these latter groups, however, the decline in the importance of the traditional agricultural taxes has as a rule been marked in recent years, as Table 2 clearly shows.

FACTORS DETERMINING TAX PATTERNS

There is, it appears, no good example of a country successfully levying heavy direct taxes on agriculture as part of a conscious development policy apart from Meiji Japan and several Communist countries. When agricultural taxes are significant today, it is because most of the population is engaged in agriculture and there is really no other source of taxation. Except for a few countries particularly fortunate in their exports, these are also generally countries in which government revenues constitute a relatively small share of G.N.P. in any case.[5] Relatively important direct taxes on the agricultural population, rather than signifying a country in the throes of planned development, as suggested by the theory sketched in Chapter 1, mean usually that the country has hardly developed at all, so that there are few other possible tax bases to support even minimal government activities.

Within this general framework, the diversity between countries in the relative importance of different types of agricultural taxes may similarly be explained mainly by the availability of "tax handles" on the one hand and by the different historical influences to which countries have been exposed on the other. The weight and form of agricultural taxation found in practice in different countries depends upon many particular factors: the vagaries of fiscal history, often including that of the former colonial power; the structure of the agricultural sector with respect to the number and average size of production units; whether production is for cash or subsistence, for export or domestic production, of food or nonfood crops; the relative political importance of rural smallholders, landlords, urban workers, foreign plantation interests, and government itself; and so on.

Such deceptively simple expressions as "farm" and "farmer" in fact cover a great variety of very different systems of agricultural organization. A country where most exports are produced on a few foreign-owned plantations is virtually certain, for example, to have a very different tax system from one in which there are few exports and most agricultural production is consumed on the farm. Indeed, highly developed, export-oriented plantation agriculture, which is often quite capital-intensive, is really a special form of industrialization. Taxing this type of agricultural organization thus raises no special problems (other than political) in most cases—plantation agriculture should as a rule be brought within the scope of the regular income tax which now exists in almost all countries—so the subject is not discussed in detail in the present study.[6]

The influence of economic structure on the nature of a developing country's tax system is, of course, much more widespread than with respect to agricultural taxes alone.[7] But the predominance of agriculture and the lack of much else to tax in very poor, traditional countries virtually ensures that taxes on agriculture will be significant revenue producers.

Whether these taxes take the form of land taxes, as in Nepal and Ethiopia, or head and cattle taxes, as in Niger and Chad, itself depends largely upon the nature of the economic structure. If the dominant form of agriculture is nomadic livestock raising or if, as in many tropical African countries, land tenure is generally communal rather than individual and the major agricultural system is characterized by the use of the shifting cultivation or bush fallow technique, land taxes will not be a suitable means of taxing agriculture, and some other form of levy has to be developed to fit the indigenous circumstances. The African personal tax system described in the next chapter illustrates this factor at work. The marketing taxes in some Middle Eastern countries reflect a very different adaptation to the problems of land taxation, one more suitable for countries with old, well-developed traditional systems for marketing agricultural produce.

Some countries have tried, at one time or another, most forms of direct agricultural taxation. Iran offers an example. The central government land tax, following a complete revision in 1925, was changed in 1933 to a 3 percent tax on the value of marketed agricultural commodities. In turn, the latter was abolished in 1943 in favor of including agricultural income within the base of the newly established income tax. Administrative problems, however, soon led to the abandonment of this attempt and the re-establishment of the old land tax on 1925 land values, adjusted crudely upward by an index.[8] Similar, if less dramatic, switches may be seen in a number of other countries.

When the economic structure begins to shift away from the traditional agrarian mold, and commercialization and modernization take place in response to internal or external changes, the tax base will also change, as, in all likelihood, will the relative fiscal importance of different taxes. If, for example, cash farming for export develops rapidly, as it did in much of Africa after World War II, this new source of readily identifiable money income is likely to attract taxation, sometimes perhaps in part accidentally, as when the marketing boards established originally to stabilize producer prices become

A QUANTITATIVE OVERVIEW

significant revenue producers.[9] In other instances (India, Mexico) either exports are not very important relative to the rest of the economy[10] and other tax bases—internal consumption, industrial wages and profits, or, most usually, imports—are available to be tapped instead, or else the country chooses for economic or political reasons not to tax exports very heavily. In all cases, however, the traditional direct taxes by their very nature are unlikely to be very responsive to increases in real or money income and hence will tend to decline in relative importance as economies develop.

This brief preliminary examination of the historical and current agricultural tax scene in the developing countries suggests strongly that the widely varying relative importance of taxes on agriculture in different countries is largely determined by broad changes in economic structure. The data are far too inadequate to support any more systematic statistical evaluation of the determinants of agricultural tax structure. Nevertheless, it is clear enough that precisely what happens in any particular country reflects both its own inherited traditions (Ethiopia, China) and the external influences to which it has been subjected (India, Latin America).

The only universal statement which can be made with much confidence on the basis of the available quantitative evidence is that land taxes (and their "direct" tax counterparts elsewhere) have everywhere lost ground in recent decades. In Latin America, for example, only Chile, where agriculture now employs less than one-fifth of the economically active population,[11] appears to have revised its land-based taxes sufficiently to maintain relative revenue yields in the face of inflation and growth in recent years, and even there the struggle has been a losing one (see Chapter 5). Very few of the other countries with conventional land taxes based on either annual rental or capital value have been able to do even this. The cruder taxes of countries like Ethiopia and Paraguay have proved almost equally ineffective in recent years, largely because effective rates have been allowed to decline.

No country with a significant agricultural population (other than perhaps mainland China in part) has proved able to emulate the famed Japanese example of the later nineteenth century, when at times the land tax provided over 80 percent of central government tax revenues (see Chapter 6). No important agricultural country appears in recent years even to have tried to raise land taxes substantially. Despite the best efforts at persuasion by model builders and fiscal advisers alike, this examination of trends in land taxation in developing countries suggests that few have reversed the apparently inevitable decline as income levels rise and the economy becomes more diversified.

In Part One it was argued that the appropriate agricultural tax system in any particular country at any particular time depended on the objectives of development policy and the initial conditions of the country in question. The discussion in this chapter suggests that in practice agricultural taxation is indeed heavily influenced by the peculiar economic and institutional circumstances of each country. Further, the one great common characteristic of the diversity of developing countries—the decline in the relative economic importance of agriculture—has been matched on the tax front by the decline in the fiscal importance of taxes levied directly on agriculture, with the exception from time to time of a few exporting countries.

It is thus no exaggeration to say that not one developing country has to date utilized the undoubted potentials of properly constructed agricultural taxes as part of a conscious development policy as well as to raise revenue, although a few, like Chile and Nepal in their very different ways (see Chapters 4 and 5), have tried to move in this direction to a limited extent. Some years ago Haskell Wald concluded that "the full revenue-producing capacities of well administered, carefully designed land taxes that are assessed according to modern land classification procedures remains to be tested in the underdeveloped countries."[12] It still does, because few such taxes exist and few governments have seriously tried to introduce them.

One reason for this striking lack of correspondence between theoretical prescription and practice may be that prescriptions for land tax reform need to be tailored much more carefully to each individual case than has usually been done. Another is, no doubt, that the administrative and political obstacles to the effective implementation of the conventionally proposed reform schemes are much greater in almost all situations than was earlier realized. The next three chapters provide ample evidence to support both of these propositions and lay the empirical foundation for the subsequent more analytical discussion of agricultural land taxes.

4

DIRECT TAXES ON AGRICULTURE

An examination of the tax systems in developing countries leaves one with an overriding impression of the great variety of fiscal instruments employed to tax agriculture. There are, for example, taxes on land area, rental and capital value, unimproved value, net income, rated potential or normal output, marketing taxes, export taxes, gross produce taxes, capital gains and land transfer taxes, special assessments, taxation through marketing boards and exchange rates, and so on and on. Each of these taxes itself usually has many subvarieties: actual or presumptive base, proportional or graduated rates, collections in money or in kind, as well as a variety of special exemptions for equity (hardship, old age), traditional (religious, public), or incentive (reclaimed land, land distributed in agrarian reform programs) reasons. The purpose of the present chapter is to examine briefly the principal alternatives to direct taxes on agricultural land—export and marketing taxes, and poll and income taxes—as well as to consider a few features of land taxes and of some land-based taxes which are closely related in concept, if not always in practice, to income taxes. In view of the scope, complexity, and rapidly changing nature of the subject matter, the analysis of these taxes does not, of course, pretend to be complete or up to date in all respects.

EXPORT TAXES

Most major tropical agricultural products are now subject to taxation either directly or through the operation of marketing boards or the exchange rate system. The objectives, forms, effects, and future of this widespread and important segment of agricultural taxation are considered in the present section.

The considerable efficacy of export taxes as revenue raisers has already been noted. There is no question that the revenue objective has been a key factor giving rise to the various systems used to tax agricultural exports in many countries. The potential utility of export taxation for other purposes has seldom, however, gone unnoticed for long.

In Burma, for example, the State Agricultural Marketing Board (SAMB) was charged after independence in 1948 with the taxation of agriculture in the face of the sharp decline in the yield of the traditional land tax as a result of inflation and the administrative upheaval accompanying independence.[1] The SAMB performed this task admirably, producing 40 percent of total government receipts in the years from 1948 to 1953. At the same time, however, the primary function of the marketing board in the eyes of the government was not simply to collect taxes but to replace the non-Burmese groups which had controlled rice-export marketing before the war and thus, in Levin's words, to serve as an "instrument of revolt" against the old export economy.[2] In this respect, Burma seems rather unique.

Two other tasks with which the Burmese SAMB was entrusted—to guarantee a stable price to the cultivator and to prevent further domestic inflation by stabilizing the internal price of rice—are shared with export tax systems in many other countries, however. The Nigerian marketing boards, for example, were set up primarily to stabilize producer prices, with the secondary purpose of financing agricultural research, disease eradication, and other expenditures beneficial to agriculture.[3] A prime function of the Thai Rice Office in the early postwar years was to hold down the internal price of rice; after 1954 the same objective was pursued through export taxes (the "rice premium").[4]

Many countries have also pursued stabilization objectives through export taxes of the "sliding-scale" type, where the rate is varied according to the market price. In Costa Rica, for example, the export tax on coffee was, after 1950, levied on a sliding scale based on the average price per quintal and varying from 0 percent if the price was below U.S. $35.00 to 10 percent of total value when the price was above U.S. $42.50.[5] Taxes of this type have existed at various times in Ghana, Nigeria, Uganda, Malaya, Ceylon, Thailand, Guatemala, and El Salvador.

Export taxation has also been explicitly used in some countries to absorb part of the increase in the local currency price of exports resulting from devaluation. In Mexico, for example, higher rates of export tax were intended to absorb the windfall gains accruing to exporters from devaluations in 1938, 1947, and 1954.[6] More recently, the Philippines imposed a stabilization tax at rates of 8 and 10 percent on a range of exported agricultural products in connection with a 1970 currency devaluation.[7] These rates were to be automatically reduced on a regular basis over the next four years, presumably in the expectation that local currency costs would rise after devaluation. Export taxes have also been employed in connection with devaluations in Colombia, Uruguay, Greece, and India.

There are three principal forms in which exports are taxed. The first is by explicit export taxes, usually of the sliding-scale type. Where specific taxes are retained, it is usually to avoid the valuation problems of ad valorem taxation for products for which there is no readily available quoted world price (such as bananas and tea). Commodities like coffee and cocoa where prices are quoted regularly on organized exchanges give rise to no problems in this respect, and by the early 1950's most export-taxing countries had shifted to ad valorem taxes, often of the sliding-scale variety.

Specific taxes have occasionally been supported as improving the quality of exports by penalizing lower-valued grades, but a similar result may be obtained by differential ad valorem taxes, as in the case of robusta and arabica coffee in Tanzania.[8] This consideration may be important where, as in the case of the International Coffee Agreement, quality improvements represent the main way in which a country can raise the value of its exports.

The second means by which agricultural exports are taxed is through state marketing boards, which usually have a statutory monopoly of purchases for export of produce within their jurisdiction. When there is a differential between external prices and the proceeds realized by domestic producers, these boards reap a surplus which is analytically equivalent to an export tax, although the exact effects may differ depending on a number of factors, such as, whether the board buys directly from producers or simply from private traders at the point of export. Marketing boards may also, of course, subsidize exports by running deficits in some years. Furthermore, not all of marketing board surplus is necessarily transmitted to the coffers of government as are other "tax" revenues. The "tax" element in marketing board operations thus requires careful analysis in each particular instance.[9] Despite these qualifications, there is little doubt that the device of the state marketing board, whether in Burma, Nigeria, or Argentina, has proved to be the most effective way of levying heavy taxes on export agriculture yet discovered, at least for short periods of time.

The third main technique for taxing export agriculture is by means of the exchange rate system. The use of exchange rates as a taxing device has a long history, although its popularity has declined somewhat in recent years. One approach is to maintain a single exchange rate that overvalues domestic currency: the exporter is thus "taxed" in that he receives less local currency than the scarcity value to the economy of the foreign exchange he earns, while importers are in effect subsidized by being able to purchase foreign goods below their "real" value.[10] This approach constitutes an important way in which real income has at times in countries such as Argentina and Pakistan been transferred from the exporting agricultural sector to the importing, and largely nonagricultural, sector, but it is "invisible" in that it involves no tax that accrues to government (except insofar as government is itself an importer).[11]

More explicitly analogous to an export tax is a differential exchange rate of the sort that operated in Colombia from 1963 to 1967, when the official exchange rate for imports and minor exports was maintained at a markedly higher level than the peso rate paid for a dollar earned in coffee exports. Some of the proceeds of this differential went to the national government budget, yielding around 14 percent of central government revenues in 1963, for example. In large part, however, much of the "tax" levied on coffee producers through this system also served to subsidize importers.[12] Even higher taxes, providing 31 percent of government revenues in 1963, have been levied on Brazilian coffee producers through the exchange rate system.[13]

DIRECT TAXES ON AGRICULTURE

These various tax instruments have been employed in some countries both consecutively and in combination. Colombia, for example, also imposed a "retention tax" on private exporters (who account for two-thirds of coffee exports), requiring them to turn over to the National Coffee Fund a certain percentage of exports, either in kind or the equivalent cash value in pesos at the current support price. From 1957 to 1962 and again after 1967, an explicit export tax was levied on the foreign-exchange proceeds of coffee exports. Most countries with marketing boards also have export taxes, often administered by the boards.

Thailand provides a good illustration of the use of all three major approaches to export taxation.[14] Until 1947, the main taxes on exports were levied by the export monopoly Rice Office. From 1947 to 1954, a multiple exchange rate system was also employed for the same purpose, while, since 1954, export taxes have been imposed. The "rice premium" which has for some years constituted the main Thai tax on rice is actually a complicated specific export tax, the rate of which varies with the grade and variety of rice. In the 1950's it accounted for close to 20 percent of total government revenues, although by 1970 its yield had declined sharply to 2 percent. In addition to other minor export taxes, the rice premium was supplemented by a complex set of export quotas and various "invisible taxes" which burdened producers but often yielded little revenue to government as, for example, the requirement that specified percentages of export shipments be sold to public agencies at low government prices.

The substantial revenue produced by this tax system actually constituted only the smaller part of the tax burden borne by Thai rice cultivators, however. One objective of this set of controls and taxes was to hold down the internal price of rice, the major consumption staple, for urban consumers. One estimate is that local rice prices were over one-third lower (and the urban cost of living one-fifth lower) as a result of the rice premium than they would otherwise be. As a result of this effect on the domestic price of rice, all rice sold in Thailand, whether exported or not, was in effect taxed through this system, which was estimated to take over 20 percent of farm income in the early 1960's.

Among the effects attributed by some to this heavy tax are the lack of modernization of Thai agriculture, the shift in the composition of agricultural production away from rice, inadequate exports, and the lack of effective demand for nonfarm products in the rural sector. The principal benefits of the system were presumably the revenues it produced and the possible encouragement to industrialization from the lower labor costs due to the reduced price of rice. The recent virtual suspension of the rice premium, while reflecting the changed situation in the world rice market, perhaps also suggests that the perceived costs of the system have come to outweigh the benefits.

Export taxes are popular revenue raisers largely because they are administratively easy to impose and collect. While they can be evaded by means of smuggling, the dimensions of this problem are unlikely to be great in most cases—certainly not compared to the evasion problems with most other possible tax sources. The administrative advantages of taxing exports are particularly marked where small producers predominate, and for this reason export taxes are sometimes considered as substitutes for the more complicated land and income taxes.

In El Salvador, for example, coffee growers are exempted from income tax on coffee earnings because there is an export tax on coffee.[15] Although the export tax is paid by the relatively few coffee buyers, it is assumed to be shifted back to the grower. No account is taken of the small amount of coffee production that is sold domestically. Similarly, in Guatemala coffee export taxes paid can be used as a credit against income taxes.

Experience suggests that procedures such as these are more likely to retard than to spread the application of the general income tax to agriculture. Furthermore, integrating export and income taxes in this fashion implicitly presumes that the incidence of the two taxes is identical, though in fact the precise incidence of most export taxes is not at all clear.

Two principal questions concerning the incidence of export taxes are: What is the extent to which export taxes are borne by foreigners? How is that portion of the tax borne domestically shared among landowners, workers, traders, and others taking part in the process of distribution and production of the taxed commodity? The first question is generally easier to answer. Most analysts agree that it is, as a rule, unlikely that an export tax imposed on primary agricultural products by a single country will be shifted forward to foreign consumers.

If a country is a relatively small producer, it will face an elastic demand curve for its products and cannot affect the world price regardless of its own supply conditions.[16] If the taxing country accounts for a large part of total world exports—Brazil, coffee; Pakistan, jute —it may have some success in shifting taxes abroad in the short run, but in the long run it is likely to face increasing competition from other producers or from competing natural or synthetic goods. Given the inherent difficulties of estimating the relevant elasticities, it is not surprising that analyses of specific countries have sometimes reached different conclusions. In general, however, "with rare exceptions, countries that are considering export duties should regard them primarily as taxes on their own producers and traders rather than as a means of taxing foreigners."[17]

The effective incidence of export taxes within the domestic economy raises more complex questions and is more difficult to resolve. The legal incidence of export taxes is generally on the exporter from whom the tax is collected. In principle, however, the effective incidence will depend on alternative opportunities open to landowners, workers, producers, and traders and on their relative mobility between different employments. One might, therefore, expect a substantial portion of export taxes to be borne by the relatively immobile cultivators themselves.

In Thailand, for example, most analysts appear to agree that the rice premium is borne by the farmer.[18] In Guatemala and El Salvador, despite their income tax treatment of coffee producers, some studies suggest that part of export taxes might be borne by hired agricultural laborers, who have very few alternative employment opportunities.[19] Occasionally government policies attempt to limit such backward shifting by controlling agricultural wages, as in Malaysia and Ceylon. In Burma and Nigeria, on the other hand, it has been suggested that in part the profits of the marketing boards may represent taxes on processors and intermediate traders and on landlords.[20]

It is not possible to disentangle here the myriad assumptions on the nature of competition and government regulation which underlie these diverse conclusions in the different countries. As a tentative general conclusion, however, export taxes may probably in the usual case be considered a tax on farmers without doing undue violence to the facts.

It is, in any case, this view of the incidence of export taxes which underlies the objection most frequently made to them: that they distort agricultural incentives and, in particular, restrict production for export. The weight of the evidence is now very much to the effect that the price elasticity of supply of primary exports is significantly positive, especially in the long run (many tree crops take five to nine years to reach commercial production).[21]

Various studies have, for example, concluded that substantial export taxes in Nigeria have at times made the production of controlled crops quite unattractive. To illustrate, from 1955 to 1961, 26 percent of potential producer income from oil palm production in Nigeria was withdrawn through export duties (13 percent), marketing board surplus (6 percent) and produce purchase taxes (6 percent).[22] It is thus hardly surprising that a recent study of palm oil concluded that "the commercial establishment of oil palm plantations is effectively precluded by marketing board pricing policies which have reduced expected rates of return to near zero. Even existing oil palm plantations cannot profitably replant, and these plantations will be (or have been) shifted to other crops or permitted to revert to bush unless these pricing policies are altered."[23]

The taxing away of from one-quarter to one-third of the potential producer prices of export crops for prolonged periods of time, as in Nigeria, appears to have resulted in reduced producer incentives, lower investment in agriculture, especially that in innovative technology, and induced migration to urban areas.[24] Similar obstacles to the commercialization and modernization of agriculture as a result of heavy export taxation have been suggested in the very different cases of Thailand, Pakistan, and Argentina, where up to one-half of potential earnings from agricultural exports were taxed away from 1945 to 1950 by the low prices paid to farmers for compulsory procurement by the state marketing agency.[25]

In general, therefore, it appears that export taxes will usually reduce exports and discourage investment in agricultural modernization. This argument is not conclusive against heavy reliance on such taxation, however, for the gain in government revenue may be judged worth the cost, and appropriate government expenditure policy can in principle redirect resources between and within economic sectors to offset the disincentive effects if desired.

A stronger argument against continued reliance on export taxation for revenue may be that revenues from this source are likely to prove very unstable. If government revenues come 'o depend to any great extent on movements in the external sector, a marked foreign-trade cycle in revenues may emerge. The abundance of revenue in the up-swing is conducive to excessive tax liberalization and expenditure expansion, while the usual downward rigidity of current expenditures leads to inflationary reliance on deficit financing and cuts in public-sector investment in the downswing. Colombia in the 1950's and 1960's illustrates the working of this mechanism perfectly,[26] and Ceylonese experience shows the same forces at work.[27] Rather than providing a strong stabilizing element in the fiscal system, export taxes may thus prove destabilizing unless very carefully managed.

On the other hand, as noted earlier, there is often a strong stabilization and equity case for absorbing through the fiscal system the wind-fall surplus accruing to the traditional export sector as a result of devaluation, and export taxes can be most helpful in this task. Marketing boards can readily adjust prices each year and hence probably provide the greatest flexibility in this regard, but an export tax graduated with respect to price can also do good service.

Furthermore, in cases where the volume of exports is limited in accordance with international commodity agreements, a principal objective of export taxes may indeed be to restrict production. Both the Colombian and the Tanzanian coffee taxes have, for example, been criticized as being inadequate for this task.

Reductions in export taxes to stimulate production have recently been much more common than increases for restrictive purposes, however. Afghanistan, for example, recently reduced taxes on the export of karakul wool and cotton to encourage production. Similarly, Paraguay abolished export taxes and other duties on hides and rice in 1971 in order to facilitate exports of these products.[28] Other recent reductions in Pakistan, Thailand, and Zaire have been intended to offset declining export prices and encourage exports.

Export taxes may thus take many forms and serve many different ends in different countries and at different times in the same country. They may be powerful revenue producers at times, but very undependable at other times. They may serve the ends of economic stabilization, or the revenues they provide may prove in the final analysis to be destabilizing. They may unduly repress agricultural development in general or with respect to particular crops, or they may not exercise sufficient restraint on production.

On balance, it would appear that, despite their undoubted defects and declining importance, export taxes are still too attractive and potentially valuable as a fiscal instrument to be abandoned completely in many countries. Instead, more attention should probably be paid to making the structure and level of export taxes consonant with the aims of agricultural and general development policy. The level of export taxes should, for example, be set in large part as one component of agricultural pricing strategy in the light of developmental objectives and world market conditions.[29] A particularly elaborate proposal of this sort with respect to Colombia, for example, recently suggested that coffee export taxes should be related to such criteria as the size and characteristics of the farm, the density and age structure of coffee trees, and the relative returns to coffee and prospective alternative crops per unit of area.[30]

Attempts to use the export tax instrument in such detail seem likely, however, to vitiate its prime virtue of administrative convenience and simplicity. If such detailed criteria are to be considered in a tax system at all, which seems unlikely given the limited administrative resources of most developing countries, the land tax would seem a much more suitable vehicle. In theory, there is no question that land taxes are a most attractive alternative to export taxes from the point of view of production incentives, but their administrative disadvantages in many developing countries are, as noted later, so great that they are most unlikely to be equally productive of revenue. Whatever the defects of the Nigerian marketing boards, for example, without the revenues they provided it is hard to see how, in the face of the grave administrative and political difficulties of all other revenue sources, any substantial public-sector development could have been successfully financed in postwar Nigeria.

Both equity and incentive considerations urge more reliance on land and other taxes, but revenue, stabilization, and agricultural development strategy, of which the greatest is revenue, often support continued use of export taxes in countries where conditions facilitate their use. Export taxes will unquestionably continue to fade in importance in most countries, but whether land taxes will then become the major means of taxing agriculture is quite another question.

MARKETING TAXES

Several countries levy taxes on marketed produce in addition to taxing exports as such. In some instances, however, these taxes are really supplemental export taxes, often imposed by local governments. In Tanzania, for instance, a "cess" of 5 percent may be imposed on any agricultural produce, fish, or livestock bought or sold within or exported from a district. Most districts in fact levy such taxes on a number of commodities, particularly those (again mainly exports) sold through cooperative marketing organizations.[31] Although these taxes, and similar levies in Nigeria and Kenya, are sometimes considered as substitutes for the taxes on agricultural land which do not really exist in these countries, or at least as an approximation to the "personal" tax, these African levies seem best characterized as export taxes.

A different, more far-reaching type of marketing tax affecting a wider range of products is found in a few other developing countries. In Mexico, for example, most of the states levy small taxes on a wide range of agricultural products, with the tax generally being collected at the time of first sale or of export from the state. Some of these taxes, which are usually specific in nature, thus amount in fact to internal customs duties collected by tax agents on roads, railways, or other control points where goods cross provincial borders.[32] In Greece, a general 3 percent sales tax is withheld by the wholesaler when he purchases agricultural products from the farmers. The apparent acceptance of this tax by the rural population has been attributed in part to the fact that two-thirds of the proceeds are earmarked for the agricultural social insurance agency, with the remainder going to support the rural police and the municipalities.[33] A number of other countries levy local taxes of one sort or another on transactions in certain agricultural products: for example, on the slaughter of livestock as in Indonesia, Colombia and Paraguay, where these taxes have at times amounted to as much as 6 percent of the value of livestock.[34]

This motley array of taxes on marketed agricultural products shares several characteristics in common. First, the taxes are normally collected only when transactions take place in relatively controlled markets. Small sales and, of course, produce consumed on the farm thus escape taxation. Second, in most cases these taxes are collected by, and the proceeds accrue to, local government agencies. None of the taxes on marketed domestic produce so far mentioned yields significant revenue on a national scale. Third, the structure of these marketing taxes is generally crude, with a premium being put on administrative convenience and ease of collection at the cost of equity and integration with other taxes. A particular administrative advantage of these taxes in some countries is that they enable the taxing authority to avoid untangling the complexities of landownership. Finally, the incidence of taxes levied on sales of agricultural produce for domestic consumption will likely be on the consumer as a rule, certainly in countries characterized by a strong urban demand for foodstuffs and agricultural raw materials.

Since most general sales taxes—in Colombia, for example—exempt unprocessed food products in order to reduce the regressivity of the tax system, levying taxes on particular basic food products appears a rather anachronistic means of financing local governments.[35] In addition, since self-consumed production is not taxed, the development of a commercially oriented agriculture would seem likely to be retarded by such taxes. Even the alleged administrative convenience of this form of taxation largely reflects the superabundance of low-grade clerical labor available in many developing countries; it is not really a simple form of taxation at all for it requires a great deal of weighing, counting, valuing, and checking in most of its forms. As societies develop, such taxes are likely to become increasingly irrelevant.

A considerably more important form of taxation on marketed produce has been imposed in some Middle Eastern countries, often in replacement of the Ottoman tithe, or tax on gross income or produce.[36] Although in the latter days of the Ottoman Empire the tithe raised around 25 percent of government revenues in Turkey, it was in all other respects a most unsatisfactory levy.[37] It was, for instance, administered by "tax farmers" who, often acting monopolistically, purchased from the state the right to collect the tax in a particular district, and then proceeded to abuse their privileges, for example, by forcing the peasants either to leave the crop in the field until it could be assessed (thus greatly increasing the risk of weather damage) or else to sell their share of the crop to the collectors at low prices in order to be assessed on time.

In 1925, soon after the formation of the Turkish Republic, this archaic levy was replaced by a "tax on soil products" marketed through railway and harbor facilities. Despite this limitation, the new tax proved very costly to administer and was replaced the next year by a general sales tax—from which agricultural products (except wheat flour) were soon exempted, leaving agriculture subject only to a low land tax. Under the fiscal stresses of World War II, however, the tithe was reintroduced in 1943 at a general rate of 8 percent on gross output (12 percent on cash crops) with collections generally being made in kind. This tax also proved cumbersome and costly to administer and was abandoned in 1946, although the equally ancient livestock tax remained in existence until 1962 when it was replaced, at least in theory, by an extension of the income tax to agriculture.

Taxes on marketed produce in Iraq and Syria were more effective and lasted longer than those in Turkey or Iran. In Iraq, for example, where the *istihlak* or consumption tax was imposed in 1931 to replace the ancient land tax, it produced 20 percent of tax revenues as late as 1952. This tax, much like the Greek sales tax, was collected at certain licensed trading centers from wholesale merchants who bought produce from farmers. In 1953 it was abolished on a wide range of agricultural products except when such products were exported, although it continued to be levied at a rate of 10 percent on the most important crops—cereal products and dates. Apparently largely as a result of this change, the combined receipts of the land tax and the agricultural produce tax fell sharply to 7 percent of current revenues in 1955–1956.[38] In 1960 the marketing tax was replaced by a revised land tax which is, however, assessed on the annual gross value of agricultural produce. In 1968 this tax produced only 1 percent of the revenue.[39] The opposite change took place in the Sudan, where a traditional land tax on crops grown on nonirrigated land was converted to a marketing tax collected from the purchaser.

These important Middle Eastern marketing taxes shared most of the virtues and limitations noted above with respect to the lesser taxes found elsewhere. In addition, however, they have at times produced very substantial amounts of revenue, though not without damaging agricultural incentives to produce and to market. The heavy taxation of agricultural produce by the Ottomans has long been castigated by historians for the damage it did to agricultural production by discouraging investment and effort.[40]

The subsequent transformation of the tithe into a marketing tax in some countries suffered generally from the same defects, although at a lower level to match the lower burden imposed, and also added its own bias against selling crops for cash. If, as argued earlier, a main objective of agricultural policy in many developing countries is to improve the supply of food to the nonagricultural sector, taxes which directly penalize marketing are obviously to be avoided as a rule.

Furthermore, these levies are generally inequitable. The fact that marketing taxes (or the tithe for that matter) neglect differential costs of production means that, insofar as their incidence is on producers, the effective tax rate on net income will vary from one farm unit to another, increasing as the fertility of the land decreases. If farmers in some areas of the country can consume their own produce while those elsewhere, who do not produce basic food crops, must market cash crops to purchase food, another source of inequity is created. Both of these problems also exist with export taxes, of course. The latter inequity will not be alleviated even if, as argued earlier, much or all of the marketing taxes levied on domestically sold produce is in fact shifted forward to consumers, in which case they act as highly regressive consumption taxes.

In short, on most counts marketing taxes do not appear to be a desirable component of the fiscal structure of developing countries. Their decline in recent years even in their traditional bastions thus appears to be a richly deserved fate. This type of levy will not be further discussed in the present study.

LABOR AND POLL TAXES

The apparent fact that many people in the rural sector of developing countries have little to do for much of the year has led, in some quarters, to a revival of interest in one of the most ancient forms of taxation—the labor, or poll tax. In one recent proposal, for instance, each individual would be liable for so many days' labor on such community development work as building roads or schools; alternatively, he could free himself of this obligation by paying a specified poll tax in cash.[41] The use of taxes payable in labor has also been proposed for India as a relatively simple way of financing community development projects in rural areas.[42] Schemes along these lines in fact already exist, with varying degrees of compulsion and apparently with some degree of success, in countries as different as Pakistan and Colombia as part of general programs of community development at the local level with central guidance.[43]

Although there continues to be substantial dispute about the extent and nature of rural "disguised unemployment" in many developing countries, there is little doubt that the mobilization of seasonally unused labor resources for local public works may be a potentially useful way to increase developmental revenues. As a rule, however, experience suggests that an unacceptably high degree of coercion may be required to direct and allocate this labor centrally. On the other hand, a number of countries have found fairly willing acceptance of direct labor contributions to erect local schools, farm-to-market roads, and other capital projects of direct and visible local benefit. Further, if the tax is paid in cash instead of kind, an additional stimulus to produce and sell agricultural produce for cash is created, thus furthering the commercialization of the agricultural sector, which is often an objective of development policy.

Many countries now have or had in the past minor taxes along these lines. The Turkish road tax of 1872, for instance, was payable in kind (four days' work a year) or cash (the equivalent salary for an unskilled worker). Under the republic this obligation was increased to a maximum of 10 days in 1929, although all except the very poorest peasants preferred to pay in cash, partly because payment in kind involved the extra costs of going to the place of work and feeding oneself while working. A recent study concluded that this tax (which was replaced in 1952 by a gasoline tax) was not in fact very useful in mobilizing developmental resources or in stimulating the commercialization of agriculture in Turkey for several reasons. First, there was not really much surplus manpower available in Turkey for most of this period. Secondly, the infrastructure needed to develop a more commercial agriculture was lacking, and the tax proceeds were apparently not spent so as to overcome this deficiency. Finally, the tax was so badly administered that most of the resources made available were wasted, and considerable ill will between peasants and the taxing authorities was created.[44] Since Turkey, like other countries, has a long and moderately successful tradition of using collective labor for locally determined public projects at the village level, it appears that a principal defect with the road tax was that it produced no benefits directly and visibly related to the welfare of taxpayers.

A similar national labor tax exists in Bolivia, where each male is responsible for two days' work on the national roads each year, unless he commutes the tax by an appropriate money payment. This tax is of very minor importance, however. More significant is the fact that some local peasant unions, after the Bolivian Revolution of 1952, undertook on their own initiative substantial community action programs providing and maintaining schools, access roads, and small irrigation systems. The desire for schools in particular proved to be a powerful incentive to "voluntary taxation" of this sort.[45] Once again, therefore, the potential of mobilizing local labor resources for local public works projects is verified by Bolivian experience, as is the difficulty of doing much on a national basis with crude labor and poll taxes.

The most that can perhaps be expected from the ancient fiscal instrument of head taxes in most countries is to regularize and channel to some extent the efforts which local communities around the world seem willing to put forward for projects of direct and visible local benefit. The historic associations of poll taxes with forced labor probably prevent them from playing a more significant role in any country with pretensions to democracy, despite their theoretical merits in situations of widespread underemployment.

THE AFRICAN PERSONAL TAXES

A much more sophisticated form of poll taxation has had a surprisingly successful existence in sub-Saharan Africa, however. Owing in part to the nonexistence of individualized land tenure in most rural areas, there is virtually no taxation of rural land as such in Africa. Partly in lieu of land taxes, a wide variety of so-called "personal taxes" have developed in many countries to reach their large subsistence agricultural sectors.[46]

The situation in Zambia, for example, illustrates the problem of taxing agricultural land in most of tropical Africa. Zambia has a long-established and well-run tax on urban property. Land titles are fairly clear, the valuation and collection process appears to afford no particular difficulty, land is taxed at a differentially higher rate than improvements, and the tax provides the bulk of local government revenues in the urban areas of Zambia. But there is no taxation of rural land, and there never has been. The principal reason for this state of affairs is that most rural land is held in the communal pattern of land tenure without registered titles, although, unusually for Africa, legal title generally rests with the government instead of the community or chief. Some state land, along the line-of-rail, is leased mainly to European farmers, and there would seem no reason why this leasehold land could not be taxed. Other than this limited possibility, however, rural land taxation is just not possible in Zambia, as in most other African countries, without definition and registration of land titles.

In this situation, the major direct tax levied in most African rural areas is the "personal tax." These personal taxes are known by different names in different countries—poll tax, hut tax, graduated personal tax, village tax, minimum tax, cattle tax, income rate. Table 3 illustrates the variety of nomenclature employed. As a rule these taxes have been levied by central governments, but collected by local governments, with the proceeds going to both levels of government in many countries. Most personal taxes are levied on those listed on the tax rolls without requiring individual tax returns, and on a decentralized basis in order to take full advantage of all available information on assessment.

In recent years some of these personal taxes have, following a pattern first established in Uganda, become somewhat more sophisticated and transformed into the "graduated personal tax," which is "a hybrid between a poll tax and an elementary form of income tax."[47] In this limited sense, then, some African countries may be said to have been relatively successful in applying a broad-based income tax to agriculture.

Despite its widespread nature, however, the personal tax system constitutes a large proportion of total government revenues in only a very few sub-Saharan countries—Malawi and Niger, for example, as discussed in Chapter 3. Little of the revenue in Malawi comes from farmers, however. Furthermore, the relative importance of the tax has declined sharply in recent years, a trend which seems likely to continue. Although the heyday of the African personal tax is thus

TABLE 3. AFRICAN PERSONAL TAXES[a]

Country	Nomenclature
Former British territories	
Gambia, The	Yard tax, "strange" farmers' tax
Ghana	Poll tax
Kenya	Hut and poll tax, graduated personal tax (GPT)
Malawi	Hut and poll tax, minimum tax, GPT
Nigeria	General tax, poll tax, income rate, personal tax
Sierra Leone	House tax, chiefdom tax
Tanzania	House tax, poll tax, GPT
Uganda	Hut tax, poll tax, GPT
Zambia	Native tax
Former French West Africa[b]	
Dahomey	Minimum tax
Guinea	Personal tax
Ivory Coast	Personal tax, *taxe vicinale*
Mali	Minimum tax, *taxe de cercle*
Mauritania	Personal tax, *zekkat*
Niger	Minimum tax, *taxe de cercle*
Senegal	Minimum tax, personal tax
Upper Volta	Personal tax
Other countries	
Chad	Personal tax, civic tax
Congo	Native tax, additional tax, personal tax
Gabon	Head tax, commercial tax
Liberia	Hut tax
Togo	Capitation tax

Source: Edward A. Arowolo, "The Taxation of Low Incomes in African Countries," *I.M.F. Staff Papers*, XV (July 1968), 328.

[a] Collection in all countries is carried out by local authorities although in most of them the central government provides the authority for levying the tax and receives all or part of the revenue.

[b] Information relates to territorial governments existing before the attainment of independence in 1959. All of these countries also imposed some form of cattle tax. There have, of course, been a good many changes in some of these countries since independence.

probably past, a closer look at it is worthwhile because of its considerable theoretical and practical interest.

In Nigeria, for example, the largest country in tropical Africa, no rural land taxes are in effect. The extremely variegated systems of land tenure and the dominance of communal landholding, particularly in the southern regions, make any conventional form of land tax impracticable. Furthermore, throughout the country, govern-

DIRECT TAXES ON AGRICULTURE

mental knowledge of the precise patterns of property ownership and use is almost nonexistent. The main direct tax on the agricultural sector is therefore the "personal tax" in its various forms. This tax is a state levy in Nigeria, so that its precise characteristics vary from state to state.

In the former Northern Region, for example, the personal tax, which predated British rule, was substantially simplified by a major reform in 1962, which integrated the tax into the income tax, so that a person with an income of over £400 became subject to income tax rather than personal tax.[48] On the other hand, where it was difficult to ascertain individual incomes, a "community" tax could be assessed on the community by the provincial authorities, based on the number of adult males and a per capita rate supposed to reflect roughly the wealth of the district. The importance of cash crops is generally a main index of wealth in such systems. The tax thus assessed was then apportioned by the local authority, on a graduated basis related to estimated individual wealth, among those individuals who were not subject to the graduated personal tax. If personal tax was paid at a flat rate, it could be credited against the apportioned community tax. Even this crude tax was not practical in the case of nomadic herdsmen, so an alternative "cattle tax" was levied on them, with rates varying according to the type of animal.

The personal tax as a whole provided an estimated 65 percent of Nigerian regional government taxes in 1964–1965; 22 percent of this amount came from the community tax and 6 percent from the cattle tax, both of which are applied only in rural areas. These personal taxes constituted around 10 percent of total regional revenues. They also provided almost 90 percent of the revenues of the local authorities which collected them.

The picture was rather similar in the rest of Nigeria, with the personal tax being most important at the local level. In 1960–1961, for instance, the personal tax constituted 48 percent of local government revenues in Western Nigeria and 25 percent in Eastern Nigeria, the most developed part of the country at the time. In these two regions also the personal tax was adopted as the lower part of the income tax structure—in effect, as the minimum rate of income tax. There are also flat-rate local taxes imposed in some areas, as in some other countries in West Africa.

An instance of a less developed system of personal taxation is provided by Zaïre (the former Belgian Congo).[49] For many years under the colonial regime of Belgium the most important direct tax in the Congo was the *impôt indigène,* or "native tax," a poll tax levied on adult males at rates set in accordance with the estimated degree of development of the area. Originally, this tax evolved partly to replace forced labor, although the latter system was also utilized extensively by the colonial administration. In 1900 the native tax accounted for over 46 percent of total current revenues, but by 1958 its contribution had fallen to around 3 percent. In addition, the various rural local authorities levied, on the same basis, supplemental taxes which in 1956 provided 37 percent of their income. These taxes had to be paid in money and were generally collected by the customary chiefs. Although a personal tax more like those elsewhere in West Africa was levied in 1950, those engaged in agricultural production were generally exempted from it, and the old tax continued in rural areas.

After independence, the name of the *impôt indigène* was changed to the "minimum personal tax," its rate was raised, and it was put on a more explicitly graduated base and allowed as a deduction from certain other taxes on income. In fact, however, the relative collapse after independence of the provincial authorities which collected the personal tax led to its virtual disappearance as an effective revenue source. Similar administrative difficulties affected export tax collections, although to a considerably lesser degree. As a result, while self-employed native farmers were apparently considerably more heavily taxed in relation to average income than other natives under the colonial regime in the 1950's, largely through the export duties and the personal tax, by the mid-1960's there was probably no significant transfer of resources from agriculture taking place through the Congolese fiscal system.

A much less significant but similarly crude tax exists in Liberia in the form of the hut tax, in 1969 levied at a rate of $16 per hut in tribal areas. This Liberian tax is closer to the original form of the personal tax—huts being easier to find than people—than most others now existing in Africa. This tax, too, is collected by local chieftains who receive a commission for their services. Because the tax is invariant to the number of adults in a hut, one would expect more persons per hut and larger huts than would otherwise be the case; there is reportedly some evidence to this effect.[50]

DIRECT TAXES ON AGRICULTURE

The taxation of agriculture is more advanced than this in the former British colonies of East and Central Africa. In Uganda, for example, personal taxes were first introduced, as elsewhere in Africa, around 1900 by the colonial administration in the form of hut taxes, in order to force Africans either to produce for cash or to work for wages in plantations or elsewhere.[51] As late as 1938 the African poll tax produced 31 percent of central government revenue in Uganda. The proportion dropped sharply in the years following the Second World War, as it did in most of British East and Central Africa.[52] This decline resulted from the fundamental inelasticity of a tax which is closely tied to the level of income of the poorest people in the country, as well as from the growing opportunity to tax export revenues.

The fall in personal taxes was not as sharp as these figures make it appear, however, for in this same period these levies came to be the mainstay of local government finance, and local governments, which had always been the tax collectors, proved much more enthusiastic about this task once they were able to keep the proceeds themselves. Furthermore, personal tax yields were further increased by imposing special rates for education (as was done as recently as 1965 in West Cameroon), and, especially, by the introduction of the graduated personal tax (GPT).

While the precise system of assessment of this tax varies from area to area, that in Buganda is of particular interest. In this case the GPT in effect amounts to a tax on presumed gross income.[53] Tax assessment in rural areas is based on estimated yields from acreage cultivated, number of coffee trees, and size of livestock herd. Each of these three items is in turn divided into nine presumed income classes, and the income thus estimated is subjected to a graduated tax. There is apparently little if any allowance for expenses of cultivation, so the tax is more on gross than on net presumed income. The tax rates are 5 to 6 percent on the minimum income of each bracket, decreasing as income rises within the bracket.

Assessment is carried out mainly by the local chiefs and assessment committees in the rural areas, occasionally on the basis of the personal appearance of the taxpayer before the local assessor, who is usually familiar with his circumstances anyway. This system is obviously very vulnerable to undesirable extraneous influences. The collection of this tax is very variable, depending in part on the whims of the local chief, and complaints about noncompliance are frequent.

In Tanzania, for example, less than 200,000 of the estimated 2.5 million adult males are on the tax register.[54] These features are fairly common to the GPT as it operates in other countries also, although the tax is reportedly effectively enforced in Uganda by requiring everyone to have an identity card showing payment of the tax. The Ugandan GPT is collected and retained by local governments, unlike the similar tax in Kenya, where it is a central government levy.

Despite its problems, African experience with direct personal taxation in rural areas suggests several lessons for other countries concerned with more effectively taxing agriculture. It represents, for instance, one of the most fully developed examples of the adaptation of tax form to local circumstances. Its relative success in some areas as a revenue raiser appears to reflect both this characteristic and the extreme decentralization of its administration and, in more recent years, the uses to which the tax proceeds are put.[55] The general economic effects of these taxes should be to stimulate effort and production for sale. The most modern version, the GPT, when working well should even attain these effects in a relatively equitable fashion compared to such alternatives as export taxes with their greater disincentive effects. Only a very limited degree of progressivity can be attained through this system, however, even if the GPT is integrated with the income tax, given the presumptive nature of the tax base.

While the importance of the personal tax has declined over time, as the character of African society has changed, and will probably continue to decline in the future, it is possible to integrate the GPT fairly neatly into an income tax structure (as in Nigeria and East Africa) so as to make transformation to a more modern direct tax structure, which will eventually be required, relatively painless. In this respect at least, the personal tax system seems potentially superior to most other forms of taxing the agricultural population yet devised, although it is of course far from perfect.

INCOME TAXES

This possibility is of special interest because to date no developing country has successfully applied a conventional income tax to agricultural income, other than in the special case of large plantations. This is not surprising since agriculture illustrates *par excellence* the general validity of Richard Goode's well-known six conditions for the successful use of mass income taxation as a major revenue source: the existence of a predominantly money economy; a high standard of literacy among taxpayers; prevalence of accounting records honestly and reliably maintained; a large degree of voluntary compliance on the part of taxpayers; an appropriate political environment; and honest and efficient administration.[56] The graduated personal tax applied in some African countries represents the most successful attempt yet to overcome the difficulties of mass direct taxation in low-income countries. Even there, however, the attempt has been most successful where at least the last three of Goode's conditions are approximately satisfied. Seldom has even this modest degree of success been attained elsewhere in applying income taxes to subsistence agriculture.

A number of different approaches to the problem are possible. One is to give up and simply exempt agricultural income from the regular income tax, as in Afghanistan, Ethiopia, Nepal, Iraq, and Indonesia, among other countries. India and Pakistan also exempt agricultural income from the central income tax, although some states levy a special agricultural income tax (see Chapter 6).

A quite different approach is to tax income derived from agriculture exactly like income derived from any other source. This is the approach followed in most industrial countries. Even there, however, the effective rate of taxation on farm income is usually substantially lower than on other types of income owing to the inherent difficulties of measuring net income accurately in the agricultural sector.[57] It is not surprising, therefore, that less developed countries like Iran, which brought agriculture within the scope of its income tax from 1943 to 1946, have usually found that a general income tax applied to agriculture does not work well. Those countries which retain this system do so despite its proven ineffectiveness. In Colombia, for example, it has been estimated that perhaps only 10 percent of the income tax legally due from the agricultural sector is in fact collected and that less than 4 percent of income tax revenues received come from agriculture, which accounted for over 30 percent of gross domestic product.[58] Thailand, Turkey, Honduras, and most of former French West Africa follow the same approach, in most cases with even more meager results. In Honduras, for example, the tax is applied only to two banana plantations.

The considerable difficulty encountered in taxing even large land-owners under the regular income tax has led some countries to adopt special forms of income taxation designed for agriculture alone. In most instances such taxes are based on the income "presumed" to arise in agriculture in accordance with some more or less arbitrary formula. The essence of the presumptive method is to assume that taxable income is related in a relatively fixed way to some factor or factors that can be more easily verified than income itself.

One basis for the presumption is the estimated value of agricultural land. This system is used even in quite developed countries. In Italy, for example, land fit for agricultural production is presumed to give rise to income on the basis of 1938 cadastral values as adjusted by a revaluation coefficient and by a coefficient fixed annually by the Ministry of Finance in relation to prevailing product and input prices. The income thus determined is then included in aggregate income for purposes of the complementary tax.[59] Similar systems of presuming agricultural income fundamentally on the basis of cadastral value exist in some Latin American countries (for example, Ecuador and Chile) and have been proposed for others (notably Colombia).

An alternative approach is to base the income "presumed" for income tax purposes on records of the physical yield of different farm products on "standard" land. France, for example, has long used this *forfaitaire* system for farmers whose income from agriculture falls below a specified level. The income assessed in each region is based on the average yield of different crops on representative farms valued at official prices. A similar system is used in Japan and, for purposes of a separate agricultural income tax, in Morocco and, as described in Chapter 5, in Uruguay.[60]

In terms of revenue yield, however, by far the most significant "income taxes" levied on agriculture outside of a few very poor African countries are those imposed in countries such as mainland China, North Vietnam, and, to a lesser extent, Taiwan and Korea. The ancient Chinese land income tax was revived after 1949 in the People's Republic of China, for example, when a tax (first with progressive, and later, after the land reform was completed, with proportional rates) was imposed on the gross estimated normal income from land, with differentials for type of crop.[61] The natural capacity of the soil, the extent of irrigation, and the normal methods of cultivation were taken into account in assessing this tax. About 90 percent of the substantial proceeds from the tax were collected in kind, thus protecting against depreciation of the tax yield with inflation.

A similar comprehensive agricultural tax was introduced in North Vietnam in 1951. This tax, payable solely in kind, was levied on the community rather than on the individual. Progressive rates were levied on normal potential gross yield. Provisions were made for tax reduction in the case of natural disaster (as was also done in China), and wasteland restored to cultivation was exempted from tax, first for one and then for five years. The most novel feature of this tax, however, was the great stress put on taxpayer participation in assessing the tax as well as on taxpayer understanding of the necessity for taxation. Extensive local participation in the assessment process, as in the better African personal tax systems, served in effect as "an institutionalized quality control mechanism."[62] The great stress on popular understanding was presumably even more necessary than in Africa because there was no local expenditure feedback to make the tax palatable to the communities which bore it.

Considered as income taxes, there is little doubt that the more sophisticated standard yield approach to presuming agricultural income is much superior to the crude cadastral value approach.[63] Although the informational base required for its successful use is correspondingly more demanding, an investment of the needed magnitude may well repay some countries, particularly those in which the agricultural sector is shrinking in size and the scope of the income tax is expanding. From the present point of view, however, it seems unlikely that any tax on presumed agricultural income, no matter how productive, will really amount in most developing countries to more than a land tax in disguise. The effectiveness of all these taxes, just like that of more conventional land taxes, depends almost entirely on the state of the basic information on land values and ownership. Taxes on presumed agricultural income, whether "potential" or "normal," are therefore considered for purposes of this study as simply a variety of land tax.

LAND TAXES

There are many ways of taxing agricultural land. An annual tax may be levied on the capital value of land, for instance, or on the value of land plus improvements, or on its rental value. Alternatively, the gross income from land may be taxed, or, with some allowance for expenses, an attempt may be made to tax net land income. The tax may be based on some simple measure such as land area or land area classified by a few factors like irrigation. A quite different approach to taxing land is to levy a periodic tax on increments in land value, or to impose betterment taxes or special assessments in connection with the financing of public improvements. A third approach is to tax land as part of a more general wealth tax or capital levy, on either an annual or a periodic basis. Finally, transfers of agricultural land may either be subjected to special taxation or else fall within the scope of more general taxes on wealth transfers. Most countries employ at least one or two of these approaches to land taxation, though with highly varying degrees of rigor and effectiveness.

The land tax is probably the oldest form of taxation. Censuses recording the names of property owners and conducting surveys of landholdings were carried out in Babylonia in 3800 B.C. and in Egypt and China around 3000 B.C., largely in order to establish a base for taxation. The oldest connection between government and rural village in most of the world is taxation, which has usually meant direct taxation in the form of land taxes, cattle taxes, or the African hut taxes.[64] In many instances, this close connection has evoked hostility: few governments have seen fit, or have been able, to work hard at creating the popular understanding and willing acceptance of direct taxation that seems necessary today. The long and relatively unhappy history of direct taxes on agriculture in much of the world no doubt in part explains the alacrity with which governments and taxpayers alike dropped the traditional direct taxes and turned as soon as possible to internal excises and taxes on foreign trade in order to finance the expanding public sector activities accompanying the transition from traditional society.

Whatever the reason, the forms of land tax now existing in most countries often represent either the withered remnant of a traditional system or a patchwork quilt of partial modifications and substitutes. In Turkey, for example, where land taxation was first introduced in 1858 as an addition to the traditional tithe (tax on gross produce), a new general assessment was started by the new republic in 1924. It proved to be very slow and unsatisfactory. As a temporary measure, therefore, the rate of the land tax was raised eight-fold in 1931 to

DIRECT TAXES ON AGRICULTURE

67

reflect the increase in prices since the original nineteenth-century assessment and to compensate for the loss of revenues from the abolition of the Ottoman tithe. This tax is still, with some modifications, in force today.

Furthermore, it is still based on more or less the same inadequate assessments since no full cadastre has ever been carried out. The tax base is the market value of land (10 times its rental value), but most valuations are actually based on values declared by the landholders themselves, a common feature of more inadequate land taxes everywhere. The failure of assessments to keep up with market values is thus unsurprising. From 1936 to 1960, for example, while land values rose an estimated fifty times, land tax revenues rose less than three times, and the share of total government resources contributed by the land tax fell from 3 percent to 0.3 percent.[65] In 1961, the old assessed valuations were again arbitrarily increased by a factor of ten—although political reaction caused this adjustment to be reduced to one of just three times the previous value only six months later. At present, agricultural land is subject to a 1 percent tax on this obviously arbitrary assessed valuation, which is also the basis of the presumptive income tax. To compound the all too typical ills of land taxation in Turkey, it has been estimated that only around 50 percent of the land tax levied is in fact collected. A new reassessment was launched in 1972 but seems unlikely to amount to much since it depends mainly on self-assessments (see Chapter 11).

Crude as it is in practice, the land tax in Turkey and such other countries as Iran and Iraq is at least in principle more refined, being based on either the value of potential net income from land or on market value. What is striking is the gap between principle and practice. One way to close this gap, the way usually recommended by fiscal experts, is to improve practice; another is to lower principle and to adopt a simpler form of land taxation in the first place. Liberia, for example, levies a tax on farmland based on area, with low rates ranging up to 6 cents per acre depending upon whether or not the land is improved or located within the corporate limits of a town. There is also a tax of 0.5 percent on farm improvements, but, since the total yield of Liberian land taxes in 1968 was only $6,000, none of these taxes appears to amount to much.[66]

An almost equally crude but much more important land tax exists in Ethiopia, where the Land Tax Proclamation of 1942 replaced the traditional (tithe-like) taxes paid in produce and services by a tax payable in money and based on land area, with the rate varying with three categories of land: fertile, semifertile, and poor.[67] At present, Ethiopia actually imposes four separate taxes on this base: the land tax proper, the so-called tithe, the health tax, and the education tax. The two latter taxes are collected by the provinces and, after transmittal to the central government, the revenues are usually reallocated again to the provinces. (Some provincial administrators reportedly do not bother with the intermediate stage in this process.) In addition, as is common in Africa, a supplemental tax is levied on the livestock herds of nomadic tribesmen who cannot be reached through the land tax.

Ethiopia has no good land survey; the land classification on which the tax is based is extremely crude; there are substantial exemptions granted to the Coptic Church (which owns close to one-third of all land) and others; observers believe there is much evasion of land taxes by large landowners—yet despite these common, and serious, faults this cumbersome land tax system yielded 15 percent of total ordinary central government revenue as late as 1966. In 1967 the tithe was replaced by an agricultural income tax levied at a progressive rate on estimated harvest income after deducting land taxes, rent, and one-third of gross income in lieu of expenses. This tax was to be based on a new assessment every five years. By 1970 it yielded 3 percent of total revenues, or almost as much as the remaining land taxes (4 percent).

Not all relatively closed traditional economies follow the same pattern, of course. The land tax has virtually disappeared in Afghanistan, for example, although a new general cadastral survey is now underway. Nevertheless, it is striking that one of the very few countries in which land taxes appear to be more important than in Ethiopia is the even more landlocked and traditional society of Nepal. Although it is almost impossible to exaggerate the complex and motley nature of land tenure and land taxation in Nepal,[68] the large revenues yielded by the land tax even in recent years (see Table 2) are striking. This tax is based mostly on area, adjusted for soil composition (four grades) and irrigation. Nepal, too, has recently undertaken an extensive land survey, initially in its more fertile areas, which will eventually cover the whole country.

The considerable success of mainland China in mobilizing resources from agriculture was noted earlier; the instrument of this success was a revival of the ancient Chinese tax under which the government collected in kind a share of the actual output.[69] The main agricultural tax levied in Taiwan today also closely resembles this tax.[70] Land is divided into 21 categories according to its utilization and nature. Of these categories, 11 are considered to be revenue yielding and are taxed in accordance with the quality of land and the "standard" yield as established by land surveys. The rates applied to the taxable base are progressive, ranging from 3.5 percent to 9.6 percent of the estimated production of the land. As is common in other systems of this sort, the tax due may be reduced or exempted when actual production is hurt by natural disasters. Newly reclaimed land is also exempted from tax for a period of from two to eight years. In order to facilitate the consolidation of farm lands, transfers of farmland are exempt from the registration tax which is otherwise usually levied at the time of sale. The enforcement of the rural land tax is considerably facilitated by the fact that Taiwan, unlike most developing countries, has a well-established and functioning cadastral survey.

The most important source of local tax revenue in Korea is the very similar agricultural land tax. In 1964, for example, almost 30 percent of local taxes and over 3 percent of total taxes in Korea came from this source.[71] The bulk of this revenue comes from a tax levied at the rate of 6 percent on the value of the "standard" output of lands used for grains. (Land used for other crops is taxed on the basis of net income at progressive rates ranging from 10 percent to 20 percent). The tax base is determined by multiplying the "standard yield" set for each parcel, based on a 1959 land survey, by the current grain prices set for purchases by government. If the actual production is 80 percent or more of this standard, the tax is based on the standard; if it is less than 80 percent of the standard, the tax may be based on actual output. Reclaimed and very poor lands are completely exempt, apparently indefinitely, a policy which appears questionable in the case of the former since public funds have usually been invested in reclamation.

Two especially noteworthy features of this tax are: first, the tax does not interfere with production incentives since the marginal rate of tax on that portion of output over 80 percent of the "standard yield" is zero. Second, while the fact that the tax base is partly determined in accordance with current grain prices insulates the yield of the tax from inflation to some extent, the same feature that provides the incentive makes its yield insensitive to increases in output. This problem can of course be overcome, with some detriment to incentives, by revising the standard yields every ten years or so, or when potential output in particular areas is altered by factors having nothing to do with the farmers' own efforts, such as irrigation schemes. These features are characteristic in one form or another of most existing or proposed taxes on the potential net income from agriculture.

Other Asian countries offer a sharp contrast to the relatively successful experience in Korea and Taiwan. The weakness of the land tax in Thailand, for instance, is striking. The Thai land tax is levied on the capital value of land at low rates (less than ten mills), with the rates varying with the location of the land. Valuations for tax purposes are in no better state than in most other developing countries, and there are substantial relief provisions in the law so the average burden of this tax is light. Since 1960 the tax has been assessed and collected by local governments, which derive 15 percent of their revenue from it. One study put land taxes in 1966 at an average of 5 baht (U.S. $0.25) per person in the rural sector, compared to an average export tax of 67 baht per person.[72]

The situation is not too different in the Philippines, where a tax on the capital value of real estate was established in 1939. Basically the same tax exists today as a local levy with 45 percent of the revenue going to the provinces, 45 percent to the municipalities, and 10 percent to the smallest unit of local government, the *barrio*. In 1968, only 16 percent of local revenues and 2 percent of total revenues came from property taxes.[73] Although there is no information as to the extent to which property tax is paid by the agricultural sector, there is no reason to doubt that the burden of the tax has declined there at least as much as it has in the economy as a whole.

The basic reason for the decline of the Philippine real property tax appears to be that so common elsewhere in the developing world: weak assessments. In 1965, for example, perhaps one-third of taxable property was not even assessed, the average assessed value of agricultural land was estimated at 41 percent of market value, and less than two-thirds of the tax assessed was collected, there being few penalties and little enforcement effort. The low nominal rate of around 1 percent in reality thus reduced to an average effective rate on taxable property of more like one-tenth of 1 percent. In addition, over 20 percent of assessed valuation was exempted for various reasons. It is no wonder that the property tax in the Philippines has been shrinking rapidly as a source of government revenue in recent years.

There have, of cou se, been various attempts to reform and strengthen this tax. In 1950, for example, the barrio councils were empowered to levy a surcharge of one-quarter of 1 percent on assessed valuation, but by 1965 none had done so. In 1965 another sustained effort for reform failed. The first major change in property tax legislation appears to have been in 1969, when the Educational Fund Act imposed an additional 1 percent tax when the assessed value of the property of a single owner exceeded $3,000. The revenues from this new levy are earmarked for the Educational Fund. The generally poor state of taxpayer compliance and tax administration in the Philippines was made painfully evident by the fact that this educational tax, a device which has been used successfully in a number of other countries, actually resulted in an immediate decrease in tax collections owing to taxpayer resistance.[74]

As noted at the beginning of this section, increments in land values over some period of time may be taxed as a complement to, or a substitute for, an annual tax. Since the experiments at the turn of the century in Germany and Great Britain, however, there have been very few attempts to tax increments in land value before they are realized by sale or transfer. Even the long-standing Danish *grundstigningskyld* was abolished in 1964. In their usual form, these levies would seem to be most relevant to urban areas in any case.

Much more common are taxes levied at the time of the transfer of property, often in the form of capital gains or stamp taxes. An example of a special tax on gains realized from the sale of land is Israel's Land Betterment Tax, which was introduced in 1949. When land is transferred within two years of purchase, the tax rate varies from 20 percent of the unearned increment (difference between sales price and acquisition cost) if the increment is less than 200 percent of cost to 40 percent if it is over 400 percent. The rate is reduced slowly the longer the land is held.[75] The estimated yield of 1 percent of tax revenues from this tax appears to be substantially higher than from similar levies elsewhere.

Many countries, for example, apply a general capital gains tax which in practice, if not in law, often reduces to a tax on real property transfers. Sometimes there are special taxes on real property gains alone, as in Colombia, Panama, or Peru. Ghana goes further and specifically exempts agricultural land from its special capital gains tax on property sales, as do Burma, Chile, and India, while Bolivia reportedly subjects certain rural property transfers to a differentially higher rate. None of these taxes appear important: a recent study suggests that capital gains taxes commonly yield 2–3 percent of income tax revenues or less.[76] Very little of this comes from agricultural land.

Special taxes on the transfer of land are also levied by means of stamp duties in many countries. In Guatemala, for example, the land transfer tax, which was established in 1921, is levied at 1 percent of the sale value of real estate on transfer of title: it produces less than 1 percent of tax revenues, although again little of this revenue comes from the largely subsistence agricultural sector.[77] It seems unlikely that the rate of this tax is high enough to have any significant economic effects. Similar land transfer or registration taxes are levied in other Latin American countries, usually at low rates. A much heavier tax is levied on the sale of real property in Greece at a rate of 11 percent on estimated market value. This tax was introduced in 1950 to replace an unsuccessful property tax and yielded 3 percent of central government tax revenues in 1962.[78] Similar high taxes on property transfers exist in France, Portugal, Chile, and India.

In principle, a heavy tax on land transfers of this sort may provide an undesirable deterrent to asset transfers, including those which would facilitate more efficient resource utilization, since its effect will undoubtedly be to reduce the average volume of transactions.[79] Transfer taxes thus may work against one of the alleged main beneficial effects of taxes on real property, namely, the pressure they exert either to utilize land more efficiently (in order to produce income out of which to meet the tax burden), or to sell the land to someone who will so use it. For this reason, approved transfers of farmlands, for instance in connection with an agrarian reform program, are often exempted from transfer taxes, as in Taiwan. On the other hand, it might be argued that high transfer taxes will deter "fraudulent" property transfers intended to avoid high property taxes, especially those levied at progressive rates.[80] The problem is how to tell the good transfers from the bad. It would seem best to follow Ricardo's advice and keep transfer taxes relatively low: "For the general prosperity, there cannot be too much facility given to the conveyance and exchange of all kinds of property, as it is by such means that capital of every species is likely to find its way into the hands of those who will best employ it in increasing the productions of the country."[81]

Special assessments to finance public improvements are not as common as taxes on real estate transfers, although they are used in various countries of Latin America—notably Colombia, but also Ecuador, Uruguay, and Mexico. Latin American experience with this device is discussed in later chapters. Other countries, too, have betterment levies of various sorts—Greece, India, Taiwan, and Tunisia, for example. Nowhere, however, do these special taxes appear to have been utilized to any great extent with respect to agricultural properties despite their considerable economic and, it would appear, political attractiveness.

Finally, a few even less important forms of direct taxation affecting agricultural land deserve brief notice. In some countries, for example, a net wealth tax is imposed. As a rule, this tax operates in a way reminiscent of Seligman's dictum that "wherever tried, the general property tax again resolves itself into the real property tax."[82] The net wealth taxes of Chile, Colombia, El Salvador, Uruguay, and, before 1962, Nicaragua in essence amount to taxes on real estate and are consequently discussed in the next chapter along with other land-based taxes in Latin America. In addition, as noted elsewhere, some countries specifically tax agricultural inputs such as draft animals, tractors, and fertilizer. Other countries subsidize some of these inputs. Farmers are also subject to general commodity taxes insofar as they purchase manufactured goods. Neither these levies nor the fiscal monopolies which operate in some countries for some agricultural products like tobacco are analyzed here, however.

CONCLUSION

This brief survey of agricultural taxation in developing countries poses some puzzling questions. Most authorities argue that a properly constructed tax on agricultural land is probably the most desirable way to mobilize and transfer any needed resources from the agricultural to the nonagricultural sectors of the economy since only this tax can perform this task without affecting agricultural production too adversely. Yet nowhere, with the exception of a few of the poorest countries in the world, does the recommended form of land tax appear to be an important revenue raiser, nor one of increasing importance. Indeed, few countries appear to have effective land taxes of any sort, largely because of universally weak valuation systems, systems which have, in many cases, remained weak despite decades of plans and programs supposed to improve them. Where agricultural taxation effectively transfers resources out of agriculture, this task appears most generally to be accomplished through some form of taxing agricultural exports, and even in these instances it appears that the importance of this revenue source has been declining in most countries.

The answers to the questions implicit in the preceding paragraph may lie mainly in the political and administrative factors discussed later in this book. More generally, until coherent policy objectives can be developed and a basic administrative framework established, the prospects for emulating the oft-cited experience of late nineteenth-century Japan (see Chapter 6) in relying on heavy agricultural land taxes as a prime source of revenues for development appear bleak indeed. Nevertheless, while their role as revenue producer may not be huge, so long as the economies of developing countries remain so segmented that special measures have to be taken to tax the agricultural sector, the proper design of agricultural land taxes to overcome the prevalent barriers of poverty and illiteracy will remain important.

Land taxes can produce significant revenues, perhaps especially for local purposes; they can, if properly designed and set up, be administered relatively simply; they can tax farmers in a roughly equitable fashion without unduly damaging incentives. That they now do none of these things in most countries reflects choice as much as necessity. One aim of the present study is to justify this statement by showing how apparent obstacles can be overcome, and why they are not.

5

LAND TAXES IN LATIN AMERICA

Agriculture is not only one of man's oldest activities, it is also one of the most complex and variegated, reflecting both the variety of soil and climatic conditions found throughout the world and the results of centuries of institutionalization of basic life patterns. It is not surprising that agricultural tax systems mirror this complexity, ranging from the personal taxes of sub-Saharan Africa to the land revenue systems of the Indian subcontinent. This chapter looks more closely at the nature and extent of this diversity within one particular region of the world—Latin America.

In some important respects, of course, the countries of Latin America differ widely from one another and even more from other parts of the world. But they almost all share a common colonial heritage, and the larger countries have probably the longest history of conscious developmental efforts of any part of the so-called Third World. A closer look at the differences and similarities in the role and pattern of agricultural taxation in several countries of Latin America should therefore prove suggestive. In particular, Latin America's extensive experience with land taxes on capital value, with progressive rate structures, and with the use of special taxes for incentive and penalty purposes repays careful examination.

Almost half the population of Latin America still lives in rural areas. In many countries two-thirds or more of the people are classed as "rural." In a few others, as Table 4 shows, three-quarters or more of the population is already "urban." While the precise meaning of these terms is often imprecise,[1] the figures in Table 4 suggest that the

TABLE 4. LATIN AMERICA: IMPORTANCE OF THE AGRICULTURAL SECTOR

Country	Percent population "rural" in 1970[a]	Percent work force in agriculture, 1968[b]	Agricultural exports as percent total exports, 1966[c]	Contribution of agriculture to GDP[d]
Argentina	29.5	15.8	92.5	15.5
Bolivia	74.6	57.1	3.6	23.1
Brazil	46.5	46.4	80.2	18.2
Chile	26.3	25.5	6.4	8.2
Colombia	45.0	45.1	75.4	31.3
Costa Rica	63.7	46.7	81.2	24.1
Dominican Republic	63.0	60.4	88.5	24.4
Ecuador	62.5	53.7	94.1	31.7
El Salvador	60.2	57.6	74.7	25.9
Guatemala	63.4	64.1	81.3	26.7
Haiti	82.4	83.2	51.0[e]	—
Honduras	74.1	65.5	82.2	35.8
Jamaica	64.0	22.4	—	9.0
Mexico	41.8	46.1	51.5	11.7
Nicaragua	56.4	56.0	85.0	28.5
Panama	53.3	42.3	57.9	21.3
Paraguay	64.2	54.5	71.9	31.4
Peru	54.0	44.6	51.4	16.5
Uruguay	15.8	17.9	97.9	15.6
Venezuela	23.6	24.5	1.2	6.8

[a] Calculated from estimated 1970 data in Social Progress Trust Fund, *Socio-Economic Progress in Latin America, Ninth Annual Report* (Washington, 1970), p. 99.

[b] Social Progress Trust Fund, *Socio-Economic Progress in Latin America, Tenth Annual Report* (Washington, 1971), p. 7.

[c] *Ninth Annual Report*, p. 7.

[d] *Tenth Annual Report*, p. 6.

[e] Coffee exports only.

countries of Latin America may be divided into three groups: (1) countries with half or more of their labor force engaged in agriculture

—Bolivia, Ecuador, Paraguay, Peru, and most of the small Central American and Caribbean countries; (2) a few larger countries where agriculture is still the most important employer but which are fairly well developed in other respects—Brazil, Colombia, and Mexico; and (3) four countries with proportionately fewer people living in rural areas and engaged in agricultural activities than many European countries—Argentina, Chile, Uruguay, and Venezuela.

In virtually every instance the weight of the rural sector in the national economy has been declining in recent years in terms of both its contribution to gross domestic product and its population. In 1960, for example, 80 percent of the Honduran population, 55 percent of the Brazilian population, and 34 percent of the Chilean population were classified as "rural"; the corresponding figures for 1970 were 74 percent, 46 percent, and 26 percent. This decline has taken place despite a very high annual rate of population growth in the 1960's of close to 3 percent for Latin America as a whole, because urban population has been expanding at more than twice this rate. These figures suggest that net rural-to-urban migration in the 1960–1970 period must have continued at close to the rates recorded in 1950–1960, when, for example, it amounted to 29 percent of the 1959 rural population in Chile, 19 percent in Brazil, and 14 percent in Peru.[2] Even so, for Latin America as a whole, and for all but the most urbanized countries (Chile, Uruguay, and Venezuela), the absolute size of the rural population was higher in 1970 than in 1960, although agriculture's share of gross domestic product was much lower in the later year.

Any realistic projection of demographic trends in the next few years suggests that this situation will persist. Despite its great metropolises and the well-developed industrial sectors in some countries, Latin America is still, in a profoundly important sense, very much a rural society. What affects agriculture affects the whole.

The recent emphasis on reducing the pace of urban migration for social and political reasons makes improving employment opportunities in agriculture even more important as a policy goal. Similarly, the new view in many countries is that reducing rural poverty is both a goal in itself and a means of hurdling the barrier to growth erected by the limited size of existing national markets. These factors accentuate the key role of the agricultural sector in development.

Agriculture is perhaps more immediately important in most countries, however, as an exporter. Only the three mineral-exporting countries of Bolivia, Chile, and Venezuela earned less than half their foreign exchange in 1966 from the sale of food and other agricultural products (see Table 4). In nine countries, including some of the largest, agricultural exports accounted for over 80 percent of total exports. As a rule these exports consist of a few primary products. Brazil, Colombia, Haiti, and several Central American countries depend for foreign exchange mainly on coffee; Ecuador, Panama, and Honduras on bananas; Uruguay on meat and wool; Nicaragua on cotton; and the Dominican Republic on sugar. Given the nature of the prevalent pattern of industrialization in Latin America to date, the need for the foreign exchange that agriculture earns may perhaps be a more pressing reason than social justice for even the most advanced countries to pay close attention to agricultural policy both in its own right and as a central part of general development policy.

Nevertheless, "one looks in vain for internally consistent policies and programs supporting conscious national strategies of agricultural development in Latin America."[3] One reason for this apparent paradox may lie in the peculiar structure of the agricultural sector in many Latin American countries. The picture of an extremely unequal distribution of land shown for several countries in Table 5 is supported by census data on the distribution of farm units by size from other countries, although area alone is of course an inadequate measure of farm size. The degree of concentration of arable land in the hands of a few large landowners is marked in almost every country. In part, the political influence of the landowning class in Latin America is still dominant because the capacity to import is totally dependent on agricultural exports.

This inequality carries over to every area of Latin American rural and national life. A recent estimate, for example, is that, while the large landholding families in Latin America as a whole—the "multifamily large" group in Table 5—constitute only 1 percent of the agricultural population and control less than 2 percent of the farm units, they control over 50 percent of the land, account for close to one-third of output, and receive over one-sixth of the total income produced on the continent.[4] The economic significance of this concentration is obvious. The considerable income accruing to large landowners may, for example, go largely for immediate consumption, often of an import-intensive luxury nature, thus creating a serious obstacle to

LAND TAXES IN LATIN AMERICA

TABLE 5. LATIN AMERICA: STRUCTURE OF AGRICULTURE,
SELECTED COUNTRIES

			Type of farm		
Countries	Sub-family[a]	Family[b]	Multi-family medium[c]	Multi-family large[d]	Total
			(percent)		
Argentina					
Number of farm units	43.2	48.7	7.3	0.8	100.0
Area in farms	3.4	44.7	15.0	36.9	100.0
Brazil					
Number of farm units	22.5	39.1	33.7	4.7	100.0
Area in farms	0.5	6.0	34.0	59.5	100.0
Chile					
Number of farm units	36.0	40.0	16.2	6.9	100.0
Area in farms	0.2	7.1	11.4	31.3	100.0
Colombia					
Number of farm units	64.0	30.2	4.5	1.3	100.0
Area in farms	4.9	2.3	23.3	49.5	100.0
Ecuador					
Number of farm units	89.9	8.0	1.7	0.4	100.0
Area in farms	16.6	19.0	19.3	45.1	100.0
Guatemala					
Number of farm units	88.4	9.5	2.0	0.1	100.0
Area in farms	14.3	13.4	31.5	40.8	100.0
Peru					
Number of farm units	88.0	8.5	2.4	1.1	100.0
Area in farms	7.4	4.5	5.7	82.4	100.0

Source: ICAD studies, as reported in Solon Barranclough, "Agrarian Reform in Latin America: Actual Situation and Problems," *Land Reform,
Land Settlement and Cooperatives*, No. 2, 1969, p. 15.

[a] *Subfamily:* Farms too small to provide employment for a single family
(2 workers) with the typical incomes, markets and levels of technology
and capital now prevailing in each region.

[b] *Family:* Farms large enough to provide employment for 2 to 3.9 people,
on the assumption that most of the farm work is being carried out by the
members of the farm family.

[c] *Multifamily medium:* Farms large enough to provide employment for 4
to 12 people.

[d] *Multifamily large:* Farms large enough to provide employment for over
12 people.

rational development policy, as has been argued was true in the cases
of Chile and Colombia.[5]

The colonial origins and persistence of this marked concentration
of landed wealth have also had a profound influence on the nature
of Latin American society. The hacienda in the valley and the village

community on the steep mountain slopes were the twin poles of social organization in many countries until recently.[6] In some areas of some countries, they still are. Although few large landholdings are now organized in as autarchic a fashion as they were even twenty years ago, land is still valued by many as much for the status it conveys as for its productive potential. Despite the economic and social changes wrought in the hacienda system by time and progress, it is not surprising that much of the political life in some countries is still heavily marked by the traditional social chasm between estate owner and peon. In no area is this truer than with respect to agricultural policy.

Exports, employment, markets, increased food marketing to reduce inflation—all these and many other conceivable instrumental and intrinsic guidelines for formulating agricultural policy have not been taken explicitly and consistently into account in Latin America largely because the policy makers and all relevant reference groups have been concerned with the "proper" distribution of land to the exclusion of almost all else. Economic arguments have, it is true, often entered these debates; sometimes, indeed, the discussion has been conducted almost entirely in economic terms. Yet on closer examination it seems clear that economics has as a rule been the rationale rather than the real reason why this or that policy measure is urged or contested.

The real crux of agricultural policy in Latin America has almost invariably been "land reform"—that is, the most basic social issue of the distribution of wealth and power—rather than the effort to improve the productivity of the factors employed in the agricultural sector which most economists envisage as agricultural policy. These two thrusts are of course related, though not in any simple or constant way; it is the underlying sharp distinction in motivation that is crucial here. Only if one interprets agricultural policy, including land tax policy, as dealing with a—sometimes "the"—vital political issue do its meanderings and general ineffectiveness in most countries make much sense. Although the interconnection between land taxation and land reform is explored further in Chapter 13, this basic proposition must be understood before embarking on any study of what has and has not happened to land taxes in Latin America.

The five countries selected for more extensive discussion in this chapter illustrate both the diversity and the common characteristics of land tax systems in Latin America. Panama's land tax is basically similar to those in such other countries as Guatemala and Costa Rica.

LAND TAXES IN LATIN AMERICA

Bolivia and Uruguay are almost polar opposites. Bolivia is a very poor country with revolutionary land reform but no land tax to speak of. In both respects, if in little else, it resembles the Mexican experience sketched in the next chapter. Uruguay on the other hand is a relatively rich country with no land reform and a sophisticated agricultural tax system. Argentina, and especially Brazil, rival Uruguay in both respects. Chile, too, has a relatively well-developed land tax, but it is included here mainly because of its experiences in the 1960's with a successful cadastral survey and a less successful index adjustment system. Finally, the chapter summarizes briefly the interesting Jamaican experience with site value taxation, which falls somewhat outside the common Latin American mold.

PANAMA

The taxation of real property in Panama is heavier than that in any other Central American country. The reason for this difference is largely historic: until 1903 Panama was a part of Colombia, and Colombia, unlike the Central American countries, already had a well-established property tax at the beginning of the century.[7] Until 1947 the rate of the Panamanian national real property tax was 5 mills (½ of 1 percent) of the capital value; from 1947 to 1960 it was generally 10 mills (1 percent), apart from a three-year period (1953–1956) when the rate was lowered to 5 mills in the unwarranted expectation that a newly launched cadastral program would result in a rapid increase in the tax base. In 1960 the present progressive rate structure was introduced. The tax rate now ranges from 7.5 mills on interests in real property valued at less than $5,000 to a maximum of 15 mills on values of $75,000 or more (see Table 6). As elsewhere, these progressive rates appear to have had little nonfiscal effect other than to encourage evasion through paper maneuvers to split ownership.

As is the general pattern in Latin America, the property tax in Panama is levied upon the property owner's total interests in real property (in personam), rather than upon the property as such (in rem). That is, the tax is attached not to the property but to whoever is determined to be its owner. The resulting increased difficulty of enforcing the tax through the seizure of property is an important obstacle to effective land taxation. Not only must the tax administra-

TABLE 6. CENTRAL AMERICA: PROPERTY TAXATION, 1966

Country	Property tax as percent of central government taxation	Property taxes per capita (in U.S. dollars)	Property tax rates (mills)	Basic exemptions[e] (U.S. dollars)
Costa Rica	5.7	2.55	3–10.5	$ 1,500
El Salvador[a]	2.6	0.74	0.5–4	4,000
Guatemala	2.6	0.66	3 and 6[c]	100
Honduras	—[b]	0.23	1.5	10,000[f]
Nicaragua	7.0	2.61	5 or 10[d]	2,850[f]
Panama	5.4	3.39	7.5–15	500

Source: Cecil Morgan, "Property Taxation in Central America," Department of State, Agency for International Development, Regional Office, Central America and Panama Affairs, November 1967.

[a] This information refers to the net worth tax which in practice is levied mainly on the value of real estate.

[b] The property tax in Honduras is solely municipal. Its yield is reportedly so low that many municipalities do not even bother to collect it.

[c] The higher rate is levied on properties valued at more than $20,000. In rural areas, the Guatemalan land tax is supposed to be levied on *all* real property, including farm animals, tools, crops, and machinery.

[d] 5 mills on owner-occupied homes or farms; 10 mills on other real or personal property.

[e] In addition to the conventional ownership and use exemptions for public agencies, cooperatives, educational and religious institutions, etc.

[f] Exemptions on owner-occupied homes or farms; in Nicaragua, the exemption is $4,300 for those located in the Central District.

tion clearly establish who owns what before taking enforcement action, often a very difficult problem, but the enforcement procedures available are also limited by the in personam nature of the tax. Real property on which taxes are delinquent cannot be seized and sold without an extremely lengthy administrative and judicial procedure, unlike the situation with most in rem taxes.

On the other hand, the fact that with this system property taxes are already explicitly personal in nature (the different interests of each owner supposedly being aggregated) has appeared to some to afford a promising opportunity to levy effectively progressive taxes on wealth with potentially desirable redistributive and allocative effects.[8] In practice, however, it appears the administrative difficulty has to date outweighed any redistributive opportunity in Panama, as in most other countries.

All privately owned real property including rural land and buildings, other than that held by nonprofit institutions, is taxable in

Panama, except for property valued at less than $500. The major additional exemption is for new construction, which for most of the last twenty years has been exempt from property tax. The cost of this last exemption alone in 1959 was equivalent to 18 percent of total property tax collections in that year.[9] Houses valued at less than $5,000 are still exempt from tax for a period of five years. Property forming part of an agricultural colonization project is also exempt.

In total, it would appear that these various exemptions are quite important in terms of revenue foregone. On the other hand, in Panama as in the many other countries in which similar exemptions are found, it is not possible to say what, if anything, the government has purchased with this "tax expenditure." The lack of information on the benefits of such exemptions, however, appears nowhere to have acted as a deterrent to their continued proliferation. At the very least, other countries would be well advised to follow the Colombian practice of making a complete census of exempt properties so that the costs, if not the benefits, of exemption policies will be at least visible.

In 1966 the real property tax yielded 5.4 percent of central government tax revenues in Panama (Table 6). Collections from the agricultural sector were very much less than this, however. The most recent figures bearing on this point are for 1961, when it appears the agricultural sector paid only around $160,000 out of total property tax collections of $3.2 million in that year.[10] Furthermore, the greater part of this amount ($100,000) was paid by one large foreign-owned banana company on its properties of less than 60,000 hectares in extent. The remaining 1 million hectares of agricultural land in the hands of private owners thus apparently paid less than $60,000 in property tax (or $0.06 per hectare). A sector which accounted for 19 percent of gross national product thus provided less than 2 percent of property tax revenues and only around one-tenth of 1 percent of total central government tax revenues.

For most of its existence the Panamanian property tax has been based entirely upon the capital values declared for tax purposes by the property owners themselves. Unsurprisingly, these values were usually low: "property owners' statements were—and are—highly undependable. Their memories are notoriously bad, both as to what they own and how much of it they own. And their modesty with respect to the value—for tax purposes—of their own property is simply incredible."[11]

In an attempt to deal with this problem, a 1961 law established that the minimum value of titled land for tax purposes was to be presumed to be $30 per hectare (or a tax of from $0.22 to $0.44), while a higher tax of $0.50 per hectare was levied on the possession or occupancy of untitled land in excess of 10 hectares. The intention of this legislation was to encourage titling and to increase tax revenues, but it seems to have had little effect in either respect. Similar problems arising from the vagueness and insecurity of titles afflict the rural areas of many other countries.

Beginning in 1953 an official assessment of property values was also attempted. Since it took ten years to assess Panama City alone, the assessment of areas outside the capital was not begun until 1964. The lengthy and costly cadastral procedure used in the capital, which gave rise to an enormous number of delaying appeals against the new assessments, was simplified for use in the rural areas in the hope that the assessment process could be accelerated. This was successfully accomplished: from 1953 to 1965, only 23,000 properties had been revalued at a cost of over $100 per property; from 1965 to 1969, 100,000 rural properties were valued at an average cost of around $11 per property.

As late as 1969, however, no additional revenue had been produced from the rural areas as a result of the cadastre, despite its cost of around $5 million. More than five years after this considerable expenditure tax yields still had not risen. Furthermore, because all assessment resources were devoted to rural areas for five years, the reassessment of Panama City, the major urban area, was halted. The net immediate effect of the rural cadastre was thus to lower property tax revenues compared to what they would otherwise have been. Further, while yields should rise substantially in the future as a result of the new valuations, which have apparently at least doubled the earlier presumed values of $30 per hectare (which applied to 95 percent of rural properties), it does not appear that adequate provision has yet been made to keep the newly established values up to date, although this problem is not as serious in Panama, with its relatively stable price level, as it is in many other Latin American countries.

The establishment of an adequate base for the property tax in rural Panama has been complicated and delayed by many factors. One problem was that the land survey had to be accurate enough to serve as a legal cadastre for purposes of regional development and agrarian reform—over one-half of the total cost is attributable to these purposes—so that the development of assessments for property tax purposes did not receive primary emphasis.[12]

Another difficulty is that there are a great many squatters in the rural areas of Panama. Indeed, it has been estimated that the majority of small farmers do not hold proper title to their land. Inadequate titling considerably complicates property tax administration especially when, as in most of Latin America, the tax is levied not on the property itself but on interests in property. The political problems created by squatters are also significant. For example, if the squatters pay the tax the landowner may feel that his title is threatened and try to evict them, or the squatters may protest payment of tax for property they do not own. If the owner pays the tax he may, as is often argued, be stimulated to start using the land himself, evicting squatters in the process. All alternatives threaten rural unrest and political instability.

Yet another reason for the insignificant collections realized from the rural property tax in Panama lies in the weak administration of the tax. For many years the tax was collected in rural areas by agents, in return for a fee based on a percentage of the tax paid—an expensive and inefficient system of collection. The administrative costs of the similar system used in Guatemala have been as high as 40 to 50 percent of property tax collections.[13]

Until 1964 no interest was charged on delinquent payments. Although more recently 7 percent annual interest has been charged on late payments, in addition to a 10 percent penalty, these monetary penalties are hardly severe enough to deter delayed payment. In view of the confused title situation and the fact that the tax liability does not attach to the property as such, enforcement by attaching property is, as has already been noted, very difficult and has, in fact, apparently never been attempted.

Similarly deficient property tax administration characterizes other countries in Central America. In Costa Rica, for example, in 1964 only 22 percent of property owners paid tax (95 percent of whom paid the minimum rate of 3 mills), with 50 percent of these filing late. In the preceding eighteen years, only 25 percent of total properties had been reassessed, with the average new value being more than double the values declared by owners. As a rule, no penalties were imposed for delinquencies. Furthermore, there were many appeals and other legal maneuvers which delayed property tax enforcement considerably. The cost of this not very productive administrative machine was estimated at 12.2 percent of revenue collected in 1962, compared to 2.4 percent for customs and 4.6 percent for income tax.[14]

In addition to the regular property tax, Panama has since 1952 levied a special tax of $1.50 per hectare on unexploited land of over 500 hectares in extent, presumably with the intent of forcing more effective utilization. This rate is very high in comparison to the regular property tax, but since only $3,100 was collected from this tax in the entire decade from 1952 to 1962, it appears that this tax, like most "idle" land taxes in Central America, has in practice proved to be a sieve.

Guatemala, for example, imposed a similar special tax on idle lands in 1956 with the apparent intention of forcing the owners of large estates (those over 90 hectares in extent) to develop and use their land or else to sell it to those who would.[15] The initial tax imposed ranged from $0.25 per hectare for the lowest of the five qualities of land defined in the legislation up to $1.25 for the best quality of land. The tax was to go up by 25 percent a year until the final levy, at double the initial tax rates, was reached. In practice, however, this law was found to be full of loopholes, all of which were fully utilized, so that the tax yielded almost no revenue. Nor is there any evidence that it exerted any noticeably favorable incentive effects on land utilization.

A new version of the idle lands tax was therefore promulgated in 1962, to take effect in 1963 under the auspices of the National Agrarian Reform Institute. "Idle" lands were defined by the 1962 law as those lacking cultivation; those supporting fewer cattle than the regulations establish; those in a state of abandonment; those exploited in an "inadequate" form; or those with a "deficient" yield. The tax rates were much higher than in the original legislation, ranging from $0.75 to $2.50 per hectare in the first year (1963) up to $1.35 to $4.50 in the fifth year (1968).

If enforced, rates of this magnitude should indeed have had some economic effect. Once again, however, it appears that in practice there have been no discernible effects, perhaps in part because of the quite unrealistic requirement that each agricultural unit must first be classified in accordance with soil, topography, availability of water, and accessibility, in order to determine the applicable tax rate. This provision appears to be as good a guarantor of ineffectiveness as Panama's reliance on the self-classification of taxpayers in its idle lands tax. It is not surprising that legal complications and lack of funds appear to have blocked this tax from being put into effect.[16] As late as 1969 the revenue produced by the idle lands tax came to only $9,200, and a thorough survey of land legislation and practice in Guatemala could say of it only that no information on its enforcement was available.[17]

It is hard to avoid the conclusion that better administration and a higher rate for the regular property tax would seem more likely to produce both more public revenues and more stimulus to efficient use of land than further attempts to put teeth into this special tax on idle lands and its fellows in other countries.

Panama's long experience with the property tax emphasizes the importance of full and current assessments, of moderately competent administration, and of an adequate legal structure if this tax is to be of much use in mobilizing resources for development. Furthermore, attempts to utilize taxes on property for nonfiscal purposes—the "idle" lands tax and the progressive rate structure of the property tax— appear to have had no perceptible effect on either the distribution of income and wealth or the allocation of resources within the agricultural sector itself. The main lessons from Panamanian experience with agricultural taxation thus appear to be negative ones.

More generally, although the six countries of the Central American region exhibit considerable diversity in the exact nature and importance of their taxes on agricultural land, the general picture in recent decades is a similar one of frequent attempts to increase the revenue and nonfiscal impact of land taxes, most of which have failed as a result of the basic inadequacies of the underlying land administration. This picture is not limited to Central America alone. A similar scenario has been enacted in most other countries in Latin America.

In Paraguay, for example, where the rural land tax, which is fundamentally based on land area, yielded 5.4 percent of government revenues in 1962, the taxation of agriculture is, as usual, complicated by the very low level of income and by the fact that many rural people hold no title to the land they occupy. Furthermore, since there are apparently no serious enforcement procedures (except the need to show that the tax has been paid in order to effect transfers of property), all tax collections are, in a sense, voluntary. It is thus not surprising that 75 percent of the taxpayers were estimated in 1963 to be delinquent in their payments and that only around 50 percent of rural properties were thought to be taxed.[18]

In light of the obvious (and common) deficiencies of the Paraguayan agricultural land tax, the most surprising thing is perhaps that it produces as much revenue as it appears to do. In 1948, however, this tax was reported to yield 12 percent of tax revenues, compared to only 5 percent in 1962 (see Table 2). Unless some drastic changes in administration, especially in valuation and collection procedures, have been made, the probability is that land tax collections have further declined in relative importance since 1962. Rather than a dynamic source of future development revenues, then, the present Paraguayan land tax appears to represent the dying remnant of a once-important tax.

BOLIVIA

Bolivia, like Paraguay, is one of the poorest countries in Latin America. Over two-thirds of its population is rural and illiterate. The country is further characterized by extreme variations in geography, climate, and agricultural conditions. Despite its large rural population, the terrain is so unfavorable that less than 3 percent of Bolivia is cultivated, and only another 10 percent or so is in pasture. Agriculture provides almost none of Bolivia's exports (80 percent of which are mineral products, including petroleum) and about the same proportion of the revenues accruing to the small Bolivian public sector. In recent years, agricultural output, destined almost entirely for domestic consumption, has grown less rapidly than the population.

In short, Bolivia would appear to be a country precisely filling the conditions needed for success of the traditional land tax remedy. Given the scarce consumption of manufactured goods and recent difficult export conditions, there is really no alternative source of revenues to support public expenditures. The stagnant, overpopulated agricultural sector and the urban food deficit similarly urge reliance on land taxes for incentive purposes. The situation is considerably complicated, however, by the fact that Bolivia, like Mexico (see Chapter 6), has undergone a major revolution that altered the nature of its rural society.

The Bolivian Land Reform Law of 1953 was implemented at a slow pace initially, as was inevitable in the confused conditions following the revolution in 1952. Nevertheless, land reform has had considerable impact on the tenurial situation in Bolivia, despite various abuses, legal intricacies, and regional variations that reflect the still important political, economic, and social role of the old elite.

Before the revolution the predominant tenure relation in Bolivia (*colonato*) offered no incentives to either landlord or tenant to adopt more productive inputs since the *colonos* supplied most of the input and reaped few of the gains. Colonos were, under this system, absolutely limited in access to land. The initial impact of the land reform on this archaic system was dramatic: peasants were made de facto owners of their usufruct parcels and were freed from the serf-like obligation of providing landlords unremunerated labor or personal services.[19] Later, and at a much slower pace, lands in excess of legally stated maximums were expropriated. As a result of the reforms most Bolivian peasants now work their own land as individual owner-operators, although there are still very great differences in the quantity of land owned by different peasants.

The immediate result of the revolution was to reduce agricultural production and, especially, the movement of agricultural products to the city. In the longer run it appears peasant consumption increased (with some effect on population growth), while production remained more or less the same or at most declined a bit. The inadequate marketing system was a big barrier to maintaining the level of marketed food supplies, which undoubtedly fell for several years. On the other hand, the new agrarian system has been able to accommodate a vast increase in rural population and provide higher living standards, as well as supplying the cities, by bringing new lands into cultivation, by intensifying production, and by switching to more labor-intensive crops such as vegetables.[20]

This pattern is very similar to that in Mexico a generation earlier and appears similarly to reflect the tremendous redistribution of income-earning opportunities (access to land) as a result of the revolution in 1952. Since Bolivia, unlike Mexico, has not undertaken extensive large-scale rural public works, this relatively beneficial result suggests even more than in the Mexican case (see Chapter 6) the importance of the private investment decisions stimulated by the land reform.

TAXING AGRICULTURE: A SURVEY

The revolution in land tenure was by no means accompanied by a similar revolution in land taxation. Indeed, as in Mexico, land reform in Bolivia appears not only to have pre-empted the major redistributive objective sometimes assigned to taxes,[21] but to have led to neglect of the considerable potential of land taxes to raise revenues for general public purposes. This "revolutionary neglect" does not mean that Bolivia has not often considered, or at least been asked to consider, the enactment of an effective rural land tax. On the contrary, since a United Nations mission in 1951 (before the revolution) recommended that tax rates, then 4 mills, be raised and assessments, then estimated at 20 to 30 percent of current values, be made more realistic, the same refrain has often been heard.[22] Nevertheless, the prerevolutionary land tax still exists, basically unchanged despite drastic alterations in both the tax base and, probably, the objectives of tax policy.

The pre-1952 rural land tax in Bolivia was based on landowners' sworn statements of the values of their properties. Market information was considered of little use because properties were seldom sold, and the sales price was often determined by the quantity of labor attached to the property through the colonato system. It is not surprising that this tax produced at most 1 percent of the low total tax revenues accruing to the Bolivian government and that the tax base was in a chaotic state. The rapid postrevolutionary inflation made these initially low assessments even more unrealistically low, so that by 1964 the yield of the tax was less than one-half of 1 percent of central government revenues, a sum which reportedly represented payments by a few landowners not yet affected by the land reform who felt that tax payments would help them secure legal possession.[23]

A tax on agricultural land in the form of a presumptive income tax of 6 percent was first introduced in 1936. The current tax, established in 1953, levies a rate of 6.4 mills on cadastral value, or the value at last transfer if higher. Since the estimated capital value continues to be derived largely from owners' self-assessments and there is no effective administration of this tax and no enforcement procedure, its yield is, as noted above, extremely low.

At present there are over seventy minor taxes affecting the agricultural sector in Bolivia, many of which are earmarked for local governments, roads, and so forth, and some of which are quite contrary to sensible development policy—for example, tolls on the value of agricultural products in order to pass through a province. The agricultural sector is in effect exempted from the regular income tax on the grounds that it is administratively impossible to levy an income tax on Bolivian agriculture at its present stage of development.[24] Although there has been a 10 percent tax on capital gains realized from the sale of rural property since 1958, it seems unlikely that this provision has been effectively enforced either.

In light of what has happened to land taxes, it is clear that at present the level of total agricultural taxation in Bolivia is very low. One estimate is that the agricultural sector provided less than 2 percent of public revenues in 1967, although it received 16 percent of public expenditures.[25] These figures are in stark contrast to those of a century ago, when the agricultural sector paid well over half of all Bolivian taxes.

Inflation and neglect thus appear effectively to have killed the existing Bolivian land tax. The major impediment to effective land taxation in Bolivia, as in many other countries, has been the lack of adequate property valuations, on the one hand, and of staff to make them, on the other. Fortunately, however, the active agrarian reform titling program of recent years has in much of the country provided the basis of a property register suitable for tax purposes.

There have been several attempts to reform the Bolivian land tax since the revolution. In 1961, for example, a proposed new tax code eliminated all agricultural production taxes (except that on coca), substituting flat-rate land taxes with specific rates per hectare varying by zone and land use. This tax was also intended to substitute for the ineffective schedular income tax on small holders, since the rates were to be set each year in accordance with average earnings in each zone. Similarly, the proposed tax could be taken as a credit against any income tax due on the net earnings of commercial agricultural enterprises.[26] Again, in 1962, a bill was introduced to establish a rural property tax applicable to small owners who received land through the agrarian reform program.[27] Nothing seems to have come of either of these proposals.

By 1967, however, not only economic but also political circumstances seemed more propitious for the proposal of a new tax on rural land. The titling program had provided much basic information; peasants were, it was thought, willing to pay taxes in order to secure their titles; and, above all, the government desperately needed revenues. An elaborate proposal to impose a "unified annual tax on the agricultural sector" was therefore prepared.

As with the 1961 proposal, the new tax was to be based on a fixed peso assessment per hectare of area, with the amount of the assessment varying in accord with the size of the property, whether the land is in pasture or crops, and eleven soil types.[28] The similarity of the structure of this tax to the one which Wald proposed to the Santiago Conference as an interim reform measure is striking.[29] The rate structure originally proposed was based on data from agricultural extension and agrarian reform studies, and it was designed to approximate roughly the income tax that would be levied on the equivalent presumed income. Although crude, this procedure seems to be about the best possible under the circumstances.

Since the proposed tax was based on land alone, it was argued that it would not discourage agricultural investment; indeed, in theory its income effect would probably encourage work effort and investment. The rate was progressive with respect to size, however, and might have tended to accentuate the already excessive fragmentation of landholdings in Bolivia if the rates were not as low as they were: 2 to 6 percent in terms of presumed income, or, say, 4 to 12 mills on assessed valuation—that is, little more than the present nominal rates. The rationale for this progression appeared to be that the land tax would substitute for a tax on agricultural income, although the substantial rate reductions later introduced into the proposal soon severed this connection.

Although based on land area, the tax was, as is customary in Latin America, levied on owners, and, further, only on those with titles executed by the Agrarian Reform Department (which are now the only legally valid land titles). The original proposal was that nonpayment for five years could lead to sale, but this provision was subsequently removed, thus considerably weakening the enforceability of the tax. An additional important feature was that 80 percent of the revenues from the tax were supposed to be destined for works benefiting the agriculture sector, with an additional 1 percent to the peasant unions, the basic political organization of rural Bolivia.

One advantage of an area-based tax is that it is, in principle, easily understood by taxpayers; this would seem especially important with a new, major tax like that proposed in Bolivia. The earmarking provisions, with their promise of visible local benefits, seem designed for the same end. Although it appears no great stress was placed on tax-payer education, the government did submit this proposal for dis-cussion to a selected group of peasant leaders at the "First Economic Conference of the Bolivian Peasantry" in La Paz in December 1968. After considerable discussion, this group approved the proposal with reduced rates and the bill was submitted to Congress. Subsequently, however, the proposal was effectively killed as a result of the opposi-tion of local peasant leaders in different parts of the country (in alliance with university students).[30]

It appears that even the removal of the old landholding class has not made direct land taxes palatable in Bolivia. Nor is this outcome unexpected. One estimate was that the yield of the new tax might amount to as much as one-third of internal tax revenue (and 20 per-cent of total government revenue) when fully in force, by, say, 1973.[31] A change of this magnitude in agriculture's contribution to the public revenues in so short a time in any country seems quite unrealistic, at least not without equally drastic changes in public spending patterns and in developmental policy, preferably accom-panied by intensive taxpayer education programs. Since such changes did not seem feasible and the administration was quite unready to handle the tax, perhaps its demise was not such a tragedy.

Nevertheless, if such a major change in Bolivian agricultural tax policy ever did prove possible, the conditions and possibilities of de-velopment in both the agricultural sector and in the economy as a whole might be markedly altered, to a degree as yet attained by no other country in South America and few countries anywhere. The principal ingredient of this potential change, apart from the crucial political conditions, thus perhaps deserves re-emphasis: a relatively simple and crude set of fixed tax assessments based primarily on land area.

URUGUAY

Uruguay may well be the richest agricultural country in Latin America. Although agricultural productivity has been stagnant in recent years, its level compared to most other countries of the area is high. The richness of Uruguay's agricultural base is matched by the abundance of taxes on agricultural land. The incomplete listing of land taxes in Table 7 suggests something of the complexity of this

TABLE 7. TAXES ON RURAL REAL PROPERTY IN URUGUAY, 1964

Designation	Rate (mills)	Base	Remarks
General National Taxes			
National Coloniza-tion Institute	0.5–8	Leasehold value	
Social Security Fund	$0.20/ha.	Area	
Rural Workers	2	Capital value	25% surcharge if absentee-owned
Railways	3.5–4.5	Capital value	$150,000 exemption
Drainage	1–2	Capital value	
Public Works	4–20	Capital	
Rural Property	1	Capital value	$50,000 exemption
Prophylaxis against Syphilis	$0.01/ha.	Area	Land used for livestock
Primary Education	10–20	Capital value	$1,000 exemption
Property Tax Sur-charge	10–40	Capital value	$100,000 exemption
Net Wealth Tax	7.5–15	Net wealth	$250,000 exemption
Special National Taxes			
Drainage	1	Capital value	Areas where works constructed
Drainage	1 or 2	Capital value	Properties fronting on completed works
Highways	$0.25–$0.50/ frontage meter[a]	Capital value	Properties fronting on highways
Special Highway	$0.80/ frontage meter[b]	Frontage	Properties fronting on Interbalnearia Highway
Railways	5	Capital value	In "zone of influence"
Departmental Taxes			
Real Property Tax	0 to 10 (varies by department)	Land value	Rates doubled for absentees

Sources: Information from Programa Conjunto de Tributación, *Sistemas Tributarias de América Latina: Uruguay* (Washington, D.C.: Pan-American Union, 1967), pp. 27–35, supplemented by the (sometimes conflicting) information in Ministerio de Ganadería y Agricultura, *Estudio Económico y Social de Agricultura en el Uruguay* (Montevideo, 1967), Vol. I, pp. 571–575.

[a] Limited to 100% of real property tax levied on property
[b] Limited to 150% of real property tax levied on property

system and of the long-standing attempts in Uruguay to do something about everything through the medium of the tax system.

The present basic tax on real property was established as a national tax in 1934 at a flat rate of 4.5 mills on appraised value excluding rural improvements.[32] By the time this tax was turned over to the nineteen departments in the constitution of 1952, the rate had risen to 8 mills. Thereafter, each department went its own way. By 1962, for example, the basic tax rate varied from 0 to 10 mills. Some departments exempted certain agricultural investments and exports; others surcharged landlords; many exempted small farmers and imposed progressive taxes graduated by the size of the property, with rates up to 9 pesos per hectare.

Although Uruguay continued to have a centralized cadastral office which recorded all property transfers and was charged with the valuation of all properties, many departments also altered the tax base. Some imposed levies on the basis of area, some taxed property as such, and some taxed ownership interests. In the early 1960's different departments applied various adjustments, usually by means of coefficients varying with the age of assessment or size, to the national cadastral values without any coordination. In many parts of the country there were two assessed valuations, one for departmental and one for national purposes. More recently, the departmental discretion in taxing land which gave rise to this complexity has been constitutionally revoked.

To further confuse the situation in the 1960's, however, the important Social Security Institute began to collect its own land tax, while the national government continued to collect the variety of levies listed in Table 7 for general and specific purposes. Most of these national property taxes, unlike the basic land tax, do not exempt rural improvements. Many of these taxes were designed primarily with nonfiscal ends in mind, such as curbing *latifundismo* or absentee ownership. One department (Cerro Largo) even went to the length of imposing a special tax on owners not resident within its boundaries!

The total nominal rates of land taxation reached potentially astronomical heights on paper: an official calculation put the maximum rate in 1964 at 24 percent on the assessed value of properties over 20,000 hectares in size.[33] The total rate applicable to properties of different sizes and valuations varied widely throughout the country, from an average of 1.7 percent in one department to an average (not maximum) of 10.1 percent in another.

A system with rates of this magnitude can function effectively in a nonrevolutionary environment only if, to paraphrase Henry Simons, it is an example of dipping deeply with a sieve.[34] And such indeed is the case. Although in terms of taxes per hectare the variation across the country was equally striking, from a low of 0.6 pesos on properties under 50 hectares in one department to a high in another of 25.2 pesos on those over 20,000 hectares, the effective rates of tax were in all cases very much lower than the nominal rates, because of the extremely low valuation basis upon which this impressive superstructure of rates were erected.

In fourteen of the nineteen departments, for example, most values in 1964 dated from 1949; in the other five departments, the last general valuation was in 1957. The considerable inflation in the intervening period ensured that the intended heavy progressivity amounted to no more than a light tax burden in reality. A new general valuation intended to correct this fault was decreed in 1960, although no adequate budgetary appropriation was made. The valuation was still underway in 1969, although by law it was to be redone each three years (compared to the previous, equally nominal, five-year cycle). Interestingly, the basis for the new valuation was to be land value plus an arbitrary markup of 25 percent, compared to the previous basis of land value less an equally arbitrary 20 percent.

In 1964 steps were also taken to offset an important loophole in the Uruguayan property tax structure—the use of corporations to hold land and hence vitiate the intended progressivity of many of the taxes —by, as in Mexico, forbidding corporations to hold rural land and to conduct agricultural activities. Subsequently, however, this prohibition was limited only to corporations with bearer shares, which were given until 1971 to comply.

These land-based taxes are estimated to have yielded perhaps 3 percent of central revenues in 1950[35] and 7 percent in 1965,[36] so the rate increases and revaluations of the preceding decade appear to have had some effect. Only perhaps one-quarter of this yield came from rural areas. The complex property tax structure yielded little more than the national tax on real estate transfers alone (whose rate was raised in 1964 to 16 percent on assessed value, multiplied by a coefficient varying with the age of the assessment), and very much less than the export taxes, which accounted for two-thirds of the total taxes paid by Uruguayan agriculture. Most of this amount came from wool, where taxes amounted to close to one-third of value-added, compared to less than 10 percent in the rest of agriculture and little more in the nonagricultural sector as a whole.

These important export taxes were much criticized both for their inelasticity and for their effects on production, although the revenue they produced was welcomed. Since 1960, when Uruguay introduced a presumptive income tax based on the potential productivity of agricultural land, a number of attempts have been made to combine the revenue yield of export taxes with the supposed incentive effects of land taxes.

A principal aim of this new tax was to promote agricultural productivity by weighing more heavily on those producing below "potential," and favoring those producing above "potential" by means of a zero marginal rate on the excess.[37] Productive investment was to be exempted, and the tax rate fell as output per hectare rose. A 50 percent deduction from gross income for tenants was allowed as estimated expenses, compared to 30 percent for owners.

The 1961 tax was to be based on a "standard yield" per hectare for land valued at 80 pesos per hectare or less. The values were determined as 80 percent of the 1956 cadastral value, increased by an arbitrary 50 percent to allow for subsequent inflation. If the value thus determined exceeded 80 pesos, the "standard yield" was to be increased proportionately. The "standard yield" was initially set as the average price of 4 kilos of wool and 20 kilos of beef. Although an oversimplification (neglecting other products, for example) this basis was perhaps not really too bad in the particular situation of Uruguay because of the dominance of these products and the relatively uniform quality of the soil.

In the first year of operation of this tax, a grand total of thirteen declarations were received. Although, by 1965, 2,500 declarations were filed, the yield of this tax remained weak, largely because the original cadastral basis was never improved. Although a new cadastre was launched in 1961, it was still not completed a decade later. This basic deficiency, although partially offset by the correction of values by an index, was accentuated by continuing inflation in Uruguay during the 1960's. Revenue from agriculture as a proportion of total government revenue fell from 30 percent in 1960 to 16 percent in 1962, and as a proportion of agricultural output from 21 percent to 16 percent, with from 70 to 85 percent of revenues throughout the period coming from the traditional export taxes on wool and meat.[38] In 1964, for example, less than 2 percent of agricultural tax revenue was provided by the "income" tax.

A revised tax on potential income was introduced in 1968. This tax, too, is assessed on the value of the "minimum required production per hectare," based on cadastral information and on the annual values established for units of wool and meat. The presumed agricultural income of an average hectare is obtained by multiplying A (the presumed physical product, in terms of wool, lamb, and beef) by B (a price index). This figure is then multiplied by C (a computed productivity index for this farm compared to an average farm), and the result multiplied by D (the farm area, excluding forests) to get the tax base. The tax base thus calculated is then subjected to progressive income tax rates of from 25 to 50 percent, although for the first two years only a fraction of these rates were to be applied.

Of the components of the tax base, A and B were to be set by the national government, with presumed production being set every five years and prices annually. D is based on the cadastre, and C is in theory to be determined by a complicated, and as yet largely nonexistent, soil analysis. In the interim, pending the classification of all Uruguayan territory into zones according to their theoretical yield of the selected products, the productivity index is to be determined by an almost equally complex calculation comparing the assessed value of each farm property with average assessed values.

This complex tax is intended eventually to replace both the income tax and the export tax on the agricultural sector. Taxpayers are to add 50 percent of the calculated presumed income to taxable income in order to determine the appropriate tax rate for their nonagricultural income. The main administrative technique for collecting the tax is by withholding a proportion (from 2 to 35 percent) of the price of exported products.

Experience is too short yet to show whether this tax will work, but it appears to be very complex and still to depend in large part upon the establishment of an adequate cadastral register and soil classification. Further, there are generous exemptions from the tax: for instance, an amount up to 30 percent of the tax may be deducted for reinvestment expenditures on certain items, with a limit of 30 percent of the tax on a 2,500 hectare farm of average production. It is not easy to see how one could prevent abuse of this and other provisions.

In short, it appears that Uruguay once again illustrates the lessons seen elsewhere in Latin America: first, that it is much easier to get large revenues from taxes on agricultural exports than from taxes on agricultural land; second, that land-based taxes, including most agricultural income taxes, stand or fall on the strength of the land survey information on which they are always, in one way or another, based.

In 1964, for example, a national tax on potential agricultural income was proposed in Argentina more or less along Uruguayan lines, but it was even more complicated since it did not follow the simple wool-meat path but attempted to take all factors into account.[39] This proposal was never implemented, in part because of the absence of the essential initial information. In general, surprisingly little progress in the basic administrative framework for taxing agriculture appears to have been made in either Argentina or Uruguay. One reason for the lack of emphasis on the fundamentals in both countries may have been undue concentration on the potential recherché benefits of the sophisticated tax gadgetry with which they have tended to experiment.

A somewhat similar situation prevails in Brazil, where agriculture is much more important as an employer than either Argentina or Uruguay. Some fifteen states in Brazil have, for instance, at one time or another introduced progressive land taxes in an effort to reduce or limit the size of landholdings. These state tax systems were quite complex. In 1957, for example, the nineteen Brazilian states employed in total seven different methods of taxing real property: four states graduated rates in accordance with assessed value; five in accordance with area; two by assessed value but differentiated by location; three others by assessed value differentiated by type of exploitation; and one, with a complexity of structure usually seen only in inheritance taxes, graduated in accordance with both value and area, differentiated by type of exploitation. One state levied only a fixed rate per hectare, although graduated by type of exploitation, while two others, including São Paulo, levied a flat-rate tax on assessed value.[40] Whatever their structure, however, all of these taxes were without discernible effects because both the rates of tax and the valuations were so low.

The basic rate of the present Brazilian national land tax is only 2 mills, which is very low even by Central American standards. The rate structure of the tax is as complicated as the state tax structure described above, however, being progressive in accordance with several different criteria—area, location, and level of utilization, for example—and the theoretical maximum tax rate is 3.5 percent, or almost up to Uruguayan levels.[41] These rates, of course, greatly overstate the effective rates because of the serious underreporting of the essentially self-declared land values.

The idea behind the tax is that the rate on the realized income of land should increase in direct proportion to its distance below the norms of the Land Statute of 1964. Since there are nine different zones (based on population potential and proximity to an urban nucleus) and six different land-use types, there are 54 different standard sizes of "modulo," or that quantity of land which is capable of absorbing all the labor of four working adults and of supporting them at a standard of living consistent with the goals of economic progress and social justice. Four size classes defined in terms of numbers of modulos are also set out. In addition, much more information than is presently available is needed to calculate the coefficients of economic yields and social conditions which are applied to derive the total theoretical tax.

Since to have full effect this complex rate structure requires information that does not now exist, in much of the country the new law may, initially, have reduced the already low yield of the land tax. There is, however, little doubt that fiscal revenues subsequently rose as a result of the effects of the cadastral survey.

Three comments may be made about the new Brazilian land tax structure. First, its very considerable complexity appears to reflect, as in some other Latin American countries, an attempt to avoid facing directly the difficult problems of agrarian reform. Second, it appears there have been no incentive effects from the new tax, largely because its effective rates are so low.[42] Third, the principal problem with the rate structure, apart from its untoward complexity, is the inadequate valuation basis upon which it rests.

It is not clear to what extent any one tax instrument can really be expected to do all the things the Brazilian tax and similar taxes in other countries are supposed to do. It is very clear, however, that the existing tax will accomplish none of these aims; nor, and this is probably more important, will it contribute anything significant to public revenues unless it is based upon decently comprehensive and current information. Even at the present relatively low nominal rates applying to most rural properties, the yield from a good land survey would probably more than repay its cost.

Once again, therefore, it appears that the technical key to successful agricultural land taxation lies in good basic information on the characteristics and value of land; a sophisticated tax like that on the statute books in Brazil or Uruguay requires an equally sophisticated information base if it is to have any effect. This requirement suggests that one should view with some skepticism the usefulness of such complex proposals either to raise revenues or to achieve their varied nonfiscal ends. Lacking this essential basis, attempts to achieve perfection through complicated land tax schemes seem likely to be at the expense of possibly acceptable if less conceptually glamorous improvements in tax structure and especially in the tax base.

CHILE

The taxation of agricultural land has probably been more effective in Chile than in any other country in Latin America. Although this result may not be completely unrelated to the fact that agriculture plays a relatively less important role in Chile than in other countries on the continent, it still stands in stark contrast to, for example, the situation in neighboring Argentina. Despite this enviable record, it appears that the relative tax burden on Chilean agriculture is still lower than that on other sectors of the economy (even ignoring the taxes on Chile's main mineral exports). Agricultural taxes fell steadily from 7 percent of total taxes in 1941 to around 2 percent in 1964, largely as a result of the failure of assessed valuations to keep up with inflation.[43] Although a major reform in 1965 raised the proportion of total taxes paid by agriculture to over 5 percent, compared to around 10 percent of gross domestic product produced by agriculture in that year, continued inflation and liberalized tax exemptions reduced the share of revenues coming from agriculture to 3 percent in 1966.[44]

Land was taxed in Chile even before it became an independent country in 1818. By 1855 there was a fairly well-established tax roll and assessment system for rural real estate. Since 1927, most taxable property in the country has been revalued around every six years on the average.[45] The tax rate on agricultural property was set at 4 mills in 1925. The rate was raised to 8 mills in 1940, and, by 1954, it was 13 mills. Part of the proceeds of the land tax was earmarked for local governments and part for roads and other public improvements. Cooperatives have generally paid taxes at only 50 percent of these rates, and there are such other conventional exemptions as that for reforested land.

A major reform was introduced in 1954 (to take effect in 1956) in which the tax rate was raised to 21 mills. More important, the tax base was changed at this time from both improvements and land to land alone in most cases. Furthermore, expenditures for clearing and drainage, and similar expenditures for land improvement were not to be reflected in the tax base until 1974, unless the land changed owners. The Chilean tax thus became, at least temporarily, one on the site value of agricultural land. The intention was to encourage investment in agricultural improvements; in practice all that was done was to reduce valuations by one-third to allow for improvements. In theory, however, the tax was levied on potential use value as determined by the capitalization of the income it would yield if the average level of agricultural technology were applied.

In another respect the 1954 reform put Chile's property tax in a class by itself. Spurred by the marked inflation which has for many years characterized the Chilean economy, a provision was introduced to automatically revalue all assessments for tax purposes in accordance with an index of the growth in money value of the output of the agricultural sector.[46] This adjustment mechanism did not, however, turn out to have the presumably desired effect of maintaining the real level of agricultural taxation in the face of inflation. For one thing, the commission set up to decide the appropriate annual adjustment factor became a political body dominated by landowners, in which a good deal of successful maneuvering designed to reduce the adjustment factor took place. More important, the pace of the official reassessment initiated in the 1950's was too slow to keep up with the inflation, so that the tax base continued to depend primarily on the almost invariably low self-appraisals by owners. The result of these factors was that the yield of the main taxes on the Chilean agricultural sector fell steadily throughout the 1950's.

In 1961, however, Chile was struck by a great natural disaster—earthquakes in the southern Central Valley—which ultimately had two decidedly beneficial effects on the yield of the property tax. The first was that the nominal tax rate was raised to 32.5 mills, thus reversing the downward trend in revenues. The second effect, which turned out to be more important in the long run, was that some of the funds collected for disaster relief by the Organization of American States arrived too late to be employed for the designated purpose. The O.A.S. decided to use them to finance an aerial survey of Chile that could serve as the basis for a general reassessment for tax and other purposes. This reassessment, based largely on aerial photographs and other mass appraisal techniques, was completed in three years, by 1965.[47] This is about as fast as one could expect to carry out a reassessment in a country the size of Chile. It stands in shining contrast to most experience with more painstaking cadastral surveys elsewhere in Latin America.

The effect of this reassessment, which was used for the first time as a basis for 1965 taxes, was to triple the real yield of the land tax in 1965 compared to 1964. In effect, the average level of rural valuations was raised from around 20 percent of market value to more like 80 percent. Although the nominal tax rate was, in an offsetting move, lowered from 32.5 to 20 mills, the effective tax rate (on estimated market value) nevertheless rose in one year from 6 to 16 mills.[48] This is probably a greater land tax increase than any other in recent Latin American history, and the cost of the cadastral survey was reportedly recouped from the increased tax revenues in four years.

As noted earlier, all this great reform managed to do was to restore some of the losses due to inflation in previous years. Although the automatic adjustment mechanism was strengthened and removed somewhat from the political arena in the 1962 reform, it has still proved inadequate to maintain this new, higher level of taxation, and tax yields have subsequently receded to pre-1965 levels.

Even after full reassessment and with an effective tax rate on market value much higher than that anywhere else in Latin America, land tax revenue in Chile in 1965 amounted to only around 4 percent of agricultural output. It is thus not surprising that various studies suggest that this highest effective property tax in Latin America has had relatively little discernible effect on the allocation or distribution of Chile's agricultural resources. The case for heavier agricultural taxation in Chile therefore continues to be made in many studies.

Schemes as elaborate as those in Uruguay and Brazil outlined above have, for example, been suggested in Chile several times. In 1964, for instance, the Ministry of Agriculture proposed that the land tax, the tax on agricultural income, the property transfer tax, and a special tax on vineyards be replaced by a unified progressive tax on land value, with rates ranging from 1 to 14 percent according to the size of the property and the type of tenancy and use.[49] This proposal was never submitted to Congress.

A similar proposal was put forward in the Ministry's 1968 Development Plan and subsequently elaborated in a study by a United Nations consultant.[50] The proposed tax would, as before, replace the present land and income tax and also the then new net wealth tax. It would be based on presumed "potential" income determined in the usual complex fashion; improvements would be exempt, and its base would be adjusted annually in relation to both the weighted prices of the most important agricultural products in each region and the improvement in productivity of the agricultural sector as a whole. More uniquely, the tax would be "personalized" by allowing credits or deductions for family responsibilities, in line with the scheme put forward by Wald some years ago.[51] The existing local supplemental taxes on the national land tax would be suppressed as part of the reform.

The probable fate of this proposal, given recent political changes in Chile, is not at all clear. A recent study, however, has attempted to adapt it to the new political situation, especially since agricultural taxation has been steadily decreasing because hardly any taxes are levied on lands distributed by agrarian reform.[52]

Despite various setbacks, Chile's attempts to reform its agricultural tax system stand up well compared to those in most other Latin American countries. The rapid and successful cadastral survey of 1962–1965 remains a model to be emulated. Gadgetry in the formulation of tax structure, while hardly unknown, has been kept within moderately reasonable bounds to date. As usual, there appear to be no empirically discernible effects of land taxation in Chile (including the net wealth and presumptive income taxes) other than to raise some revenue.[53] Most important, the development and operation of a system of annual automatic adjustments of the tax base, starting from an adequate cadastral survey in the first place, although defective in practice, provides a rare Latin American example of concentration on the fundamentals of land taxation and adaptation to local circumstances. The Chilean land tax system is far from perfect, but it is largely sensible and workable, which is more than can be said for that in some other countries.

JAMAICA

Although not strictly included in the usual understanding of "Latin America," the case of Jamaica is discussed briefly here because it has recently taken a particularly interesting step in the taxation of agriculture by introducing a tax on unimproved land values to replace a more conventional property tax levied on capital value.[54] Although in effect a somewhat similar change has been made in such Latin American countries as Uruguay and Chile, it has seldom been done so explicitly or with so much preparation.

The change to the unimproved value basis had been recommended in Jamaica before by, among others, a Royal Commission in 1943 and a World Bank mission in 1952, but it was finally made as a result of a 1956 report by a United Nations expert.[55] The resulting Land Valuation Law of 1956 provided both for a change in the basis of the existing property tax to unimproved value and for the revaluation of all land in Jamaica. The revaluation process started in 1956, and the first parish (unit of local government) adopted the new tax basis in 1959. Since then, the work of revaluation steadily, though slowly, progressed, until now more than one-half of the island is taxing on the basis of the new unimproved value assessments. The major urban areas have not yet been reassessed, however, and the revaluation has been halted, leaving two different systems in effect in different parts of the island.

Under the new law the land tax is based on the unimproved value of land, defined as the value of the new land alone without taking into account such improvements as houses, crops, and so forth that may have been put upon it. The removal of the original land cover (timber or vegetable growth) is not considered to be an improvement of land for purposes of taxation. In other countries taxing on the unimproved value basis, like Australia, "invisible" improvements of agricultural land such as the cost of clearing it, drainage, and the like, have been found to create by far the greatest problems of valuation.[56] The Jamaican law has thus simplified administration considerably by turning the land tax into one on "site value" rather than on "unimproved value" as such. By far the most difficult and costly part of the conventional property tax assessment procedure is the valuation of improvements, which cannot be handled by mass appraisal techniques alone but requires a degree of individual attention by relatively well-trained technicians. Indeed, a principal argument in Jamaica for the adoption of the revised land tax system was its relative simplicity of administration.

Jamaica has consistently emphasized the importance of practical rather than theoretically "perfect" administrative techniques. It has thus been able to accomplish a very substantial revaluation with a limited technical staff. In 1957, for example, there were only 2 fully qualified professional valuers on the island, and even as late as 1965 there were only 8 plus supporting technicians for a total of 77, compared to a staff of 700 in Puerto Rico in 1960. Of course, the pace of the revaluation was correspondingly slow.

As in Chile, the Jamaican revaluation process was based on the elaboration, mainly through large-scale aerial photography, of a set of property maps and related information just sufficient for fiscal purposes, rather than, as in Panama, the much more demanding elaboration of a legal cadaster sufficient to establish title. The Jamaican Commissioner of Valuations has, for example, referred to much of this mapping exercise as nothing more than "controlled sketching."[57] While the area figures thus obtained cannot be completely accurate, they are considered good enough for tax purposes, especially since the other factor determining tax liability, appraised value, is itself inevitably an estimate with a much greater range of possible error.

Another administrative simplification adopted in Jamaica was that all landholdings worth less than £100 were exempted from the formal valuation process. Such properties were instead subject to a token parish tax of four shillings. Over 70 percent of rural parcels (but only 14 percent of value) were exempted from valuation as a result of this procedure, which, like the similar provisions found in other countries, may perhaps be criticized as encouraging still further fragmentation of the already greatly fragmented rural landholdings in Jamaica, but which certainly made the general revaluation much simpler.

Relief was also provided to certain taxpayers who found it hard to meet their new land tax liability because the tax was based on the potential use of the land (for example, a resort hotel) while their income was based on the actual use (for example, fishing or agriculture). In such cases, taxpayers may apply for relief, which will be granted if the Taxation Relief Board decides it is reasonable for the land to continue in its present use because, for instance, of the limited skills and mobility of its owner. While the effect of such relief may be socially desirable, it may in a minor way reinforce some of the characteristic problems of underdeveloped regions. Similar provisions lightening the tax burden on agricultural lands which, although potentially suitable for more productive purposes, are retained in agricultural use, may be found in many countries, both developed and less developed, notably in the case of land on the fringe of growing urban areas.

Three taxes are at present levied in Jamaica on the unimproved value of that land taxed on this basis. The first is a national property tax, levied at progressive rates on property whose unimproved value is over £1,000. The effective rate of this tax reaches almost 3 percent on properties over £31,000 in value, although the fact that land taxes are deductible from taxable income for income tax purposes reduces the effect of this progressivity, particularly for the owners of properties of high value. The tax is progressive with respect to properties rather than the property holdings of persons. It is thus less personal but probably more practical than the graduated property taxes found in a number of other countries in Latin America, which are, without exception, levied on the interests of owners in property rather than on the property as such. Less than 2 percent of all property holdings in Jamaica—but over half of all land value—is in fact subject to this tax, much of which is probably paid by plantation agriculture which is usually characterized by the large acreage of individual properties.

The second tax levied on the unimproved value basis is the parish rate, set by the local (parish) council subject to national government approval. This tax has no exemptions: the first £100 of unimproved value is, as already noted, subject to a flat tax of four shillings, and values above this amount are subject to moderately progressive rates (of which none go as high as 1 percent) which vary to a limited extent from parish to parish in accordance with local revenue needs. Owing to the lack of exemptions, this parish tax actually raises more revenue than the much more steeply progressive national property tax and constitutes an important, though not rapidly growing, source of local revenues. In addition to these two taxes, service rates for specific municipal services (fire protection, water, and so forth) are also levied on the unimproved value basis.

The economic effects of the new Jamaican land tax system are not wholly clear. To begin with, the parish rates were set to yield the same revenue in the first year as the old system, so the effects were those of a tax substitution rather than a tax increase. But the general revaluation of land also changed relative tax burdens substantially. The most careful examination of the Jamaican experience to date suggests that as yet there have been no dramatic effects as a result of the adoption of the new tax basis, largely because of the relatively high exemption levels and the moderate tax rate.[58] There appear to have been some instances of properties being divided or sold as a result of the introduction of the site-value tax, but it is not clear to what extent this division reflects successful attainment of one of the nonfiscal objectives of the tax rather than legal maneuvers designed to avoid the full effects of the progressive rate structure.[59]

On the whole, it appears that Jamaican experience (as well as that in Barbados and Trinidad) provides strong support for the argument that unimproved value taxation is administratively feasible in the agricultural sector of a developing country, if desired.[60] Jamaica, it appears, has now—provided it completes the cadaster—a sound basis for fuller and more effective taxation of property in order to mobilize resources for development as well as to encourage the efficient utilization of agricultural land (and perhaps, although this is more questionable, to affect favorably the distribution of income), if this is the path it decides to follow. There are very few other developing countries, in Latin America or elsewhere, about which this much could be said at the present time.

CONCLUSION

There appears to be no country in Latin America in which agriculture has been taxed heavily enough in recent years either to provide substantial resources for public developmental purposes or to affect significantly the allocation and distribution of resources within the agricultural sector. The most effective taxation of agricultural land has perhaps been in Chile. Even there, however, no government has yet enunciated an explicit policy as to the appropriate size and nature of agriculture's contribution to the development effort. Some interesting experiments in land taxation have been carried out in other countries, notably in Jamaica, or have been studied, as in Bolivia, but in general the record has been rather discouraging to reflective advocates of bigger and better land taxes, with some Latin American countries, notably Venezuela and until recently Peru, levying no tax on rural land at all, and some—Paraguay, Guatemala, Panama, Brazil, and others—doing so only very unsuccessfully.

Perhaps the major lesson which Latin American experience suggests is that the most rewarding path to follow, if an agricultural land tax is to contribute much to development, is to concentrate on establishing a simple property tax with significant rates on the basis of solid valuations, rather than, through graduated rates of tax, special taxes on idle lands, and similar devices attempting to achieve primarily nonfiscal purposes. It is true that any tax will in fact exert nonfiscal effects, and that the heavier the tax the more important these effects will likely be. These side effects must certainly be considered in evaluating any fiscal instrument. But there would seem to be good reason to focus on the primary revenue purpose of the tax in proposing any reform in land tax systems.

In the past the inherent problems of levying effective land taxation have been unnecessarily complicated in Latin America by the propensity to attempt to achieve many complex nonfiscal purposes through the land tax: bringing idle lands into production, discriminating against absentee landowners, breaking up large landed estates, and so on. In each and every instance of such attempts, however, the relatively low nominal tax rates and the inadequacy of the basic information on land have resulted in such low effective rates of tax that none of these nonfiscal objectives appears to have been realized. These same factors, of course, lie behind the relatively low burden of agricultural land taxes characterizing Latin America today. The key role of land valuation in an effective land tax system emerges clearly from Latin American experience.

Furthermore, as Daniel Holland noted about Jamaica, the experience there suggests strongly "the wisdom of choosing procedures that may be 'second best' in theory but 'first best' in practice. Basically, Jamaica was able to get off the ground because at a number of steps in the process where there was a choice between an unalterably correct or completely thorough procedure and one that fell short of perfection but could be basically satisfactory, Jamaica opted for the latter."[61] Much the same might be said about Chile. The evidence in support of this proposition from the long history of unsuccessful attempts at taxing agricultural land in Latin America is strong. If land taxes are to play a more important role in the future than in the past, it is clear the apparently inherent human tendency to let the perfect be the enemy of the good must be overcome.

6

LESSONS FROM HISTORY

The historical experience of three countries—Japan, Mexico, and India—is examined in this chapter. In each case there is a special reason for the choice. First, the apparent success of nineteenth-century Japan in utilizing heavy land taxes to transfer resources out of agriculture while at the same time rapidly expanding agricultural output has long been used as a standard which presently poor countries should strive to emulate. Second, although Mexico's relevant experience is both much shorter and to date less successful, the "Mexican model" of relatively rapid agricultural development through concentrating on a small number of commercialized farmers seems more likely to be the path followed by other countries today than the "Japanese model" of widespread improvement on the part of small-holders. The Mexican case is also interesting because of the insignificant role played by land taxes in transferring resources out of agriculture and because of the important Mexican land reform. Finally, although India is hardly a "model" of success in the same sense as either Japan or Mexico, it has been so often studied by economists, Indian and foreign, that notions based on interpretations of Indian experience are almost equally common in the development literature. In addition, nineteenth-century India was itself the scene of one of the greatest attempts in history to alter land taxes to conform to the dictates of economic theory, and the failure of this experiment may have as many lessons for poor countries today as the better-known Japanese success.

THE MODEL OF MEIJI JAPAN

One of the few concessions to political realities made by some proponents of land tax reform is their frequent recourse to the hortatory device of pointing to some other country exemplifying their solution and its desired outcome. Since most writers on this subject are apparently not willing to propose imitating totalitarian regimes, which appear to be the only recent practitioners of the heavy land tax path to development, the inevitable result is a reverential mention of the case of late nineteenth-century Japan, with or without qualifications as to its applicability for the case in hand.

The Japanese experience with land taxation is important not only because it is so often postulated as a model for presently developing countries but also because the conventional interpretation of this experience has shaped many "general" models of agricultural and economic development. The conventional dual-sector development model, with agriculture serving essentially as a source of savings and labor for the nonagricultural sector, has, for example, been heavily shaped by nineteenth-century Japanese experience. The argument that the nonagricultural sector is the engine of growth and that tax revenues from agriculture are the necessary fuel rests as much on a particular interpretation of Japanese economic history as on general development theory.

The generally accepted interpretation of the role of agriculture and agricultural taxation in the Meiji era (after 1867) may be stated succinctly as follows:

Agricultural production and real income are said to have risen at more than 2 per cent per year which is somewhat more than twice the 0.9 per cent growth rate of population. Since the agricultural labor force declined somewhat during this period, it is claimed that the speed of growth is attributable to agricultural developments which caused labor productivity to increase at about 2.6 per cent per year. A proposition of major importance is therefore advanced that this remarkable increase in agricultural labor productivity released a cheap and "unlimited" supply of labor to other sectors since most of the population growth was taking place in farm families. Meanwhile, it is said, a large part of agricultural income was appropriated by the government through various taxes that weighed heavily on the agricultural sector. It is also said that agricultural saving mounted, inasmuch as consumption in the agricultural sector rose slowly if at all, and the tax burden is believed to have declined owing to inflation. During this period net agricultural investment is believed to have remained at low levels. This led to a second important proposition; namely, that the speed of growth of agricultural production was responsible for a large transfer of savings to other sectors. Landlords are believed to be responsible for most of these savings, and they invested a large part of their savings in the nonagricultural sector as entrepreneurs in their own right.[1]

The general view is thus clearly that Meiji fiscal policy was a great success from a developmental point of view: "Meiji fiscal policy was able to raise large amounts of funds internally to finance the enormous expenditures required for the development and modernization of the economy. It did this mainly by taxing heavily the agricultural sector, without interfering with the healthy growth of the sector."[2] The thesis is thus that a rapid growth in agricultural productivity with very little capital investment in agriculture provided a surplus that could be used for capital formation elsewhere and that through the land tax, which provided over two-thirds of total government revenues in the 1870's and took 10–20 percent of agricultural income (see Table 8), the state was able to rechannel much of this "surplus" to industrial activities without hurting the growth of agricultural productivity; landlords themselves did the rest of the job.[3]

One essential fact that must be noted at once about Japan's extensive use of the land tax in the Meiji period (1868–1911) is that it followed logically from the well-developed system of land taxation in pre-Meiji Japan. By the 1860's, as one author has put it: "Because of efficient and productive taxation systems and its tradition of economic activity and control, government was well placed to play an important role in the process of economic modernization."[4]

At the end of the sixteenth century, for example, early in the Tokugawa era, a comprehensive survey was carried out to identify, measure, and classify land for tax purposes. Although it was later revised only partially and irregularly, this early cadaster provided the basis for the establishment of the well-entrenched land tax which formed the essential starting point for the later Meiji reforms.

TABLE 8. LAND TAXES IN JAPAN, 1868–1911

Year	Land taxes as percent of total government revenues[a]	Land tax as percent of central government taxes[c]	Direct taxes on agriculture as percent of net agricultural income[g]	
1868–72	—	(80)[d]	—	
1873–78	(72)[b]	(88)[e]	—	
1879–83	64	—	17	(8)[h]
1884–88	57	(60)[f]	22	(12)
1889–93	46	86	16	(9)
1894–98	35	80	12	(8)
1899–1903	26	63	12	(8)
1909–1911	15	43	13	(9)

[a] Source: Calculated from Harry T. Oshima, "Meiji Fiscal Policy and Agricultural Progress," in William W. Lockwood, ed., *The State and Economic Enterprise in Japan* (Princeton, N.J.: Princeton University Press, 1965), p. 359. *Ibid.*, p. 360, estimates that, in 1880–1889, 90% of land tax receipts derived from farm land.

[b] *Ibid.*, p. 358.

[c] Source: Kazushi Ohkawa and Henry Rosovsky, "The Role of Agriculture in Modern Japanese Economic Development," *Economic Development and Cultural Change*, IX (October 1960), 61. These data cover slightly different periods than those shown in the lefthand column.

[d] Source: Motokazu Kimura, "Fiscal Policy and Industrialization in Japan, 1868–1895," in International Economic Association, *Economic Development with Special Reference to East Asia* (New York: Macmillan, 1964), p. 277.

[e] *Ibid.* A lower estimate of 80% is given by Oshima, "Meiji Fiscal Policy," p. 358.

[f] Average of 1886 and 1888 only; from data in Harley H. Hinrichs, *A General Theory of Tax Structure Change During Economic Development*, p. 52. I have no explanation, other than different statistical sources, for this low figure.

[g] Gustav Ranis, "The Financing of Japanese Economic Development," *Economic History Review*, XI (April 1959), 448.

[h] The figures in parentheses represent Nakamura's correction for the undervaluation of agricultural production in the official statistics (James I. Nakamura, *Agricultural Production and the Economic Development of Japan 1873–1922* (Princeton, N.J.: Princeton University Press, 1966), p. 161). As noted elsewhere, many scholars think this correction is too large, though most would probably now agree that some downward revision of the conventionally accepted figures is desirable.

The main Tokugawa land tax was based on the estimated gross yield (in rice or rice equivalents) per area of land in normal years.[5] Taxes were levied on villages as a whole rather than on individual plots and were then allocated by a consultative process within the village, the mechanics of which are not known in detail, but which

LESSONS FROM HISTORY

may well have resembled in its virtues and defects the process used to this day in some African countries for personal tax assessments.[6] Originally, taxes were paid in kind, but by the nineteenth century commutation to cash payment was increasingly accepted.

In principle, the land tax was basically levied on gross produce, as estimated either on the basis of generalizing from sample harvests or by regular or irregular resurveys. In practice, wide differences in tax rates, land and harvest measurement practices, and tax administration resulted in a very diverse system with substantial differences in tax burdens among individuals, villages, and provinces. By the end of the Tokugawa period land taxes took over 55 percent of estimated crop yields in some parts of the country and less than 25 percent in others, with the modal burden apparently around 40 percent.[7] In fact, owing to the obsolete nature of assessments, many of which were 100 to 150 years old by the middle of the nineteenth century, the real burden of the tax in many areas was almost certainly less than this. Both increased productivity and the inevitable initial assessment errors point in this direction. In other areas, however, tax policies appear to have been considerably harsher, as suggested by various stories of tax revolts and peasant impoverishment.[8]

For the first few years of the Meiji era the Tokugawa land tax system was simply carried on by the new leadership pending the formulation of a new tax system. The first major reform legislation was enacted as the "Land Tax Revision Act of 1873." This law and subsequent revisions ensured that the land tax would remain the major source of government revenue and that the cadastral survey would remain the basis for land tax assessment and collection. The tax rate was initially set at 3 percent of assessed value.

As Table 8 suggests, the yield of the land tax was probably not much changed by this reform.[9] Other aspects of the old system were altered considerably, however. For example, payment was to be made in money rather than in kind, both in order to alleviate problems of storage and handling and in the expectation that better use would be made of land; the preference for rice payments in the Tokugawa period had allegedly encouraged the uneconomic use of land for rice.[10] More important, the tax base was changed to land value instead of the estimated annual harvest. Further, the 1873 law stipulated the land tax rate would be reduced to 1 percent as soon as revenues from other sources exceeded two million yen. In response to pressure from landowners following a fall in rice prices in 1876 the rate was in fact lowered to 2.5 percent in 1877, where it remained for the next sixty years.

As with all land taxes, the most difficult aspect of the Meiji reform concerned the valuation of the land. Legally, land value was to be derived by applying the following formula:

First, the money value of the average yield (over a five-year period) from one tanbu (0.245 acres) of land was calculated on the basis of the price of rice prevailing in that area. From this was deducted the cost of fertilizer and seed rice (legally fixed at 15 per cent), the land tax, and the local tax which was usually one-third of the land tax. What was left was called the "net profit" despite the fact that no deduction had been made for the cost of labor. Then the "net profit" was capitalized at a rate ranging from 6 to 7 per cent, giving the "legal value" of the land. The land tax was to be 3 per cent of this. . . .[11]

The Meiji land tax was thus usually based on the capitalized value of "normal" net farm income rather than market value.

The necessary information for these calculations was gathered by an elaborate new cadastral survey, which was begun in 1875 and completed around 1881. The procedures followed in this survey were similar to those in any cadastre except that, despite the shift of responsibility for tax payment to the individual himself, primary reliance continued to be placed on the village to report area and production.

As was true in other countries, no other general revaluation was ever carried out in Japan. Indeed, in a move reminiscent of some British legislation in India at an earlier date, a new Land Tax Law in 1884 abolished the previous stipulation for periodic reassessment, which had never actually been carried out, and fixed assessments at the 1875 levels unless land was reclassified. There were only minor revisions in tax assessments (notably in 1898–1899 when total assessed land values were reduced) until the 1930's.

Dissatisfaction with the Meiji reform, especially with the requirement that the tax should be paid in cash and in an amount not correlated with harvest conditions, resulted in several immediate amendments to the 1873 legislation. In 1875, for example, a rice deposit system was instituted permitting peasants to pay up to one-third of their taxes in kind. In 1877 it was further determined that paddy field taxes could be paid one-half in kind on the basis of the prices used in calculating the "legal value" in 1873. In addition, as noted above, the tax rate was lowered in the same year from 3 to 2.5 percent in response to a rash of peasant revolts.

Some of these problems were more significantly alleviated by an inflation in rice prices as a result of the Meiji government's general political and fiscal plight. The immediate beneficiaries of the inflation were the landowners, who could increase the rent in kind received from the peasant and convert it into cash profits while at the same time their tax liability was fixed in money terms. One estimate is that the landowners' share of the proceeds from the land rose from 18 percent before 1868 to 56 percent in the inflationary period of 1878–1887, while the state's share fell correspondingly from 50 percent to 11 percent.[12] A substantial reduction in land tax burdens was thus the result of inflation in nineteenth-century Japan as in many other countries since.

In an attempt to reform the chaotic currency and fiscal situation, a severe deflationary policy was instituted from 1881 through 1885. Rice prices, which had doubled from 1877 to 1880, fell back almost to their previous levels, so that the fixed land tax in effect doubled (as is suggested also by the figures in Table 8, above). The result was that substantial numbers of peasants were forced to sell their lands to meet tax arrears, thus clearing the way for a considerable concentration of land holdings. After the late 1880's, however, prices rose again, and agriculture appears to have generally prospered while tax burdens fell.

The account to this point of the nature and workings of the Meiji tax reforms should contain few surprises for those familiar with land taxes elsewhere. Before 1873 the principal tax on Japanese agriculture was a tithe or gross product tax. The basic Meiji tax legislation enacted in that year converted this traditional levy into a land value tax by capitalizing the gross value of production (less certain arbitrarily defined costs, notably the land tax and the costs of seeds and fertilizers) at the prevailing interest rate. This value of production was, in turn, determined by the area of cultivated land, the yield per unit area, and the price level. The first two of these elements were, in accordance with Japanese tradition, based primarily on reports by landowners and villages and were hence almost certainly subject to some understatement (also by tradition) although these estimates were supervised and reviewed by tax officials.[13] The general level of tax burden was probably not much affected initially by this change in the nature of the tax although its distribution may have been. Thereafter, however, owing to the fixed assessments, the impact of the land tax on Japanese agriculture became dependent primarily on movements in the general price level and in particular on the level of rice prices. Its real yield first fell sharply in inflation, then rose equally sharply in deflation; thereafter it declined gradually as prices again rose.

Controversy arises only when we consider, first, the impact of this tax on agricultural production and, second, the role which the land tax played in transferring resources out of agriculture during the 1868–1911 period. There are opposing views on each of these crucial matters. The conventional view has already been stated: agricultural productivity grew moderately rapidly from the 1870's on, complementing the rise of modern industry in Japan through the resources provided from the increased surplus created in agriculture. Most but not all of those who hold this view point to the land tax as the main transfer mechanism utilized.

Recent literature suggests that there are several important contentious points in this conventional interpretation. First, there may not really have been much of a net outflow of resources from the farm sector in Meiji Japan anyway.[14] Second, while the tax system clearly transferred a good deal out of agriculture to the public sector, much of this appears to have been wasted from the point of view of development (largely in military expenditures).[15] Third, recorded agricultural productivity was based largely on land tax records, and there is evidence of substantial initial underestimation of agricultural production for tax purposes, so that the rate of productivity growth was probably much lower than was at one time thought.[16] Finally, there appears to be growing sympathy for the view that "the extraction of large sums of money from the farm population was generally detrimental to the healthy development of agriculture, especially as so much was used relatively unproductively for military purposes."[17] While the fixed nature of the land tax clearly exerted favorable (if unmeasurable) incentive effects, the sheer size of the payment and its regressivity may well have offset these effects in the initial years by draining liquidity from the countryside and destroying smaller peasants. On the other hand, the decreasing land tax burden as prices rose suggests strongly that the key to resource transfer in Japan lay in the hands of the private landlords, who in a very non-Ricardian way became the vanguard of the capitalist class.[18]

It is not possible for a nonspecialist to arbitrate in the battle of the giants as to just how fast agricultural production rose in the early Meiji era.[19] Nor, in a sense, is it necessary to do so. Clearly the contention that, in the case of the government, savings were transferred from agriculture by the land tax is correct. But it seems equally likely that Nakamura's arguments that there was considerable evasion of the land tax as well as Oshima's arguments on the extent to which these savings were wasted have merit, certainly from the point of view of agriculture.

The real question that must be answered is the extent to which this heavy tax burden penalized agricultural growth (and perhaps, as Oshima has suggested, even social stability?).[20] As Ishikawa has argued, even if there was a net resource flow out of agriculture and agriculture continued to grow under its heavy tax load, this result was probably due to exceptionally favorable initial conditions in Meiji Japan.[21] Either there was a pre-existing surplus at the beginning of this period or else partly fortuitous technological progress may have served to generate agricultural surplus simultaneously with industrialization, as, for example, when the removal of the feudal restraints of the Tokugawa period permitted the wider diffusion of already known agricultural techniques.[22] While public expenditures on agriculture were apparently very small in the early Meiji era, a substantial infrastructure of land development, market access, and knowledge had been built up over the previous centuries and was consequently on hand when the opportunity came to utilize it. The basic capital-intensive investments in land—flood control, irrigation, and drainage —undertaken in the Tokugawa period were a necessary prerequisite for the widespread introduction of fertilizer, better seeds, and better farming techniques in the Meiji period, just as the tenurial and other reforms of the Meiji restoration were needed to release the pent-up talents of Japanese farmers.

On closer examination, then, while many key aspects of late nineteenth-century Japanese economic history are still in dispute, the Japanese "land tax miracle" appears much less miraculous—and considerably less different from experience elsewhere—than most accounts would lead one to believe.

The common view is that Japanese experience is atypical. Landes, for example, has noted that, "in general, then, the land did not perform in western Europe the function of generator of savings for industrial development to the same extent as in Japan. On the contrary, not only did it compete for funds with the modern sector on purely rational grounds, but it drew more than its share of capital resources."[23] In Germany, for example, during the same period the land tax provided a far smaller proportion of government revenue than in Japan, and it appears the intersectoral flow of capital favored agriculture, largely because of the capital-intensive nature of the land clearing and drainage operations which made possible the increase in agricultural output. But, as already noted, these expenditures had actually been made in Japan prior to the Meiji period.

Similarly, "in the years of Britain's industrial revolution, agriculture was taking as much capital as it was giving; indeed, in the period from 1790 to 1814, when food prices rose to record levels, the net flow of resources was probably toward the land."[24] The Japanese response to similar pressures may not, according to recent studies, have been much different. "We may conclude that the final judgment as to whether or not the net result of resource flows between the farm and the nonfarm sectors was an outflow from the former sector, must wait for further investigations. Even if it was, as usually thought, the outflow, its magnitude does not seem to be so large as to be the major source of financing Japan's early industrialization."[25]

Rather than heavy land taxes financing industrialization, the real economic key to Japanese success, as to that of the United States, may have been "the ability to generate a continuous technology biased towards saving the limiting factors,"[26] just as it has been argued that a crucial aspect of India's relative failure to date has been its difficulty in successfully adapting foreign models to its own needs, customs, and capabilities.[27] It is easy in these circumstances for the economist to draw the lesson from this that presently developing countries should, as did Japan, direct their efforts to exploit the opportunities created by the trend toward modernization in the light of their peculiar factor endowments.

But this recommendation neglects completely the crucial significance of history: Japan's history had not only equipped her agricultural sector well with capital, it had also, and more importantly, provided her with a well-ordered and disciplined population that was capable of implementing, adapting, and diffusing new technologies

LESSONS FROM HISTORY

121

at a rapid pace. The role of such minor instruments as the land tax in this process, while not wholly clear, was certainly not nearly as significant a determinant of whatever happened as was Japanese history of the previous six centuries. The same could be said of Western Europe and is to some extent probably true of China today. India, on the other hand, like many other poor countries in Asia and elsewhere, appears to have a long way to go before its institutional development in most of the relevant respects comes close to that of Japan a century ago. In addition, there are greater disparities between traditional and modern technologies, greater openness (and vulnerability) of most developing countries to outside influences in general, and greater differences in the scale of institutional adaptation required, all of which make the task of development increasingly hard in some important respects.

THE MEXICAN MODEL

The "Japanese model" is thus a labor-intensive, capital-saving approach to agricultural development which utilizes yield-increasing innovations which are neutral to the scale of farming operations and can therefore be widely diffused throughout the agricultural sector. This model, it has been suggested, has also been followed in Taiwan and, to a considerably lesser extent, perhaps in parts of East Africa.[28] Whether this path to agricultural development is open or not would seem to depend largely on the extent to which the requisite economic and social agricultural infrastructure is already in place, as well as on the ability of the governmental authorities to stimulate and guide the countless decision points in this kind of decentralized system.

In sharp contrast to this approach, there is an alternative path which countries like Pakistan and India seem to be following more closely. This alternative relies more on increasing yields through mechanization accompanied by the introduction of improved seed varieties. The results of this approach—which has recently been proposed as conscious policy in Egypt and other Middle Eastern countries[29]—have usually been a dualistic structure within agriculture with the output increases concentrated in a small group of capital-intensive large farms while most farm units remain too small and poor to purchase the new inputs or even simple consumer goods.

Since no country has progressed further or faster on this path than Mexico, this approach has been labeled the "Mexican model."

Mexico presents a puzzle to the fiscal economist when he attempts to analyze Latin American development experience. Mexico had a wide-ranging revolution in the decade after 1910. It carried out a substantial land reform before 1940. At the same time, it expropriated major foreign companies in the mineral extractive industries. Since then, it has experienced a tremendous increase in income, in agricultural output, in urbanization, and in population. Despite numerous continuing problems, Mexico clearly constitutes one of the few success stories to be found in Latin America.

Both development theory and casual observation suggest that the state must, indeed did, play a very considerable role in all of this. Yet, in the usual terms in which these comparisons are made by public finance economists, Mexico appears to have almost the smallest public sector in Latin America. As late as the 1960's, for example, tax revenues amounted to only 10 percent of GNP, and Mexico came close to the bottom in the various international league tables comparing "tax effort" and similar presumably "good" characteristics of the aspirant to developmental success. Nevertheless, it is clear that the role of the public sector in directing and financing investment through the fiscal and, especially, monetary system has been crucial in Mexico for forty years or more and that, albeit in a very indigenous fashion, the central bureaucracy has exerted far-reaching control over the shape and size of economic development.[30]

A similar puzzle exists with respect to Mexican agriculture. It seems clear that Mexico's industrialization and urbanization must have been financed in the crucial early years primarily by the agricultural sector: foreign capital was not significant before 1942, and there was really no alternative domestic source of finance. Indeed, it has been argued that the effects of this massive transfer of resources out of agriculture are still evident in the depressed condition of life in most of the Mexican countryside today.[31] Despite this, agricultural production appears to have risen faster and in a more sustained way in Mexico (at least after the initial years of political turbulence) than in any other Latin American country.[32] How were these resources transferred, and how did agricultural productivity continue to rise in the face of this apparently adverse policy?

LESSONS FROM HISTORY

One point at least is crystal clear: Mexico has at no time followed the conventional prescription of visiting experts and relied on direct taxation of agricultural land to effect this transfer. Indeed, the immediate impact of the land reform of the 1930's was to lower the already small yield of the rural land tax. Not only are the "ejidal" lands which constitute around 50 percent of Mexico's cultivated area constitutionally exempt from land taxation, but other taxes may not exceed 5 percent of annual production.[33] Even these low taxes were hard to enforce on land which cannot be alienated or mortgaged. The low nominal rates of local land taxes (which varied considerably from state to state, and even among municipalities within the same state) were made even less meaningful by the inadequate and out-of-date nature of the equally varying cadastral assessments to which they were generally applied.[34]

The relative unimportance of land taxes was accentuated by the effects of inflation on the tax base and by the rapid increase in other revenue sources. Land taxes as a percentage of total tax receipts fell from 7 percent in 1942 to 5 percent in 1947 and to less than 1 percent in 1962. In the latter year land taxes amounted to only one-tenth of 1 percent of the value of agricultural production.[35]

Nor was the fiscal balance redressed by other taxes on agriculture. As elsewhere in Latin America, export taxes have for many years been the most important means of taxing farmers in Mexico. The yield of these taxes has varied sharply from year to year, in accordance with stabilization purposes, as higher rates of export tax were employed to absorb the windfall gains accruing to exporters from devaluations (see Chapter 4). In general, however, it does not appear that either export taxes or the small local taxes on agricultural products employed in a number of Mexican states to make up for the deficiency of the land tax were important agents in mobilizing and transferring resources out of Mexican agriculture. All taxes on agriculture amounted to perhaps 10 percent of total government revenues in 1947 and only 5 percent in 1962, compared to the 19 percent of GNP from the agricultural sector in the latter year.[36] Since the value added by agriculture has since fallen still further, there is every reason to expect that the relative fiscal burden on Mexican agriculture has continued to decline.

The weakness of agricultural taxation means that resources must have been transferred out of agriculture by nonfiscal means if at all.[37]

The mechanism employed appears to have been a somewhat complicated one, and to have evolved more by accident than design.[38]

First, over a fairly long period of time (up to 1940) an extensive land reform was carried out. The full costs of this reform were basically paid by the landowners. Second, from 1925 to 1947 most public investment was financed through deficit spending, which resulted in substantial inflation. The capital levy on landlords which was initially distributed to the peasants was thus partly taken back through inflation since agricultural prices and industrial wages lagged well behind the general price level. Profits also rose substantially in this period, so that some of the forced saving generated by the inflationary process accrued to private entrepreneurs, while the balance was channeled to public investment through deficit financing.

"The peasants," according to one interpretation, "tolerated the ensuing forced austerity because it came from the same government that was giving them free land and was engaged in unprecedented efforts to build dams, highways, and schools."[39] Indeed, one estimate is that the public transfers of investible funds from industry to agriculture more than offset the flow of private savings from rural to urban areas, though others dispute this.[40] In any event, it is clear that there was heavy public investment in agriculture from the 1930's to the 1950's.

At the same time, other public investments combined with strong protective and subsidy policies which fostered import substitution to provide an attractive outlet in the industrial sector for the savings of those *hacendados* whose lands were not confiscated, in some instances through the intermediate stage of the urban real estate market.[41] The increased monetization of the agricultural sector also increased the market for labor-intensive consumer goods production.[42] The profits generated by inflation in the nascent industrial sector were largely reinvested in response to the investment opportunities thus created. This growing domestic industrial production for a sheltered market further tilted the terms of trade against agriculture as did, at a later period, government subsidy policies which held down food prices for urban consumers.

In large part the process of Mexican development thus appears strikingly close to that envisioned in the labor-surplus model of Fei and Ranis, which stresses the need to transfer the agricultural surplus and the importance of the "connectedness" between the agricultural and industrial sectors both for pushing resources out of agriculture and for pulling them into industry. The basic unanswered question is therefore the same as that raised in Chapter 1 with respect to the general applicability of the Fei-Ranis model: how did agricultural productivity continue to rise in the face of this resource drain?

Land reform in Mexico was not at the expense of agricultural productivity. On the contrary, recent studies suggest that agricultural production at least kept up with the growth of population in the early years and has risen even faster since about 1940. The secret of this success was in part public investment in new irrigation systems. Most of Mexico has insufficient rainfall for the production of staple crops, so that irrigation is unusually important. By 1962, following decades in which 10–12 percent of the federal budget had been so directed, almost U.S. $1 billion had been invested in irrigation.[43] An equally impressive amount was spent on creating a network of highways and roads over Mexico's difficult terrain.

Even more important, however, was extensive land clearance and intensification of farming—that is, increased private investment in agriculture. Despite the initial damaging effects of insecurity on production, in the long run "by redistributing income and wealth and improving political stability in the countryside the agrarian reform program represented a major investment in social infrastructure."[44] This investment, especially after the onset of the more centralized and institutionalized reform of the post-1935 era, proved a powerful stimulus to more efficient factor use and productivity. The increased investment in labor-intensive agricultural growth as a result of the land reform has, it has been argued, served the capital-scarce Mexican economy well, and has also kept large numbers of people employed on the land in a relatively productive fashion.[45] Another view is that substantial public investments in agriculture raised both rural savings and total private investment in agriculture by raising the private rate of return on capital in commercial agriculture.[46]

The destruction of the old agrarian system in the years from 1910 to 1940 thus laid the foundation for Mexico's economic upsurge since 1940 in both the agricultural and the nonagricultural sectors. In part, however, Mexico's successful agricultural development doubtless also reflects other favorable and fortuitous developments— good weather in some crucial years, a favorable export market for

Mexican cotton, import-substituting possibilities for its northern wheat, and the ready availability of both technology and capital across the U.S. border.

Since 1960 these factors have been supplemented by the remarkable rise of output owing to new application of the improved seeds and technology encompassed in the term "Green Revolution." Yet, where the old revolution may have enabled Mexico to make considerable progress in a relatively stable political framework precisely because it meant a substantial initial change in that framework, this new revolution seems less likely to be accommodated within the framework of the old.

Mexican land reform was never as great a sociopolitical success as is sometimes thought, largely because it was never applied severely enough to redress completely the tremendous income inequalities characteristic of prereform Mexican agriculture. Although the expropriation process as actually applied amounted to outright confiscation of part of the property of the rich—a capital levy—it was, for example, offset in part by the benefits large landowners received with respect to the rest of their property from public irrigation projects. These strong residual inequalities have been accentuated since 1960 by the effects of the Green Revolution. Most of the recent growth in farm output has been due to a relatively small group of commercial enterprises. Subsistence agriculture has been largely untouched by these developments. The persisting maldistribution of wealth in rural Mexico has been further accentuated by the unequal distribution of benefits from the new technology, and the already huge rural unemployment problem has grown.[47]

Substantial new policy efforts seem likely to be required in order to accommodate the technological change of seeds without impeding the seeds of technological change. The question, then, is whether the bureaucracy developed to "institutionalize" the first revolution can respond as well to the challenge of the second.

If Mexico's experience has any lessons for other countries in Latin America or elsewhere, they are perhaps three in number. First, when a country wishes to transfer substantial resources out of agriculture, a land reform may help not only by the direct release of resources involved in expropriating from the unproductive rich but also, through redistributing land, in making the poor accept more willingly a state of continued poverty. Second, this process will be assisted if public investment is directed both to increasing agricultural productivity and to creating attractive investment opportunities outside of agriculture. Third, although considerable progress may be made along these lines, there will likely come a point in any country with unchecked population growth at which a substantial re-evaluation of the policy of mulcting agriculture will be needed to avert political upheaval from the ever-growing number of rural dispossessed. As John Sheahan recently put it: "Mexico vividly illustrates the growth possibilities of the Arthur Lewis model of the 1950's, and almost as dramatically makes clear that this is not enough."[48]

So far as taxation is concerned, the most striking lesson from Mexican experience is that the only country in Latin America which has managed to develop mainly on the basis of its own resources did not attempt to avoid drastic social and economic restructuring by tinkering with the tax system or other indirect (and usually ineffective) methods. If land reform is needed, then it is needed; tax gimmicks are no substitute (see Chapter 12). Direct, crude measures may in some situations be both politically more acceptable and administratively more feasible.

On the other hand, if a large resource flow out of agriculture is needed, it may be easier to effect if it is not done openly, as through direct taxes, but rather indirectly through inflation or through turning the terms of trade against agriculture by protecting domestic industry, or in other ways, while at the same time softening the blow by land reform and at least in part offsetting the effects on productivity by strategic investment policy.

Ironically, effective direct taxation of some segments of the agricultural sector may be needed more in Mexico now in order to offset the tendency of the Green Revolution to accentuate inequalities within the rural economy than it was fifty years ago. The growing general rural-urban inequality as agricultural output rises may again require a net resource flow to rural areas, especially in the form of investment in people rather than water and roads, although one might expect the main result of such a policy in the immediate future to be better-educated migrants (and thus a transfer of human capital) from the rural sector. Land taxation coupled with appropriate expenditure policy may be neither a substitute for nor a complement of land reform policy, as has sometimes been suggested (see Chapter 12). It may, as in the Mexican case, be a necessary sequel.

LAND TAXATION IN INDIA

India has always been an overwhelmingly agricultural country. Today, as for thousands of years, most of the Indian people live on the land. Despite a substantial growth of nonagricultural activity in recent decades, the agricultural sector still accounts for close to half the national income. In sharp contrast to the continuing importance of agriculture in the economic picture, however, the agricultural contribution to fiscal revenues is small and diminishing. The repeated pleas of most development and fiscal economists to reverse this trend have as yet had no effect; nor do they seem likely to have any in the immediate future. The roots of the present situation appear to lie deep in India's past.

Elements of the present Indian system of land taxation can be traced back thousands of years to the *bhaga,* or the king's share of agricultural produce.[49] The rate of this tithe was ordinarily one-sixth, although it varied with the nature of the soil and the crop and could be as high as one-fourth in times of emergency. A system of land measurement and classification was early developed to support this levy.

After various ups and downs over the centuries, a thorough revenue reform was carried out in the sixteenth century under Akbar, the great Mogul emperor of India. Although the nature of the system varied considerably from place to place in the diverse Mogul empire, fundamentally the reform involved a careful survey and classification of lands in terms of soil and productivity in order to estimate their gross produce and a conversion of the tithe into a cash levy, with average gross produce being valued at local grain prices. In some areas the revenue assessment (at first annual, later decennial) was levied on the village, as in Japan, rather than on the individual cultivator. Later, it became increasingly common for the emperor to grant land to individuals with the right and responsibility of collecting revenue for the government. The rights of these "tax farmers" became hereditary in some regions, and they abused their privileges in most. Somewhat similar reforms, and subsequent deterioration, appear to have taken place in other parts of India not under the Moguls. The foundation of the traditional revenue system remained the village organization in one way or another, and its main form remained a cash levy based on estimated gross produce.

The British conquest of India in the eighteenth century presented the new rulers with the task of effectively re-establishing this land tax system, the essential basis of government revenue and, hence, of power. Both Indian traditions and the newly developed doctrines of English classical political economy were influential in this process, the latter largely through the instrument of James Mill's constant emphasis on the Ricardian doctrine of rent.[50]

"Rent," or net produce (defined as gross produce less the cost of wages and the ordinary rate of profit on the capital employed), was in this view an unearned increment accruing to landlords which could be taken entirely by the state with no adverse effects on productivity. In the context of India, the extreme implication of this view was that, in Ricardo's words, the government should be considered "the sole possessor of the land, and entitled to all the rent."[51] The immediate policy advocated by those holding this view was frequent re-assessment on the basis of estimated net produce.

Three predominant types of revenue systems were in fact established by the British in India.[52] The first was the system of permanent settlements set up under Lord Cornwallis in Bengal, Bihar, and Orissa in the late eighteenth century. This system not only recognized the existing institution of tax farming but went even further and established the tax farmers or *zamindars* even more firmly as landlords where they were responsible for collecting the revenue. Equally important, the existing level of the land tax assessment was declared fixed for all time—at ten-elevenths of the current net rental receipts of the zamindars in Bengal in 1793, for example. The virtue of such a system was the steady flow of revenue it assured on the one hand and the certainty of taxes on the other. Its defects arose from this same rigidity, for the state would not share in any improvements in yields; nor would it lower its taxes if yields fell.

The second system followed Mill's ideas much more closely: the tax assessment was temporary, supposedly based on net produce, and arranged between the state and the peasant cultivator himself. This *ryotwari* system did not, however, attempt to take the entire surplus in accord with the extreme rent doctrine; instead it generally aimed at a levy amounting to around half the net produce. Its exactions often appear to have been much higher than this, however, and to have resulted in considerable agricultural distress in some parts of the country.[53] The period during which the assessment was fixed varied from fifteen to forty years, again largely with the object of obtaining stable revenues, but with the secondary effect of imposing a zero marginal rate of tax on increases in production over a fairly long period of time.

The third land revenue system was a variant introduced into the North-Western Provinces (now Uttar Pradesh) during the 1820's in which the assessment levied on net produce was made on the village as a whole rather than on the individual cultivator. These *mahalwari* systems combined elements of the other two systems, but were closer to the second in conceptual rationale.

Some parts of the country operated one or more systems simultaneously, while others, especially among the princely states, had large portions of unsurveyed land and no regular system of land revenue. In tax administration, as in most other respects, no simple statement can accurately capture India's complex diversity.

There are two main reasons for sketching this brief capsule history here. The first is that the systems established by the British in the late eighteenth and early nineteenth centuries were essentially still in existence when India became independent in 1947. To some extent, traces are still evident today. Different methods of calculating land revenue that continue to exist in many parts of India, for example, reflect these varied origins. "In Punjab, Uttar Pradesh, Madya Pradesh, and the temporarily settled parts of Bihar, Orissa, and West Bengal assessment of land revenue is based on the "net assets," determined by estimating the gross produce, valued at the average price of the crop for a specified period ("commutation price") and deducting the landlord's estimated costs. In Madras the assessment is based directly on the value of the net produce, determined by deducting cultivation expenses and certain adjustments for bad seasons from gross produce valued at the commutation price."[54] Gross produce, the ancient system, is still the basis of assessment in Assam. In Bombay, Mysore, and certain other parts of India the standards to be used by the assessing officers in determining the basis of assessment are not fixed by law: they are left to the judgment of the assessing officers, who are supposed to take into account such factors as soil fertility, crop yield, climate and rainfall, proximity to markets, prices of agricultural produce, and the rental and sales value of agricultural land. In practice, owing to the infrequency of revision of assessments even in the nonpermanently settled areas, the land tax now probably amounts to little more than a fixed area tax in most parts of India.

LESSONS FROM HISTORY

The second reason for looking briefly backward is that, in an effort to implement the theoretical ideas on which the attempt to tax net produce was based, British administrators spent a large part of the nineteenth century engaged in cadastral surveys and similar attempts to gather the needed information. The tale is familiar to aficionados of more recent land tax literature: "There was no alternative but to set out on a laborious and detailed inquiry into the circumstances governing the existing assessment on each field. Only when all information on crop, soil, stock, agricultural caste, and past history, had been carefully gathered, would there be grounds for arriving at an equitable assessment in each separate case. . . . The cultivated area would need to be accurately measured, and, where payment was made in kind by means of a division of the crop, the gross produce would have to be ascertained. . . . Where payment was made in money the accuracy of the village accountant's records would need to be tested."[55] An even more thorough attempt in the Bombay Deccan "involved the calculation of the average gross produce per *biga* (⅔ acre) for nine separate soil qualities, turning this into a money value, and finally deducting the cost of production and interest on the stock employed, so as to arrive at the net produce."[56]

These and other attempts, and they were many and prolonged, to found the assessment of the Indian land revenue on a consistent and logical theoretical criterion failed. As one writer remarks, "basically this theoretically precise system floundered [*sic*] under the weight of its own precision."[57] In practice, revenue officers found the required information too difficult or impossible to attain and fell back on enlightened estimates based on pragmatic considerations of what given areas could afford to pay. These empirical as opposed to theoretical methods were not always simply rough and ready guesses. In the better areas they were to the greatest extent possible based on careful analysis of available data (for example, cash rents actually paid), and the objective was generally still to proportion taxes in accord with net produce. The theoretical standard for land tax in most parts of the country was one-half of the net produce or rental value. The result of the ensuing wide variations in assessment practice and the great difficulties of administering a complicated and detailed tax with an inadequate administrative staff was substantial interprovincial, interpersonal, and interclass inequalities in tax burdens.

The subsequent history of Indian land taxes reflects these varied origins. In general, the burden of the land tax in the permanently settled areas became, as one would expect, substantially lighter as the area under cultivation was extended and the price of agricultural products rose. In the larger part of the country in which assessments were supposed to be revised every few decades, there were in practice a wide variety of assessment practices and a consequent variety of adaptations to changing circumstances. The general trend, however, was toward a decline in the importance of land taxes in government revenues and a corresponding decline in their burden.[58]

Land revenue receipts constituted 69 percent of total central and state revenues in 1793–1794, 36 percent in 1891–1892, 16 percent in 1938–1939, and only 9 percent by 1953–1954.[59] This decline has continued, apart from a temporary increase in the yield from land revenue during the 1950's as a side effect of the land reform program, to the point where, by the late 1950's, the land tax took only about 1 percent of agricultural income in the country as a whole, compared to perhaps five times that much in the prewar period.[60] Land taxes produced one-half of state revenues in prepartition India. By the immediate postwar period, however, this proportion fell to one-fifth in both India and Pakistan.[61] As a proportion of state taxes, land revenue in India fell from 26 percent in the First Five-Year Plan period to 23 percent in the Second Plan to 17 percent in the Third Plan. As a proportion of total (central and state) tax revenue, land revenue fell from 8 percent in 1958–1959 to 5 percent in 1964–1965.

The marked decrease in the importance of land revenue, despite continued growth in the area under cultivation, progressive monetization of the economy, development of internal transport, growing commercialization of agriculture, and rising food prices, appears to have been due to several factors. The growth and significance of new forms of taxes, both central and state, such as income tax, customs duties, central excises and sales taxes, has, for example, obviously meant a decline in the relative importance of land taxes. As significant, however, has been the marked inelasticity of the land tax in response to increases in income and prices. In practice, land revenue in effect generally amounts to no more than a proportional tax levied at a flat rate per area, with the rates varying according to the fertility classification of the land and being fixed for very long periods of time (often forty or fifty years). Since the assessments generally remain fixed during the currency of the settlement, increases in production or in prices above those at the time of settlement tend as a rule to reduce the real burden of land revenue.

This inherent problem with any system of fixed levies has been accentuated by the fact that reassessments have not been made in many Indian states for many years, owing first to the depression, then the war, and later the reorganization of states. An interesting variation on this general pattern is found in the Punjab region where, since 1935, a "sliding scale" system of land revenue has existed under which, whenever agricultural prices decline below the base level (commutation prices) set at the time of the tax settlement, the annual tax due is reduced proportionately.[62] The tax is not increased when prices rise, however, so the added flexibility of this system has not served to maintain yields in the face of postwar inflation. In the province of Sind in Pakistan, however, the assessments may vary with either increases or decreases in prices, so that in theory the yield of the land tax should be responsive to growth in money income owing to price increases, although not that owing to increases in real output.[63]

Since the rates of land taxes have been changed as infrequently as the basic assessments, little flexibility came from this source either. Several states have, however, imposed special surcharges on large estates, notably Uttar Pradesh, where the Large Land Holdings Tax is graduated according to the value of holding and exempts those cultivating less than thirty acres. The impact of such special levies is, in total, slight, so that on the whole land revenue in India is a tax in rem levied at a flat rate. This lack of progression and personalization, while it makes the tax much easier to administer, is another factor that reinforces the inelasticity of assessments and infrequency of tax rate changes in causing the decline in importance of land revenue in India.

Finally, but not least important, states tended not to increase land taxation because of the immediate political opposition such increases generated. This opposition came not just from the larger landowners; it was much more widespread, perhaps in accordance with the sentiment recently expressed by one prominent economist that "during the British occupation only agriculture was taxed. . . . Now the historical injustices are being corrected."[64]

Under the changed political and economic circumstances following independence in 1947, the land policy evolved during the British rule, with its inequity in the distribution of tax burdens and the inelasticity that crippled state tax resources, cried out to be altered. Two significant reforms implemented in India since the attainment of independence are the abolition of the permanent settlement and the abolition of the (usually related) *zamindari* system of land taxation. The principal object of these reforms was to provide security of tenure for tenants, but they also affected the importance of land revenue in a number of states, principally by converting the rents paid by tenant farmers to intermediaries or zamindars into land revenues paid directly to the state.

Together with the larger territorial coverage arising from the integration of the princely states, this aspect of the land reforms led to a substantial increase in land revenues in the early 1950's. The beneficial effects of land reform on state revenues were offset, however, by the need to pay monetary compensation to the displaced zamindars. In Uttar Pradesh, for example, "the costs of conducting the operation, paying compensation, and paying rehabilitation grants was just about balanced by the increase in land revenue resulting from the state collecting the former rents as land revenue."[65] The net effect of these reforms on tax revenues was therefore negligible since this conclusion can be safely generalized to other parts of the country affected by the land reform.[66]

Much the same is true of a much newer tax, that on agricultural income, which is also a state tax. First levied in Bihar in 1938, taxes on agricultural income are now in force in eight states, enacted but not in force in two states, and nonexistent in 4. Where it does exist, the agricultural income tax is usually (except for plantations) basically a presumptive levy dependent on the usual rent and assessment information, though with significant variations in methods of presumption, exemption levels, and rates from state to state. In 1965–1966, the agriculture income tax yielded only around 100 million rupees in all India (or less than 1 rupee per hectare) compared to 1,100 million rupees from land revenues (7 rupees per hectare).[67] Most of this yield appears to have come from tea plantations in a few states. Agricultural income is constitutionally exempt from the central income tax. The state tax on agricultural income, where it exists, has nowhere been merged with the central tax on nonagricultural incomes, and proposals to this effect do not appear to have received much attention in India.

Betterment levies (or special assessments) also exist in one form or another in many states, particularly with respect to increases in land values owing to irrigation. But these charges are nowhere significant revenue producer. The betterment levy in India is normally calculated as a percentage of the increase in the value of land, which is itself computed as a multiple of the increase in income owing to irrigation. In fact, however, only two states have ever enforced the betterment levy. Even there, enforcement was not very effective because of the administrative difficulty of assessing the increase in land values and the political difficulty of levying the tax anyway. On balance, instead of financing irrigation projects through betterment levies, Indian policy is better characterized as extending a substantial subsidy to agriculture through low irrigation water rates. The same is true, to a lesser extent, with electricity.

It has been argued that it is difficult to recoup the benefits accruing to the rural sector from irrigation projects because of the difficulty of getting Indian farmers to use enough water in the first place.[68] In line with this thinking, in many parts of India, the use of irrigation water is actually subsidized rather than charged for. The existing betterment levies have also been criticized as being regressive because they tax increases in land value at proportional rather than progressive rates.[69] These arguments are suspect, and there would seem to be much more scope for special assessments and user charges in India, as in other countries, than has been exercised to date.[70] This theme is developed further in later chapters.

The only significant taxes on Indian agriculture are thus land revenues and the agricultural income tax, which together now yield only around 1 percent of agricultural output and less than 5 percent of total revenues. Of these two taxes, by far the most important is the old land revenue which, as noted above, is declining fast. In addition, it has been argued that concealed taxes have, at various times, been levied on Indian agriculture especially through the compulsory procurement by the state of food grains at fixed prices and through the monopoly distribution of fertilizers. It appears, however, that the "taxation" through these sources has in total been offset in most years by the concealed and open subsidies extended to agriculturists in various ways, so that the key factor in the mobilization of resources from Indian agriculture remains the two direct taxes mentioned above. If, however, direct government expenditures on agricultural development are also taken into account, it appears that there may well have been a net flow of public sector resources to the agricultural sector in most postwar years.[71]

In view of the recent tendency to abolish surcharges on land revenue (seven states did so by 1967, for example) and even land revenue itself (in Bihar in 1967 and, for small holdings, in four other states), the apparent unwillingness in all states to tax agricultural income effectively, and the failure to revise the assessments on which land revenue is based (which were made mainly in the 1930's), it is hard to see that this situation has changed in recent years. The mainstay of the present Indian agricultural tax system, land revenue, is being either removed or allowed to dwindle away, and it appears that nothing is being put in its place. An attempt in 1969 to extend the central government's net wealth tax to previously exempt agricultural properties seems most unlikely to provide an adequate substitute.

Unless there is some drastic change in policy in the immediate future, it appears that India will continue, on balance, to mobilize no significant public developmental resources from its huge agricultural sector. This result may, of course, make sound developmental sense. Nevertheless, the increased rural income inequalities arising from the Green Revolution, accentuated by the distorted factor prices facing the larger farmers who benefit, add new urgency to the repeated formulas for reforming the land tax put forward by almost every observer of the Indian scene.[72]

Many proposals for reform may not unfairly be characterized as renewed striving for the same pristine theoretical certainty (and desirable economic effects) as was sought in vain by nineteenth-century British colonial administrators. One recent proposal would, for example, convert the present land revenue system (which is, as noted above, little more than a crude acreage tax) into a tax based on "the potential income from each holding under average conditions of production . . . estimated on the basis of a soil classification according to productive capacity."[73] This tax should, the author suggested, take on as many features of the income tax as possible; aggregation of all household holdings, personal exemptions, progressive rates, exemptions of particular forms of saving, are, therefore, all recommended.

LESSONS FROM HISTORY

Certainly no one can criticize these proposals as "too simple," "too crude," or "too arbitrary," to use some of the phrases by which the same writer characterized some earlier reform proposals.

Indeed, a major problem with the recommended system, as with most of its fellows, is almost surely that it is not simple and arbitrary enough. The cost and difficulty of assessing potential output in India (or anywhere) appears to be underrated in relation to the benefits to be gained in terms of increased tax revenues or agricultural productivity. The lessons of nineteenth-century experience in this respect do not appear to have been fully absorbed. The ease of evasion is also underestimated, as is suggested by the stress in most proposals on the need for progressive rates. After all, a principal reason for the present inadequacy of the Indian land tax system is the debility of the administration, so it is surely incumbent on those proposing new and more complicated systems to undertake a serious examination of the land tax administration and its potential for improvement. An ideal tax badly administered may well be less desirable than a simple, crude, and arbitrary tax badly administered, and that may well be the choice.

The other principal reason for the relatively light taxation of agriculture in India is of course political. Most economists proposing land taxes do not consider this crucial factor sufficiently to justify much confidence in the future of their proposals. As discussed at greater length in the concluding chapter, the political circumstances in many developing countries today, and India is certainly to be counted among this number, are such that serious proponents of tax reform must view their proposals as exercises in political economy rather than in economic analysis alone. The alliance between big landlords and business and labor leaders linking low food prices and low land taxes is, for example, a more important determinant of tax policy than doctrinal prescriptions for increased agricultural taxation.[74] To an extent the attempt of some Indian land tax reformers to do all things perfectly on paper with their chosen instrument appears, as it has in the case of many Latin American countries, to have played into the hands of those who would do nothing at all in practice. At least this has been the result in India so far.

CONCLUSION

One interpretation of ancient history is that the vast empires of China, the Middle East, and Meso-America did not progress, despite highly successful agricultural systems, because they were too good at what some economists consider a primary task of a development-oriented government: transferring capital and labor out of agriculture. Of course, the crushing tax burdens (and labor obligations) imposed on the peasantry in ancient times were largely wasted from a developmental point of view on defense (the Great Wall of China) and monuments (the Pyramids), which again points up the vital importance of how resources are used. Such employment of public funds is not unknown even in this enlightened age. More important, however, "the chances that the peasantry might raise their own standard of living significantly and thus provide a broadly based market were severely circumscribed. Tax burdens were so onerous and collection was (all-considered) so efficient that local consumption was kept at a low, often a subsistence level, and might be further depressed in times of stress."[75] As we have seen, some have suggested that in and of itself heavy land taxation may have had similar effects even in Japan.

In a similar vein, it has been argued that nineteenth-century Italy, too, provides an example of the successful use of the fiscal mechanism to transfer resources out of agriculture, though not without the usual cost:

[The state finances] . . . constituted a powerful mobilizer of capital in Italy, transferring it from agriculture to the infrastructure, both through taxation and through the public debt. But agriculture, which was flourishing in no region and was in a very poor condition in some regions, suffered heavily from this haemmorrhage . . . it is easy to understand the economic result of this primitive fiscal policy: contraction of internal demand, a serious obstacle to the formation of a national market. . . . What it [Italian agriculture] gave, in financial terms, was torn from it more or less coercively; one should remember that entire regions lived in a virtual state of siege for some decades after Unity. In consequence, as already stated, agricultural demand for industrial products was restricted, creating an obstacle to a balanced and continuous industrial expansion which was not overcome for half a century.[76]

LESSONS FROM HISTORY

The similarity of this historical interpretation to that which other authors have recently drawn with respect to Nigeria and some other presently developing countries is striking.

When economies, whether in Europe or Japan, underwent the transition from basically agricultural to nonagricultural, they were enabled to do so, it appears, by a constellation of noncapital-intensive biological and organizational improvements and agricultural innovations which substantially increased productivity and produced a food surplus.[77] These changes were on the whole adopted on a widespread basis only in societies prepared by centuries of commercialization of large sections of their agriculture which had produced many "deviant" individuals.[78]

One result of this process almost everywhere appears to have been the creation of that rural inequality noted earlier in relation to the Green Revolution—though perhaps less socially destructive than in countries like Mexico today because of the relative size of the adaptive population in Europe and, in Japan, by the marked strength of tradition and social discipline. Everywhere and always it appears true that new technology has first been adopted by the better-off farmers and that the net incomes of the less efficient are likely to be hurt by such innovation: This is the "farm problem" in North America today. So was it, in a very different context, in Japan in the nineteenth century, and so is it in India, Mexico, and elsewhere today. The major notable difference appears to be that some countries—those, including Japan, that we call "developed"—appear to have been much more successful at enlisting, in relatively few decades, the bulk of their active population in the innovative ranks than others—the "less developed"—have.

Today, developing countries face higher rates of population growth and more difficulties in taxing agriculture in ways that do not damage production incentives because of the responsiveness of most governments in one way or another to the mass of the people.[79] Furthermore, as a result of the great backlog of innovations now existing and the availability of foreign loans, developing countries are pressed —a pressure sometimes greatly accentuated by their own policies—to adopt more capital-intensive technology in both industry and agriculture regardless of their own factor endowments. The availability of this technological backlog on a worldwide basis may make social and institutional reforms a less necessary prerequisite to innovation in any particular country, but the extra leeway provided as a result of being backward may eventually accentuate rather than alleviate the development problem by leading most countries to follow an extreme version of the "Mexican model" to agricultural development without even the initial primary redistribution that took place in Mexico.

"The pitfalls of the historical perspective as a guide to policy are many," a noted historian has said.[80] The conventional facile interpretation of the Japanese experience as a mandate for heavy land taxes provides a good illustration of such pitfalls. Yet without a sound conception of the overwhelming importance in any given situation of the historical development of ideas and institutions, one may go equally wrong. The real "lesson" of history is that no one guide to policy is readily applicable either to developing countries in general or to any one country in particular. Each historical instance appears, on close examination, to be complex and unique in many important respects. This, perhaps, is the real lesson of historical experience for present-day policymakers.

The main lessons suggested by these historical and comparative studies are, first, that no one small instrument such as a land tax can do much in and of itself and, second, that tax structure and desirable and possible changes in it can be analyzed sensibly only in the context of each particular nation.

PART THREE

ANALYSIS OF AGRICULTURAL LAND TAXES

7

CLASSIFICATION OF LAND TAXES

A variety of bases has been a feature of the land tax since earliest times. Since the tax base is a major determinant of the economic effects of a tax, it provides a convenient and meaningful criterion for classifying the varied assortment of land taxes found in the world today. Following Wald, land taxes may be grouped into four major categories, depending upon whether they are assessed according to land area, a rental value concept, an income concept, or for some special purpose.[1] Not every land tax fits neatly into this or any other classification system, of course. Moreover, some land taxes combine the characteristics of two or more categories as shown in the earlier discussion of specific taxes. On the whole, however, this four-fold classification provides a useful framework for discussion.

TAXES BASED ON LAND AREA

Land taxes assessed on the basis of land area are the simplest in structure and administration and among the first in historical sequence. In its most elementary form, the land tax is levied at a uniform rate according to the area of the farm or of each taxpayer's landholdings, without regard to the income-producing capacity of the land. The amount of the assessment is determined by multiplying the tax rate, expressed as a flat amount per hectare or other unit of land area, by the number of units in each taxable tract.

In principle, rough allowances for differences in the productive capacity or economic value of the land can be made by adjusting either the tax rate or the value of the tax base. As a practical matter, however, the classified rate area tax can recognize only a few broad economic categories of land, such as might be identified under the more rudimentary systems of land classification. The most useful single distinction that can be made in most countries is probably that between "wet" and "dry" or "irrigated" and "nonirrigated" lands. As suggested, for example, in a recent study of Nepal, the tax burden resulting from this simple classification may be distributed in a surprisingly equitable fashion.[2]

It has been suggested that the area basis of land taxation may also have some justification as a benefit tax, especially in urban areas, since area is sometimes related to the benefit received from government services.[3] There would seem to be little merit in this argument in the agricultural context, however. Although differential land taxes or assessments have apparently been employed in Mysore, India, to recapture part of the private benefits accruing from such public works as irrigation,[4] it is more common to levy supplementary special taxes for this purpose, as noted later in this chapter.

Further research needs to be done into the regressivity of taxes based on land area, but if the burden distribution produced by a simple classified land area tax is found to be roughly consistent with prevalent equity norms, then the overwhelming administrative advantages of taxing on the basis of area alone should lead to this form of land tax receiving more careful consideration than it has in recent years. Many poor countries have been prevented from introducing the elaborately graduated land tax systems long urged by native and foreign experts alike because of the administrative impossibility of satisfying the stringent land classification requirements on which such systems invariably rest, quite apart from any political problems of implementation.

An area-based tax, on the other hand, requires knowledge of only four facts: the area of the property, its location, its classification, and the name of someone to whom the tax bill can be sent. While there are opportunities for cheating and corruption with respect to the area and classification recorded, both of these can be checked through such techniques as controlled aerial photogrammetry. The combination at one level of this highly modern and capital-intensive technique, which is readily obtainable in most countries from foreign sources and often with foreign financing, with a simple field enumeration procedure that can easily be done by workers with only elementary schooling under the supervision of a few well-trained experts holds promise for many poor countries (see Chapter 11).

The simpler the classification scheme which accords with rough notions of equity, the more equitable the system may prove to be in fact. This is in contrast to the usual approach of postulating highly refined and equitable classification systems that cannot be properly administered in practice and, hence, often prove inequitable. An area-based tax is, however, inherently crude; it would probably be tolerable in most countries only at fairly low rates, though even a low-rate tax may be an improvement over the present situation in countries which now in effect collect little or nothing from much of their agricultural sector, and it might be especially suitable to finance local government activities (Chapter 12). An area-based tax is also inelastic; this can be remedied by adjusting tax rates or assessments in some appropriate fashion to encompass increases in the money value of output as a result of either productivity improvements or inflation.

Finally, as always with crude make-do policies, there is the danger that too much emphasis on doing what can be done with the resources at hand may in some way preclude the adoption of an inherently more satisfactory tax base, such as some form of capital value. This hypothetical danger should not, however, preclude paying more attention to the design and implementation of simple, feasible land taxes. More work along these lines would be a better use of resources in many countries right now than undue concern with "ideal" land taxes.

TAXES BASED ON AN INCOME CONCEPT

The second major category of land taxes employs an income concept to measure the tax base. The fundamental distinction between these taxes and the more important group of taxes based on a rental value concept, which is discussed later, is not usually a matter of outward form. The rental value concept, whether expressed as annual value or capital value, aims at identifying that income attributable solely to the properties of the land: the quality of the soil; the topography of the field; and location as related to climate, irrigation, and accessibility to markets. Land revenue in India is an excellent example. The income concept, on the other hand, is more inclusive. It covers not only the income of the land itself but also the income of other factors of production, such as the value of the labor of the cultivator and his family and the return on capital invested in improvements on the land and in productive equipment.[5]

The income concept may be interpreted in different ways. The tax base may, for instance, be measured in terms of either physical production or its monetary equivalent. It can be either total income or cash income, either "gross" income or "net" income (that is, after deduction of expenses). There may or may not be personal exemptions and other deductions.

The oldest example of a tax assessed on the basis of gross harvest or gross income is the tithe, now almost extinct but long dominant in countries like Turkey (see Chapter 4). A few countries still have land taxes based on gross yield or gross income, but, unlike the tithe, determined by the rated productivity of the land rather than by inspection in the field at harvest time.

There are only a few examples of land-based taxes on a net income concept, most of which are integrated with a general income tax. Since income tax legislation often requires presumptive assessment of agricultural income, such taxes on agricultural income can usually be described as "quasi" land taxes. The presumptive assessments in these cases are, as noted in Chapter 4, often dependent on land surveys and, like most forms of land tax, usually remain unchanged from one year to the next. Sometimes these agricultural "income" taxes are really based on a rental value concept of the tax base, often for incentive reasons.

The central issues concerning the use of the income concept as a basis for taxing agriculture are the same as those concerning the use of this concept as a tax basis in other sectors. There is nothing unique about either agriculture or agricultural income that warrants discussion except the crucial point that it is almost impossible to assess agricultural income accurately in any country, no matter how advanced. The administrative difficulties of taxing farmers like those engaged in any other activity may be great enough to warrant the application in most developing countries, where agriculture is the most important economic activity, of special, and inevitably more crude and arbitrary, systems of taxation such as those based on "presumptive" income.

Once the decision has been made to proceed in this fashion, however, we are no longer talking about a tax on income but, rather, a tax on the factor or factors from which the tax base is derived. This is true whether the agricultural income tax is run separately or whether the presumed tax base is amalgamated into a general income tax, as one may wish to do, for example, in order to increase the degree of progressivity in the system. The usual basis from which income is presumed to arise at some rate in these systems is the assessed value of agricultural land, in which case the tax is not based on the income concept at all but rather on the rental value concept.

"The presumptive method of estimating taxable income is . . . mainly a guessing game organized according to variable rules."[6] As noted in Chapter 4, this is as true of the yardstick method (which is based on the determination of the yield and profits, gross or net, per acre for each crop in a sample of farms) as of the assessed value method (which usually takes estimated income to be a percentage of the assessed capital or annual value). These techniques are inevitably inequitable to some extent; their application may discourage wider use of bookkeeping and, hence, the spread of a proper income tax. Their undeniable short-run incentive effects owing to the zero marginal rate applicable to increases in production may be offset by adverse effects on investment if, as is likely, the presumption of income is based on criteria that would be affected. The usual type of tax on the presumptive income of farmers is, from the present point of view, not an income tax at all but simply a variety of land tax.

The widespread resort to presumptive assessment in land taxation has at times been encouraged by another consideration, which is more a matter of principle than of administrative necessity and which applies to many land taxes. It is sometimes claimed that assessments which vary each year in accord with actual income and expenses or actual rents are inconsistent with the conceptual framework of these taxes because the intention is to tax "normal" or long-term value, and not necessarily the actual value at any particular time. If the tax assessment is stabilized for long periods for any reason, the administrative burden is greatly reduced. On the other hand, this system also ensures a rapidly diminishing role for the land tax insofar as there is in fact any increase in real output or in its price level. Experience in both Japan and India illustrates this process (see Chapter 6).

TAXES BASED ON A RENTAL VALUE CONCEPT

The most important land taxes by far are those assessed according to a rental value concept. This approach derives in part from the Ricardian theory of rent. Briefly stated, this theory, developed in England in the early nineteenth century, is that the amount of rent for any given plot is determined by the excess of its yield over the yield on "marginal land," defined as the poorest land in actual cultivation. Marginal land is assumed to produce just enough to cover production costs, including the wages of the cultivator, and hence leaves nothing for rent.

In the specific case of agricultural land, then, rental value is the payment that can be obtained in a competitive market for the opportunity to apply common techniques of agriculture to the cultivation of the land, taking into account its location and other inherent qualities as well as additional qualities it may possess as a result of past human action. In practice, it is usually close to impossible on long-used land to distinguish the effects of nature from those of nurture. This rental value can be expressed either as a rate of payment for the use of land during a specified period or as an equivalent capital sum. The former method, which is ordinarily stated as an annual rent, is the basis of assessment for some older land taxes, especially the Indian land revenue, while capital value is the basis for most modern property taxes. Various differences in fact exist in both theory and practice between these alternative applications of the rental value concept in land taxation.

Annual Value

When rental income is included under a modern income tax, landlords are generally required to report their gross annual receipts from rentals, from which they can deduct expenses attributable to the rented property. A land tax, however, is usually imposed as a form of mass taxation intended to apply to all landlords, large or small, or at least to most of them. No land tax could work, except possibly in plantation economies, if it were dependent upon taxpayers' accounting records, because most landowners simply do not keep adequate records.

A possible compromise might to be to base the land tax on actual rents paid by tenants to landlords, with standard allowances for expenses. Uruguay, for instance, employs capitalized rental values derived from an examination of rental agreements. In the case of owner-cultivated land, the assessment might be determined with reference to rentals and expenses for similar properties cultivated by tenants. Even with this system, however, a satisfactory land classification is still an essential initial requirement in order to establish appropriate rental rates and allowances on a standardized basis for all the different grades and uses of land in each local area.

Furthermore, not only may there be many obstacles to ascertaining what rents are actually being paid and to keeping abreast of successive changes in rental rates, but also the rents actually paid cannot be accepted at face value for tax purposes.[7] For example, the rental agreements may be for varying terms of years, with all sorts of provisions as to security of tenure, or the respective responsibilities of landlords and tenants may be divided in different ways. What is included in actual rents may vary widely from area to area and contract to contract, or the rents may diverge from "normal" rents because they are the outgrowth of a long history of unequal bargaining power between landlord and tenant. Moreover, rents are sometimes paid in kind rather than in cash and must be converted to a monetary value unless the tax is also collected in kind. Finally, and most important, the absence of an openly competitive and active real estate market in the rural areas of most poor countries severely limits the use of actual rental data for the determination of the tax base.

The better assessment methods used for taxes based on annual rental value fall into two groups: those which require officials to estimate the income-producing capacity of each class of land, following presumably standardized land classification and assessment procedures, and then to separate out that part representing rental value; and those which require officials to appraise the capital value of the land, either by reference to the prices at which land is being sold or in accordance with established standards of appraisal, and then to compute rental value on the basis of an assumed rate of return on the capital value. Sometimes one method is used to corroborate the other. Under either method the result is a presumptive assessment, rather than an assessment based on any record of individual experience. Its accuracy and equity can be only as good as the way in which it is in fact administered.

Among the underdeveloped countries the leading examples of land tax assessments in accordance with an annual rental value concept are India and Pakistan. As noted in Chapter 6, however, the nominally rental value assessments in these countries have been reduced by time and attrition to, in effect, little more than taxes on land area, crudely classified.

Capital Value

The most important land taxes to employ a rental value concept are those assessed on appraised capital value, a concept often defined in the law as exchange or market value, that is, as the price at which properties are being sold or can be sold.

In a hypothetical case in which the value of land is determined exclusively by economic factors operating in a competitive land market, the capital value of the land is nothing more than the capitalized net annual rental value. The two measures of value, if appropriately defined, are reciprocally related, as principal is to interest. To illustrate: if a plot is estimated to yield a net rental income of $100 per year for an indefinite future period and the going rate of interest on capital is, say, 10 percent, the selling price under theoretically ideal circumstances would be $1,000; with a rate of 5 percent, it would be $2,000.[8] From the viewpoint of the purchaser of land, who may prefer to look at the interdependence the other way around, rent is nothing more than the return on his capital investment.

In theory, any income stream can thus be converted into a capital value, and any capital value can be converted into an income stream. All that is required for the conversion is an appropriate rate of discount. It follows, therefore, that, if income and capital are defined in the same way, a tax on income and a tax on capital should have the same economic effects. Even different timing of the two taxes would not affect this identity, except through its influence on liquidity.

In practice, however, "annual value" for land taxes levied on this base is generally not defined in the same way as "capital value." Consequently, despite fundamental interdependence between bases of capital value and annual rental value taxes, it is important to classify each tax separately since there are generally far-reaching differences between them in actual operation. If, for example, two pieces of land of equal economic value were assessed according to annual rental value in one jurisdiction and according to capital value in another, there is only a remote possibility that the resultant tax bases would be reciprocally related, as they should be under ideal conditions.[9]

As already indicated, the annual rental value assessed for land tax purposes is largely a notional value. The tax base is no less artificial or hypothetical in the typical case of assessment according to capital value. Only a very small portion of taxable landholdings in most rural areas are in fact sold in any assessment period. Even for those that are sold, it is doubtful whether the selling prices can be accepted as true indexes of capital value since they are usually influenced by a host of institutional forces and by market imperfections.

To administer the land tax properly, officials must therefore place primary reliance upon land classification procedures and other indirect methods of valuation. The relation of the assessed value to the legal standard will, as usual, depend upon what information is available to the officials and upon how well they do their work.

Moreover, the concept of value that is most appropriate for tax assessment is not necessarily the same as that which would be most relevant for determining value in the market place. Rental value is open to several interpretations: for example, actual rental value at the time of assessment; "normal" value as measured, say, by past experience; or value anticipated in some future period. A further distinction is possible when land is not being put to its optimum use: rental value can be measured with reference to either expected income from present use or potential income from optimum use.

To the extent that the selling price of land is determined by the economic benefits of proprietorship, rather than by intangible benefits such as prestige of landownership, it reflects the discounted value of anticipated rental income and not necessarily the capitalized value of current rental income. Furthermore, the selling price is likely to be associated more closely with the value of land at its optimum economic use than with its value under less favorable alternative uses. In some countries, where land is a favorite object of speculative investment, the value of land may reflect the expectation of continued inflation or the relatively greater security and prestige of investing in land compared to other assets.

Most laws which tax on the basis of capital value establish the selling price of land as the measure of value. "Value" is thus usually construed as "market value," which is understood to be either the price which the property would bring in an open market in a free sale between a willing buyer and a willing seller or, more realistically, the most probable selling price in the prevailing market circumstances. This value, too, is in most cases only a notional value, just as is the value of a property to its owner. The value actually used for tax purposes in most countries is itself notional in the sense of being established in accordance with prescribed standards: its reliability will always depend primarily on what the assessor knows and what he does with his knowledge. The more complicated the legal requirements the more arbitrary their application is likely to be, despite the theoretical advantages of a tax based on a notional value derived from the productive capacity of land. Imperfect as market values are in most countries, these considerations suggest they should be regarded as relatively "hard" information and play as important a role in the assessing of land taxes as notions of rated productive capacity. Chapter 11 elaborates this point.

In contrast, when annual value is assessed for land tax purposes, it is likely to be determined with reference to current, or even past ("normal"), rather than anticipated income, and with reference to the income of the land in its present use even though a different use of the land might be more profitable. In effect, then, taxing capital value provides in principle a means of reaching both current income and wealth, whereas taxing annual value reaches only the former. These differences between the two bases can be of paramount importance as regards the economic effects of the respective classes of land taxes and suggest strongly the relative merits of a properly applied capital value approach in developing countries.

A particularly striking disparity between the results of the two methods of assessment can be found in the case of idle land, especially when the land borders upon an expanding urban area or is in an agricultural area which is expected to experience rapid development. In either of these situations the market value of the land can be expected to exceed the capitalization of current rental value. This will also be true for newly planted orchards or land recently shifted to crops having a long period of gestation, though in these cases special relief provisions are often applied: whether they should be is a question which cannot be further explored here.[10]

Divergences between assessments on capital and annual value may also result from differences in the treatment of improvements on the land. Some countries with a capital value tax base exempt all visible improvements and tax only "site value"; others go further and attempt to tax only the value of completely unimproved land. Ordinarily, however, capital value assessments cover at least a few types of improvements; some countries even include the value of farm animals and equipment as well as the value of structural improvements on the land itself. The more equipment is included, the closer the tax base approximates to the income concept mentioned earlier.

In addition, because it is relatively easy to identify the specific assets to be taxed or left untaxed, the capital value approach lends itself more readily to selectivity in the definition of the tax base than does the annual value approach. On the other hand, the annual value basis would appear to permit more sensible "personalization" of the land tax, if that is a desired goal.

When agricultural land is taxed on the basis of capital value, the tax is very often part of a property or real estate tax applied in both urban and rural areas and is, hence, perhaps less likely to be viewed as a tax in lieu of income taxes. Indeed, in most countries it would seem advisable to view the tax in this way so that the expansion of the income tax into the agricultural sector as modernization proceeds will not be unnecessarily blocked. Furthermore, taxes on wealth, even on only some forms of wealth, have their own justification and do not need to be assimilated to income taxes in order to be acceptable and desirable fiscal instruments (see Chapter 10).

Assessment practices in most developing countries employing the capital value approach, most of which are in Latin America, are poor. The number of specially trained assessors is usually very small. Many assessors fail to apply such elementary appraisal tools as simple soil classification schedules and unit value tables. More modern techniques, such as scientific soil mapping and productivity surveys as well as official assessment manuals, are still rare despite substantial improvements in this respect in recent years. Nevertheless, on the whole there are considerable economic merits in capital value as compared to annual value assessments, and no significant administrative difficulties in the circumstances of most developing countries, so the capital value approach would appear to be that most suited for expansion and development in all countries, except those few in which some other system is already well established and functioning, so that transition costs could reduce the net benefits of adopting the capital value approach.

There is no reason to believe that capital values are more difficult to assess correctly than annual values. Contrary opinions[11] appear to be based on the fact that most capital value taxes in Latin America are very badly administered, even compared to the annual value taxes of South Asia. This association, of course, tells us nothing of the feasible standards of administration of either tax in either region. The differences some see would appear to reflect more stylistic differences in tax culture than inherent characteristics of the tax bases. In particular, the lack of adequate land surveys, which is undeniably the main fault of most existing capital value taxes, has nothing to do with the capital value approach; it is a defect in most annual value taxes too.

SPECIAL PURPOSE TAXES

This final group of land taxes, being a catchall category, does not lend itself readily to a general description. Most of these taxes, however, are designed primarily to serve nonfiscal objectives of an economic, political, or social nature. The numerous Latin American taxes described in Chapter 5, which are intended to penalize absentee owners or to force idle land into cultivation, illustrate both the use of such devices and their apparent ineffectiveness in most countries.[12] Special purpose land taxes of one type or another are found almost everywhere, often as integral parts of a country's over-all system of land taxation. Many examples were given in Part Two. Even though their revenue yield is usually unimportant, these special land taxes are often of interest as being closely related conceptually to the government's development program and broad fiscal objectives.

Many writers have stressed the peculiar taxable capacity of increases in land values on the ground that such increases are often due to the ordinary progress of society and not to any expenditure of capital or any exertion or sacrifice on the part of the owners.[13] There are several possible methods of taxing this so-called "unearned increment" in land values. A one-time levy may, for example, be imposed on the basis of the increment in land value from a fixed date in the past. Past increments in value may alternatively be taxed at the time of transfer, possibly at rates which vary according to the class of land and the length of time held. Finally, provision may be made for taxing future increments in value at specified intervals.

Special capital gains taxes on land are justified in many countries on these grounds. These taxes do not in practice amount to much, however, and, as noted in Chapter 4, there are few other examples anywhere today of taxes aimed at tapping the "unearned increment," with the exception of special assessments. Despite the possible merits of general land value increment taxes as a supplement to property or capital gains taxes in some cases,[14] conceptual, and especially administrative, difficulties seem likely to preclude them from playing a fiscally significant role in any less developed country, especially in the agricultural sector.

When increments in value are localized and result from a specific public improvement, such as an irrigation project or a new road, however, an excellent opportunity exists to impose a special assessment, or betterment levy. In theory, a special assessment aims to determine the portion of the cost of a public improvement that gives rise to a special as opposed to a general benefit, and to apportion that part of the cost among the property owners in the area where the special benefit is localized.

In view of the fact that special assessments are specifically designed for financing such development projects as irrigation works, flood control systems, and farm-to-market roads, all of which are extremely important for underdeveloped countries, it is surprising to find that they have not been employed more widely. Part of the explanation seems to be that special assessments are an effective and efficient method of finance only when they are planned and executed with great care, and that this administrative requirement may be beyond the capacity of most underdeveloped countries. Until recently, for whatever reason, few developing countries have shown much interest in seeking out refined fiscal tools of this type. An outstanding exception is provided by Colombia, where a particular form of special assessment called the valorization tax has proved to be of considerable value in recent years.

CLASSIFICATION OF LAND TAXES

This tax is similar to the "special assessment" or "betterment tax" levied in some English-speaking countries.[15] As in other developing countries, some areas of Colombia are still without any transportation but horses and mules, and construction of a road or railroad may have such dramatic effects on land values (by lowering transportation costs) that a large proportion of the cost of the new road or railroad can in principle be paid for through taxes roughly related to the increases in land values. In addition, projects to increase the value of agricultural land through dikes to prevent flooding or canals to provide drainage may have very high benefit-cost ratios in developing countries, so that financing them also with valorization taxes may be feasible. Colombia has to a limited extent realized this potential, though much less so than it has in certain urban areas. It could do much more.[16] Even so, other countries can perhaps profit from Colombian experiences to date.

As early as 1887, for example, a law authorized valorization for flood control and land reclamation projects. The tax could cover only the cost of the public investment, and it was to be assessed on the basis of appraised land values. This law was poorly drafted and little used. In 1936 the law was extended to cover municipal improvements in Bogotá. Two years later all major cities were authorized to carry out public works and to impose the valorization tax. The new laws required land valuations before and after the investment to determine the benefits, and they again limited the tax to the cost of the public investment. It was at this time that the first valorization activities were underaken in Bogotá. The law was still both too vague and too restrictive for wide application, however, and it was not until 1943 that the valorization tax was established in the form in which it is found today in Colombian municipalities.

The 1943 law allowed all municipalities to charge a valorization tax on all public improvements, whether financed by the municipality, department, national government, or other public agency, up to the total amount of the benefit received, without reference to the cost of the public improvements. This law also left it open to the municipality to determine the methods by which the benefit in increased land values to the property owner would be determined; gave municipalities almost complete freedom to establish the organization and methods for administering the valorization tax; made it clear that any public improvement which increased land values could be covered by the tax; and gave the municipalities clear rights to collect the tax, providing the sanctions of embargo and seizure of property if the tax were not paid. In an important ruling a year later the Council of State provided that municipalities had the right to assess and collect the valorization tax as soon as the plans and budget for a project had been prepared and approved and before actual work had begun on the improvements. An additional section in the 1943 law stated that the municipalities must give property owners the right to be consulted in the formation and execution of the project and in the determination of the way in which the valorization tax was to be allocated among property owners.

It is on the basis of this broadly drawn law, which provides almost complete autonomy to the municipalities, that the modern valorization tax has been developed in some Colombian cities. The primary check on abuse of the municipal valorization tax is provided by the ability of local citizens to put effective pressure on the city government and the valorization agency rather than by safeguards against abuse written into the law. Perhaps surprisingly, it appears to work fairly well.

While the laws for municipal valorization thus give great freedom of action to municipalities, the laws for flood control, drainage, and irrigation, and other projects executed by the departments, the nation, or regional development authorities remained quite restrictive until 1966. The valorization tax in these cases could not, for instance, be assessed and collected until after the public work was completed. Further, the total tax was limited to the cost of the investment plus at most 33 percent of the difference between the total benefit to land values and the investment cost. The tax had to be in proportion to the benefits, as calculated by special valuations of the properties before and after the work was done. The 1966 law finally gave national and departmental valorization authorities the same freedom of action enjoyed by municipalities.

Even before this law, however, the valorization procedure had been used in rural areas for swamp drainage and water projects and highways by both departments and regional agencies. A recent project financed in part by valorization, for example, was the construction by the Cauca Valley Corporation, a regional power and water agency, of dikes to protect lowlands near Cali from floods. Although it proved fruitless, serious consideration was also given to financing part of the Magdalena Valley railroad by valorization, and the proposed use of valorization to finance new intercity highways was the main reason for the enactment of the new national valorization law in 1966.

The difficulties of applying valorization taxes under the old stringent laws for nonmunicipal agencies are well illustrated by the experience of the Cauca Valley Corporation in levying valorization taxes to finance a dike project which, by preventing seasonal flooding, opened up much new land for urbanization on the outskirts of Cali.[17] Although the project was authorized in 1958, and by 1962 the work had been substantially completed and over ten thousand people were living in the formerly flooded areas, no valorization tax had yet been collected by the middle of 1964.

The principal difficulty was that the law required special property valuation surveys before and after the dike was built, and these surveys were not completed until mid-1964. Only then could the tax be determined and collections begun. Since the interest rate charged to the taxpayers between the time the expenditure was made and the time the tax was assessed was only 6 percent, whereas the purchasing power of the currency dropped by about 10 percent per year during the period since construction, the tax did not cover the total costs of the work in real terms. The delay in collection therefore forced the corporation to finance the work for three or more years from other sources in a situation of chronic credit shortage. If the 1966 law works as well in rural areas as it has in some Colombian cities, and there seems no reason why it should not do so since the administrative capabilities of the regional corporations and the national government are at least equal to those of the city governments, the financing of capital works through benefit taxation should proceed much more smoothly in the future.

Colombia is not the only country in which such development projects as irrigation and road building give rise to large increments in land value in the immediate localities benefiting from the projects.[18] Taxing away the value increments by means of "betterment levies" or "special assessments" would be economically advantageous and would probably meet with more ready acceptance by the taxpayers than most taxes, owing to the presence of visible local benefits.[19] Earmarking the proceeds of a tax levy for specific projects benefiting the taxpayers may increase the agricultural savings available for development purposes within the rural sector.

From an administrative point of view, too, some variant of betterment tax may seem an attractive potential source of finance to developing countries, for land cannot easily be hidden from taxation (though landowners can—an important factor in countries with the Latin tradition of in personam taxes). The tax is collected in large sums from a relatively small number of taxpayers, which makes enforcement easier though it may make compliance more difficult. Collection of special assessments must normally be spread over a number of years.

The crucial factor in administration is that the tax and the public improvements go hand in hand. If poor administration leads to badly planned or executed projects, projects which are not executed promptly, or poor allocation of taxes among landowners, and if, as a consequence, a significant number of taxpayers find that the tax they have paid is more than the increase in the value of their property, the tax may easily be discredited and appear to be only an arbitrary and capricious capital levy.

Extensive experience with the valorization tax in Colombia suggests that it has been most successful where the greatest efforts have been made to put it on a true benefit basis, as was done in the city of Medellín. To do this seems to require the following elements: freedom from any fixed formulas for distributing the tax among property owners; careful study of projects at the initial stage to determine those that will result in increased land values equal at least to the cost of the project; participation of property owners in the planning and execution of projects without giving them obstructionist or veto powers; careful costing and prompt construction of projects; prompt and complete collection of all taxes assessed on the property owners while the project is being built; extensive publicity of valorization construction projects; and a general statement of the rules for hardship cases permitting, but not requiring, reduction in tax or delayed payment in certain circumstances.

The development of a valorization system is also a matter for careful planning; Medellín's experience suggests the importance of starting with small projects that can be completed quickly and with certainty and thus earn taxpayer trust; at a later stage it might be better to concentrate on large multifaceted projects. While there are no empirical studies available to show how closely valorization tax assessments have corresponded to subsequent increases in site value in Medellín, there is a general feeling on the part of officials and other

CLASSIFICATION OF LAND TAXES

observers that the tax has been levied, by and large, on a basis proportional to benefits. Preserving a popular identification between the tax and the benefits by all possible means is repeatedly emphasized in Medellín.

Public finance textbooks tend to condemn earmarked revenues because they limit the flexibility of government budgeting, glutting some activities with too much revenue while other activities starve. This can be avoided if the rate of the earmarked tax is changed regularly to bring it into line with actual revenue needs, as is the case with the valorization tax. Further, the financing of investments from the earmarked valorization tax gives an added incentive to examine the prospective benefits of projects more closely than would otherwise be done and hence promotes good budgeting and project appraisal procedures.

Benefit taxation may be made politically popular in the way outlined above. There is a danger, however, that those activities which can be readily financed on this basis will receive too much support at the expense of other activities which, for technical reasons, cannot be benefit financed. Too much emphasis on benefit taxation may also limit the scope for income redistribution through taxation. The force of these charges is lessened to the extent that benefit taxes can be shown to be in addition to other taxes rather than substituting for them. On the basis of admittedly crude and impressionistic evidence, the valorization tax does seem to be a net addition to public financing in Colombia. The need in Colombia, as in many other poor countries, is for additional technically sound benefit taxes to expand the public sector, not for less use of those now existing.

In summary, betterment taxes in theory seem attractive for many developing countries. They are suitable only for financing public investments that will be demonstrably productive. They have a clear benefit justification to help muster political support for the tax. As shown in Chapter 9, their effects on saving should be at least neutral and may be positive, and their incentive effects should be favorable. They should be relatively easy to collect. But skilled administration is needed if they are to work well in practice, and skilled people are often the scarcest resource in developing countries. That such administration is not beyond the reach of an underdeveloped country is demonstrated by Colombian experience; whether it is the best use of limited resources is another question.

AGRICULTURAL LAND TAXES

8

SHIFTING AND INCIDENCE

The basic theory of the incidence of a land tax is simply that the burden falls on the owners of land. Furthermore, if the supply of land is completely fixed, if all farmers are profit maximizers, and if factor markets are perfect, the effect of the tax is basically to lower the price of land.

What the theory really says is that a tax on the "pure" economic rent of land will always be borne by the landlord, provided the amount of the tax does not exceed the economic rent.[1] Under competitive conditions of supply and demand, the market prices of agricultural commodities are determined by the cost of production on marginal land. But marginal land carries no tax when the tax base is restricted to economic rent because, by definition, such land yields no rent. The market prices of agricultural commodities will thus be unaffected by the tax.

This initial principle has two important corollaries. First, the incidence of a tax on economic rent is independent of whether the land is rented or owner cultivated, or whether the landlord or tenant is the statutory taxpayer. The market rental which landlords can exact from tenants will be the same before the tax as afterward, because the supply of land to be rented and the number of tenants seeking land will be unchanged. This assumes, of course, that landlords exact the full rent permitted by market conditions. Should the tenant be the statutory taxpayer, his rental would tend to be reduced by market forces to just the extent required to shift the tax to the owner.

A second corollary is that landlords cannot shift a tax on economic rent to farm laborers or to suppliers of such inputs as seed and fertilizer. There is thus no reason why the tax should induce profit-maximizing landlords to make any adjustments in production levels or techniques.

On the other hand, a tax that is greater than the economic rent of land but less than the total rent will be shifted to the extent that the tax discourages landlords from replacing capital improvements, the return on which accounts for the difference between economic rent and total rent. Total rent may include, in addition to economic rent, the return on such elements as permanent land improvements like clearing and grading, fertility elements in the soil due to the application of fertilizer and adherence to crop rotation and other beneficial practices, and other improvements such as buildings and fences. A tax that exceeds the economic rent impinges on the reward to labor and capital invested in land improvement.

Landlords have some choice with respect to the upkeep of their land; if the after-tax return is not sufficiently attractive, they may decide to allow the land to deteriorate and buildings, fences, and the like to fall into disrepair. The eventual effect of the tax may, thus, be a decline in agricultural production. In this case, part of the tax will in the long run be shifted to consumers of agricultural products in the form of increased prices.

If, however, the imposition of a land tax causes capital to move out of agriculture, the return on capital will be reduced in the non-agricultural sector also. Prices of goods produced outside of agriculture would then be reduced, thus serving to compensate for at least part of the price increases on agricultural commodities. The results would be different, however, if total savings were curtailed as a result of the effects of the tax on the rate of return because the level of investment in both sectors would then decline.

If the tax is in excess of total rent (economic rent plus the return on the landlord's investment in the land), it will tend to curtail all investment in agriculture and to encourage the abandonment of marginal land. The result is that such a tax tends to be shifted both forward to consumers and backward to laborers and tenants. The greater the tax-induced retirement of land, labor, and capital from agriculture, the larger the reduction in agricultural output and the larger the price rise that can be expected. If, however, the tax on agricultural land is part of a general uniform-rate tax on property, there would be no incentive for an exodus of labor and capital from agriculture in particular, although there would still be an incentive for factors to leave property-intensive lines of production, including agriculture. The extent of shifting would depend on how much agricultural land was withdrawn from use and on whether the volume of total savings was affected by the tax.

Finally, a tax that is uneven in its initial impact on different classes of land, or that applies to some classes of land and not to others, tends to be spread evenly among all landowners to the extent that land in marginal use is shifted from heavily taxed to lightly taxed categories. The resulting price increases for the produce of heavily taxed land tend to be counterbalanced by price decreases elsewhere. If the total tax is less than the economic rent, so that it does not drive any land out of production, there will be no appreciable shifting on balance to consumers (unless the goods purchased are very different for different groups of consumers); nor will the burden of the tax be spread to investors outside of agriculture. The main burden of the tax will then be on the net rents received by landowners as a group.

These propositions contain the sum and substance of the basic theory on shifting of land taxes. Like all generalizations in economics, however, they should be applied only with caution to specific situations. It should be noted, in particular, that the theory outlined above rests on two key assumptions: first, that production is responsive to tax pressures, and, second, that prices (including rents) are competitively determined in the marketplace. The latter seems especially dubious in the circumstances of most developing countries.

INTERSECTORAL TAX SHIFTING

If one assumes that the introduction of a land tax has no direct effect on other parts of the tax system and that land tax revenues are not spent in ways that increase agricultural production, the burden of taxation on resources in the agricultural sector will be increased relative to the burden of existing taxes on resources employed elsewhere. If this tax increase reduces agricultural output, however, some of this initial burden will probably be shifted to other sectors of the economy.

Even when land taxes employ a rental value concept, the tax base will in practice almost always reflect the value of some of the improvements which have been made to the land and not simply the raw site value. The inextricable merging over the centuries of man's effort and nature's bounty ensures that few, if any existing land taxes can claim membership in that fiscal elite which includes taxes paid entirely out of economic surplus. As Dumont once wrote:

> Above all, agriculture modifies the soil. Unlike climate, this should not be regarded as part of the natural endowment of a region, the only exception being in the case of certain virgin soils which have retained their original vegetation of grass or forest. . . . Our own soils are highly artificial. In many cases they have been worked with plough and harrow for thousands of years, corrected for deficiencies and enriched with manure, and every kind of fertilizer, natural and artificial.[2]

If land taxes encroach upon returns to labor and capital in agriculture, these resources will tend to leave the industry. If as a result production declines, the stage will be set for intersectoral tax shifting. The extent to which a tax on agricultural land remains on the agricultural sector therefore depends in large part upon the elasticity of supply in agriculture.

One possible source of supply elasticity in agriculture is that owners of poor land, or of any land that is taxed for more than its economic rent, may decide to abandon it rather than continue cultivation at a remuneration which means a reduced living standard. But farmers are often reluctant to abandon land. Landowners in many developing countries place a high value on the intangible benefits of landownership, such as independence and social standing in the community, and they may be willing, if necessary, to accept smaller monetary rewards than might be obtained elsewhere. Moreover, the fluctuating and uncertain nature of income from agriculture may conceal the impact of the tax for long periods and may encourage farmers to continue working the land in the hope of an eventually favorable turn of the market. In addition, landowners may be tied to their land because of the cost and other hardships of relocating themselves and their families. Short of abandonment, farmers may tend to decapitalize the land by applying too little fertilizer or cultivation input.

The likelihood of a tax-induced abandonment of land would seem to be especially small in overpopulated countries. Greater opportunities for the tax to reduce the supply of land under cultivation exist in countries where rapid industrialization creates attractive employment opportunities outside of agriculture. On the other hand, in a country in which new regions are still being opened for settlement, the tax may not reduce the total amount of land under cultivation; it may, instead, induce farmers to settle in new areas.

In some countries, cultivable land may be withheld from production for speculative purposes or because of inertia or disinterest on the part of the landowners. Alternatively, where monopolistic or oligopolistic market power exists, land is likely to be used at less than the social optimum (the point where the value of the marginal product equals the marginal cost of land use) on quite rational profit-maximizing grounds similar to those which lead monopolists in other sectors of the economy to restrict output.[3]

In these cases a land tax would increase the cost of holding land idle. If the added cost were heavy enough, it might force the landowner to cultivate the land or to sell it to someone else for cultivation, which would benefit the country as a whole. Instead of being shifted forward to consumers, the tax would then rest on the landowners, or other factors of production if the cultivation process becomes more intensive or extensive, while at the same time consumers would benefit as more products became available at lower prices. Precisely this ideal result of increased land taxation is the target of many schemes for land tax reform.

From this point of view, then, taxes on land are virtually ideal taxes. Quite apart from political problems, however, a principal difficulty in achieving these results in practice is that we have no way of distinguishing between those returns to land (and other resources) which constitute true economic rent and those which are actually opportunity costs of production. Agricultural land is not costless. The supply cost of land may be taken to be equal to the annual interest payments on the original capital cost of clearing, leveling, draining, and bringing it into use, plus annual maintenance charges.[4] (Since properly kept land does not depreciate, there is no amortization cost.) The rent, or scarcity value of land, will then equal the annual cost of bringing the marginal unit of land into use. While for much of agricultural land the extent of these charges will be obscured by the passage of time, they will usually be clear enough at the margin.

Much of the return to agricultural land is thus really interest on capital improvements, and a tax which impinges on this return can usually be shifted, as noted earlier. Land usable for agriculture is not the free gift of nature; nor is it indestructible. Both to bring it into use and to keep it there involves costs. It therefore follows that agricultural land is not perfectly inelastic in supply. Taxes on the imputed wages and interest involved in land can be shifted either backward to other factors or forward to consumers, and, in the long run, usually will be.

Land markets in developing countries are often imperfect, and tenants are immobile through law or custom. At the same time, however, land supply is in fact elastic in many of these same countries, or at least land supply can be elastic, provided necessary infrastructure and institutional changes are made. In an important sense, then, the elasticity of land supply reflects policy, not nature.

Even arguments about market imperfections, although obvious to the eye, sometimes turn out to be rather different on closer examination. For example, it is common currency in countries such as India that markets for agricultural commodities do not operate efficiently owing to monopolistic elements which lead to large spreads between prices paid by consumers and those received by producers. In fact, however, an extensive study of the Indian grain trade recently found that there were far too many intermediaries to permit monopolistic practices. The high profits earned by some traders reflected not monopoly power but their skill and their command over scarce capital.[5] The relative ignorance of the cultivators and their inability to store their produce also, no doubt, had some influence on this result.

Since the supply of rural land is not fixed—it can be increased or decreased by man's action—there is almost always some possibility of shifting substantial land taxes, even where there are owner-occupiers and certainly where there are immobile powerless tenants and where landowners are in collusion. Even without monopoly power, however, the usual effect of a tax on land (no matter what its particular base) would probably be to reduce the amount of land employed, with some effect on production and perhaps on prices. The burden of the tax in terms of its effects on gross rents will, of course, be shared between landlord and tenant in accord with their relative elasticities of supply and demand (see below).

In a situation in which capital flows freely between agriculture and industry, then, the effect of a land tax, assuming it is a discriminatory tax that is not counterbalanced by equivalent taxes on industry, may be to divert an increased share of the total supply of capital to less heavily taxed branches of industry. The resulting restriction on agricultural production, combined with the stimulus to production outside of agriculture, would shift the sectoral terms of trade to favor agriculture and would correspondingly lighten its real tax load.

Some of the conditions necessary for a tax-induced diversion of investment are unlikely to prevail in underdeveloped countries, however. Much investment in agriculture is in the form of accretionary capital formation, or on-the-spot investment in kind created through the labor of those who work the land.[6] Only an extremely heavy tax would discourage such investment since most of the labor is firmly attached to the agricultural sector and would otherwise remain idle. Of course, the result might be different for investment in the form of equipment purchased from outside agriculture. Inclusion of the value of such equipment in the tax base, or acceptance of its ownership as evidence of taxable capacity for purposes of a presumptive assessment, would reduce the advantages to the farmer in making the investment and may discourage purchases of equipment. This result may, of course, be desirable in the present circumstances of some countries, as is noted in the next chapter.

The rate of economic development in a country may also influence the elasticity of supply in agriculture. A rapid rate implies a continuous opening of alternative employment opportunities for labor and capital and probably some intersectoral transfers of resources. Supply obviously is more likely to respond to tax pressures in a fluid economy than in a static, sluggish one. Tax policy should, of course, be directed toward stimulating intersectoral resource transfers in line with national economic objectives—yet another reason why an appraisal of intersectoral tax shifting should be made within a broad economic context in which the relationship of taxes to taxpaying capacity is not necessarily the paramount consideration (see Chapter 10).

A land tax may also tend to decrease the yield on reproducible capital generally.[7] Even if the tax is limited to agricultural land, it is still widespread in its effects in the typical developing country and might therefore affect the rate of return of capital. Total savings and investment, not just that in the taxed sector, may be reduced to some extent, with resulting changes in relative commodity and factor prices and shifts of capital and population. So long as the tax is differential between sectors, however, some intersectoral shifting might also result unless all factors are completely immobile.

On the one hand, a land tax will have disincentive effects on production because it absorbs part of the return on a farmer's labor and on his investment in production requisites; on the other hand, however, the income effect of the tax provides a positive inducement to the taxpayer to find ways of increasing his income so that he might maintain his living standard despite the tax payment. Economic theory is inconclusive as to which set of opposing effects is likely to be the stronger.

The effect of reduced domestic output on market prices will be softened if the gap is filled by additional supplies of agricultural products from abroad. Insofar as international competition is a factor in the internal markets of some countries, it may set a limit to tax shifting.

More important, changes in the volume of production will not always be transmitted into equivalent changes in the volume of marketings. A substantial portion of the production of food crops, for example, is ordinarily consumed on the farm and never moves out of the agricultural sector. In deciding how much to market, a farmer takes into account not only the requirements of his family, but also the prevailing price in the market and his own need for cash. One reason why he may need cash is to pay taxes. A land tax, by raising the farmer's cash requirements, might actually encourage him to market more, which would depress selling prices. In effect, the burden of the tax on the farmer would then be compounded: in addition to paying the tax, he would receive a lower price for his produce.

A tax-induced incentive to larger farm marketings would not occur, however, if such marketings were themselves the object of taxation, as in some Middle Eastern countries. Instead, the more likely effect of a marketing tax would be to discourage producers from bringing their crops to the marketing centers—an effect distinctly favorable to tax shifting.

There are several categories of agricultural income which a land tax might absorb before creating pressures for tax shifting, such as economic rent, rent on permanent improvements, and income that is counterbalanced by the psychic values of landownership and the hardships of farmers in moving elsewhere. Finally, should production be curtailed by the tax, a price rise for agricultural products might be partly prevented by an inflow of supplies from abroad or by the failure of the loss of production to reduce the volume of crops marketed. Broadly speaking, the likelihood of the full tax incidence remaining on the agricultural sector would seem to be greatest for taxes based as closely on a rental value concept as possible and least for marketing taxes.

TAX CAPITALIZATION

The relative immobility of the factors of production in agriculture in most developing countries tends to restrict the shifting of land taxes. To the extent that factor immobility prevents a tax-induced change in the market prices of agricultural products, however, it encourages a tax-induced change in the market price of the income-producing asset, which is land. The latter price change is a manifestation of tax capitalization.

A tax is said to be capitalized if it is paid by the property owner at the time when it is imposed. Insofar as the land tax is thus discounted in the purchase price of land, the tax is no burden to any subsequent owner, and discussion of its incidence becomes relevant only if changes are considered.

The analysis underlying tax capitalization is simple. The capital value of an asset equals the discounted value of an expected net income stream. A new tax on the asset will immediately reduce expected net incomes and, hence, the capital value of the asset. (The more general in scope the tax imposed, the more it will tend to alter the discount rate proportionately and hence not be capitalized.) Since future purchasers of the assets will pay only the reduced capital value, the current owners bear the full burden of tax, except insofar as they may over time be able to shift some of it to consumers or other factors through failing to maintain the property.

If, therefore, substantially higher effective taxation of agricultural land is introduced, and markets function at all, one would expect land values to fall and, perhaps, though this is less certain, the maintenance of land (clearing, drainage, irrigation) to decline. In situations where land values reflect nonmarket factors like prestige and status, the results may be less clear-cut. In the short run there may also be some capitalization of taxes on improvements, though over time downward shifting of the supply of improvements will tend to restore a normal rate of return on capital invested.

To maintain that a given land tax is fully capitalized presupposes an active land market. It also presupposes that the supply of agricultural land is inelastic with respect to changes in the return on land (otherwise at least part of the tax would be shifted rather than capitalized); that the pattern of future tax liabilities is foreseeable and fully anticipated; that the government does not spend the tax revenue in a way that affects the value of land services; and that the tax does not affect the rate at which land income is capitalized.

There can be few situations where the necessary conditions for full tax capitalization are completely satisfied. Whenever the value of land is affected by changes in taxation, however, at least part of the tax is being capitalized; from this standpoint, therefore, tax capitalization is probably a fairly prevalent phenomenon, no matter how imperfectly it operates. In fact, tax capitalization may be occurring continuously in some countries, simply as a reflection of changing expectations regarding future taxes.

There appear to be no empirical studies of tax capitalization in developing countries. There are, indeed, few studies anywhere, but what scanty evidence is available does support the notion that higher property taxes tend to lead to a fall in the value of the taxed property.[8] To produce this result, the supply of property has to be inelastic in the short run, and the general level of interest rates should not be affected by the tax. Neither condition seems as likely to be fulfilled in a poor rural country where land may be held out of use for monopolistic purposes, where "land" is a variable anyway (depending on maintenance expenditure), and where the general level of rates of return is more likely to be affected by a significant land tax.

The impact of a capitalized tax on land prices will depend upon the size of the tax and its expected duration, as well as the extent to which the government expenditures presumably made possible by the additional tax revenues provide benefits which are themselves capitalized into property values and, hence, offset the effects of the tax. There may also be some "threshold" of size of tax increase which needs to be crossed before any capitalization effect may be expected. A significant tax increase not offset by direct benefits to land ought, however, to result in some decline in the level of land prices. This conclusion assumes, of course, that some market for agricultural land exists, even if it is distorted by noneconomic factors.

It is in part the expectation of this price reduction effect that seems to underly some proposals to utilize land taxation for purposes of land reform.[9] Landlords may want to sell more of the now lower-priced land since their wealth (and perhaps also their consumption) will be decreased as a result of the tax: tenants will also be able to buy more since, in effect, the capitalization of the land tax converts a down-payment (the higher pretax price) into a running cost (the future tax liability), thus making it possible for those with lower liquid assets to buy land.[10]

In a perfect world the capitalization effect alone will not spur development, however, for in effect the tax raises the running costs on the new lower value to equal the annual interest cost before tax. But the world, and particularly the capital market in developing countries, is not perfect, so this liquidity effect can be important in increasing the accessibility of land to the poorer inhabitants.

In theory, then, heavy land taxes can be a powerful wealth-redistributing instrument in any society with a substantial nonlandowning class: the doubling of a 1 percent tax on the capital value of land may, for example, reduce the wealth of present landowners by 20 percent (assuming a discount rate of 5 percent). This very power may perhaps explain the substantial difficulty of increasing land taxes in most countries.

The argument that a tax on land cannot be shifted assumes that landowners are charging as much as the market will bear, which they may well not be doing in a primitive rural society. In addition to the direct effect on prices, the costs of holding land in less than its best use are increased, so that the tax will stimulate landowners either to put land to better use or to sell their land, thus further tending to lower prices. On the other hand, that part of the usual land tax which falls on improvements will increase their carrying cost and penalize further investment in land. The net result depends, as usual, on the specific circumstances at hand.

More formally, if the supply of land is completely fixed, all farmers are profit maximizers, and factor markets are perfect, the burden of a tax on agricultural land alone will be completely on the landowner.[11] Furthermore, since the effect of the tax is to reduce the net income from the land that can be retained, the value of the land to the owner will fall—in the extreme case of full capitalization to the point where the rate of return on the land is restored to its original level. The land tax will then have been completely capitalized in the form of a reduction of land prices.

The fall in land prices is likely to be less than that required to restore the pretax rate of return, however, if, as is often claimed, land produces for its owners more nonpecuniary returns than other assets, or if land forms an important part of total wealth or even, if capital markets are imperfect, an important part of the wealth of those who own land. All these conditions are likely to be satisfied in the typical underdeveloped country. When much wealth takes the form of land, the rate of return on capital as a whole may also change as a result of the imposition of the tax. The final result depends on many interdependent factors, for example, the pattern of savings and investments, the use of revenues generated by the tax, and time preferences. But it seems likely that as a rule the effects of land taxes on land prices will be considerably muted.

Furthermore, this discussion incorrectly treats land as an original and indestructible factor of production. In fact, as argued earlier, the value of any rural property depends to a large extent on how much man has improved it over the centuries. This means that any land tax will invariably decrease the rate of return to investment in land and hence discourage it to some extent.

In the upshot, if investment in land is either very important in the total investment picture or capital markets are highly segmented, the result may as well be an increase as a decrease in investment, at least in theory. In practice, however, one would normally expect the imposition of a tax on any particular form of investment, including that in land, to lead to a decline in it, and, consequently, to an increase in the price of goods produced by the agricultural sector. This presumably undesired result is a reason for exempting as many improvements as possible from the land tax in countries like Jamaica and Uruguay. Since it is administratively highly desirable not to attempt to distinguish all improvements from bare land value (see Chapter 11), however, there will in the general case probably always be some disincentive effect to the use of land and probably to agricultural production from any feasible land tax. If the marginal rate of the tax is fixed in the short run, however, the disincentive may only be minor, as noted in the next chapter.

INCIDENCE WITHIN THE AGRICULTURAL SECTOR

How the burden of the land tax is distributed among the economic groups within the agricultural sector is an even more difficult question than the extent to which the burden is shifted between sectors. The possibilities for intrasectoral shifting depend upon the nature of the economic relationships among the groups living in the agricultural sector. The analytical problem is enormously complicated by the variety and complexity of these relationships and by their dependence upon local institutional factors that restrict the free interplay of economic forces. In many respects, therefore, the problem does not lend itself to analysis in terms of general principles of tax shifting; instead, it must be examined in the context of a particular tax in a particular country and with the aid of as much inductive evidence as possible.

Land taxes are paid initially either by landowning or tenant groups. The remaining economic groups in agriculture—landless laborers, traders, and moneylenders—may share the tax incidence only if some part of the tax is shifted from the original payers either backward or forward through adjustments in the prices paid or received by landlords or tenants. (Insofar as the normal land tax includes in its base not only agricultural land but also the land, and perhaps buildings, of traders and others in rural villages this argument must of course be amended.)

One way in which taxes may be shifted within the agricultural sector is through the operation of government regulations: for example, an increase in the land tax might be accompanied by an upward adjustment in the official prices paid by traders for crops purchased from farmers, or by a lowering of the legal rate of interest charged farmers, or by the subsidized sale of feed, seed, or fertilizer. Such price adjustment, if effective, would be a form of tax shifting because it would provide partial tax relief to the immediate taxpayers. Although wages paid to farm laborers are sometimes subject to government control, it is difficult to conceive of a situation in which a government would attempt to enforce tax shifting to laborers, who are usually the lowest-income group in agriculture. It is more probable that wage controls will seek to prevent shifting to laborers.

If the land tax does not curtail agricultural production, the basic supply-and-demand relationships determining wages and interest rates will be unchanged.[12] No shifting of the tax to factors of production other than land would, in these circumstances, occur through market adjustments.

The problem cannot be dismissed so simply, however, because of likely restraints on the operation of market forces and because tax shifting might assume subtle forms that are not readily noticed by the parties who are affected. For example, employers who are required to pay an increased tax might respond by economizing on the housing furnished laborers or on other forms of wage payments in kind. In countries where wage rates in agriculture are determined largely by custom, where labor is unorganized and lacks political strength, and where workers tend to be immobile, backward shifting of this sort cannot be effectively resisted. Even a reduction in money wages may be possible in the absence of active competition for workers.

The payment date for most land taxes comes at harvest time. This timing is convenient for the tax collectors but not necessarily for the farmers, who may be forced to sell their crops when prices tend to be at a seasonal low. If the necessity of raising funds to meet taxes depresses the prices obtained by farmers, the tax is made doubly burdensome on them, while traders' or moneylenders' profits may tend to increase, reflecting the increased return on holding stocks of agricultural commodities, which farmers are unable to do. The plight of farmers will be aggravated if, because of the timing of the collection of the tax, they are pushed further into debt.

Aside from the price inelasticity of production, perhaps the paramount consideration with respect to the possibilities for tax shifting through price adjustments other than rent is that traders and moneylenders are likely to have the upper hand in dealing with farmers and are able, therefore, to protect themselves against tax shifting, unless they can somehow be prevented from doing so by legislation. Agricultural laborers are probably in the weakest bargaining position of any group in the economy. The fact that in most countries they earn little if any more than a bare subsistence may be an effective barrier against much of the tax being shifted their way.

If the preceding avenues of tax shifting are without much practical significance and if for some reason the prospect of forward shifting to consumers is also limited, then land taxes imposed on landowning groups which do not rent—peasant cultivators, plantation owners, and communal units—are unlikely to be shifted.

Finally, there is the possibility of tax shifting between landlords and their tenants. If it is assumed that the amount of land available for rental is unaffected by the tax and that rents are competitively determined so as to equate the supply of and demand for the available land, a land tax imposed initially on owners will, as noted earlier, not be shifted to tenants because the owners will not be in any more advantageous position to obtain higher rents after the imposition of the tax than before. A tax imposed initially on tenants in these circumstances would, however, be shifted to owners because marginal tenants would be unwilling to continue renting if landlords did not make allowance for the tax and persisted in collecting rents at the old rates. If some tenants decided to drop out of the rental market rather than pay the tax, competition among profit-maximizing landlords for the remaining tenants would force a reduction in rents or otherwise some cultivable land would remain idle. Rental relief granted initially to only part of the tenants would similarly gradually spread to all of them through the working of competition.

It has long been argued that sharecropping systems, in which the rent paid varies with gross output, engender tenant insecurity and hence deter innovation and intensified cultivation.[13] The same is true of a tithe or ad valorem excise tax on output. In principle, a fixed rent or tax, whether in cash or kind, gives the tenant more to gain from increasing production and seems therefore more conducive to risk-taking and effort, although a fixed levy too may squeeze out marginal producers if it exceeds their returns.

These contentions are debatable. In the first place, sharecropping has the virtue from the tenant's point of view of ensuring that he is not squeezed out by fixed obligations in bad years, since rent is reduced when output is low. He is also insulated against falling prices if, as is usual, the rent is levied in kind. The greater security provided by sharecropping arrangements may thus offset the admitted deterrent to innovation of having to share the gains also.[14] In the second place, landlords, like tax assessors, are likely to press fixed rents upward if production in fact increases. In the third place, it has recently been argued that there is no more reason to expect misallocation of resources under sharecropping than under any other form of tenure.[15]

Basically, the argument is that the percentage increment taken in rent by the landlord is itself determined in part by economic forces, so that the optimal amount of land will tend to be used. Of course, if the amount of land in production is nonoptimal, gross rural product will be lower than it should be. Also, even if it is optimal, population pressure or rapid productivity increases such as those resulting from the Green Revolution may create a new disequilibrium situation, the solution to which may well be to expand land utilization through, for example, the provision of easy credit.[16]

One implication of this analysis is that the tithe, that now largely vanished levy, may well not have been as black as it has generally been painted. Similarly, the fixed nature of a land tax paid in money may be a curse as well as a blessing, as both Japanese and Indian experience in the nineteenth century at times suggested (see Chapter 6). As always, the appropriate procedure is a complete and thorough examination of the particular circumstances of each case rather than a blanket condemnation of particular fiscal instruments, even (or especially!) old ones.

When rental rates are determined by local custom or by law, rather than by competitive bidding in an active rental market, they respond slowly, if at all, to changes in land taxes. An additional source of rental inflexibility also exists when land is under long-term leases.

Adjustments to tax pressures need not take the form of a change in the landlord's stated share or in the actual rental payment. They may occur through a change in the allocation of production costs between owners and tenants. An owner who finds his tax liability increased may decide, for example, to stop providing plowing livestock or to give the tenants less seed than formerly. Although the respective obligations of owners and tenants are usually defined by custom or legislation, leeway for variations always exists in practice. Any leeway will generally be under the control of the owner rather than the tenant; thus it will facilitate tax shifting by the former to the latter, but not the reverse.

Another aspect of landlord-tenant relationships warrants attention in this connection. By definition, a true competitive rent is a "rack rent," or a rent which reserves to the owners the maximum possible share of the produce. In the densely populated areas of the world, such a rent would be ruthless in its impact on tenants. Rental practices are undeniably harsh in many countries, as evidenced by the miserably low living standards of the tenants and by the necessity for governmental action to protect tenants from excessive exactions. Paternalism is not entirely absent, however, and it may well be that many landlords do not exploit their position to the fullest possible extent. They may, instead, collect rents that are lower than those that would be established if the impersonal forces of competition were controlling.

Whenever the actual rent is below a rack rent, owners may take advantage of the opportunity, within the limits of the law, to shift part of a tax increase onto their tenants, provided that the tenants can absorb it without being pushed to starvation level. On the other hand, if tenants are the liable taxpayers and their taxes are increased, it would probably be of little avail for them to apply to the owners for more favorable rental terms unless they have a bargaining weapon in the form of alternative employment possibilities. Where rents are controlled, tenants may also gain relief from taxes through the government's manipulation of the rent ceiling.

In summary, it appears that intrasectoral shifting of that portion of land taxes that is neither shifted to consumers nor capitalized in lower prices is likely to be important only with respect to the division of the tax between landowners and tenants. For a variety of reasons farm laborers, traders and moneylenders tend to be insulated from the impact of land taxes. Impersonal economic factors are most likely to be important as determinants of the direction and extent of intrasectoral shifting in countries where land is relatively plentiful and landlords must compete for tenants. A tax on landlords in such countries will tend to remain with them and not be shifted to tenants, except when the tax reduces the supply of land under cultivation; whereas a tax on tenants might well be passed on to landlords because it would tend to discourage some tenants from seeking land to farm. The opposite conclusion holds for countries which are land poor. Land taxes may well be shifted to tenants unless they are somehow protected by governmental regulations. Tax shifting from tenants to owners would not seem likely in densely populated countries, although governments may conceivably compel owners to share in a new tax imposed on tenants.

9

ECONOMIC EFFECTS OF LAND TAXATION

The economic effects of land taxes are difficult to analyze without careful attention to the institutional organization of agriculture. A plantation, for example, may be analyzed like any other business firm, while the traditional *latifundia* is basically a unit of authoritarian political control and requires a quite different analytical framework. Whether the dominant tenurial form is peasant proprietorship, sharecropping tenancy, or commercial landholding is often a significant determinant of the effects of policy measures. When, as is common, different institutional settings exist within the same country, matters can be even more complicated. As Myrdal has well said: "In the absence of common valuations, a uniform response to common incentives and stimuli cannot be expected."[1]

Under any circumstances, for effort and production to be encouraged by government policy a number of conditions usually need to be satisfied.[2] There must, for example, be a desire for increased material welfare. There must also be a realistic expectation on the part of the innovator that change will in fact increase wealth and that he himself will participate in the net increase in wealth that accompanies successful innovation.

The idea that peasant farmers are unresponsive to economic opportunities has been refuted by many studies in recent years. There is now an impressive body of evidence that the behavior of farmers everywhere can be largely understood within the framework of traditional economic analysis. As Hunter put it: "The peasant may be uneducated: but he is an adult, he is experienced, and he has as high a degree of intelligence as any of us. He has time to think and calculate, and, within the limits of vision, his reckoning is right."[3]

No one who examines agricultural practice throughout the world can fail to be impressed with the tremendous diversity and complexity of the tasks facing farmers in most poor countries—and by the obvious need to reduce this complexity to manageable proportions by means of ritual and traditional rules.[4] To quote Hunter again: ". . . farmers have repeatedly proved as good or better economists than those who advise them—and not unnaturally: their life depends on it."[5] When farmers fail to respond to the economic pressures created by taxation, then, the reason seems more likely to be an inability to bear the risk of loss or the expectation of being unable to get ahead in any case than it is sheer lack of interest in material well-being. This reasoning may or may not be based on accurate information, but it is clearly not irrational.

THE MARGINAL TAX RATE

The marginal tax rate, that rate at which the last increment of production or income is taxed, is the focal point of analysis when the economic effects of a tax are at issue.[6] In theory, an individual will be disposed to work harder or to invest more, the smaller the tax collector's share of the rewards for additional effort or investment.

In part, of course, the marginal tax rate depends on the rate schedule specified by law. Since many land taxes are imposed at proportional rates, the statutory rate often does not vary with the size of the tax base. In addition, the marginal tax rate depends on both the definition of the tax base and the frequency of reassessments.

Land taxes are usually assessed on the basis of either the estimated productive capacity of the land, as indicated by such factors as soil type, location of field, and availability of irrigation, or its estimated market value. The tax base, therefore, reflects primarily long-run values and is, in theory, relatively independent of the actual income which individual cultivators of varying skills and diligence are able to derive from working the land. Furthermore, tax valuations are generally only revised at long intervals. Thus, by reason of the nature of the tax base and of the infrequency of its revision, the tax tends to be a fixed annual charge against the land. For all practical purposes, the marginal rate of the land tax in the short run is therefore, in the usual case, zero.

A tax like the land tax will not tax an increment in production. The need to pay the tax will reduce the income available for other purposes, however, and this income effect would normally be expected to induce more effort and production—the more so the higher the marginal utility of income—or alternatively, as noted earlier, to encourage the sale of underutilized land. The effects of heavier land taxes on land use will in fact depend also on what happens to other taxes, for heavier taxes on land alone will of course make it a less attractive investment relative to other assets. On the one hand, then, since land taxes always tap some returns other than pure economic rent except perhaps in the very short run, there may be less investment in improving land as a result of the tax, while, on the other hand, there will be an incentive to utilize land more efficiently in order to pay the tax.

The most common argument appears to be, as noted in Chapter 1, that a tax on land value or on the presumptive net income of all rural land, regardless of the actual type of production or degree of exploitation, will increase agricultural productivity by inducing owners to bring idle land into use and by increasing the efficiency with which land already in production is utilized. In the case of a tax on presumptive income, for example, the tax acts as a penalty to underutilization until the return on the land equals the presumed amount. Once actual returns are higher than the presumed rate, since the marginal rate of tax on the excess is zero, there is every incentive to earn still more.

All this is true enough, in the short run. But what will the farmer do with the extra income (after tax) he receives from increased production? Since presumptive income taxes, like land taxes, are often based in one way or another on assessed property values or on certain characteristics of the land, new investment in land may over time raise the assessed value, and thus the presumptive income and the tax, unless great care is taken to assess only bare land values—the "original productivity of the soil"—a most difficult, complex, administratively costly task, and inherently almost impossible.

Some land taxes have marginal effective rates greater than zero. Tithe-like levies and taxes on marketed produce, for example, are assessed on the basis of current actual production or sales. Farmers subject to these taxes can ordinarily expect the government to take some part of any increase in output. (By the same token, of course, the government will also share with farmers the burden of a reduction in production.) These taxes would therefore appear to create more of a deterrent to innovation and effort than other forms of land taxation.

In some situations the marginal rate of tax may play a crucial economic role. If, for example, submarginal land could be brought into production through reclamation, irrigation, or other means of land development, taxing the newly reclaimed land or its produce would clearly reduce the return to the developers. Where the prospective return (exclusive of tax) was not overly attractive in the first place, the imposition of a tax might be sufficient to deter potential developers. The deterrent effect would of course vary with the size of the tax in the event that the land became productive.

Many countries seeking to encourage land development have therefore expressly exempted reclaimed land from taxation for a stated number of years. Tax administration practices which delay placing rehabilitated land on the tax rolls for several years can serve the same purpose as statutory tax exemption. Two points might be made about these and similar exemptions. First, the rate of tax in most countries is so low that the stimulus provided by such policies would be miniscule at best. Secondly, insofar as land reclamation is due to public rather than private investment, not only should the reclaimed land not be exempted, but it should also, if possible, be subject to special betterment levies designed to recoup the public expenditures which have resulted in increased private land values.

Other investment would appear less likely to be affected by the marginal tax rate. In many instances assessment formulas look only to the economic value of the land alone, irrespective of improvements on it. In these cases farmers contemplating many types of new investments need have little fear of subjecting themselves to increased taxation.[7] Investments needed to maintain the fertility of the soil will enter into the tax base and hence, as noted earlier, will tend to be deterred by the tax.

Even when the law requires inclusion of the value of improvements in the base of a land tax, there is a high probability that the assessments lag well behind reality. Especially in countries with price inflation, the deterrent effect of the tax will thus be minimal. On the other hand, where tax assessments are based not upon inherent soil characteristics but upon outward evidences of productive wealth such as actual crops or the tangible assets possessed by the farmer, the prospect of a heavier tax might discourage the acquisition of new wealth, just as any taxation of capital may be expected to differentially favor investment in human rather than nonhuman wealth. Neither effect seems likely to be of major significance, however, given the low rate of most actual land taxes.

On the whole, the potentially favorable incentive effects of exempting improvements would seem to be smaller in agricultural areas than in cities where improvements represent a larger proportion of the tax base. Moreover, business decisions to invest in residential, commercial, and industrial buildings are likely to be more closely tied to detailed calculations of expected profits than are the investment decisions of a typical farmer.

More important from an economic standpoint than the policy with respect to taxation of improvements on agricultural land is the policy with respect to taxation of marginal producers. Imposition of a tax on a field which is capable of yielding only a bare subsistence standard will either force the land out of production or else so impoverish the cultivator that he cannot possibly become an efficient producer. A farmer barely able to feed and clothe himself and his family is unlikely to be interested in soil conservation and cannot risk experimenting with new techniques of cultivation. Moreover, economic incentives are easily blunted by poverty. All land taxes which fail to provide adequate allowances for production costs, including the risk of crop failure and the cost of transportation to market, are potentially damaging to production for these reasons.

This point is especially significant in view of the apparent importance for the achievement of developmental objectives in most countries of the introduction and widespread adoption of new technology in agriculture. It is, indeed, surprising that more attention has not been paid to the effect of taxes on social risk taking and to the possible use of fiscal incentives in this connection.

The primitive farmer can be viewed as an optimizing risk averter.[8] His aim is less to maximize profits than to survive. Security, like status, is an important goal for him. If he is to be induced to adopt new, risky techniques, the potentially terrible price of failure will have to be reduced.

It is curious that the voluminous literature on the use of land taxes to penalize nonproductive farmers is not matched by much thought on how to reward productive ones. Although it is clear, for example, that the risk attached to improvements in agricultural techniques will be reduced by imposing lower tax rates on increases in output than on "normal" returns, there is no equivalent under the land tax to the loss offset provisions of the income tax except for the often limited "hardship" provisions for relief. If, as has been argued, such factors as the creation and development of entrepreneurs, risk taking, and supply capacity are as much or more important to growth than allocative efficiency, more attention to the role of taxes in affecting these factors seems necessary.

Two initial points may be mentioned in this connection. First, any tax pressures to increase production will work much better in countries with a well-developed agricultural infrastructure, in which, for example, farmers will know that they will have ready access to credit at reasonable rates in order to help them survive in the event of failure. This consideration suggests that the incentive effects of increasing fixed land taxes might perhaps be stronger in semideveloped countries like Argentina or Chile than in poorer countries like Ethiopia or Nepal. Again, then, the effects of particular taxes cannot easily be analyzed without detailed reference to the institutional framework.

Secondly, if there are particular forms of innovation which are considered desirable, such as more use of fertilizer or water or tractors, a policy of subsidizing the favored input directly would seem to be much more efficacious than exemption (de facto or de jure) of increases in output. The problem with subsidy policies is, of course, that governments often know less than farmers what might work and how well. Some sort of general subsidy to change is often therefore preferable to specific input subsidies: again, however, cheap credit policies would appear more likely to succeed than tax exemption policies which do not help if the innovation results in disaster.

Another problem is that subsidies must be financed somehow. As noted earlier, some of the requisite resources may have to come from outside agriculture, but there would also seem no reason why those farmers who are successful should not be taxed to help those who encounter disaster. If the deterrent to innovation is, indeed, less the prospect of taxes on increases in output than the prospect of personal disaster in the event of failure, a tax policy which underwrote failure by taxing success might prove to encourage innovation more than one with a zero marginal rate. As suggested in Chapter 8, the much maligned tithe, when correctly administered, cushions losses by lowering the tax burden and thus partially redeems the disincentive created by the fact that it taxes success.

One useful way of gaining more knowledge on how to employ fiscal instruments to stimulate nonconventional inputs might be for national governments to underwrite fiscally and in other ways experimentation on less than a national scale, for policies like this might work better on the local level, where knowledgeable judgment on the contribution of personal effort to success or failure could be brought to bear. Although political circumstances and administrative constraints are a serious problem in most countries, limited experiments along these lines are even more necessary in the developing countries, with their greater needs and lesser knowledge, than they are with respect to social and economic policies in the industrial countries, where this approach is coming into vogue.

EFFECTS ON PRODUCTION

Three views on the supply response of traditional farmers can be perceived: (1) it is no different than that of anyone else to relative price changes; (2) institutional constraints ("human inelasticity") make any supply response to price changes negligible or perverse; (3) marketed surplus in particular may be inversely related to price, either because farmers have relatively fixed monetary obligations and a high marginal utility for food consumption or because the income effect outweighs the substitution effect. In analyzing these views, one must distinguish, for example, the effects on total production from those on marketed surplus and from those on a single crop, as well as consider the relevant time period (tree crops have longer gestation periods and hence may—not will—respond more slowly).

The question about supply response is essentially an empirical one, and most empirical studies appear to support the hypothesis that farmers in poor countries respond significantly and substantially to economic incentives.[9] The evidence is especially strong for production of particular commercial crops. The heavy Thai taxation of rice, amounting at times to about 30 percent of the export value of rice, appears, for example, to have affected supplies and export earnings adversely.[10] This adverse effect may have been partly offset through beneficial pressure to diversify, which may have moved the country closer to its real comparative advantage position or at least reduced uncertainty and risk, but this seems unlikely.

From a tax point of view, important factors in determining the nature and strength of such effects are the extent to which food crops are involved, the length of the gestation period, and the tenurial situation. Thai tenurial systems, for instance, appear to provide no barrier to the operation of economic incentives. Furthermore, since the price elasticity of the marketed surplus of Thai rice should be greater than that of total supply, a reduction in export taxes and hence a rise in domestic prices should lead to a response in marketed output. In general, as one would expect, the elasticity of supply is greater when other economically profitable crops can be grown, regardless of tenancy, literacy, or any other factor.

Not all agree with this assessment, of course. It has, for example, been argued that in other parts of South Asia, where over two-thirds of agricultural production is consumed within the agricultural sector itself, most farmers are still so poorly fed that their response to an increase in agricultural prices is likely to be to sell less and consume more. On the other hand, since nutritional deficiencies are marked, more food intake will tend to increase production somewhat, so that the net effects of a change in prices on marketed output are far from clear even in this extreme case.[11]

Whatever the theoretical case may be, another lesson suggested by experience in various lands is that higher or "better" land taxes alone will likely do little to increase production unless, at the same time, roads and marketing organization are improved, price policy is correctly structured, and needed inputs, including credit, are provided. Without these conditions, economically rational farmers cannot realistically be expected to believe that risk-taking innovation would indeed improve their position in life.

Land taxes may also influence the composition of production. The opportunities for such influence tend to be limited in economies dominated by a single crop or where the land is not readily adaptable to growing other crops. Some diversification in production is almost always present, however, and in many countries growing conditions favor a wide range of crops. The possibility of redirecting agricultural output is especially great where cash crops are grown, because of the more market-oriented attitude of cultivators and their greater use of purchased inputs. Rice producers have, as noted above, proved very responsive in this regard. Other commercial crops, which usually constitute only small portions of the total cultivated land, can have an even more elastic supply response than a crop like rice or most subsistence crops, which take up most of the cultivated area. Attempts to control food prices while allowing those of commercial crops to rise, as in India, may therefore sometimes result in an increase in the production of the latter at the expense of the former, which is presumably not the desired result.[12] Other goals of agricultural price (and tax) policy may be to encourage crops (or other forms of agricultural output) which promise higher returns relative to the input of productive factors, or are a lucrative source of foreign exchange, or are needed to improve national dietary habits.

Almost any type of land tax affords opportunities for favoring certain kinds of agricultural activity and penalizing others. For a tax to be neutral in its effects on the composition of production, it would have to exact precisely the same proportion of net income from each product, thereby leaving undisturbed the relative attractiveness of different productive activities. When a tax exacts unequal proportions, it tends to encourage farmers to shift to more lightly taxed products. It is of course impossible to specify how sizable the tax differentials must be before such shifts will actually occur in specific circumstances.

With gross production or land area as the tax base, the tax may represent considerably different proportions of net income for crops that require relatively large outlays for seed, fertilizer, irrigation, and hired labor than for crops that are more easily cultivated, and the resulting differentials might be large enough to induce some shift of production. Marketing taxes also fall with uneven weight on net earnings from different kinds of output. Rental value taxes, based on either annual rental value or capital value, probably are more nearly neutral than most other types, since the rental value base allows for differences in the productive capacity of land. As seen in Chapter 11, the effects depend more on how the tax is actually administered than on the formal definition of the tax base.

All land taxes will of course have some nonfiscal effects even though these effects are indiscernible in most countries because of the extremely light weight of the tax. Such other factors as the absence of complementary inputs needed to increase production, the lack of marketing channels (or monopsonistic buyers), or the inability to innovate because of fear of losing in the "game against nature" also usually outweigh the importance of tax effects. Nevertheless, since tax effects on the composition of production do exist and are largely under the control of government, they should clearly be taken into account in the formulation of agricultural and tax policy. The rental value basis for land taxation scores most highly in both its basic neutrality and its susceptibility to conscious manipulation of nonfiscal effects.

Another point which deserves passing mention is that, if agricultural taxes result in lower domestic prices for agricultural inputs to processing establishments than they would pay on world markets, then in effect they constitute industrial subsidies. Export taxes are most likely to yield this result. It has been argued that in Tanzania, for instance, relatively low levels of export taxation on primary products may be used to offset the disincentive to domestic processing afforded by the high rates of effective protection (owing to higher rates of duty on more highly processed goods) imposed in many importing countries.[13] The effective protection of 160 percent in the European Economic Community for its processors of soybean oil could, for example, be offset by an export tax on soybeans of only 10 percent. Given the importance of protective policies around the world, this factor adds to the case made in Chapter 4 for careful re-evaluation of export tax policy.

EFFECTS ON MARKETING

An increased volume of agricultural marketings is sometimes a policy goal to support growing consumption requirements in urban areas, to expand exports, or to displace imports. At the same time, the proceeds of larger marketings may permit farmers to improve their own living standards or to acquire new productive equipment.

The fact that land taxes strike the nonmonetized sector (and self-consumed production) is thus both an administrative disadvantage and an economic advantage. While it is unlikely that land taxes per se have much effect in increasing output, they may have more effect on marketing because the need to have cash to pay them creates a money income effect. Supplies of food to urban areas might be increased and their price lowered, thus turning the terms of trade against agriculture. (The personal tax or hut tax can have similar effects if it is not limited to a money income base.) This move may or may not be beneficial from a development point of view. The argument that adverse internal terms of trade for agriculture will increase total saving and investment and allow a more rapid growth of the nonagricultural sector is counterbalanced by the fact that the same adverse trend will slow down or arrest the diffusion of innovations, the absorption of new inputs, the utilization of idle capacity, and the needed institutional adjustments fundamental to development.

In any event, those small-scale producers who are largely outside the money economy may be induced to bring more of their product to the market if their commitments for cash tax payments are increased. Otherwise, the chief impact of land taxation on the proportion of output made available to the nonagricultural sector will arise where there is a differential tax on the proportion marketed and the proportion retained for the farmer's own use. Since a marketing tax creates such a differential, it is generally a deterrent to the marketing of products.

Marketing taxes may be a more serious deterrent for farmers who are not oriented to the commercial market and, therefore, need to be induced to bring their products to the marketplace rather than deterred from doing so. The force of this objection to marketing taxes will, of course, vary with the particular conditions of agriculture in each country.

TAXES ON SURPLUS

A distinction is often made in theory between income that is economic surplus and income that is a necessary economic reward. A tax on the first type of income has no deterrent effects on production since the income that is taxed accrues to a passive agent. A tax on the second type, however, does tend to discourage production since the income accrues to an active agent and is necessary to induce economic activity. This fundamental contrast provides the conceptual foundation for the proposition that taxes on surplus income have unique qualifications as ideal revenue measures. A land tax based on pure economic rent, as defined in Ricardian theory, is one of the model taxes in this category.

This ideal type of land tax, however, is merely an intellectual construct. With the exception of "site value," the productive qualities of soil are exhaustible, and any tax on the value of these soil qualities acts as a deterrent to their replenishment. The rental value taxes found in many parts of the world today thus fail to satisfy the Ricardian prescription because the tax bases invariably include some return on the value of capital invested in the land.

A more workable approximation to a tax on "surplus" appears to be a betterment levy similar to the Colombian valorization tax outlined in the previous chapter. The incentive effects of betterment taxes are, for example, favorable to investment and development.[14] As a tax on pure site values, the betterment tax does not penalize development of unimproved land, and in practice its use will also probably lessen reliance (currently or in the future) on the regular property tax, which does penalize such development.

The payment of the tax itself is probably an even more important stimulant to investment, however, in practice and perhaps also in theory. It is often stated that a tax on site values should, in theory, have no incentive effects on land use since it does not affect the most profitable use of the land. This argument implicitly assumes that land is always an investment good. In fact, in developing countries much land is held idle not for speculative purposes, but to provide pleasure and prestige to its owners, so that it is in a real sense very often a consumer good. Under regular site value taxation, the income effect (there is no substitution effect) of site value taxation can be expected to lower this consumption since land is probably not an inferior good; land formerly used for consumption purposes may therefore be put to productive use as a result of the tax.

For the betterment tax the analysis is different since payment of the tax is, by definition, matched by an increase in the site value of the land. The improvements financed by betterment taxes increase the value of the land for productive purposes, not for prestige consumption, however. As a result, the tax and public investment combined increase the opportunity cost of using land for consumption purposes, so the substitution effect in this case also tends to induce more productive use of the land.

In practice, the effect of site value taxes in forcing more intensive land use may depend most on the lack of liquidity and capital markets facing many landowners and on the common failure of landowners to calculate carefully the most profitable use of their land. Owners may underutilize land when not faced with cash payments, but when a betterment tax must be paid they may either realize the opportunity cost of holding the land idle and hence put it to more profitable use in the monetary sector or they may have to sell it to someone else who will do so. Since the betterment tax is a relatively large tax assessed over a short period of time, its impact in forcing better land use through its effects on liquidity and attention to use should be stronger than a regular site value tax, where the rate may be too low to threaten the liquidity or arouse the interest in land use of most landowners.

In the underuse of land in developing countries a factor as important as the existence of large estates held for prestige purposes may be the large amount of land held by absentee owners, usually professional and commercial people from the cities, who cannot find good farm managers and who do not themselves have the time, inclination, or ability to provide good management. The analysis is the same as in the prestige case: under pure site value taxation the income effect might be expected to lead to greater owner work effort, probably in managing his land, while under the betterment tax the owner must supply greater effort and develop his land if he is to realize in cash the greater gross income it can now provide, or else sell the land to someone who will develop it. The effects are similar if the farm property is being held for recreational purposes.

A tax of this sort is also probably progressive since it is usually levied in some relation to property ownership, which is more unequally distributed than income in almost all countries, and it cannot be shifted. Using the more inclusive concept of the "fiscal residuum," the tax is neutral, for all taxpayers would receive benefits equal to or greater than the tax payment. Compared with alternative ways of financing public improvements, betterment levies probably favor the poor over the wealthy and yield a more equal income distribution. This presumption is somewhat confirmed by the fact that the strongest opposition to valorization taxes in Colombia has come from some of the wealthiest groups in the country.

EFFECT ON LABOR SUPPLY

The amount of labor employed in underdeveloped rural areas can be explained in many ways. One explanation, which is intuitively appealing to economists, is that the wage and amount of labor employed will depend on the nature of the supply and demand curves for labor, precisely as in conventional economic analysis. The wage rate will thus be determined at the point where the supply of labor equals the value of its marginal product, with the modification that up to some point higher wages will enable workers to increase their productivity through a better diet.[15] In these circumstances, wages and employment will be set at levels reflecting the degree of monopoly in the produce market and of monopsony in the labor market: the more concentrated either market—for example, because of geographical isolation or because of the feudal nature of the labor force—the lower wages and employment will tend to be. In the extreme, the result of rational market forces may be wages so low that calorie intake is insufficient for workers to be productive, or there may be substantial underemployment of both labor and cultivable land.

This analysis is not materially affected if we assume the supply curve for labor is normally sloped or, as some have argued, backward sloping, because workers work only until they reach a fixed target income. In view of the apparent significance of the demonstration effect, provided it is not damped too much by misguided "luxury" taxes on incentive goods, it would seem likely that the supply curve of labor is forward sloping in most rural areas today, even in countries with allegedly "unlimited" supplies of labor. Since increases in the demand for that labor undoubtedly raise its reserve price, from the employer's or landlord's point of view, as the number of workers increases, the wage offered should decrease because the marginal value of production per worker will decrease.

When wages are thus optimized, rents are of course maximized. If social pressure or government legislation were to force landlords to employ more people than this equilibrium amount, both wages and rents would fall. Both owners and existing tenants thus have an interest in creating employment on other than existing holdings, even if the new farms compete with the old. If wages are artificially kept higher than equilibrium and employment is also fixed, then the landlord's situation becomes truly an unhappy one, and one might anticipate substantial evasion of regulations by both parties or else the necessity of nationalization, which would not, of course, alter the underlying economic realities.

In a more general framework, the supply of labor may be taken to depend on the relationship between the farmer's preferences for leisure, income, and risklessness on the one hand and the technical characteristics of the cropping patterns on the other. Leisure demand depends in large part on social status and arrangements, while the demand for cash income depends on the availability of cash goods, financial commitments (including taxes), family size, and so forth. Security depends on all of these things, plus especially familiarity with the prospects before him (the degree of uncertainty). In terms of this model, then, "the higher the demand for cash, and the less strong the extended family system, and the less demanding the social organization in terms of time for social functions, the greater the income effect [of a tax] is likely to be in relation to the substitution effect."[16] That is, the economic analysis stressed earlier is sound, but it must always be remembered that it operates within a sociological framework which affects the magnitudes of the relevant variables.

For example, the conventional analysis of land held in common, a tenurial scheme particularly frequent in sub-Saharan Africa, is in effect that investment in such land is equivalent to the creation of a public good. We should therefore expect that factor utilization in such areas will be suboptimal because the fruits of any one man's investment will have to be shared equally with all of his fellows, whether they contributed anything or not.

Three resolutions to this problem are perhaps conceivable. First, privatize the common land. This is the most frequent recommendation of Western economists, and in their terms it makes a lot of sense. On the other hand, it also reflects a highly ethnocentric (albeit implicitly so) approach to communal land tenure and a failure to utilize the insights derivable from functional and evolutionary analysis as to the reasons for the existence of this tenurial system at the present time and in the light of history. In turn, this neglect reflects the economist's tendency to eschew "noneconomic" matters as beyond his ken and consequently of less importance than the aspects he can, and does, bring under his analytical gun. In this light, the privatization recommendation as it is commonly made smacks of an attempt to make uncomfortable reality accord with the dictates of a model with which the economist is familiar. It may indeed resolve the problem, but it cannot be simply assumed that it provides the only possible solution.

A second possible approach is to let the government provide the "public" good, that is, to accept the boundaries of property rights as now established and to attempt to approach the optimal allocation of resources via the political rather than the economic arena. The pitfalls of this path are well known. In brief, there is no *a priori* reason to anticipate strikingly better results than those already in existence since imperfections in the political market are even more prevalent than those in the economic market. Furthermore, the traditional tenurial pattern in a way already represents a "political" as well as an "economic" solution—though perhaps to different problems than those which concern the development economist.

A third approach recognizes that the geographic domain of common lands is, by definition, limited, so that in certain instances one might expect voluntary cooperative provision of investment in land (a "club good" in this case) to at least approximate optimality.[17] Again, the particular circumstances of each case require careful study before making facile generalizations on the inherent economic inefficiency of communal land tenure or on the effects of taxes on economic incentives in particular tenurial situations.

EFFECTS ON FACTOR MIX

In the long run, there is no doubt that in most countries the path to development lies in reducing the size of the agricultural labor force and in accelerated migration out of rural areas. In the short run, however, these objectives may conflict with those of increasing agricultural production and countering the apparent tendency to employ unduly capital-intensive means of production—a tendency which has, in many instances, been in part artificially created by other government policies. A proper factor mix in agricultural production may require more, not less, labor. Furthermore, the urgent need for more employment and to reduce the pressure, economic and social, arising from rapid migration to urban areas makes it even more desirable in some countries to increase agricultural employment opportunities.

Taxes may affect employment, factor mix, and migration in a number of ways. The basic policy that can be followed if one is concerned about this concatenation of factors is undoubtedly to improve the relative position of the farmer. In some countries, for example, a reduction in export taxes might be seriously considered for this reason alone. In general, then, so far as migration reduction is a policy goal, rural tax and other policies should be changed so as to favor rather than penalize farmers relative to industrial workers and urban residents.[18] Since, as we have already seen, most countries do not in fact tax farmers harshly now (other than through export taxes), there would appear to be little leeway for further concessions on this score, except perhaps to offset adverse nontax policies.

A more interesting question concerns the effects of taxes on choice of techniques. While a number of recommendations for tax change emerge out of an examination from this perspective—to reduce incentives to invest in capital goods; in some instances, indeed, to levy taxes on capital goods; and to reduce any special taxes on labor such as payroll taxes[19]—few of them are related to land taxes, so that the question, despite its importance, cannot be pursued too much further here.

A few additional points may be made, however. It has been argued that factor-saving innovation (of very different sorts) has been an important ingredient in both Japanese and American agricultural development. Incorrect factor prices might bias substantially, and undesirably, the direction of such induced innovation. Policies which increase the price of capital and land relative to that of labor would thus seem desirable in some developing countries, at least to the extent of offsetting reductions in the relative prices of these factors as a result of such government policies as tariffs and exchange controls. Similarly, if land taxes act to increase the cost of land relative to other factors, land-saving technologies, which tend to be labor-using, may tend to be induced. This point may be the most important economic argument for heavier land taxes in some countries.

The needed direction of input change will of course often vary among regions. In some it may be toward more water; in others it may be toward more machinery. A tax policy designed to induce the adoption of the optimal factor mix—or, more modestly, at least not to hinder it—will hence also differ from place to place and time to time. In Pakistan, for example, one analysis found a significant divergence between private and social net benefits from mechanization, owing largely to the undervaluation of capital and foreign exchange and the overvaluation of labor to the farmer interested in mechanization. The result was that mechanization was privately profitable but socially costly. To eliminate this divergence a direct tax on tractors of at least 200 percent was recommended.[20]

In this connection, however, it should be noted that the real problem is often that imported capital equipment is relatively underpriced so that those techniques involving the more sophisticated equipment, imported at overvalued exchange rates, are favored. Only these assets should be differentially taxed as a corrective measure. Further, farmers using family labor, since they cost labor well below the market wage, are likely to choose more labor-intensive techniques. The same results cannot be achieved by subsidizing wages paid by large farmers in view of the problems of financing the subsidies. But they can be approximated by raising the prices of capital-intensive techniques above their true social cost to offset the distortion in the labor market. The design of a tax policy intended to optimize factor mix can thus be a complex and subtle exercise, although one which might be worthwhile for many countries.

DISTRIBUTIVE AND ALLOCATIVE EFFECTS

The economic aspects of the distributional patterns of different taxes are many. In the first place, the extent to which taxation affects the allocation of production between consumption and investment is partly dependent on its distributional pattern. The risk that essential investment will be curtailed because taxes on upper-income groups will absorb necessary funds does not seem to be a serious one in many underdeveloped countries, where much of the private investment in agriculture does not require large cash outlays and where other factors are the chief obstacles to increased private investment.[21] Relatively heavy taxes on high-income cultivators and landlords will probably less often absorb funds needed for investment than funds that would otherwise be spent for luxuries or accumulate as idle savings. When this is the case, concern over the effects of taxes on savings and investment need not act as a restraint upon the progressivity of the tax system in the agricultural sector.

The distributional pattern of land taxation is in fact likely to be of more decisive importance because of its effects on the volume of private investment. In many countries there are large rural populations barely subsisting on extremely low annual incomes. To lift these people out of their poverty is more than a humanitarian goal; it is also an economic necessity, because poverty gives rise to much waste of manpower and productive talent. If the tax system is so heavy as to reduce the level of consumption of the mass of the rural population below the level of their maximum productivity, a reduction in taxation may actually increase production by reducing absenteeism due to illness as well as through the longer-range effects on the physical and mental growth and development of children. The increase in consumption might also, of course, lead in the long run to more and larger families, which is not an unmixed blessing.

For many land taxes the distributional pattern may often be regressive, so that the proportion of net income absorbed by the taxes declines as income increases. This is generally true, for example, when the tax base is gross production, assuming that the tax rate is proportional and not graduated, because of the failure of the base to include allowances for differences in unit costs of production. Fields producing the same gross harvests may yield substantially different net incomes. The pattern need not be regressive when the base is annual rental value or capital value, however. When properly assessed, rental value or capital value taxes distinguish between high-cost and low-cost productive units by making allowances for cost differentials attributable to the qualities of the soil, availability of irrigation, climate, accessibility to markets, and other factors affecting land value. These taxes, however, do not allow for net income differences traceable to the cultivator's skill and diligence. Furthermore, under prevailing administrative practices wealthy farmers generally seem to fare better with the tax assessors than taxpayers who are financially less well-off (see Chapter 10).

The more regressive the distributional pattern, the larger the relative impact of the tax on essential consumption and the smaller its impact on luxury consumption. In addition, a regressive pattern tends to widen existing income inequalities. Mose countries would probably prefer to avoid such effects and instead to distribute taxes so that they are paid primarily at the expense of nonessential consumption and uninvested savings. To achieve these results with a land tax alone may require both an exemption system and a tax base that represents a constant or a rising proportion of net income at successively higher income levels. The appropriateness of graduated tax rates also needs to be considered. The problem with all these ameliorative measures, of course, is that they complicate the administration of the land tax and hence remove one of its principal virtues. The equity aspects of land taxes are discussed further in the next chapter.

In countries which have had an equalizing of agricultural incomes, as, for example, from land reform, these distributional issues may recede in importance. An example of the possible effects of a land reform of this sort, which may be of some relevance in the circumstances of a number of Latin American countries, follows.[22] Suppose that there are two distinct land markets for different-sized farms, that the small farms are more efficient than the large ones, and that the tax is levied on the large sector only. The resulting fall in price of the large farms may make it more possible for the small farmers to buy them (or parts of them), with positive results on all sides. Alternatively, the large landowners may utilize the land more efficiently than before or rent it to someone who will do so. This will also increase output and probably employment, but it may make small farmers worse or better off depending on the competitiveness of the output of the two sectors.

The first possibility is that envisioned by those who would use land taxes to bring about land reform, and who see land reform as involving not only a better distribution of income and wealth but also as increasing total agricultural output (see Chapter 12). Unfortunately, despite the considerable number of times this model has at least implicitly been put forth, there is still almost no empirical evidence on the crucial links in it. Furthermore, as noted later, it is fatal to schemes of this sort to analyze them in a political vacuum since they must inevitably be implemented through the political system, and it is all too likely that the major reaction to them will take place in that same murky arena rather than in the clear cool atmosphere postulated in this kind of abstract theorizing.

As noted earlier, a key fact to remember in appraising traditional agriculture and its susceptibility to change is that many practices are intended to increase security. Where the margin of survival is small, risk taking is an expensive activity. Only those who can afford to do so will indulge in it, and, if government policy permits too wide a divergence between the few and the many, trouble lies ahead: ". . . the policy of 'backing winners'—encouraging the wealthy and better educated farmers—really involves, in peasant societies, a policy of 'the devil take the hindmost'; there are too many of the hindmost in peasant economies for this to be acceptable."[23]

It is mainly the poor who are most dependent on tradition for their livelihood and life. Changes may, therefore, mean not only enriching the farmers best able to take advantage of them, but ruining the weakest as well. The probably regressive nature of the shift of the tax burden within the agricultural sector as a result of the fact that the better-off farmers are, as recent experience with new technology has shown, much better able to take advantage of the carrots and to avoid the sticks created by tax measures is a troubling element of this mode of procedure, particularly in situations where the maldistribution of income is itself a barrier to progress.

The dual economy at the village level that is thus established is not only socially but economically dangerous. Furthermore, as noted elsewhere, there are in many countries strong economic arguments for a more equal distribution of incomes (size of the market, chance for talent), in addition to the desire to avoid destructive effects on smaller farmers, with a resultant increase in the landless unemployed.

If, as has been argued by some, one key to agricultural success for poor countries, especially those with high labor-land ratios, lies in the adoption of yield-increasing technology, it will undoubtedly be the wealthier farmers who will lead the way in innovating in the absence of a substantial governmental educational effort. Such farmers are better able to take risks and have greater access to information and a supply of innovations. This argument is disquieting. It suggests that for most countries the "Japanese path" to development is foreclosed by the need to build up a considerable infrastructure in order to spread the benefits of the new technology widely. The more likely model is then the "Mexican path" of "devil take the hindmost" which other countries seem to have taken in recent years, in part at the urging of economists conscious of the need for generating a larger agricultural surplus.[24]

This path is not one which countries are forced to follow because, for example, only large farms can introduce the new techniques or because only large farms are well managed. The size of the farm is technologically irrelevant for most of the new technology and, at least in some countries, it can be argued that small farms tend to be better managed.[25] The real deficiency leading to the choice of this path of "backing winners" lies in the extremely weak infrastructure of the public sector in most underdeveloped rural areas. In view of the probable social, political, and economic costs of thus accentuating rural inequality, however, and the desirability in many countries of retaining more people in the agricultural sector, there would seem reason to examine anew the feasibility of the Japanese approach of combining the generations-old wisdom of traditional farmers with the technology made available by modern science. Some efforts have already been made in this direction in India and elsewhere; more probably should be.

CONCLUSION

The discussion of this chapter is best summarized by reviewing a number of policy goals and commenting on how, in different initial conditions, different land tax instruments seem likely to affect their attainment. Some of these goals are ends in themselves. Some are means to more ultimate ends. In any case, all have been of policy concern in one country or another and hence have sometimes entered into the design of appropriate land tax structures. In all instances, it should by now go without saying that no direct inference of the policy suitability of one or another form or level of agricultural taxation can be drawn from a general discussion, no matter how detailed. In the final analysis what is good for a country can only be decided on the basis of a close examination of the actual situation and possibilities in that country, especially in regard to the state of the public administration on the one hand—since so many of the characteristics of land taxes depend upon how they are administered rather than on how they look in the statute book—and to the land-labor ratio on the other.

If land taxes are increased, and the revenue thus raised is not employed in the agricultural sector, the effect of the tax on agricultural production will depend primarily upon the relevant elasticities in the factor and product markets and secondarily on the form of the tax. Since the best forms of land tax in effect impose a short-run marginal tax rate of zero on increased production, and since the income effect of the tax induces in the normal case an attempt to recoup income, the production effects of the tax have often been considered to be positive.

This view is naïve, however. As a rule the land tax will inevitably impinge to some extent on investment and hence act as a deterrent to increasing production if one assumes, as seems reasonable in most cases, that some additional investment will have to be incurred in order to increase production. If the supply curve of land is completely inelastic, if all landowners are at their profit-maximizing position, and if all markets are perfect, the tax will have no disincentive effect on production. But these conditions are unlikely to be met, and, hence, one might expect some decline in output as a result of the tax.

As usual, general statements are dangerous, and it is not possible to make any prediction of the effects of the tax on production, whether positive or negative, without a close examination of the particular circumstances in question. Almost the only conclusion which can be drawn with much assurance is that export taxes and tithes are likely to be more discouraging to production than more strictly land-based taxes.

The effects of increased land taxes on marketed supply are very similar. One extra feature which requires comment in this context is that the levying of taxes payable in money only provides an extra stimulus to marketing and to monetization. A tax levied directly on marketing of course discourages it. Although many writers imply that anything which discourages marketing is detrimental to development, this is not necessarily true. If the result of less forced marketing is better-fed and healthier farmers, this is not only one of the desired ends of development in itself, but it is also likely, at the nutritional levels prevalent in the rural areas of many underdeveloped countries, to lead to more productive effort and then more production—and eventually more voluntary marketing.

The effects on prices of land taxes of course depend primarily on the effects on production and are therefore dependent on the particulars of each case. If production rises, relative agricultural prices would be expected to fall, other things being equal; if it falls, they will rise. The traditional view is undoubtedly that they will not rise, but for the reasons suggested above this is not certain. To the extent that they do, of course, the burden of agricultural land taxes will rest on the consumers of farm products, not solely on the farm sector itself.

The composition of production may be affected in a number of ways, intentionally or otherwise, by the tax structure. Heavy taxation of particular crops, through export taxes, for example, will reduce the relative attractiveness of those crops for producers and thereby deter their production. These effects may be particularly important in countries short of foreign exchange, as most less developed countries are. Very light taxation of land will favor the production of land-using crops such as livestock, with relatively low labor requirements, which may also not be particularly desirable.

As noted above, in the general case land taxes are likely to exert some, if not necessarily much, deterrent effect on investment in agriculture. A problem of particular interest in this connection is that, unless considerable care is exercised, the investments which are most likely to be deterred are those in the land itself, which are usually highly labor intensive in nature and make little if any use of scarce foreign exchange. This would be a most undesirable result in most less developed countries and would appear to suggest the desirability of approximating the site value basis of assessment as closely as possible. This point is discussed further in Chapter 11.

The effect of any particular land tax on the distribution of income is a very complex matter to analyze. Even ignoring the important question of the possible shifts of tax burden outside the farm sector, the distributional effect will depend on the distribution of land by income class, the valuation for fiscal purposes of landholdings of different sizes, and other factors which, as always, vary from place to place and time to time. As noted in the next chapter, however, even a proportional tax levied on land may well be progressive in its incidence, perhaps highly so, in most developing countries, given the great maldistribution of land which appears to be common. On the other hand, there is also much evidence to suggest that the per unit tax tends to be substantially higher on small than on large units, thus partly canceling this progressivity. The reasons for this result are in essence administrative, as discussed in the next chapters.

It should also be noted that the same zero rate of tax at the margin, which makes the land tax less of a disincentive to effort than most taxes also reduces substantially the "dynamic progressivity" of the land tax,[26] that is, makes it singularly ineffective at sopping up increases in income accruing to those groups whose incomes are rising rapidly with development. Since the benefits of the agricultural revolution appear in fact to accrue most rapidly to the already well-established, this means that the static progressivity of the land tax is also declining over time.

The remedy to these problems is, of course, to keep assessments more up to date, at the cost of losing the alleged incentive effect. On balance, few poor countries could probably afford to base their fiscal system on an inelastic and increasingly regressive land tax for the sake of some hypothetical incentive effects on production, although this policy might be sensible for a semideveloped country with other elastic revenue sources. A better policy for poorer countries would appear to be to improve the tax administration to make it more responsive to price and production changes as soon as possible and at the same time to foster, and hopefully spread, productivity increases through public expenditure policy. Undue concentration on supposed marginal benefits from this or that feature of the tax system carries with it the danger of detracting unduly from what is likely to be, for some time at least, the principal task of the land tax in most developing countries: namely, to produce an increasing amount of revenue in a noninflationary way.

One reason why the distributional effects of any tax are important is that a principal factor governing the composition of demand is the income distribution. The relationship is in reality interdependent since there will be effects on both the sources (income distribution) and uses (prices) side which, combined, will determine the outcome. If food prices rise as a result of a land tax, its effects are clearly regressive, though perhaps less so than if the tax is wholly absorbed by the generally poorer agricultural sector. In any case, a rise in domestic prices of mass consumption items will shift demand away from these items to other items, often with higher import content, thus accentuating possible development problems.[27] There is therefore something to be said for cheap food policies in some countries quite apart from their distributional and political effects, provided always that they do not get in the way of the more fundamentally important need in most countries to increase agricultural production. Again, part of the answer would seem to lie in appropriate public expenditure policy. To try to do too much with any tax instrument alone is to ask for ineffectiveness on all counts.

In principle, and very likely to at least some extent in practice, another effect of increasing land taxes will be to reduce land prices. The increased tax will also increase the cost of holding land out of use and will therefore tend to reduce land speculation and to encourage better land utilization. These factors may in total lead to an improvement in the distribution of land, as large landowners sell off their land in smaller parcels to smaller landowners who can now afford the lower prices and who are, in the nature of their operations, more likely to utilize the land efficiently in terms of prevailing factor endowments. Alternatively, the landlords may be willing to strike a more generous bargain with their tenants in the changed circumstances.

There is no reason to anticipate these results any more than their opposites, however, for the new tax would seem as likely to lead to more consolidation as less. For example, as noted elsewhere, the principal effect of the new yield-increasing technology which is being adopted in many developing countries has been to make the rich, at least the productive rich, richer. Heavier land taxes then are likely to lead to the sale of underutilized lands to those who have the resources to buy them and put them into use rather than to the small farmers who are already usually suffering from the competition of the successful rich.

It should also be noted that, if the effect of a land tax is to reduce the real value of land held by farmers, its effects on savings may well be slightly positive according to conventional economic theory. Its effects on risk taking are likely to be the opposite, however, particularly if it presses hardest upon those at the lower end of the wealth distribution who lack the security, and in some cases even the strength, to take chances anyway.

The effects of land taxes on work effort were discussed above. Their effects on population are ignored here as too problematical and insignificant to be worth a word. Their effects on migration would seem to rest more on their weight than their form, except insofar as their form affects the degree to which the tax burden is shifted outside of agriculture. In general, the considerations of employment and urbanization which are coming to have such weight in so many countries suggest strongly that this is not the time to attempt to get large new revenues out of agriculture, for the more successful the effort the greater the impact on migratory flows.

On the other hand, employment in the rural areas may be increased by encouraging the use of land-saving technology, which is also as a rule labor-using. To be successful, a policy of this sort will require substantial government support in other areas, but it would appear that a strong case could be made on this ground in a number of countries at the present time for levying heavier land taxes. These taxes would raise the relevant price of land (the annual marginal outlay required to keep it in operation) and provide a stimulus to economize on its use, while the revenues yielded could be utilized to provide necessary complements to increased agricultural production such as access roads, water, fertilizer, and education. Many of these expenditures might most efficiently be carried out at the local level, where the tax revenues might also be most readily forthcoming (see Chapter 12).

In the end, this quite different rationale to that often put forward in the literature seems to provide the most persuasive case for increased land taxes in many countries today. Land taxes may not, as is often claimed, always lower land prices, provide incentives to higher production, or facilitate the transfer of resources out of agriculture. In any case, these objectives may not have the highest priority for many countries right now. A more important argument for land taxes in these countries may simply be that they encourage the more efficient utilization of land which in turn, if factor prices are not badly distorted by other inappropriate government policies, will lead to the employment of more labor on the farm. At least to some extent this alleviates a major economic and social problem and helps the country utilize all of its available resources more efficiently. Land taxes may indeed produce some revenue for transfer out of agriculture. What is more important, however, is that, in conjunction with special assessments, they may be able to provide, in a more economically and politically acceptable way than any other levy, the money needed for expenditures within agriculture that will increase agricultural production, increase agricultural employment, and, at the most optimistic, induce appropriately biased innovation.

10

EQUITY ASPECTS OF TAXING LAND

A common approach to the study of agricultural taxation is simply to assume that "heavy agricultural taxation can do wonders from the point of view of economic development."[1] The only question to be examined, then, is whether the heavy taxes can be supported by the "taxable capacity" of the agricultural sector. Laborious statistical exercises along these lines have now been carried out in a number of countries.

The usual result of these studies is to demonstrate that the "burden" of taxation is relatively lighter on agriculture than on the nonagricultural sector. The average tax burden (including inflation "tax") in the Brazilian rural sector in 1962–1963, for example, has been estimated at 5 percent compared to 21 percent in the urban sector.[2] The comparable figures for India were 4 percent and 9 percent, respectively.[3] In India, it has been further argued, the higher-income groups within the agricultural sector are especially "undertaxed" relative both to those of comparable income levels outside agriculture and to low-income farmers. The inference usually drawn from these results is, of course, that there is a prima facie equity case for increasing agricultural taxes.

This sort of information is certainly interesting and valuable for some purposes. The general usefulness of this sort of study is suspect, however. In the first place, there are very substantial difficulties in measuring both sectoral "capacity" to pay taxes and the "burden" of existing taxes. These problems are much more than statistical, serious though the latter are. "Tax burden" tables, for example, even apart from the inevitably disputatious nature of the many arbitrary assumptions needed to construct them, cannot really yield any useful information about the distribution of the tax burden, because the basic assumption underlying the exercise—that the pretax distribution of income would be the same if the tax system did not exist—is palpably false.[4] This is not to deny that comparison of two such tables might not yield useful information on the distributional effects of potential tax changes, a purpose for which these burden studies might prove useful, but it does mean that such statements as "per capita net burden . . . forms 3.22 percent of the per capita income of an agriculturist in India"[5] have no real meaning.

Secondly, there are of course a great many governmental policies other than taxes which affect the intersectoral allocation of resources: the protective effect of tariffs and foreign exchange systems, subsidies, credit policy, and so on. While at least one recent study of India has gone a long way toward dealing with this aspect of the question,[6] the use of these studies as a basis for policy inferences is still highly questionable. The desirability of higher taxation of agriculture, or of particular groups within the agricultural sector, must be assessed in light of its effects on the relevant objectives of national policy, not merely in terms of static indexes of tax capacity and tax effort. One danger of the burden approach is that it leads to overconcentration on relative burdens and inadequate attention to absolute burdens, effects on agricultural saving and investment, and other things that are generally much more relevant from the point of view of developmental tax policy.

Even for hortatory purposes, the results of comparing indexes of intersectoral tax burdens seem likely to convince only those who were already convinced. It is, for example, very hard to know exactly what "intersectoral equity" means. The relevant standard of equity in these studies appears to be that the same proportion of income should be taken in taxes from each sector of the economy. Sometimes the tax ratios are adjusted for differences in average per capita income, but never do they get much more sophisticated than this. In view of the wide discrepancies between sectors in the level and distribution of incomes and in the availability of government services, it is hard to see why this standard should be particularly compelling as an equity guide to policy. The meaning to be attached to intersectoral burden index comparisons within a country is at least as subject to conceptual and statistical questions as similar comparisons among countries.[7]

THE EQUITY OF LAND TAXES

The traditional equity case for subjecting land to special discriminatory taxation is that land values primarily result from the bounty of nature, public investment, and the presence, efforts, and investment of individuals other than the landowner. Land is therefore qualitatively different from other forms of property and can be properly subjected to special taxes. As Wald noted in his severe and generally convincing criticism of this line of argument, however, it is hard to see that this position has much merit in the rural areas of most less developed countries.[8]

A case for land taxes can still be made on equity grounds, however. Through use of land taxation, for example, it is easier to reach a broad income base, including the nonmonetary income which is so important in the predominantly subsistence agricultural economies of many countries. Home-produced food and fuel, the imputed value of owner-occupied dwellings, and similar nonmonetary forms of income may amount to a very large proportion of total rural income, and not just that of the poorest groups. The complete exclusion from the tax base of nonmonetary incomes which are unequally distributed would result in substantial departures from any attempt to attain some standard of taxpaying capacity. Land taxes act to offset this tendency.

Similarly, like any tax on nonhuman wealth, property taxes have some special justification in that they act to offset the discrimination in favor of property income inherent in most income taxes. There is no question that income from labor ought, in an equitable tax system, to be taxed more lightly than an equal amount of income from property. The reason is simply that property income, dollar for dollar, is obtained with less effort and more permanency than income from work. It is therefore more "pure" or "net" than income from the sale of personal services. One way of compensating for this bias in the income tax is to levy supplementary taxes on property income, or on property itself.

In addition, the possession of wealth provides advantages of opportunity, flexibility, and security (for example, in the face of income fluctuations) over and above the income enjoyed from the employment of capital. It is therefore in itself an appropriate subject for differential taxation. A wealth tax is thus needed to complete an equitable tax structure, especially when there are important forms of wealth which do not produce anything recognized as taxable income.[9] Furthermore, land taxes may have special justification in terms of ability to pay in poor countries in which real property typically constitutes a large part of wealth, and where property ownership is much more concentrated than income.

Land taxes thus have some justification as a form of wealth taxation. Their defects in this respect are serious, however. They apply to gross wealth of one type only. They are often regressive in their incidence, owing in part to the way they are administered. If heavy, they may cause an unpalatable degree of hardship for those with low cash incomes. Above all, they are hard to administer fairly and effectively in practice, given the very limited administrative resources of most poor countries.

Whatever the merits of the equity arguments for land taxation, it is thus unlikely that the results in practice of most land tax systems accord closely with the conventional norms of either horizontal or vertical equity. Expediency, that great fiscal criterion, perhaps justifies the violation of horizontal equity which any nongeneral tax gives rise to as a result of differences in the asset preferences of taxpayers.

As for the alleged adverse distributive effects of land taxes, two counterarguments are possible. First, it is the distributive impact of the fiscal system as a whole, not that of each tax, that is relevant from an equity point of view. Secondly, it is well established that wealth is distributed more unequally than income and that agricultural land constitutes a substantial part of wealth in most poor countries. To some degree, therefore, land taxation, even if proportional in rate, is likely to contribute something to redistribution. Even a roughly classified area-based land tax may in some instances prove to be surprisingly progressive in its incidence.[10]

In an effort to strengthen the redistributive effects of land taxes, they are frequently levied at progressive rates. When considering the possible desirability of levying progressive taxes on land, two factors must be kept clearly in mind. First, a tax on land is not a tax on persons. It therefore cannot be made progressive as among persons with any degree of distributive efficiency. Any attempt to discriminate among individuals on the basis of either the value or size of land-holdings alone is inherently quite arbitrary.

No tax on real property can be easily modified to take explicit account of the taxpayer's net economic position relative to others largely because, even in the rural economy of developing countries, real estate is only one form of wealth. In practice, as noted earlier, attempts to levy taxes on total net wealth in poor countries usually become taxes on real estate and, hence, subject to the same strictures. Two particular problems with more refined attempts to tax net wealth through personalized land taxes are that the tax may be shifted in part and that the attribution of debts to this particular part of wealth opens many possibilities for evasion.

The second point on the desirability of progressive land taxes has already been noted above. Whether any particular tax is progressive or not is of relatively little importance compared to the question of the incidence of the fiscal system as a whole on the distribution of private incomes (which is itself a very hard thing to determine). The only policy-relevant point is whether the entire fiscal system has a progressive impact or not.

Progressive land tax rates should therefore probably never be attempted at the local level. The appropriate place for redistributive fiscal policy is at the national level, and the degree of progressivity of any one levy is meaningful only in the context of the total system of taxes at all levels of government. More important, it has proven impossible in practice, even in highly developed countries, to avoid artificial splitting up of properties in order to escape the higher marginal rates. This problem is especially acute since the higher ranges of the rate schedule usually apply in practice mainly to larger land-intensive agricultural enterprises. As argued in the remainder of this chapter, attempts to personalize the land tax generally succeed only in making it more complex, which in turn both makes the administrative task more difficult and also affords more opportunity for opponents to block and weaken its impact.

IMPERSONAL (IN REM) FORM

Most land taxes outside of the Latin countries are cast in an impersonal, or in rem, mold. The main legal characteristic of an in rem tax in theory is that the tax liability is limited to the assessed property and does not extend to any other assets of the taxpayer. On the other hand, the liability is clearly attached to the property and not to the more elusive owner.

The economic distinction between personal and impersonal taxation, on the other hand, turns upon whether the amount of the tax is determined with reference to the status of the liable taxpayer. The source of the tax payment has no bearing upon the distinction, since all taxes, regardless of their form, must ultimately be paid out of personal income or wealth. Nor is the object of assessment a valid criterion for this purpose since, with the exception of a head tax, all taxes are apportioned according to some impersonal magnitude such as the value of property, income, production, or transactions.

In its origins, the land tax was doubtless conceived as a method of personal taxation. In mainly agricultural economies, land value or produce is not a bad measure of taxpaying capacity. In medieval Europe, for example, the common levy was a cattle and land tax, similar to those existing in much of Africa today.[11] As the forms of tangible wealth multiplied, however, the land tax in most countries became an essentially impersonal levy.

The impersonal form finds its clearest expression in those land taxes which employ a rental value concept, measured by either annual or capital value. Although land taxes often attempt to promote the equitableness of the tax burden distribution, the aim is necessarily an equitable distribution of taxes among different farms, rather than among different farmers. Moreover, the concern is with equity only within one segment of the community, the agricultural sector. Even within that sector, the degree of equity actually achieved is ordinarily far from complete because of the generally conspicuous lack of success at the administrative level.

The impersonal character of land taxation may be evidenced in numerous ways. For example, there is the Indian practice of a "land settlement," which fixes the revenue demand for a considerable period of years. Even when there is no formal settlement, land taxes in practice are seldom adjusted annually with income or rental value changes. In addition, most countries impose the tax at proportional rather than progressive rates, although the latter are frequently assumed to accord more closely with ability-to-pay considerations. When exemptions are allowed, they are usually to be explained as measures of expediency: for example, the saving in administrative costs resulting from an exemption of very small farms may more than make up for the revenue loss.

Another manifestation of the impersonal form of land taxes is that the tax is usually assessed separately on each plot of land, rather than on each taxpayer's aggregate holdings. Furthermore, it is levied at the situs of the property instead of at the domicile of the taxpayer, and the assessment customarily is made without regard to the existence of encumbrances on the land, such as a mortgage, that is, the land tax is a tax on gross, not net, wealth.

In one way or another, these practices and provisions of the law are related to the view that the land tax falls on property rather than on persons and, therefore, need not take note of the landowner's position. Clearly, however, land cannot have any taxpaying capacity apart from that of its owners, so many land tax systems provide for relief in cases of particular hardship owing to natural disasters or other uncontrollable events.

Only one argument can really be made in favor of the in rem form of land taxation: it may work. It avoids, for example, such overwhelming administrative disadvantages as requiring that the government must first determine who has the legal title before it can take any action to claim a property for delinquent taxes.

Those less developed countries which have attempted to apply more "personalized" land taxes with such commonly recommended features as progressive rate structures and aggregation of all lands owned by one individual or family have invariably encountered such substantial administrative difficulties that the tax has foundered in a morass of good intentions and bad execution, producing neither equity nor revenue.

The confused title situation in many rural areas is in itself sufficient to guarantee such endless litigation and argument that a more "personalized" form of land tax is unlikely to function well. When added to the possibilities for evasion and abuse discussed below, the invariable failure of personalized land taxes is not surprising.

Again, then, as at various other points throughout this study, careful consideration of experience throughout the world suggests that the protagonists of "personalized" land taxes have put their money on the wrong horse. What is needed in most developing countries is not the closest approximation to a personal income tax that the mind of man can fashion out of the unpromising timber of a land tax applicable to a large number of poor and illiterate people, but, rather, a simple mass tax that works. Levying the tax on an in rem basis is almost certain to be one ingredient of the successful formula to achieve this end.

It is perfectly true that this approach does not lend itself to many conceivable beneficial applications, but, much more important, it may aid in the establishment of a soundly functioning tax in the first place. It is the latter, not the former, which is crucially needed in most developing countries today. Once this has been done, additional refinements could be added later, if desired.

RATE STRUCTURE

A commonly desired characteristic of the revenue system in a developing country is that it be income-elastic. By this standard, taxes on land generally show up poorly.[12] The rigid rate structure and inflexible base characteristic of land taxes in most poor countries combine to reduce elasticity sharply. One way to overcome this problem would appear to be by relating the tax to actual output and prices, with, however, concomitant disincentive effects. Alternatively, a similar effect might be achieved by keeping assessments up to date or, as noted in the next chapter, by levying taxes in kind which ensure the treasury against the adverse effects of inflation.

Built-in revenue inflexibility of most land taxes is, as mentioned above, intensified by the rigidity of the rate structure. This rigidity is partly an administrative phenomenon: an invariable tax is easier to administer than one which must be calculated anew each year. Rigid rates appear also to have strong roots in the politics of taxation since few people anywhere are willing to provide governments with carte blanche to increase rates. In view of the ordinarily large representation of agricultural interests in the national assemblies of the underdeveloped countries, the land tax rate is likely to be a sharply debated political issue. Once an agreement is reached, legislators may have little desire to see the question soon reopened. The practice in the

United States and Canada of setting the local property tax rate annually in accord with estimated revenue needs seems to be unknown in most underdeveloped countries, although Uruguay permits subnational governments to levy supplemental variable rates.

Resistance to upward adjustments in tax rates can also be explained by other considerations. As cadastral values become outdated, it is probable that the original assessments will become less equitable. The impact of inflation or development on property values and income is not likely to be spread evenly over the agricultural sector. To raise the tax rate without first equalizing the assessments would therefore result in compounding inequities inherent in obsolete assessments. Because of this fact, inflexible assessments and stable tax rates tend to go hand in hand.

The superficially plausible notion that rate changes can be used to compensate for assessment values that are outdated is not an acceptable solution from an equity point of view, despite its apparent attractiveness to revenue-hungry governments in a number of countries. Whenever an increase in rates is ruled out simply because it would aggravate existing inequities, however, there exists an immediate need for reassessment of the tax whether one is primarily concerned with revenue or equity.

In addition to the temporal inflexibility of property tax rates, rates are set nationally in many countries, even when the revenues, or part of them, accrue to the coffers of local or state governments. While, as noted in the next chapter, there is a very strong case for centralized assessment administration, there is almost no case for imposing uniform national rates on the usually diverse situations to be found in different parts of a country.

If there are to be local governments at all, there is much to be said for having them exercise at least some degree of discretion in setting land tax rates, even if only in the form of supplements to a uniform basic rate in order to prevent the creation of tax havens. In view of the inherent immobility of the tax base, no severely deleterious economic effects are to be expected from mild subnational differentiation. Further, the administrative, allocative, and distributive effects of some local autonomy in this respect are, as is noted in Chapter 12, likely to be favorable on the whole.

The major problems of rate structure, however, hark back to the issue of personalization of the land tax. The inequality of the distribution of income in most poor countries is well documented. Although less studied, it appears that the distribution of real property is yet again more concentrated. Progressive land tax rates (and exemptions for small producers) are sometimes justified in these terms.

A common objection to heavy reliance on proportional land taxes, indeed, is that the incidence of the tax is regressive. This is not necessarily true, given the uneven distribution of agricultural land in most countries. Indeed, a proportional tax on agricultural land (especially with a basic exemption, even one determined on administrative grounds alone) may turn out to be more progressive in practice than a net income tax, certainly as the latter is often administered in developing countries.

In practice, however, a nominally proportional tax rate is all too likely to be regressive despite the maldistribution of property. Apart from the obvious danger of bribes and political pressure, it is often easier to conceal or to understate the value of large properties. Further, the usual assessment practice is to assess small properties at a higher value per unit of area than large ones because of the alleged greater difficulty of selling big properties, though they could be subdivided in most instances, and because of the lower value of output per acre usually observed in large properties, though this is one reason why they are often said to be "underutilized." In addition, there is some evidence that, perhaps for similar reasons, small properties are usually assessed at a higher rate of assessed to true value than larger ones.

Administrative deficiencies may accentuate these inequalities. It has been suggested, for example, that large farmers in Pakistan often paid their land taxes in arrears whereas small farmers had to pay immediately in order to protect their shaky land titles.[13] This sort of problem might be accentuated by progressive rates, although the regressive nature of assessment practice (see also Chapter 11) could be partly offset in this way. Once again, then, the details of how the land tax is administered, rather than how it looks on paper, turn out to determine its effects in practice.

Another argument for progressive rates is that land tax rates which are progressive by size of unit will encourage the use of techniques employing less land and more capital and labor to produce a given quantity of output. It is hard, however, to see this as a good argument in countries that are short of capital, especially where the shortage of arable land is acute. Furthermore, rates that are progressive by size of holdings are not necessarily equitable since, for example, average holdings tend to be larger in regions where the fertility of the soil is lower.

EXEMPTIONS

Perhaps the most common exemptions from land-based taxes are those for agricultural improvements. A 1964 Spanish law, for example, grants exemptions of up to 50 percent for those who make investments, improvements, and research expenditures in order to improve farm productivity, as well as a further reduction when newly irrigated lands are put into use. Iraq similarly exempts from national taxes lands which are, by means of improvements, turned into cultivated uses. Portugal and Yugoslavia grant tax exemptions for improvements. Uruguay favors those who fertilize or invest in artificial pastures in addition to excluding improvements from the assessed valuation.[14] Other countries favor particular crops by exempting from land tax the lands thus planted. Similarly, tax favoritism has often been used to encourage the development of agricultural cooperatives. Many other examples were noted in Part Two.

Two points should be made about exemptions and preferential tax treatment. First, although there is reason to suspect that this means of stimulating investment and efficiency in agriculture is costly, most countries do not know what this cost actually is. Secondly, while in most countries there is continual pressure for more and more "incentive" exemptions for various worthy purposes, it is impossible to say what, if anything, has been the effect of such property tax incentives in stimulating the various good things at which they are purportedly aimed, though such ignorance nowhere appears to deter the granting of new exemptions. Tax exemptions are subsidies and cost the government revenue just like any outright expenditure.[15] Adequate information on these costs should obviously be collected to permit some evaluation of the usefulness of each exemption in furthering its policy objective. Where the cadastral system forms the basis of the property tax system, such a census should be perfectly feasible.

While the general tenor of the arguments to this point would seem to be against any minimum exemption from property taxes for equity reasons, administrative exemptions of this sort can be significant: in Jamaica, for example, 70 percent of rural parcels are exempted from the national land tax.[16] These exemptions act to reduce tax consciousness and, just like graduated rates, provide an incentive to fragment. The former problem (if it is considered to be one) can be obviated by levying a small, flat-rate levy on obviously low-valued properties (like the parish rate in Jamaica), without going to the trouble and expense of making an accurate valuation which could not possibly be paid for out of the prospective tax proceeds. The evasion problem, of course, persists with any differential tax.

Some experts would go much further and provide personal exemptions similar to those in the income tax. A powerful argument for personalization of the land tax along these lines was made by Wald, who suggested that there should be personal exemptions allowing for numbers of dependents, that allowances should be made for loan obligations and catastrophes, and that all land parcels belonging to a single individual should be aggregated.[17] The aim of these proposals was of course to make the tax base approximate more closely a particular concept of abilty to pay.

As noted earlier, however, it is hard to see that any but very crude measures in this respect are either feasible practically or desirable conceptually. The principal argument against this line of reasoning, even if one accepts the dubious proposition that "ability to pay" is a viable standard at which to aim in the context of a partial wealth tax in one sector of the economy, is that it would enormously complicate the administration and hence work against levying effective taxes in agriculture for any purpose. Even less ambitious schemes intended to personalize land taxes by means of exemptions related to the personal circumstances of taxpayers will vitiate the basic virtues of simplicity and potential revenue-raising power which are the major reasons for turning to land taxes in the first place in most countries.[18]

AN "IDEAL" LAND TAX

The threads of the argument in this chapter may be drawn together by considering a recent typical plan to levy a progressive tax on the potential net income of agricultural land, that put forward by Joshi and his coauthors in a recent study of India's agricultural tax system. To implement the recommended tax, the government would first have to reclassify and measure lands in terms of "standard areas" related to potential net produce "defined as the produce that could be obtained from a piece of land under normal climate conditions and proper management when efficient methods of cultivation which are within the reach of cultivators are applied."[19] The price level to be employed for valuing this produce, they suggested, might be the mean of prices in the previous ten years. From the gross product thus calculated, the "normal" cost of production could be deducted. Once these calculations were carried out for each class of land, and the necessary classifications and conversions made to apply them to each parcel, a special graduated tax would then be imposed on the resulting estimate of potential net income. Further, in order to make the tax yield more elastic, the rates would be revised according to price changes. On the other hand, the tax could be forgiven in the event of natural disasters.

The advantages of this scheme were alleged to be four. First, there would be little evasion. To reduce the obvious pressures to fragment landholdings and to evade the provisions for consolidating landholdings, they would tax all family members as one unit, recognize only registered transfers, and rely on jealousy, mutual distrust, informers, and harsh penalties to do the rest. Clearly, the efficacy and acceptability of such devices depends very much on a country's "tax style." India's past record does not appear to suggest that it provides the most congenial environment for success in this respect.

Second, the incidence of the tax should be progressive, because of the consolidated personal (or family) nature of the base and the graduated rate. This conclusion clearly depends upon the validity of the "no evasion" hypothesis. Third, the proposed tax should provide incentives to efficient land utilization. This point was discussed in the previous chapter, but it should be noted here that any heavy land tax would exert much the same effects and that a simpler one could be more effectively enforced.

Finally, the tax yield would be elastic—an objective which of course tends to vitiate the desired incentive effect to the extent that it is successful. To be elastic, the marginal rate of a tax must exceed its average rate; to encourage production the marginal rate must, as a rule, be lower than the average rate. Both conditions cannot hold at the same time.

The limitations of schemes like this have perhaps already been adequately suggested. The main one is clearly administrative. In this connection, as the authors themselves note, this levy, or *any* tax on "potential net income," requires a lot of estimates, estimates which, no matter how full the information on which they are based may be (and it is not very full in most developing countries), will "dilute the scientific nature of the scheme."[20] It cannot be stressed too much that complex schemes such as this carry with them the very real danger that they will largely defeat their own purposes in the circumstances of most developing countries. Their outwardly scientific appearance not only tends to degenerate into crude guesses in many cases, but it also provides an endless series of points on which astute taxpayers can focus their protests and block the effective implementation of significant land taxes.

To take a simple example, in Nepal in 1959 a progressive surcharge was levied on the total land tax paid above a certain minimum. Immediate protests and difficulties led to the retroactive abolition of this surcharge, which had yielded hardly any revenues, in 1962. The intended purpose of this tax was to force land owners to transfer part of their holdings to their tenants. The result, as one commentator later noted, was "large-scale evasion through fragmentation of individual ownership units and little, if any, actual redistribution of ownership," partly because of the inadequacy of the land administration and the poor state of land titles.[21] These same problems render the task of collecting a progressive agricultural income tax too formidable to be contemplated.

There are many ways of evading land taxes in most countries. Progressive rates can be vitiated by the formation of several companies who nominally split the ownership of the land in question. This avoidance technique is especially simple when, as in most of Latin America, bearer shares are permitted.

One way to counter this technique is to place special penalty taxes on those forms of business organization most likely to be abused. The rationale behind this procedure is basically the same as that which leads some countries to levy schedular income taxes at higher rates on those sectors of the populace deemed most likely to evade the tax. It is questionable, first, because of the still greater inducement the higher penalty rates will create for evasion and, second, because of the distorting effects, presumably undersirable, inevitably arising from the discriminatory taxation of particular forms of business organization.

Similar objections may be made to the suggestion that high land transfer taxes might be used to discourage the division of holdings to avoid taxes progressive by size. The possible merits of this notion would appear to be outweighed by the general undesirability of high transfer taxes and the practical impossibility of telling "good" transfers from "bad" ones. In any event, taxes on real estate transfers may often be easily avoided by creating a private company to hold the land, so that the transfer is carried out, not by a change in the title of the land, but by a sale of stock. Similarly, absentee taxes can readily be rendered ineffective by this device.

In short, although it is always possible to make relatively fine equity distinctions in a land tax or a tax on presumptive agricultural income, it is not nearly so clear that these will be realized in fact. For example, farmers whose output suffers because they cannot get credit or seed just when they need it, owing to the uncertain agricultural infrastructure characterizing developing countries, pay the same tax as the man for whom the system works perfectly. The usual hardship exemptions do not meet this case. Low realization of potential productivity by no means necessarily demonstrates culpability.

More importantly, if we judge the land tax on how closely it resembles an income tax, it is virtually certain to look inferior.[22] Nothing resembles an income tax as much as an income tax. Indeed, even what passes for the income tax in some developing countries bears only a faint resemblance to the "income tax" of theory.[23] Land taxes have some independent justification of their own on equity grounds both as a tax, however crude, related to wealth and also as one way of partially blocking one of the more common holes in the income tax.

In most circumstances, however, this equity role of a land tax does not call for a refined progressive tax based on the potential value of land, as so many reformers have long and unsuccessfully urged. Such a tax is really conceivable only in a well-administered country with individual land tenure and politically weak landowners. If these conditions prevail, neither the incentive nor the equity results of the tax are likely to be worth the effort; if they do not, the tax in all probability cannot be effectively enough administered to produce significant results. With the possible exception of a few semi-industrialized countries with particularly recalcitrant agricultural sectors, a roughly classified land tax or, better, one based on capital values, would seem in most countries to produce results which, while they are not completely equitable, do offer a high enough target for reform efforts right now. As time and the appraisal process go on, of course, initial somewhat crude efforts can be refined, while at the same time other, more personalized, levies might increase in importance.

11

LAND TAX ADMINISTRATION

The importance of administration has been stressed throughout this study, for no tax can be better than its administration. A tax that looks ideal on paper may well turn out to be abysmal in practice. Indeed, in one view the administrative constraint on effective land tax administration is so severe in most developing countries today that virtually all the more refined fiscal devices beloved of theorists can and should be discarded for this reason alone. Not only will they not be well administered; they will in all likelihood be so poorly administered as to produce neither equity, efficiency, nor revenue. Furthermore, their very complexity and oft alleged panacea quality provide endless opportunity for procrastination and delay in carrying out the basic administrative tasks required for effective implementation of any land tax, no matter how simple.

The general case dealt with in this chapter is the realistic one in which only limited administrative resources, and those of a low quality, can be devoted to land taxation in the near future. The tax system employed should therefore be as simple and as free of error and corruption as possible. Its objectives are assumed to be to yield revenue in accordance with some rough notion of equity and with the least possible damage to production and marketing incentives. While, as argued elsewhere, the particular objectives of any tax are peculiar to each situation, this summary is probably adequate for most countries. The tax which best fits the circumstances of most developing countries is probably a tax on the capital value of land, which in the case of rural land is not usually the same as market value; this distinction is elaborated below. A simpler compromise which may be satisfactory in some countries, especially if the revenue demand is not too great, is a classified land area tax.

The design of the tax employed with respect to such features as exemptions, rates, and the treatment of various improvements ought of course to be varied as necessary to suit the conditions and objectives in different countries, as discussed elsewhere. But the need for simplicity is pervasive, even at the expense of some loss of paper equity and of theoretically desirable incentive effects. If desired, for example, supplementary levies on personal net wealth, on income earned from large-scale agricultural operations, and on land controlled by absentees or corporations may be imposed to achieve one or another social or political objective, but it is important that the basic land tax instrument not be weakened by attempting to do too much too soon.

Undue complexity leads to confusion, corruption, and evasion in the circumstances of most poor countries. It is rather ironic that, by the time the public administration and the attitudes of taxpayers are sufficiently developed to permit the effective utilization of land tax gadgetry, other, better instruments are usually also available to achieve the intended purposes.

In general, therefore, there would not seem to be too good a case anywhere for introducing some of the more complex agricultural land tax devices put forward by scholars, except perhaps in a few well-developed countries with peculiarly recalcitrant agricultural sectors of relatively small political importance. Even in these cases, it is perhaps questionable whether the benefits in terms of equity and additional output gained as a result of using scarce human skills for unduly sophisticated soil studies, valuations, and so on, will be worth the opportunity cost of doing so. The principal exception to this line of argument might be when, for such other reasons as a land redistribution program, it has been decided to carry out the needed investment in skill and knowledge anyway. An improved agricultural tax system may, in these instances, be an obvious and relatively cheap side benefit that naturally should not be neglected.

The fundamental reason for this stress on the virtues of simplicity in tax design is not to help the public understand the tax, though, as noted elsewhere, this is important in developing that key ingredient of any effective tax—a cooperative public. Simplicity is stressed because of the general condition of public administration and consequently of tax administration in most poor countries. The quality of staff under the conditions prevailing in poor countries is low. This limitation is especially serious with a tax like the land tax which requires administrative action to identify and value the object of taxation.

The steps needed to improve the present abysmal situation in tax administration are so well known as to require no special attention here except to emphasize the special vulnerability of land taxes to untrained and unmotivated staff, inadequate information, taxpayer antipathy, and inadequate legal and administrative collection and enforcement procedures.[1]

The basic assumption one has to make with respect to land tax administration is that the present poor administrative machine will continue to exist for some time in most countries. Whatever can be done to improve administration should of course be done, and as soon as possible, but even with the best will in the world not much can realistically be expected from such efforts in the near future. The maladies of tax administration reflect the general state of economic and political development and cannot, as a rule, be expected to alter very much faster than the pace of development itself. It is therefore incumbent on the tax policy adviser to suggest only reforms that can be handled by a relatively weak administration. This thrust underlies the entire discussion in this book. The remainder of the present chapter discusses briefly from this point of view the basic requirements of land tax administration: identification, valuation, collection, and enforcement.

THE FISCAL CADASTRE

Once the initial conditions in terms of objectives, politics, and the opportunity cost of administration have been met, the basic administrative requirements for the effective implementation of a land tax are deceptively few in number. They include knowledge of the location of each parcel; its physical extent and boundaries; the tenure in which it is held and interests in it; the productive capability of the soil; and relevant value, cost, and price information.

Even the simplest in rem area-based tax requires the first two of these items; the more complex taxes require them all. Each poses severe problems. The first three, for example, presuppose a clear set of titles and ownership registration, good map coverage, and a basic cadastral survey. The fourth presupposes that an elaborate cadastral base exists, or can be created. The last depends upon the existence of a well-informed and flexibly up-to-date land administration. The problem is that in many countries none of these prerequisites exist in adequate degree. The solution which has generally been proposed is to carry out a complete cadastral survey at once in order to serve as the needed backbone of land tax administration.[2]

The term "cadastre" refers to an official record of the location, size, value, and ownership (or other basis of occupancy) of each tract of land in a specified area.[3] The record normally consists of a set of large-scale maps on which each "survey plot" appears as a recognizable unit and corresponding registers which contain in tabular form the information needed to describe and identify each plot. In addition, a system of cross-references between the maps and registers is needed.

As a minimum a cadastre provides the tax officials with the location and boundaries of all taxable properties and the names and addresses of the liable taxpayers. For that reason alone the cadastre is a virtual necessity for proper administration of any land tax.

The information on land productivity and value provided in existing cadastres does not follow any set pattern. Much depends on how the land tax is assessed. Where the tax is based on capital value, the cadastre may not go beyond listing the official appraisal, possibly with the value of land shown separately from that of improvements. If the assessors rely chiefly upon sales information and simple unit value formulas, the cadastre may not record specific information on factors affecting the economic value of each tract. In some rural areas of Latin America the cadastral values are self-assessed by the landowners and are hardly ever verified by tax officials. Under such conditions the information in the cadastre will be most rudimentary and quite unreliable.

Some countries of South Asia, on the other hand, tend toward the opposite extreme as regards both the informational detail in the cadastre and the painstaking care with which the cadastre was originally prepared, often many years ago. Apart from a complete description of each field and various findings as to soil characteristics, there may also be data on the potential yield of various crops and on certain production expenses, such as payments of water rates, wages, and cost of transportation to a marketing center.

The large investment of money and technical skill that is required in the preparation of a satisfactory cadastral survey is a unique phenomenon in the field of tax administration in underdeveloped countries. It is doubtful that the investment in the administration of any other tax in these countries is nearly so costly as it is for the land tax, although the cost of the cadastre should in some cases be apportioned between taxation and other uses that are served by cadastral surveys such as agricultural development and land tenure reform policies.

"It can now be said with some confidence that the administration of a satisfactory tax on real property is no longer beyond the possibilities of countries which are even at a fairly low level of development, provided that the introduction is well prepared and the organization of the tax service is carefully planned."[4] The basic requirements for success are:

(1) a comprehensive property tax law, including clear statements of who is responsible for paying the tax, the precise nature of the tax base, an adequate penalty structure, and so forth;

(2) a coordinated cadastre system, designed to discover and identify properties and record them in tax maps as well as to ascertain ownership to the extent possible—a task that will be greatly facilitated if land can be seized and sold if no owner comes forward;

(3) a proper organization of qualified, trained, and sufficient people; and

(4) proper equipment.

With these ingredients the job of establishing a cadastral register can unquestionably be done. Of course, the same could be said of most other things. The relevant question is, as always, whether this is the best use of the required scarce resources.

That developing countries can establish satisfactory cadastral records is demonstrated, for example, by the case of Chile, where aerial photography at various scales, photogrammetry, photomosaics, photo interpretation, and other techniques were used.[5] Photo interpretation, supplemented by field operations on a sampling basis to verify the results, determined the present use of land. Although it was a much more complex operation, a potential capability was then established for all land, on the basis of a similar combination of aerial and field techniques. The precise identification of property boundaries also required extensive field interviews and visits in view of the inadequacy of existing title records. Finally, this information was combined with other information on location and accessibility and on such socioeconomic factors as the availability of human resources to establish potential land values. While not a panacea, it is clear that the procedure followed in Chile resulted in low costs and output and reliability at least as good as more painstaking commercial methods.

The Panamanian story recounted briefly in Chapter 5 is perhaps more typical of attempts to establish and update land surveys, however. The original base for the land tax in Panama was self-assessed values, protected only by a provision that the National Bank would lend up to a maximum of 60 percent of declared value. The first official cadastre started in 1953. It took ten years to assess Panama City alone, partly because of the enormous number of appeals launched against the new assessments. By 1965 only 23,000 properties had been valued at a cost of over $100 each.

Not until 1964 did a rural cadastre start. Even then its progress was greatly hampered by the confused title situation (epitomized by the large number of squatters) and at least as much by its multipurposed nature since it was intended to serve agrarian reform and regional development as well as tax purposes. Although this cadastre was much more rapid and cheaper—in 1965–1969 over 100,000 properties were surveyed at an average cost of $11 each—as late as 1971 there was still no additional revenue as a result, owing to the failure to process the cadastral data, set up adequate administrative procedures, and collect the tax. Furthermore, there were few preparations to maintain the cadastre, a never-ending job in any country because of changes in ownership and values. After almost twenty years of cadastral work, then, over 75 percent of the rural land taxes collected in Panama were still yielded by a totally arbitrary valuation of $30 per hectare on titled land.

Experience in other countries, ranging from Afghanistan to Nicaragua, also suggests that the general impact of cadastral efforts on land taxation has, as a rule, been modest.[6] At best, a cadastre is to land taxes as infrastructure is to economic development in general; it is a necessary but not sufficient condition for success. Even in cases such as Chile, where there have been apparent results in terms of increased revenues and a more equitable tax, a number of years generally elapsed before these beneficial effects appeared.

The standard detailed cadastral survey developed on European lines is simply too slow and too demanding of scarce administrative skills to be worthwhile in most developing countries. Even if, for other reasons, such detailed information is desired, tax bills should not wait on its completion as has too often been the case. Two alternative approaches seem more feasible: one is the tax mapping and mass appraisal approach; the other is the "yardstick farm" approach, possibly supported by the use of local assessment or review committees.

A cadastral survey for tax purposes is quite different in principle from a survey which, like the traditional legal cadastre, is carried out for purposes of establishing title to land. The fiscal cadastre involves two stages: first, the preparation of a set of maps showing the location and area of each parcel of property in the taxing jurisdiction; and, second, the estimation of the value of each parcel of taxable property. Both stages can be carried out much more cheaply and rapidly than has in fact been the case in many countries, though admittedly at the price of some degree of arbitrariness and approximation.

The mapping, for example, can normally be done through aerial photography, as in Chile. Some supplemental field work will be needed in certain areas, but primary reliance can be put on modern aerial survey methods (which lend themselves to foreign financing). Any error arising from this procedure is much less than that inherent in the determination of appraised value.

Since a complete soil survey is a very expensive operation, the cost of which cannot be justified simply to provide a basis for the valuation of rural land for purposes of taxation, a much simpler land classification system might suffice in many countries. The United Nations has, for example, suggested a scheme that is similar to that of the ancient Chinese land tax: crop land, pasture, forest, and waste, each with from one to four subclasses by quality.[7]

Values can, as noted below, be satisfactorily determined for tax purposes, provided the tax is not crushingly heavy, by relatively un-skilled technicians using a written manual developed by a few skilled appraisers. Mass appraisal involves comparison of each parcel of land with a standard value unit for the standard parcel in each class and subclass, with appropriate modifications for location, topography, availability of water, salinity, stoniness, erosion, and drainage. The needed soil capability studies can be done on a sample basis in con-junction with the aerial work or, alternatively, by intensive studies on the basis of certain parcels selected in each region as "yardstick farms." If the latter approach is used, it may in some instances prove possible and useful to involve local people with special knowledge of the area in selecting the representative parcels and in developing the coefficients to be used in the assessment manual. The value units can be determined on the basis of sales information, where available, or, more often, by sample productivity yields and commodity market prices. Semitrained field appraisers usually record the field data, and final valuations are then done at a central office by higher-level tech-nicians.

The key to mass appraisal is clearly the classification system. It must be sound enough, for example, to be defensible in appeal and review procedures. Mass appraisals along these lines can, if executed properly, yield results that are fairly uniform and acceptable in terms of most standards.

Much of the information in the cadastre may quickly become dated, especially in periods of rapid change. Because resurveys are expensive and require technically trained staffs, they are generally made at infrequent intervals. Most countries do not have any firmly established policy with respect to the frequency of resurveys and tax reassessments, although some fixed period for reassessment, such as five or ten years, is often specified in the law. Since reassessment of the land tax must ordinarily await a resurvey, the tax assessments remain unrevised over similarly long intervals, except that most countries permit downward changes in individual assessments in hardship cases, and some countries reassess land which changes hands at the selling price if it is higher than the assessed value.

Apart from the need for periodic resurveys to check changes in boundaries and land use, there is a continuing requirement for regu-lar recording in the cadastre of topographical changes, such as occur when land is washed away or new land is formed by the diversion of rivers or by other natural or man-made forces. For the particular needs of tax assessment, information on current changes is most essential when the agricultural sector is undergoing rapid change, but that is just when the task of keeping the records up to date is most difficult. An accurate, scientific soil classification survey, despite its substantial initial cost, may, however, be valid for extended periods, which is one reason why that kind of survey, as opposed to a mere recording of field boundaries and assessed valuations, can be very advantageous for land tax administration, although the cost can seldom be justified on this ground alone.

As always, those concerned with the design and implementation of tax policy must keep objectives and alternatives firmly in mind when it comes to the question of a cadastre. What is required in most countries is not the best cadastral system of which man can conceive but rather the minimal information needed to levy the required taxes in a politically and economically tolerable fashion. Furthermore, in carrying out this task, it is essential to do so in a manner that utilizes the least possible amount of scarce budgetary and human resources. If this formulation of the problem is accepted, it is highly improbable that anything but the simplest cadastre, utilizing the fewest possible experts and the maximum amount of existing underemployed resources (for example, local knowledge) will be desirable in the immediate future in most developing countries. Further, overemphasis on the importance of the cadastre has apparently led in some instances to undue neglect of the general administrative reform needed in order to collect and enforce taxes levied even on a newly determined base. Efforts in these other areas of administration are a necessary complement, not a substitute, to cadastral surveys if the latter are to be of much fiscal use.

THE VALUATION OF LAND

Valuation is an art as much as a science. Few taxes involve more judgment in their determination than the land tax. Its suitability for developing economies must therefore depend upon the extent to which it can be made automatic and simple in application without becoming too grossly inequitable or economically distorting.

The extensive use of notional or artificial values instead of real or actual values as the basis of assessment is perhaps the characteristic of land taxes which most distinguishes them from other taxes. The typical land tax is levied on a "presumptive" base, although the emphasis properly belongs on the hypothetical or fictitious nature of the value taken as the base, rather than on the usually unwarranted presumption that the assessed value is indicative of the actual value.[8]

To say that the tax base is a fictitious value is not necessarily the same as saying that it is unrelated to "actual value," assuming for the moment that such a thing exists. When reasonably refined methods of appraisal are followed, the resultant assessments should in fact be systematically related to real values, as these are usually defined. In any case, the objective of most assessment systems is not so much to measure actual values as it is to distribute the tax load among the individual properties in a way that is generally considered "fair." This objective may well conflict with levying the tax on, say, a basis approximating the current selling price of the property. The dominance of "fairness" over "accuracy" is, for example, clear in the property tax relief provisions common throughout the world favoring the agricultural use of land near growing urban centers.

For reasons noted in Chapter 7, it is ordinarily neither feasible nor desirable in the case of assessment according to net annual rental value to base the tax on the actual rents paid by tenants to landlords. Heavy reliance must therefore be placed, even with an annual value tax, upon appraisal formulas for converting the physical characteristics of the land into corresponding economic values. Many such formulas are tied to a fictional concept of a cultivator of "average" skill, who employs "standard" amounts of seed, fertilizer, and other production requisites. The hypothetical rental value of the land to such a hypothetical cultivator is then taken as the norm.

Some formulas in use are crude, as when land is classified into only a few broad categories—such as dry fields, wet fields, orchards, and so on—and the presumed yield is valued at uniform prices. Indeed, these methods come close to a classified land area tax. On the other hand, some methods employ highly refined formulas, at least in theory. They may begin, for example, with an estimate of gross income, from which are subtracted standard allowances for costs of production; or they may require rating each field in relation to the rental value of a "yardstick farm" or some other standard producing unit. The objective of these different approaches, however, is in all cases to obtain a reasonably accurate index of relative rental value rather than a realistic estimate of actual value.

A similar situation exists with respect to capital value assessments. Selling prices are not a reliable source of information since they are so easily influenced by special circumstances surrounding the sale, as well as by short-term market factors. Capitalization of rental income, while limited to rental properties and open to the many weaknesses of rental data, is often as useful as sales information as a basis for a capital value appraisal.

The most common approach for rural land, however, is to rely upon such rule-of-thumb appraisal standards as a table of unit values classified by soil types, land use, location, and other factors. If the standards are carefully worked out and honestly applied, they may yield quite acceptable results. Few countries seem to be able to meet these requirements. Appraisal manuals along these lines are absolutely essential for a successful mass approach to land tax administration. In all too many cases, examples of which can be found in developed as well as in less developed countries, appraisals are made cursorily, according to haphazard methods, by poorly trained staffs. Standards set forth in the law, such as a requirement for full market value assessments, are openly ignored.

Another reason why the quantitative expression of the tax base is often a figment of the assessor's imagination is that empiricism necessarily plays a large role in the assessment of many land taxes. Assessors may, for example, be guided primarily by the previous appraisal and the record of past taxes, making only rough adjustments for observed changes in the condition of the land and in the uses to which it is being put. Errors in the initial assessment thus stand a good chance of being carried forward from one survey to the next. The assessors may continually put off the day when they will start afresh to reappraise each field in accordance with uniform standards with the aim of equalizing the assessments. There is no way to get around this problem except to do it right in the first place.

Three types of land taxes, however, are avowedly based on real rather than hypothetical values. The simplest is the area tax, which is assessed according to the size of each field. A second is the tax on marketed produce, which is assessed according to the value of each load of produce when it is brought to the trading center. When the valuation of produce is according to official rather than actual market prices, however, as has often been the case in practice, an element of unreality is introduced into this tax base also. Finally, there are the tithe and those taxes patterned after it, which are assessed by inspection teams in the field at each harvest time.

Basing the tax on observable values supported by readily available evidence does not necessarily make it easier to obtain fair and accurate assessments or to control tax evasion. Apart from the area tax, the simplicity of which gives it a very large administrative advantage in poor countries with limited technical skills, the other two tax types with bases which can be measured in concrete terms at the time of assessment—marketing taxes and tithe-like levies—require a close check over the activities of many authorized middlemen in the one case and field inspectors in the other. All the Middle Eastern countries which have relied on these levies appear to have encountered difficulties in these respects. Moreover, once the object of assessment moves into distribution channels, usually within a short time after the assessment, there is no longer any direct evidence to substantiate the valuation. Subsequent verification must rely upon indirect proof.

The dominant characteristic of most land taxes as they in fact operate is thus that they are necessarily based on estimated rather than observed values. It is this feature that gives rise to the greatest conceptual and administrative difficulties with the tax.

Land valuation may basically attempt to approximate one of several standards: market value as represented by either the perfectly competitive market price which would emerge if "the whole world was hypothetically there, making hypothetical bids,"[9] or, more realistically, the most probable selling price in the actual market situation; the "normal" or "average" value of the land in its present use as measured by past production records and the like; and the potential use value for agricultural purposes. In practice, most valuation systems applied to rural land attempt to estimate the last of these on the basis of soil classification systems and the like.[10]

A tax on the potential income basis is often put forward as being easier to administer than either a tax on actual income or a tax on the market value of land. This seems questionable, however, as may be illustrated by listing the administrative requirements in a recent proposal to levy a tax on the normal potential income from agricultural properties:[11]

(1) Divide the country into ecological zones of uniform climatic-economic characteristics.

(2) Determine the characteristics of the land in each zone, on a sample basis. These samples are also used to calculate coefficients of divergence from the "ideal" land on the basis of such characteristics of the land as altitude, topography, thickness of arable stratum, salinity, permeability, stoniness, and distance from shipping centers or graveled roads.

(3) Determine the important crops or products in each zone in accordance with these characteristics.

(4) Determine for each zone and crop that size of farm which represents a "rational unit" (that is, an economic unit of "average" capability).

(5) Determine the average physical production over the last ten years for each region and crop.

(6) Determine the average annual price of all products last year.

(7) Determine the operating expenses of each unit last year, taking into account depreciation of all assets, financing and credit costs, production and transport costs, and uninsurable risks.

(8) The net income for each crop will then be determined by multiplying the average physical production (5) by last year's prices (6) and subtracting from the result all expenses (7). This figure is then divided by the number of hectares of the typical farm unit selected (4), in order to give the net income per hectare for each crop.

(9) The income per hectare for each zone is then determined by the weighted average of the incomes for each crop important in the zone.

(10) Finally, the income of the "ideal" land in each zone is fixed by multiplying the average unit income (9) by the reciprocal of the coefficient of divergence of the land chosen as a sample (2).

(11) Given this figure, the next task is to establish the divergence of each individual property from the "ideal" land. It was suggested that this might best be done by a self-assessment system which would require all taxpayers to compare their property to the "ideal" for their zone, as presented in a table of coefficients on the relevant characteristics. That is, they were to describe their property in terms of these objective criteria. Potential income would then be calculated as the product of the appropriate coefficients and the area of the property. Rent would be deducted by the individual. Officials would of course check these declarations on characteristics and area to the best of their ability.

(12) The standard estimates would be updated each year by altering

the prices to those of the immediately preceding year and by employing a moving average of the previous ten years' production.

Clearly, the implementation of a system like this or that described for India in Chapter 10 presupposes a high level of technical knowledge of a country's geographical and climatic composition. It would be much easier to administer in countries in which these conditions were relatively uniform over large areas (such as Uruguay; see Chapter 5) than in countries encompassing substantial variations. Furthermore, the efficacy of the scheme in increasing agricultural productivity—the usual reason for proposing this form of levy—depends to a very large extent upon the reliability of the self-classification by owners. This is a very slender reed upon which to erect a tax system. If, as is likely, owners' self-reporting cannot be relied upon (see later discussion), the tax would be effectively blocked until all farmlands were individually classified and assessed by officials. In most countries, this requirement would suffice to kill the whole scheme for years to come.

The alternative "market value" standard is likely to fare little better in practice. The sales price of land may differ from its capitalized value based on actual or potential income-earning capacity for a number of reasons. Land is valued not only because of its ability to produce, but also because of its relative risklessness and certainty compared to the limited range of available alternative assets, because its price is assumed to be especially responsive to inflation, because taxes on it are low, because it confers social status, because it acts as an apparently permanent and indestructible store of wealth, because it provides power over labor or political influence, or because it provides a vacation spot. This list suggests strongly that only the "fair market" price can capture all these influences and hence provide an equitable basis for the assessment of taxes.

A basically insuperable problem in relying heavily on "market value" assessment in developing countries, however, is the thinness of the real estate market in most rural areas. Effective enforcement of a market value standard necessarily rests on extensive use of comparative sales information. There are few sales in most rural areas, and what few transactions do take place reveal the gross imperfections of the typical rural real estate market with such special factors as financing arrangements and personal relationships influencing the price (assuming the actual sales price can even be determined). In some countries, there may of course be no private property in land and hence no sales. Alternatively, there may be excessive offerings of land in others due to fear of land reform. Certainly any alert assessment office should collect all the information it can on land sales, but on the whole this information would appear best used as a guide and check rather than as a reliable basis for assessment unless one has more confidence in the reliability of inferences from sold to unsold properties than would seem warranted in the typical rural area.

Market value is, as noted above, influenced by many factors, including speculation, inflation hedge, tax shelter, expected price changes, land reform policies, and others. Viewed as a tax on wealth and a progressive element in the total tax system, the land tax should presumably reach these values; viewed as a tax on the agricultural sector in a developing country, the case is much less clear. On balance, the incentive and administrative arguments seem strong enough to suggest approximations to potential value assessments where feasible, with a close check being kept on divergences from sale values. There is, of course, no bar to levying a supplementary net wealth or income tax on richer farmers for redistributive purposes, if desired and administratively feasible.

A major problem with this suggestion is that "there is no such thing as *the* just, fair or equitable form of land valuation. . . ."[12] These are all culturally relativistic concepts which must be assessed carefully in the light of the existing distribution of power—including private control of public power—in society and, hence, of the possibility that in practice the alleged intention of particular valuation approaches will be substantially distorted. The potential land use value criterion is suspect in most countries because it provides too much latitude for discretionary distortions and because it does not necessarily provide a culturally acceptable standard of fairness. The market value criterion is also suspect because of the ease of falsifying sales values, the limited number of transactions, the lack of relation to the capitalized value of potential yields (if this is considered closer to "true" value), and the fact that it too may not be "fair" by local standards.

While there is no certain answer to this dilemma, two rules to guide action in this difficult field of valuation standards do seem to emerge fairly clearly from an examination of the literature and experience to date. The first is to give up the quest for the Holy Grail of the "true" value of land; there is no such thing, and, as with the medieval search for the "just price," the quest is more likely to hinder than to facilitate constructive analysis and action. The second rule is that one must decide, first, what the objective of policy is and then determine an administratively convenient base on which to operate; *only then* can a plausible looking formula linking the two be developed.

To implement this suggestion, the first task is to determine the desired distribution of the burden of the land tax among taxpaying groups; the second is to determine the appropriate base (for example, the area or capital value of land); and the third is then to set up the assessment system so as to achieve the desired distribution. This is, in effect, what will happen anyway. There can be two substantial advantages in looking at the problem in this fashion, however. Much useless discussion of "the" correct standard is avoided, and, more important, there is perhaps a better chance that the intentions of the designers will be achieved in practice than if all the necessary adjustments are left to take place unseen and unchecked, legally or illegally, within the interstices of the land tax administration. Of course, if the objective is itself expressed in circular terms as distributing the tax in proportion to the "true" value of the land, then nothing is gained by this suggestion.

A particularly important factor in determining the value of rural land is its location and accessibility with respect to markets. This factor is much more important in developing than in developed countries. Unfortunately, the influence of location on value tends all too often to be determined quite arbitrarily and qualitatively. It is obviously a wise investment of limited resources to make as accurate a quantitative determination of the value increment associated with location as possible, even though it will still be rough and ready. The same can be said of the other outstanding determinant of land value in many countries—water supply. Since in both these cases, the major direct contribution to increased land values often lies in public investments in infrastructure, there is also a strong case for recouping some of the increment directly through betterment levies, thus expanding budget capacity to undertake such investments. The new assessments needed for this purpose can also, of course, serve as a basis for levying the general land tax. There is no element of double taxation in doing this since the two taxes have quite distinctive rationales.

To turn to another problem, a commonly noted assessment phenomenon is that low value properties tend to be overassessed relative to high value ones, and small ones relative to large. Apart from the influence of political connections and legal costs on this result, a particular feature of the appraisal process which often contributes to this bias is the common use of a "size coefficient" which reduces the unit area value of larger properties.[13] The rationale for this reduction is presumably that the market value per unit of area of a parcel is likely to fall as its size increases. This convention may make some sense in the urban context if, for example, there is some "typical" lot size.[14] Even there, however, the fact that larger lots can often be subdivided into smaller ones would seem to argue against its blind acceptance.

In the rural context it makes no sense at all. In the first place, not only is it inequitable to tax owners of small plots more heavily than those of large areas, it is also economically inefficient. As noted elsewhere, if the potential capacity per unit is equal, that potential is probably closer to being realized in small farm units than in large ones. Taking the lower activity per unit of area to justify a lower valuation is perverse in its incentive effects. Secondly, land tax policy is often intended to discourage large land accumulations; it is therefore ridiculous to introduce an artificial "correction" coefficient that has the opposite effect. Finally, the way in which different-sized parcels are treated by the market (if there is one) is not necessarily an appropriate basis for deriving assessment standards suitable for the rural areas of poor countries.

Once again, then, the rule suggested above of first determining the desired effects and only then deciding on the instruments to be used to achieve them is supported. Conventions like the size coefficient have no merit in themselves; their suitability for application in any particular circumstances must be very carefully considered. In this case, it seems likely that the effects of the correction as often made are undesirable. It should therefore not be made, no matter what the appraisal manuals may say. As usual, the mechanical transmission of techniques developed for one set of circumstances for use in another set of circumstances is more likely to lead to bad than to good results.

To mention quite a different "convention," the major problem in assessing farmland in most industrial countries today concerns land near expanding urban centers. If the traditional standard of full market value in "highest and best use" is followed, the present use of property is of course irrelevant if it is less valuable. With the spread of suburbs near major cities, land values have risen sharply on many lands still used for farming—and so should property taxes, under prevailing standards, often to such an extent that farming would probably no longer be profitable. To counteract this, many jurisdictions in the United States and Canada provide, by assessing farmland at value in present use or some other way, for preferential treatment of land kept in agricultural use.[15]

Analogous "hardship" exemptions are not unknown in developing countries, and the probability is, given the rapid growth of metropolitan areas, that the urban fringe problem will also arise there, if indeed it has not already done so. The implications of continuing to assess land which is ripe for urban development at agricultural values need to be carefully considered, however. It is by no means clear that the practices followed in most developed countries are suitable for adoption in developing countries, or indeed if they are suitable for the developed countries either!

The appropriate tax treatment of land on the urban fringe depends upon whether one considers the holders of such land to be virtuous farmers or vicious speculators—the first leads to preferential assessment, the second to differentially higher taxes on unimproved land— as well as upon one's conception of and control over urban development. Since most rural land taxes are in fact levied on some sort of notional "potential" value in agricultural use, it is in these cases that the divergence between market value and assessed value will be greatest. If there are many farms in urban areas, they should in principle be encompassed within the urban property tax and assessed at market values. If this procedure is felt to create undue hardship, at most the tax on the excess of market value over the value in agricultural use might be deferred (not exempted) until the land is sold. Alternatively, a special capital gains tax or other levy might be imposed to capture the unearned increment when the land is transferred to urban use. Either solution is likely to give rise to administrative complexities. In any event, the "fringe" problem is really one concerning urban rather than rural land taxes and will not be discussed further here.

Site Value Taxation

There can be no question that a land tax is workable whether its base includes only land or all real property. Referring to the extensive Australasian experience with site value taxation, for instance, Woodruff and Ecker-Racz concluded: "Many decades of experience have convinced even the most hardened skeptics that while it may be considerably more difficult to appraise the land component of a single improved parcel apart from the building on it, the reverse is true when great numbers of properties have to be evaluated for tax purposes."[16]

There is also no doubt that in either case there is an inherently high degree of arbitrariness in the determination of the "value" of any parcel of land. What is perhaps more subject to dispute is whether a tax based on land value alone or one based on the value of real estate as a whole is more arbitrary.

On the whole, it appears that when mass appraisals are to be carried out, which is the only way land taxes are ever likely to amount to anything in most developing countries, land must as a rule be valued separately from buildings. The valuation of structures is inherently much more difficult than that of land because of the multiplicity of structural characteristics. Although some success has been achieved in recent years in adapting mass appraisal techniques to certain classes of structures in developed urban areas by means of extensive computer-based studies,[17] there would appear to be little carry-over to underdeveloped rural areas, both for technical and institutional reasons. Outside of local market centers, buildings as a rule are not significant in determining rural values. On farms, improvements such as fences and ditches are generally more important.[18]

Since most farm improvements in poor countries are the result of the direct investment of the farmer's own labor, the incentive aspect of freeing such improvements from tax is probably desirable in many countries. On the other hand, exemption of all improvements from tax may tend to induce more capital-intensive methods of farming, a result that is presumably less desired. Average rural land has few buildings, however, so taxes on structures would appear to cause relatively little resource misallocation.

The combination of the desire to encourage accretionary capital formation and production on the one hand and, more important, the difficulty of assessing many improvements on a mass basis on the other suggests that an agricultural land tax may be both simpler and slightly more desirable economically if its base does not include visible improvements. This omission will not necessarily make it any "fairer" in terms of ability to pay, but, as has already been suggested, the search for exact "fairness" in this sense is a will-o'-the-wisp anyway. If anything, taxing only land values may make the tax more acceptable in rural communities. On the other hand, if it should be decided to tax land and all improvement values, the task would be easier in rural than in urban communities because of the simple nature of most rural improvements.

In any event, it should be emphasized that omitting visible improvements from the land tax base does not mean that the object of assessment can or should be the "original and indestructible powers of the soil" in Ricardo's phrase. It is in practice impossible to disentangle the work of man in clearing forests, draining swamps, and other activities over hundreds or thousands of years from that of nature, and it is futile to try to do so even conceptually, at least in settled agricultural areas.

Countries such as New Zealand, which have successfully employed the "unimproved value" form of taxation in rural areas for decades, have found that it gives rise to increasing difficulties as the agricultural sector becomes more settled and capitalized. The major problems are the lack of sales evidence for unimproved rural lands, the difficulty of taking into account such "invisible" improvements as underground drainage, land clearing, stumping, reclamation, and good husbandry, as well as the premium placed on underdeveloped land by tax incentives to agricultural production which make the few sales of such properties as exist an increasingly unreliable guide to the general level of unimproved values.[19] The essence of these complaints is that more and more "improvements" are in fact being taxed.

A careful study of New Zealand practice in this respect recently proposed that "land value" replace unimproved value, thus obviating the practically impossible but legally required task of estimating the added value due to unexhausted invisible improvements and increasing the sales evidence available to check on assessments: "By the term "land value" . . . is meant for rural land, the land in grass as we see it today, excluding 'visible' structural improvements such as buildings and fences, but including the often called 'invisible' improvements which embrace all the development activities necessary to put the land into grass from its original state."[20]

The relation of unimproved value and land value varies a great deal depending upon both physical factors affecting the cost of bringing land to grassland state as well as factors offsetting this by high demand owing, for example, to location. In general, however, it seems clear that on administrative grounds alone the case for the "land value" approach as compared to "unimproved value" is overwhelming. "Land value" need not, of course, be defined precisely as in the New Zealand study cited above. But the general idea of not trying to separate the inseparable is correct for other countries, too, as recent studies in Jamaica and other areas also suggest. It is therefore the "land value" standard which ought to be employed in those developing countries which choose to exempt improvements, despite its disincentive effects compared to the unimproved value basis, in order not to put too great a strain on the analogizing capacity of the valuer.

Self-Assessment

The obvious difficulties of administrative assessments have given rise to a number of proposals to get around some of the problems stressed in this chapter by relying on a self-assessment system. In essence reliance on self-assessment of property taxes is an attempt to alleviate the recognized deficiencies of public administration by shifting the burden of tax enforcement to the private sector. The quest for some magic device to bypass the administrative roadblock to effective land tax administration is a very old one, as Hirschman has noted.[21] Its recent revival owes much, however, to the advocacy of Harberger and Strasma, who have respectively suggested and developed a way of getting around one of the major defects of the usual self-assessment systems.[22]

The main problem with most self-assessment schemes is that their success depends upon the political tolerance of the community. In the case of the usual scheme in which, as in Colombia in 1963, the pressure for declaring an adequate value comes from the threat of forced sale to the government at the self-declared value (plus some fixed margin), the crucial question is the credibility of this threat. As a rule the results of such schemes have been meager.[23]

In the case of the "market-enforced" variant in which anyone can purchase the property at the declared value plus margin, community tolerance would, it appears, be an even more crucial determinant of the workability of the scheme. If, as has been persuasively argued, such forced sales would in fact be unpalatable in most communities, this threat is not credible either.[24] Furthermore, the usual provision in these schemes to the effect that a bid may be frustrated by raising the declared value accordingly and paying a fine, to be shared with the would-be buyer as compensation for his trouble, in effect makes market-enforced self-assessment a glorified informer scheme. Even with private tax administration, there are strong incentives for corruption and blackmail. Since the state of public sector morality generally reflects that of the society as a whole, there is little reason to expect that shifting the administrative burden to the private sector will improve matters.

Another undesirable result is the differential effects on property value that will result from varying risk preferences, information, and other factors. Under self-assessment, owners of properties of similar market value would place very divergent assessments on their properties, reflecting their risk preference, income, knowledge, and the extent to which they incorporate "consumers' surplus" into their valuation.[25] The variations in assessments might be as great, and as inequitable, as those with a system of administered assessment. There is no reason to believe that these differentials will be either policy-relevant or desirable. Self-assessment has also been criticized for its questionable legality in some countries and for undermining private property as well as for its uneven impact on the unwary.

Finally, self-assessment systems must really be based on properties "as is," that is, on land plus improvements, if any. Even so, this device is unlikely to reduce the social costs of attaining a given standard of assessment; instead, the costs are simply shifted to the private sector, as many owners will have to engage appraisers to ascertain the value anyway.

In summary, it would appear that the idea of relying on the self-assessment system has little to be said for it as an alternative to more conventional administrative practices. Shoup's summation seems sound:

Assessors, auditors, and tax collectors being expensive, fallible and sometimes corruptible, a search continues for a tax system that is self-enforcing, one that reduces the role of the tax official to that of storing records and receiving freely tendered tax payments. New hopes are stirred by new devices. But in the end they all come down to reliance either on a desire for pecuniary gain by someone other than the taxpayer or on fear by the taxpayer or his agent that he will lose either money or freedom. Neither stimulus amounts to much without some degree of active administration; realistically, the goal cannot be a completely self-enforcing system staffed by completely passive administrators.[26]

Even as an interim measure, despite its relative cheapness and apparent ease of implementation, experience and the above arguments suggest that self-assessment does not offer a low-cost path to an effective property tax. In some circumstances, however, it might be useful to leave the option of altering assessments to the landowner in order to avoid overburdening the appeal machinery, particularly if an index adjustment is used to compensate for inflation since the last official valuation, as may be considered desirable to improve the responsiveness of land tax yields to increases in money national income.

If such index adjustments are carried out, they should probably be made as simply as possible: for instance, by adjusting assessments annually to reflect significant changes in price and production indexes relating to the principal commodities in different agricultural regions or in some other way. Such global adjustments will not, of course, offset inequities among taxpayers. Indeed, they will accentuate them by maintaining or increasing the weight of the tax. An index-adjusted land tax thus makes it even more imperative to start from an acceptable base if one is concerned with equity.

On the other hand, a rapid increase in revenues from an existing land tax can often be most quickly attained by an index adjustment that does not require the same long period a general reassessment requires before taking effect, and does not run the same danger of being compromised into ineffectiveness. Self-assessment might perhaps help as a temporary measure to get the system off the ground. Declared values should, however, as a rule be replaced by officially assessed values as soon as possible, though the option of self-assessment (with appropriate penalties for subsequently discovered undervaluations) might be retained to escape the enormous burden of expected appeals to the courts against the new assessments. In the final analysis, there is no shortcut available to effective land tax administration.

COLLECTION AND ENFORCEMENT[27]

The administrative requirements of any tax are determined primarily by such aspects of the local setting as the land tenure structure, the nature of existing land records, the typical scale of production, the average size of plots, the variety of products, the extent to which agriculture is market oriented, the scope of the monetary sector, the marketing and distribution system, and the proportion of output exported. For the most part policy makers must concentrate their efforts on designing taxes that are appropriate for the local setting and do not create unduly burdensome administrative requirements.

Perhaps the most obvious single factor determining the cost of tax administration is the number of taxpayers. Broadening the coverage of a tax will almost certainly add to the administrative cost, while narrowing the coverage should permit cost saving. To maximize tax revenue, the administrative budget should be so allocated that the revenue return for the marginal dollar spent on each aspect of administration is everywhere the same. Other standards are, of course, also possible, and the general rule for efficient resource allocation (equalize at the margin) applies in this case as in most others.[28]

To illustrate, in most countries there is probably a cutoff point established by law or administrative practice that serves to exclude very small taxpayers. Although this exemption level is often determined by equity or ability-to-pay considerations, an exemption can also be justified on efficiency grounds. If, for example, spending an additional dollar on assessing a given property will yield less than a dollar in revenue, it is unlikely that it will be worth doing. Indeed, unless the dollar spent on assessing the last little property yields as much in terms of revenue or equity as a dollar spent on, say, a more intensive valuation of larger properties, it is not well spent. A minimum exemption or, alternatively, a low fixed levy on small properties thus makes good sense in the circumstances of most developing countries.

The number of taxpayers can be changed not only by adjusting the minimum exemption, but also by shifting the point of collection or the point where the ultimate liability rests. Where there is plantation agriculture, a tax on the owners would involve a comparatively small number of taxpayers. Where tenant farming is prevalent, the number of taxpayers can be reduced by imposing the tax directly upon landlords rather than upon individual tenants. In a populous country of owner-cultivators, a tax collected when the produce moves to the market probably would involve fewer taxpayers than one collected at the farm. In tribal societies it might be expeditious to levy a collective assessment on each tribal unit.

A second cost factor is the assessment procedure. At one extreme are assessments according to land area, with a minimum number of land classifications; these are probably the least costly to administer satisfactorily. At the other extreme are assessments according to the economic value of the land. There are many degrees of possible refinement in the calculation of economic value, but the administrative requirement is considerable, even for a rudimentary value calculation. The cost of well-administered capital value taxes is likely to be far out of line with that of other taxes unless a lower standard of equity is deliberately designed into the system. This lower standard was suggested earlier so that such a system could be attained with available administrative resources.

Cost calculations necessarily influence decisions regarding the degree of refinement to seek in classifying land for tax purposes. Where the prevailing classification system recognizes only gross variations in land value, the cost of introducing a more discriminating system might be a worthwhile investment for nontax as well as tax reasons. There are certain types of refinements, however, such as those which reflect changing economic factors, which may permit more equitable taxation but may be considered too costly because they do not yield complementary advantages either for revenue collection alone or for land administration programs. Even these adjustments can be made by simple formulas, however, if the resulting crudeness is politically acceptable.

Starting from the premise that the higher the tax yield the greater the need for more accurate classification methods, policy makers must seek to balance the estimated additional cost of improved methods against their expectation of equity gains. Ultimately these judgments rest upon intuition and political considerations, though they should be formed with the aid of as many facts as can be assembled.

The desire to reduce administrative costs has strongly encouraged the practice of keeping land tax assessments unchanged for long periods, as has the lack of trained surveyors and soil experts needed for land surveys. Apart from saving the cost of resurveys, a stable assessment also simplifies administrative procedures by making it unnecessary to recalculate each taxpayer's liability and by reducing the occasion for taxpayers' appeals. On the other hand, it practically ensures an eventual reduction in real tax yield in most developing countries.

The cost of land tax administration is affected, as are all taxes, by other factors: provisions in the law which lead to controversy because they are difficult to interpret and apply; tax relief and exemptions; frequency of tax collection and the method of enforcing payment; and extent of coordination between tax administration and other government programs, such as loan programs, fertilizer distribution, grain collection, and rent control.

The cost of taxpayer compliance is less important for most land taxes than for other kinds of taxes. Under the typical land tax there are no record-keeping requirements for taxpayers and no tax returns for them to file. In most phases of land tax administration the initiative rests with the tax officials. This statement does not apply, however, to marketing taxes enforced with the aid of detailed accounting records kept by traders or to self-assessed taxes.

Some provisions that would reduce the government's cost of land tax administration will also reduce taxpayers' compliance costs. For example, when assessment standards are easy to interpret and apply, the government's job is simplified, and the taxpayer is less likely to dispute his tax bill. In some instances, however, by spending more on administration the government could lighten the taxpayers' compliance burden. This might happen, for example, if the government increased the number of local offices where payments might be made and where appeals for adjustment of assessments might be adjudicated.

Another aspect of the compliance burden is related to the size of the tax. The heavier the tax, the more the taxpayer will be interested in finding ways to reduce his liability. As the tax rate is raised, it becomes more important to close any avenues of escape and also to simplify and standardize tax relief provisions, including any special arrangements for hardship cases. For example, instead of requiring each taxpayer to apply for remission when he believes that he is eligible, it might be preferable to grant automatic relief to groups of taxpayers on the basis of some general criteria. A poor growing season or a sharp price decline might provide the occasion for granting such relief.

Holding underpayment of taxes to the lowest practical minimum is the third principal area of concern in tax administration. The consequences of widespread uneven underpayment can be fiscally disastrous not only because of the revenue loss but also because of the damage to the equity of the tax and to taxpayer morale.

Under a tax that is assessed by administrative officials and is not dependent upon taxpayers' returns, the completeness of collection depends largely upon the ability of the officials to locate the taxpayers, determine with accuracy each person's liability, and enforce collection by being able and ready to penalize those who fail or refuse to pay. Whether the form of the tax will assist or obstruct the exercise of these administrative functions is sometimes an important policy consideration.

In those few countries that have a full set of cadastral maps and complete land registers, the administrative effort required to make taxes that are tied to landownership difficult to evade is not great. In areas where field boundaries or titles are not clearly established and recorded, and where ground surveys are not immediately feasible, aerial photography usually affords a practical and speedy means of identifying ownership units and making rough estimates of their size. When government ownership records are inadequate, or when it is impossible to locate some owners, the tax assessment might be levied on the occupier or cultivator. If no one can be found to pay the tax, the land might revert to the state. Because of these opportunities for tax enforcement, identification of taxpayers and of taxable property need not be a serious barrier to effective collection of taxes imposed directly on either ownership or use of land, except in areas where there are no recognized rights in land or in sparsely populated regions characterized by nomadic agriculture. In the latter cases administrative considerations might favor a marketing tax or a form of poll tax.

Second, authorities will be aided in checking on taxpayer compliance if the form of the tax permits verification of the assessment on the basis of cadastral records or other official sources of information. Thus a tax that is assessed according to land value as established by official surveys, the results of which are made part of a permanent land record, would appear to be more easily enforced than one which relies upon field inspections at harvest time. In the latter case, verification of the assessment is difficult after the crop is gathered and marketed. The policing problem would seem to be even more troublesome for marketing taxes since the object of assessment may escape detection and lose its identity after it moves into distribution channels.

Third, there is the problem of controlling delinquent taxpayers. Many countries have had great difficulty in dealing with this problem, but the source of the difficulty seems to be largely unrelated to the form of the tax. Because tax laws often fail to provide adequate penalties for nonpayment or because tax officials are lax in applying these penalties, taxpayers often find that the administrative machinery is ineffective. Land taxes have one feature conducive to effective control over delinquencies: land or its produce often stands as security for the tax and is subject to forfeiture to the government for taxes due. The credibility of this procedure, of course, as always depends on political and social attitudes in the country in question.

Various simple steps can be taken to make collection more effective. For instance, interest should be charged on delinquent payments along with a penalty for lateness, and the tax might be made payable in installments.[29] In Colombia, for example, various studies have stressed the importance of improving collection procedures by such measures as imposing higher interest charges and fines on delinquent taxpayers and by altering the tax to an in rem basis in order to facilitate enforcement procedures by permitting the attachment of land regardless of the whereabouts of the owner or the nature of his rights to the land.[30] Effective enforcement of a property tax is likely to prove extremely difficult unless a lien is enforceable against the property itself.

The mix of central and local administration can vary from complete centralization on the one hand to complete local autonomy on the other. In most countries, however, some mixture would seem more appropriate.

For the last decade property tax assessment throughout most of Colombia, for example, has been in the hands of an independent public institution, the Agustín Codazzi Geographic Institute, which maintains sectional offices in most of the departments. (Separate cadastral offices exist in the Special District of Bogotá and in Antioquia, however, and these two areas account for over one-third of the total taxable assessments in Colombia.) On the whole, the level of assessment technique used throughout the country has been considered good, though the techniques employed by the Geographic Institute are also thought by some to be too painstakingly exact to cope with the constant problem of keeping property valuations reasonably up to date in an inflationary environment.[31]

Countries which levy progressive personalized land taxes require an even more centralized administration. Others may wish to follow the interesting New Zealand pattern in which valuation is the function of a central government department quite independent of the tax authorities; either taxpayer or tax assessor can appeal the valuations made by this department to an independent valuation tribunal. Still others may combine valuation and tax assessment as well as centralized billing with local collection or local review committees. An older pattern is to involve local landowners in the initial determination of assessment, as was done in the famous Domesday Book land survey of England in the eleventh century and is still being done in some countries today. Depending on the particular circumstances of each country, any of these patterns, or some variation, might make sense. As a rule, however, some degree of centralization is probably advisable in many countries, although not at the expense of neglecting the importance of local knowledge and local involvement.

Collections in Kind

In countries such as the Soviet Union, China, South Korea, and Taiwan, land taxes have at times been collected in kind instead of in cash. The method of in-kind collections has lost its original attraction in most areas of the world, largely because agriculture is no longer so completely outside the monetary economy. For the most part, any country which would now contemplate extensive use of in-kind collections would probably do so primarily because the system offers special advantages over cash collections as an instrument of economic policy, especially as applied to food distribution.[32]

Whether collections are in kind or in cash need not affect the basic structure of the land tax. Nevertheless, the economic effects of the two types of taxes offer some significant contrasts. In the first place, in-kind taxes may provide more opportunities than cash taxes for influences on the composition of production. A government may wish to avail itself of these opportunities, provided that it has a consistent agricultural development policy and can reasonably expect agricultural development policy and can reasonably expect agricultural producers to respond to tax inducements. The government may, for example, accept in-kind payments in only a limited number of staple crops, usually grains. Thus, producers of, say, vegetables or fruits must be permitted to pay in cash, or else their tax liability must be expressed in terms of a basic crop even though their harvest consists of other products. Whenever the resulting tax differentials among farmers fail to correspond with differences in net income, farmers are given an inducement to produce lightly taxed commodities and to refrain from producing those that are heavily taxed.

Also, in-kind collections appear to offer advantages over cash collections when the government has set a very high revenue goal for the land tax. Centrally planned economies in particular have made considerable use of this fact. One explanation for the comparatively high yields of in-kind taxes is that such taxes are not limited by the availability of cash resources in the agricultural sector. A tax contribution can be obtained even from very small producers who customarily restrict themselves to barter transactions and do not market crops for cash. A more important explanation for high yields is probably that countries which have employed in-kind taxes have been in a stronger position, for political and institutional reasons, to impose relatively heavy fiscal burdens on the agricultural population than are most other countries.

The income from in-kind taxes may also include some profits that would otherwise accrue to private distributors of agricultural commodities. When the government collects grain or other products from farmers, stores it, and later moves it into wholesale, retail, or export trade channels or distributes it in other ways, the government is performing the middleman's functions and carrying his risks. The net receipts from the in-kind collections, the difference between the aggregate market value of the commodities when they are distributed and the total cost of storage, transportation, and distribution, represent, in this case, a combination of taxes and profits.

In-kind taxes are again, in an important sense, superior to cash taxes when a country is experiencing inflation. Cash holdings depreciate in value as prices rise, but inventories of goods retain their value. In-kind taxes thus provide the treasury with a kind of insurance against loss of purchasing power of its tax receipts in the event that prices rise; by reducing the need for deficit financing, such taxes are more effective than cash taxes in combating inflation. Should prices fall, however, the treasury would be better off holding cash instead of goods; on the other hand, it can be argued that in-kind taxes help to stabilize prices and income in a depression because they do not reduce private spending to the same extent that cash taxes do.

Finally, in-kind taxes represent a convenient means for the government to acquire a sizable portion of each harvest and thereby exert some control over the distribution and prices of agricultural products. This consideration seems to have been of paramount importance in the past in South Korea, for example, where the in-kind tax served as a key instrument of national food policy and was also important in the government's effort to control prices and wage rates. The substitution of in-kind for money taxes eased many of the government's problems with respect to food distribution and wage-price control.[33] In India, on the other hand, it appears that compulsory procurement of marketed surplus at controlled prices has been a failure, thus again suggesting that the political and institutional requirements for successful use of heavy in-kind taxation are high.[34]

Taxation in kind is difficult to administer. It lends itself readily to harshness and has a long history of misuse in many lands. In-kind taxation is much more difficult where the agricultural output varies substantially in type and quality. Efficient operation of such a system requires precisely that infrastructure of storage and distribution facilities that is usually missing in poor countries. The storage problem is especially troublesome as administration becomes more centralized.[35] If a country is capable of levying heavy in-kind taxes on its agricultural sector, it can presumably levy money taxes, too, if it wishes to do so. Taxing in kind may tend also to retard the monetization of the subsistence sector that inevitably accompanies modernization of agriculture. On the other hand, money taxes can be misused, too, as has often been the case with the heavy taxation of cash crops and the consequent discouragement of expansion into these dynamic areas. In general, however, little can be said for reversion to the ancient system of collecting land taxes in kind.

CONCLUSION

It is impossible to devise a simple and uniform set of valuation rules to deal equitably and adequately with land on a mass basis. No two parcels of land are identical. Transactions in rural areas are infrequent and subject to many special factors. Owners have a strong incentive to undervalue. Attempts to "normalize" or "standardize" values weaken the already tenuous administrative process by providing a wider latitude for administrative laxness and potential abuse.[36]

The good administration of any tax on real estate requires a considerable amount of specialized training, especially in valuation, as well as extensive familiarity with the particular area involved, not to mention industry and integrity. The last two of these qualities are rare everywhere. The first constitutes a main argument on the one hand for not trying to do too much with the limited resources available and on the other hand for keeping the valuation function centralized. Assessment administration is almost universally condemned in the United States because of its poor quality. The principal reasons for this quality deficiency are that staffs are too small and too poorly trained, which in turn reflects the small size of the basic assessment jurisdiction. Underdeveloped countries have enough problems without falling into this same trap. On the other hand, there is much to be said for involving local knowledge in the assessment process, either through local assessment or review committees or through some other means. Local administrative devices of this sort, though they inevitably slow down the administration process, are valuable in securing some degree of cooperation from taxpayers. Chapter 12 discusses some of these points further.

Finally, perhaps the most serious problem raised here concerns the equity of the rather rough and ready assessment methods that have been suggested as suitable for most countries. If valuations are primarily based on such readily observable differences as access to water and market roads, the results may be acceptable. If there are over-riding equity-directed taxes, which is rather unlikely, this question is less important. Sometimes, however, even crude differentiations produce surprisingly equitable results, as was suggested by the previously cited study of Nepal where poor land tax administration was long held to result in serious tax inequities, hence making it very difficult to increase land taxes. In reality, it appears that the Nepalese land tax is equitably distributed between rich and poor districts, although dry lands are overtaxed relative to wet lands.[37] A simple rate or base alteration between these classes of land would alleviate this problem. If these results can be generalized, the prospects for effective and acceptable land taxation may be less bleak in many countries than either past experience or a reading of the impossible "prerequisites" postulated by some authors would suggest.

LAND TAX ADMINISTRATION

PART FOUR

TAXING AGRICULTURAL LAND: AN APPRAISAL

12

LAND REFORM AND LOCAL GOVERNMENT

The role of land taxes in relation to land reform has received a great deal of attention in the literature, perhaps even more than it deserves. The opposite is true of the connection between land taxes and local government. This chapter discusses briefly these two questions which, though important, do not fit neatly into the more general conclusions in the next chapter.

LAND TAXES AND LAND REFORM

The problems that are expected to be resolved by "land reform" are as manifold as the meanings assigned to that term by different authorities. Sometimes farms are considered too small and fragmented to be economically efficient; sometimes they are too large and concentrated to be socially desirable. Sometimes tenancy arrangements are thought to be too insecure or too adverse to encourage innovation; sometimes efficient plantations are in the hands of foreigners or absentee owners. "Land reforms" may be aimed at rectifying any or all of these problems and other economic, political, and social ones. While some "reform" proposals are motivated by the desire to increase agricultural production, it seems less confusing to reserve the term "land reform" for policies aimed primarily at redistributing property rights in land.

Perhaps the most important question in connection with land reform in most developing countries is whether it is possible to achieve more egalitarian land distribution and increased production at one and the same time. As pointed out in earlier chapters, in some countries it has in fact been the larger farmers, not all of them, of course, who have led the way in introducing yield-increasing technology. Partly for this reason, some have argued that land reform is inherently an economically costly measure, reducing the rate of growth of agricultural production.

The opposite inference has also sometimes been drawn from the same experience: that is, that "reforms" aimed primarily at increasing production are in fact likely to block redistributive measures, both because they favor the prosperous who are most able and willing to respond to incentives, thus accentuating the initial inequality, and also because they will probably prevent the undertaking of more radical reforms.[1]

Both of these propositions assume that there is a direct trade-off between redistribution and increasing output in agriculture. A similar trade-off has often been assumed, also on the basis of little or no evidence, in the economy as a whole. The relation of policies to reduce inequality and policies to produce growth is in reality as uncertain, and as unlikely to lend itself to productive generalization, in the agricultural sector as anywhere else.[2]

A quite different line or argument, for example, runs as follows. The possession of land in many societies is of more than strictly economic significance. Land not only provides security against inflation but also social prestige and power in the form of control over labor. In these circumstances, where the concentration of land underlies the concentration of political and economic power, there is unlikely to be any "trickle down" of productivity increases from the rich to the poor. "Thus if in response to tax, price, and other 'carrot and stick' policies, inactive owners either sell to commercial farmers or become more active themselves in introducing new technology, it will probably decrease employment and increase labor unrest. Investment in technical measures within the present institutional context may achieve optimistic short run results only to run afoul of costly social and political upheaval."[3] In order to make widespread economic improvement possible in the rural areas of developing countries which fit this pattern, social and political reform is not a luxury that cannot be afforded in the name of growth; rather, it is a necessary prerequisite for growth.

Few would go so far as to argue, however, that the breakup of large estates will in and of itself increase output. Although there is substantial evidence that output per unit of land is inversely related to land size and that this relationship holds even when existing farms are split up into new, smaller units, as in a land reform, peasants will usually require substantial complementary inputs of equipment, credit, and technical assistance over a long period of time before this result can be expected. Indeed, it can be argued that the provision of cheap credit to peasants is itself the key to agricultural growth in a sense since, by directly lowering the supply cost of land, it will stimulate the extension of the margin of cultivation into underutilized land, thus increasing the peasant's surplus over subsistence and reducing the risk of lending to him, so that interest rates will fall still further.[4]

Where landlords have monopolistic or oligopolistic power in particular market areas, the extent of underutilized land will, of course, be even greater and underemployment of both land and labor will exist. These conditions, which will come about with perfectly rational profit-maximizing landowners, may well, of course, be accentuated by managerial sloth on the part of many larger landowners. In these cases, a necessary complementary policy to any effort to increase agricultural production or to redistribute land without hurting production is to undertake the development of farm-to-market roads and similar investments in order to reduce monopoly and its attendant social inefficiencies.

Some would be more optimistic than this in predicting beneficial production effects from land reform per se. If, for example, one believes that the owner-occupiers of efficient-sized parcels would be quicker to adopt new cereal varieties or other improvements than would tenants, the effects of land reform on production will look better in the long run.[5] Similarly, it can be argued that land reform will not only make the distribution of incomes more equal, but that it will also encourage work effort. Owners, unlike tenants, will apply more labor to land, even if the marginal product of labor is low, because they receive not only wages but also property income and are therefore interested in the average product of their effort.

More importantly, "in rural areas, landownership or other secure forms of tenure which assure the farmer of some control over the returns from his labor and the land he works is the real and practically the only means of participation in the social and economic life of one's country. . . . Land reform is deeply relevant. . . . Land must be viewed as a vehicle for human development as well as a resource for food production."[6] Similarly, a recent massive A.I.D. study of land reform concluded that "the social and political goals of wider distribution of opportunity, power and employment among farm people is *not in conflict with* but *consistent with* increased agricultural productivity or efficiency."[7]

These variant views on the nature and effects of land reform suggest the difficulty of generalizing from one (often implicit) set of assumptions to make sweeping policy prescriptions for all countries, as writers in this field seem prone to do. The discussion of the relationship between land taxation and land reform is similarly complicated by the wide variety of existing and conceivable objectives and circumstances.

Three approaches to land reform may perhaps be usefully distinguished: total revolution, direct nonrevolutionary reform, and vigorous and progressive taxation of land. The usual arguments against the first method are its high direct social, political, and economic cost and the fact that revolution alone does nothing to provide an alternative to the landlord for supply of credit, market, and similar functions.

The second method may be similarly opposed because it requires an effective political will for reform that is hard to generate and a considerable amount of administrative ability to carry out the reform needed at the local level. Both the will and the ability are in scarce supply in most countries. Furthermore, it can be argued that an incomplete or unsuccessful reform of this sort may do more harm than good by destroying mainly the smaller and politically weaker farmers and still further corrupting the administration.

For these reasons some authors have favored the tax road to reform. Hunter, for example, recognized that taxation, too, needs political will and effective administration. Nevertheless, he argued that "it does not interfere so directly with social development. . . . It is a good deal easier for the small man to give a vote to a national party which supports it than to enforce newly granted tenant rights against a patron."[8] Both the relevance and the accuracy of this statement are open to serious question, however.

Taxes have traditionally been a favorite method, in theory at least, for altering land-use patterns in the rural areas of Colombia, for example. Land taxation has long been seen, by both Colombians and foreigners, as the key to successful "land reform." The culmination of various earlier efforts in this direction in Decree 290 of 1957 was in some ways a model for this sort of legislation, providing for a classification of agricultural land into four types with detailed requirements for the use of each type if the owner was to avoid severe tax sanctions. Like so many models, however, Decree 290 was never put into effect, nominally because of the tremendous technical difficulty of classifying the land as the law requires. (Nonetheless, certain tax exemptions in the law were put into effect at once since it was left to the initiative of the taxpayers to claim them!)

It has been plausibly suggested that this law, and its predecessors and successors, was not really a failure, for the continued inability of such tax measures to solve the land "problem" eventually made it quite clear that any desired changes in the land tenure system would have to be brought about by other, more direct means, such as the Colombian Institute of Agrarian Reform, which was indeed set up a few years later.[9]

Colombian experience also suggests that land taxes in themselves are unlikely to produce substantial land reforms, in part because of the technical difficulties of implementation and the consequent scope for endless arguments on technical points. In general, if direct changes in land tenure are politically unacceptable, it is unlikely that any tax gadget designed to achieve the same end can be effectively enforced. In order to achieve the same goal, taxes will have to exert the same pressure as more direct measures. They are thus likely to stir up the same opposition and to have at best the same chance of success.

Nevertheless, the land reform objective has usually been one reason behind proposals for the heavy progressive taxation of land, especially that held by absentee owners, of idle lands, and so on. Without saying anything about the merits of the various changes in

LAND REFORM AND LOCAL GOVERNMENT

land tenure and utilization patterns designed to be brought about by such measures, it does seem fair, on the basis of the discussion in earlier chapters, to say that most claims for drastic nonfiscal impacts from such land tax changes are naïve, for both technical and political reasons. In a different context, Hunter recognized the same point when he said "since camouflage deceives no one except perhaps the government itself, what the government wants to do it had better do openly, and had better take care to do well."[10]

All land reforms are fundamentally political in nature. So are all tax reforms. Both are, in a sense, concerned primarily with the distribution of power in society. In some cases, direct measures, such as expropriation, may shade into indirect measures, such as a capital levy, and may be analyzed similarly. For example, in both instances the disincentive effects of any change, or reform measure, will be greatly accentuated by delay and uncertainty. More generally, the effects of any reforms depend heavily on initial conditions. Peasant attitudes, economic holdings, and the capability of the government for speedy implementation are all important.[11]

In Latin America, for example, most land reform laws are permissive rather than mandatory in their major provisions, so that the extent to which any reforms are actually carried out depends primarily on the will of the government and the resources it makes available for the purpose.[12] Little has been done with this legislation in most Latin American countries. This is as true of the common supplementary proposals to impose heavily graduated taxes on idle land as it is of direct land redistribution.

The basic reason for this inaction is undoubtedly political. To cite a rather extreme formulation of the Latin American dilemma: "The landowning oligarchies have never encountered any social or political force to counteract their power. *Any* kind of reform is therefore extremely difficult; progressive land taxation meets with as much resistance as expropriation and distribution."[13] Although most dramatic in Latin America, the characteristic problem of underdeveloped latifundia accompanied by substantial rural underemployment occurs elsewhere.[14] There is no reason to believe that any desired degree of income redistribution, which is not directly attainable in such cases for political reasons, can be indirectly achieved by taxation with any less pain and trouble.

In another view, however, land reform and tax reform may perhaps be regarded as good substitutes. If a major barrier to industrialization is considered to be the lack of effective demand owing to the unequal distribution of income, which in turn largely reflects the unequal distribution of land, then redistributing either income via the tax-transfer system, or land via agrarian reform might in principle serve to break this bottleneck. This effect of land reform might be especially marked where it results in increased monetization of the economy. At least two conditions are necessary for the desired result: that there exist an industrial base, whereby the supply of domestically produced industrial goods is elastic and, presumably, nonforeign-exchange-intensive; and that "land reform" include not just land redistribution but such complements as more and cheaper credit, irrigation, and a stronger infrastructure.[15]

In another view, land reform can be seen as essentially a redistributive measure that acts as a delayed corrective for regressive tax systems and extensive evasion.[16] The lack of effective progressive taxation is thus likely to increase the demand for land reform which, in effect, is a capital levy intended to redistribute wealth from the rich to the poor.[17] It follows from this argument that, unless an effective tax system is introduced subsequent to a land reform, the original conditions tend to reappear over time. Furthermore, land taxes will be needed even more than they were before the reform in order to finance the complementary inputs required to sustain production. The new distribution of the benefits should, however, make it easier to establish the tax system on a firmer basis.

A related approach to the connection between land taxes and land reform is that land reform may facilitate and indeed make necessary land taxation: "It is only *after* land redistribution and the establishment of a family-farm system that the political will to tax agriculture in the interests of economic development is likely to emerge."[18] Indeed, since the state must to at least some extent replace the landlord as accumulator in this model, the beneficiaries of the land reform must certainly be taxed if a net flow of resources out of agriculture is an essential component of development policy.

Even if all tax revenues are reinvested in agriculture, care will generally have to be taken to maintain the land tax after a land reform since it has usually been one of the first things to disappear in countries that have undergone such reform. Land reform accompanied by appropriate land tax reform may greatly increase the potential mobilization of capital from rural taxpayers, especially for such desired investments as education for their children. The cost of providing services such as education, market systems, local roads, water supply, and law and order is a potentially heavy burden that should be more willingly shared if the land tenure structure is accepted by all.[19] In this connection it is especially important not to exempt new landowners from direct taxes for fear of spoiling them forever as taxpayers.[20]

A summary of the main conceivable relationships between land taxation and land reform might run as follows:[21] (1) Land reform will be facilitated by the existence of land tax records and in some cases may indeed depend upon them for success, especially when the land values recorded for tax purposes provide the basis of compensation. (2) Heavier land taxes will tend to reduce land prices and to increase the cost of holding land as a status symbol, thus increasing the feasibility and reducing the cost of nonconfiscatory land reforms. (3) Any land tax has nonfiscal effects and hence should be structured to the extent possible to help rather than hinder reform objectives (for example, the point concerning the "size coefficient" noted in Chapter 11, above). (4) A successful land reform may reduce land tax revenues if the tax is progressive by size of holding or if production is adversely affected. (5) Even a confiscatory land reform generally requires complementary expenditures, as noted earlier, and hence requires financing through taxes, including land taxes. (6) Land reform may strengthen the land tax system by widening the tax base, especially if production increases, and making it politically more feasible to levy taxes which can then recoup in part some of the benefits previously distributed as a result of the reform. (7) An adequate land tax system may indeed be needed subsequent to a successful land reform to prevent the reappearance of the conditions requiring reform in the first place.

In general, land taxes of any variety are unlikely to prove adequate substitutes for more direct land reforms, no matter how ingeniously the tax rates may be varied by size or value of holding or by degree of departure from some optimal use level. The liquidity and incentive effects which stimulate more rational use or sale of underutilized lands are usually minor in practice as are the taxes themselves in most instances. If a country has the political power to tax heavily enough to induce major changes in land holdings and the administrative ability to collect the taxes, it could also generally alter the tenurial system directly and should in all likelihood do so. "Land reform" is at least likely to get the support of the landless, while tax reform is all too often supported by no one. It is also probably easier to evade taxes than direct controls, although the latter are more costly to administer. Reliance on land taxes may even be counterproductive in that, while achieving no reform themselves, their mere existence may be taken to mean no other reform measures are needed.

On the whole, then, land taxes and land reforms are best viewed as complements rather than as alternatives. In designing a land tax system, close attention should be paid to any land reform policy objectives and, to the extent that they are consistent with its principal objectives, the tax should work to support and complement land reform rather than to be at cross-purposes with it. Land reforms should similarly be structured with an eye to their consequences for the land tax system.

LAND TAXES AND LOCAL GOVERNMENT

It has often been suggested that a strong local government is an essential ingredient of rural development. Mellor, for example, argues in his important text on agricultural development that the net extraction of capital from agriculture can be substantially higher if local government bodies are developed.[22] Taxation for local purposes may then be considered less onerous by taxpayers. Also, more opportunities exist to tax unemployed local resources for rural public works if there is some local control.

On the other hand, many see a considerable danger that local self-government in many poor countries will simply strengthen the hold of the traditional rural elite. In India, for instance, where the village is "the stronghold of stagnation,"[23] it has been argued that only a fundamental land reform which changed the basic economic and social structure could alter the existing situation, where all too often, "whatever the basis of power and the degree of cooperation, the chief function of local self-government was to preserve the social and economic balance in a stagnant, largely self-sufficient community closed to outside influences."[24] Without such reform, local rural public works, for example, are most likely to benefit only the upper stratum of rural society, thus accentuating existing inequalities. In this situation it is also doubtful to what extent labor and resources can be mobilized for such investment without substantial coercion.

Nevertheless, the tremendous local diversity of agriculture in most poor countries requires at the very least substantial provision in some way or other for local adaptation of centrally determined policies if they are to be made workable. The desire, common to the planners of many countries, for uniform application of measures throughout the whole of a diverse nation has in practice often been a death warrant for innovation, both locally and nationally. It is a mistake to say that making room for local initiative acts against rational national planning; it may, on the contrary, facilitate it by increasing total resources available for developmental purposes, utilizing more intensively the available skills, knowledge, and interest, and permitting modest degrees of social experimentation without courting national disaster.

Local government is an obvious means to this end, at least conceptually, and the same is true for land taxation. The possible problem of tax competition among localities, especially for more mobile market centers and other nonagricultural rural capital, can be obviated by establishing a minimum national rate and a uniform assessment basis, administered centrally. Decentralization will likely raise taxable capacity in the rural sector. When farmers can see some return for their money, they will be more willing to pay for the services they want.

Another result, of course, would be an uneven pattern of development as some areas would do more than others, but it is hard to see why it would be bad to let those most willing to help themselves do so since the central governments in poor countries are usually unable to provide uniform standards anyway. The main argument against decentralization is not administrative but political, understandably so in countries usually made up of diverse peoples each with their own contending local leaders. Those in precarious power at the center are most unlikely to weaken their authority by strengthening subordinate units of government. Once again, then, the need for relatively stable political conditions seems a primordial condition of development.

Given the tremendous shortage of administrative talent common in most countries, efforts should be concentrated not on trying to run everything in detail from the center but rather on setting up general policy rules so that people at the local level are induced to make their own decisions as far as possible and to make the right ones from the point of view of national policy. This sort of decentralization may not be so superficially tidy, but in diverse countries it is likely to be more economically efficient than further unnecessary centralization.

The virtue of putting the decision closer to the consumers and perhaps using otherwise wasted entrepreneurial talents is obvious. There is substantial evidence, for example, that in some rural areas local community development programs have been quite successful in mobilizing both resources and entrepreneurial talents and in efficiently allocating them.[25] It can even be argued that unless farmers have a substantial amount of influence and control over the local governmental and service agencies with which they are concerned, they will in many cases be neither willing nor able to absorb the meaning and method of improving their economic and technical performance. Participation increases both the level of knowledge and the quality of rational decisions, so that the potential virtues of local government are not just political but also economic in nature.[26]

In addition, establishing a clearer connection between government services and the taxes levied to pay for them by decentralizing some government functions will force more revelation of preferences and simultaneously slow the demand for public services while increasing their supply. Centralization, in contrast, almost inevitably ensures that the demand for expensive public services exceeds the supply.[27] Not only may the total resources for development be increased by encouraging local areas to finance more of their own expenditures, but the allocation of resources might also be improved through heavier reliance on local taxes where possible.

An important factor in development taxation is tax consciousness or, more broadly, a sense of civic obligation. Difficult as it is to quantify the existence or degree of this attribute of a society, there can be no question of its relevance. A principal argument for increasing the role of local governments in both raising and spending revenues lies in this area. The argument is really the same as that with respect to any other earmarking: people are more willing to pay if they can be made to believe that they derive some tangible benefit from the activities of the taxing government.

LAND REFORM AND LOCAL GOVERNMENT

What is often missed, however, is the especially crucial importance of this simple proposition in societies with no tradition of voluntary support of government. There are few things more important in a sound developmental tax policy than efforts to reduce the ancient and all too often well-founded distrust and fear of tax collectors and "alien" (meaning colonial or urban) governments. Even if one believes that the political power of elite landowners is the key factor blocking the adoption of heavier land taxes, one of the few hopes for progress is to get a tax at least associated in their minds with expenditures they may see as advantageous. This may not do much to reduce evasion and the use of political power to counter taxation, but even a small step in this direction would help in some countries. The traditional suspicion of outsiders manifested by peasant communities makes all of these arguments even more powerful when considering agricultural taxation than they are for taxation in general.

If there is one thing almost all students of tax reform are agreed upon, it is that there must be fairly general public acceptance of the need for change if a reform—any reform—is to be acceptable. Since tax reform almost always means more taxes on somebody, public acceptance of the need for change requires some degree of public acceptance of government expenditure policies and of government in general. If the public attitude is one of dislike and contempt, as expressed in the alleged Brazilian saying, "Our country grows by night, when the politicians sleep," prospects for meaningful reform are dim. In the case of the property tax, which directly affects almost every articulate citizen, effective publicity is an absolute necessity. Such publicity, aimed in part at justifying the expenditures carried out with the tax money, is not impossible, as experience in some countries shows.[28] People will never like taxes, but they can sometimes be made to accept them by a good public relations campaign. The need to thus "sell" the product of government is usually unduly neglected by tax policy makers and administrators. A punitive attitude toward taxpayers can seldom produce as satisfactory and frictionless results as inducing them to pay more or less voluntarily.

A possible virtue of land taxation that has not received the attention it deserves is that it lends itself to levying separate rates for each public function financed. This virtue is not particularly applicable to the major increase in agricultural taxation discussed elsewhere, but it could be most useful if the land tax is also viewed, as it should be in many countries, as the principal financial resource of local governments in rural areas.

Although the economic case for increased land taxation is often strong in theory, the political possibility of achieving substantial increases in revenues from this source may well depend on how and where the money is used. Budgetary unity is an important principle of fiscal policy in any country, but the need for public revenues is more important in most poor countries. If this need can be satisfied only by setting up independently financed autonomous institutions or local governments, or by the partial equivalent of earmarking a tax, then earmarking may be justified. In the particular case of the land tax, a substantial increase in rates or a general revaluation program would probably be politically acceptable in many countries only if taxpayers knew the money would be spent on something of tangible benefit to them or their immediate neighbors.

To illustrate, if development programs are to touch the lives of most peasants significantly, it will doubtless in part be through increased access to public services like education. If local communities are not interested in sacrificing something to improve their children's lot in life, it is perhaps unlikely that there is much hope for substantial national progress of any sort. In many areas the attractiveness of education as a public expenditure has already led to substantial contributions by landowners to community development programs for the construction of schools, for example. In these circumstances, it may well be that a land tax increase tied to education may be the only way to improve both the financing of education and the general municipal fiscal situation.[29]

The usual arguments made against earmarking in underdeveloped countries give too little weight to this all-important factor of political acceptability. The danger of undue distortion of the development program from the particular earmarking suggested here seems remote, at least for years to come in most countries, especially if the rate of the earmarked tax is kept flexible.

Major problems with such suggestions might arise, however, because of the incapacity of many smaller rural municipalities to take on any responsibility at all for the raising and spending of more money on anything, or because of the hierarchial control exerted by the rural elite. There are other problems as well. The heritage of colonial years, the poor record of some postcolonial governments, overcentralization, and corruption have, for instance, been said to hamper considerably progress toward sound local administration anywhere in such countries as Indonesia.[30]

These remarks must not, therefore, be taken to constitute an invariably persuasive case for "local government" in the traditional Anglo-Saxon sense. Quite apart from the problems already mentioned, few central governments in developing countries are eager to delegate power. Yet there is no easy way to establish the necessary political conditions for development, and it seems likely that many countries will in one way or another have to turn in the future to such devices as increased delegation to local governments and increased regionalization of administration in an effort to cope with the overwhelming problems they face. The results may not always be good, but in at least some instances they may well be better than any feasible alternative.

In any event, if local governments are to exist and to be viable, they will need some local revenues. Property taxes are the most obvious source of such revenues. As noted above, it may well be easier to tap this revenue source at the local level for local spending purposes, and there may also be some administrative advantage in doing so in terms of information and compliance. But, in general, experience suggests strongly that substantial centralized assessment and administrative guidance is generally needed if this policy route is chosen. Centralized assessment is the only efficient way to utilize modern mass appraisal techniques and to keep values up to date. Local administration can also usefully be strengthened by, for example, centralized preparation of tax bills as well as by providing technical assistance to local governments through regional development corporations, special municipal institutes, or other agencies. While, as always, the particular circumstances of each country must govern, there is probably good reason in most countries to urge closer attention to the sorts of interconnections noted here between good land taxes and good local governments.

13

THE DESIGN OF AGRICULTURAL LAND TAXES

A principal argument in this book is that the level and form of agricultural taxation appropriate for any particular country depends upon the initial conditions in that country and its developmental objectives and possibilities. The conventional argument that heavy agricultural taxes are an essential ingredient of development policy is, for instance, derived from an oversimple model of agriculture's role in development and an unrealistic view of the feasible structure of agricultural taxation in most poor countries. It cannot, therefore, be lightly applied to any particular country without close examination of individual circumstances.

Countries where the population is mostly agricultural, whose export earnings depend heavily upon agricultural exports, which are trying to develop through exploiting their internal markets for consumer goods, and which are in some sense politically responsive to the current well-being of the mass of the (rural) population are much less well advised to attempt to tax agriculture heavily than countries which can better afford, in both economic and political terms, to reduce incentives to agricultural productivity and to encourage migration to urban areas. Even in circumstances where heavy agricultural taxes are needed, much of the surplus thus mobilized will often have to be reinvested in agriculture itself (even in cases where there is "slack" in one form or another which may potentially be utilized) if the rate of growth of agricultural productivity is to be maintained. The potentially more refined effects of various tax measures must always take second place to these basic decisions on the appropriate tax level.

There are few developing countries in which agriculture has been taxed heavily enough in recent years either to provide substantial resources for public developmental purposes or to affect significantly the allocation and distribution of resources within the agricultural sector. Quite apart from such political factors as the resistance of farmers to taxation and the unwillingness of governments to tax food, there are at least two good reasons why agriculture is lightly taxed in many countries. One is that farming enterprises are not administratively easy to tax, as experience in all countries at all income levels clearly suggests. The other is that most farmers, whether self-employed, tenants, or laborers, are poor.

When the agricultural sector has been taxed moderately heavily, it has usually been by means of taxes on exports of agricultural products rather than through direct taxes on income or property. The administrative ease of taxing exports appears in these instances to have outweighed the usual political difficulties of taxing agriculture, whereas in the case of land taxes the considerable administrative complexity of the conventionally recommended approach has combined with political problems to block the development of an effective tax system.

On economic grounds alone, however, heavier reliance upon taxes on agricultural land would seem the most desirable way to obtain increased public revenues from the agricultural sector for developmental purposes, if this is the appropriate policy goal. Only through land taxes can desirable incentives be created within the agricultural sector, which will, at the same time, increase its contribution to public revenues. Severe noneconomic constraints have, however, generally prevented the governments of less developed countries from following this particular path to development. For example, the weight of history lies heavy on attempts to revive land taxation in many countries because land taxes have long been seen by peasants as instruments of oppression by colonial powers—the British in India or the Belgians in the Congo, for example—or by indigenous ruling classes.

For these and other reasons, it is hard to see increased land taxes realistically replacing export taxes as revenue producers in the near future. If it is desired to increase agriculture's contribution in the short run to the public treasury in many developing countries, it may even be advisable in the first instance to improve and strengthen export taxes rather than to pin one's hopes on land taxes.

In the long run, of course, export taxes on agricultural products are not a promising fiscal instrument on which to rely because of their disincentive effects and the instability of the revenues which they produce. Heavier taxes on agricultural land have much more merit if political circumstances allow their use and sufficient time and effort can be devoted to establishing the necessary legal and administrative framework. There is no question that, with sufficient expenditure of resources, land taxes can, if desired, be made much more effective fiscal instruments in most countries than has been true to date.

The most rewarding path to follow if an agricultural land tax is to contribute much to development would seem to be to concentrate on establishing a solidly based simple property tax with meaningful rates, rather than attempting to achieve primarily nonfiscal purposes through graduated rates of tax, special taxes on idle lands, and similar devices. The difficult task of levying effective land taxes has been made more difficult in some countries by the propensity to attempt to achieve through the land tax nonfiscal purposes such as bringing idle lands into production and breaking up large landed estates. As a rule, however, the effective rates of tax have been so low that few, if any, of these nonfiscal objectives have actually been realized. Indeed, one might perhaps even suggest that undue complexity of form tends to be associated with a light tax burden since the effort needed to clarify the nonessentials diverts attention from the central question of tax level.

TAX POLICY AS A DEVELOPMENT TOOL

The changing function of agricultural tax policy as the nature of the economy and the objectives of development policy change may be illustrated by considering briefly the range of problems created for agricultural taxation by the import-substituting industrialization policies long favored in many countries. These policies have on the whole generally worked to the detriment of agricultural development. The higher industrial prices resulting from protection turn the internal terms of trade against agriculture, especially when, as is often the case, they are combined with price controls imposed on agricultural goods in order to maintain urban real wages. Furthermore, the overvalued exchange rates which often accompany these policies also hurt agriculture by making agricultural exports less profitable. The allocation of most investible resources to industry also means less is available for agriculture. The means chosen to foster industrialization thus often stifle incentives for agricultural production. Argentina is the classic illustration of this.[1]

The effect of industrialization policy as typically pursued is to alter the relative price structure of labor and capital in such a way as to reduce the rate of labor absorption and to increase the search for, and adoption of, capital-intensive techniques. While these policies have their greatest effect in determining the structure of industry itself, they are also significant in accentuating the dual nature of agricultural production, especially since the range of technological choices is probably more flexible in agriculture than in industry. Many tax policies have helped in biasing factor prices and the choice of technology.[2]

Capital-favoring policies affect not only the choice of technology but also the distribution of income, tending to increase already existing inequalities and, hence, social pressures. Unless offset by explicit redistributive government policy, the growth of new incremental demands is thus slowed down—in particular, demands for lower-income consumer nondurables most likely to act as incentive goods to encourage increased marketing or agricultural production.[3] The regional concentration of income characteristic of this situation accentuates the general rural-urban inequality. Increasingly, it is being argued that the distribution of income needs to be changed to overcome the obstacle to industrial expansion created by the past pattern of industrialization.

One problem with changing the profile of demand through changing the distribution of income is that the structure of industrial production may take quite a while to adjust to the new consumer demand pattern. Another is that one would expect pressure on food supplies to tend to increase, thus accentuating the urgency of transforming traditional agriculture.

Another problem is that in many instances it appears that the labor-intensive technique is less productive, so that there is indeed a conflict between output and employment, at least with respect to manufacturing industry. If there is a choice between output and employment, it would appear that only very shortsighted policymakers would choose the latter, for the higher growth path will over time yield both more output and more employment. There are, however, both economic and political factors contravening this simple conclusion. The political factor is simply that increasing open unemployment is not conducive to a stable political environment. Over time, therefore, one might expect that either the policy will change or the government will. It seems likely that political factors will force change before long-run expansion in employment opportunities from a strictly growth-oriented policy can be realized.

The economic situation is more complicated. In the first place, not all labor-intensive techniques are less efficient in terms of requiring a higher capital-output ratio than more capital-intensive techniques (that is, techniques with a higher capital-labor ratio). In particular, this appears to be more likely in the case of agriculture with its less rigid technical coefficients of production and its greater rewards to intimate individual knowledge of the unique characteristics of each parcel of land. In the second place, there is the problem, already mentioned, that with the more growth-oriented policy, particularly in the import-substituting form it has taken in many countries, there goes an increasing personal and regional concentration of income which in turn means a relatively slow growth of demand for the products of mass industry.

The immediate effect of the Green Revolution has often been to add to the incomes of the already rich, partly because the inputs are not truly neutral to scale in that, for example, credit to buy fertilizers and technical assistance on how to use it is only extended to larger farmers. The only way to offset this may be through some land redistribution combined with complementary changes in institutional infrastructure.

It is far from clear that a simple redistribution of income, whether through fiscal or such other means as land reform will lead to a breaking of the industrial structure and import constraint bottlenecks now found in a number of countries.[4] Nevertheless, it seems likely that policies affecting the composition of demand will become increasingly important for many countries in the immediate future as they struggle to regain growth momentum. In this new policy perspective, agriculture will assume increasing importance.

In the first place, the importance of agricultural exports, both traditional and new, will receive new stress. Taxes on these exports will, hence, become increasingly unattractive as revenue sources in view of their well-demonstrated effects in discouraging exports. Secondly, if income is successfully redistributed downward, this will have profound implications for the agricultural sector both as producer and consumer. The high income elasticity of demand for food by the lower-income groups, both urban and rural, which will benefit from the redistribution means that an increase in marketed food products will be needed in the urban sector at the same time as an increase in home-consumed production will be demanded by the rural producers. The only solution is to increase total food production more rapidly than before.

There is now overwhelming evidence that farmers throughout the world are very sensitive to changes in the relative prices of different crops. Although less certain, it appears that total agricultural output is also responsive to changes in the agricultural terms of trade, however engendered. This suggests that lower taxes on produce sales, for example, might provide both incentive and resources for increased investment in agricultural production. There is also, however, usually a requirement for increased governmental financing of agricultural investment which must, in the circumstances of most countries, be financed by increased taxation of the agricultural sector itself. Taxes on marketed production, and indeed on production as such, are thus undesirable, while all the traditional arguments for levying substantial monetary taxes on the rural population acquire new power.

On the other hand, the supposed aim of the new policy is to alter the structure of industry by expanding the size of the domestic market for mass-produced industrial products. In countries where a high proportion of the economically active population is still in the rural sector, this can be done only by increasing the monetary income of that population. Tapping the rural sector through heavy taxes on inputs or on consumer goods works against the supposed goals of the policy. The only solution to this dilemma again lies in an increase in marketed production. Fortunately the new developments in agricultural technology appear to make this possible in at least some circumstances provided that the benefits of the technology are made available to all and not permitted to add in the first instance to inequalities within the rural sector itself.

The rather curious conclusion suggested by this brief sketch of some emerging issues of development policy is that the traditional argument for a heavy direct tax on potential income from agricultural land may come into its own more in partially industrialized countries that are trying to get out of a structural bind created in part by their own industrialization policies, rather than in the more primitive agrarian societies for which it is usually proposed. Only through such a tax can a stimulus to production be given without adding to price distortions or income inequalities. Equally significant, only in moderately developed countries is there much hope of setting up and administering such a levy successfully.

Even the political situation should be more conducive to success. On the one hand, in a semi-industrialized country there are, by definition, important political forces, other than the traditional landholding class, which might perhaps be mobilized in support of such a policy. On the other hand, there is no question in this instance of using land taxes to transfer resources out of agriculture, as in the traditional argument. Instead, what is involved is mainly a reallocation of resources within agriculture and perhaps even a net inflow. Some resort to earmarking of revenues for local expenditure purposes may thus not only make the needed direct taxes more palatable but also be in accord with the dictates of development policy.

The appropriate goal of agricultural tax policy in this situation would appear to be twofold: to increase agricultural production and to alter the distribution of income in the rural sector. The net balance of fiscal policy will probably be to favor the agricultural sector, especially the poorer farmers. The income effect of a tax on land will encourage the productive use of existing resources in the agricultural sector, while the increased flow of public investment resources and credit to agriculture will facilitate this expansion, and the enlarged availability at lower prices of both inputs and consumer products will stimulate it. Except for the stress on increased rural consumption of industrial products and the crucial fact that there would be no increased outflow of resources from agriculture to industry, this scenario bears close resemblance to the conventional case for the taxation of agricultural land. Instead of coming as an essential prelude to any significant industrialization, however, the suggestion here is that this tax policy may fit in best, and be more feasible, as a part of the transitional stage from industrialization propelled by import substitution to that aimed at satisfying the demands of a broader-based domestic market.

THE POLITICAL ECONOMY OF LAND TAXATION

The reasons why few countries appear to have effective land taxes of any sort probably stem from administrative and political factors. A number of analytical and factual puzzles—such as the incidence of export taxes and the virtually universal lack of information on the volume and pattern of savings and investment—in the agricultural sector itself, however, also confuse matters. When combined with the growing uncertainty of many as to the role that mobilization of resources from agriculture plays in development, these factors may be almost as important as politics in explaining both the absence in most countries of a clear and coherent policy direction on the vital question of agriculture's appropriate contribution to development resources and the corresponding presence in most developing countries of a confused and confusing mass of contradictory public policies affecting land use, agricultural production, and the distribution and allocation of agricultural resources.

The outstanding impression conveyed by any survey of agricultural taxation in developing countries, apart from the weakness of some vital primary information, is how little basic empirical work has really been done in this field, despite twenty years of continual discussion of agricultural tax problems.[5] Furthermore, much of the existing empirical work has been concerned mostly with the "relative burden" of taxation on the agricultural and nonagricultural sectors, although the relevance of information of this nature for the design of agricultural taxation is, as argued in Chapter 10, far from clear.

There are, no doubt, good reasons why there have been so few empirical studies of the effects of alternative land tax structures. The subject matter is, it must be confessed, inherently tedious. The data could hardly be worse. The complexity and peculiarity of the institutional context is marked. The taxes are usually low, and their consequences are hopelessly intermingled with those of other governmental policies affecting agriculture.

For all of these reasons, the lack of solid research on agricultural tax policy is not surprising. Another reason may be that so much development research has been conducted by itinerant scholars. Agriculture and public finance are not only grubby, institutional subjects with low professional prestige within the economics fraternity, but they also require, as a rule, substantial local knowledge in order to be able to say anything useful about them.

Despite the tenuous nature of the evidence, however, one conclusion seems clear: as matters now stand, the direct taxation of agriculture in most developing countries contributes very little to financing public expenditures either within agriculture or more generally. Where much revenue is collected, as through some export taxes, the effects on agriculture itself are not likely to be desirable; where the effects are at least in theory desirable, as through well-ordered land taxes, little revenue is collected. No less developed country today appears to be emulating the oft-cited experience of late nineteenth-century Japan in imposing heavy agricultural land taxes as a major source of public revenues.

Whether the reasons for this apparently regular pattern are political or otherwise, the prospects of a drastic change in this situation in the immediate future do not appear to be strong. From a developmental point of view, therefore, the results of this look at the taxation of agriculture must be considered somewhat depressing, certainly by those who believe that agriculture should make a net contribution through the tax system to development elsewhere in the economy.

The fact that few countries appear to tax agriculture very heavily is unlikely, however, to reflect very deep thought about the many and complex conceptual issues at stake. Three other explanations are commonly offered for this general failure to obtain much of a contribution for public revenues from the agricultural sector.

Feasibility Constraints on Tax Level

One explanation is "that insufficient recognition of the strategic role that agriculture can and should play in contributing to the capital requirements of economic development has been a factor in the failure to realize the potential for a higher rate of capital formation."[6] In view of the lack of explicit discussion of most of these matters in many countries, there may be some truth in this proposition that the failure to tax agriculture reflects some such perceptual deficiency on the part of policy makers. On the other hand, they have been told about the conventional reasoning often enough by foreign advisers. Their failure to act on this advice may equally well reflect a different perception of the appropriate reality on their part. Yet again, to argue that "correct" knowledge will necessarily lead to "correct" action suggests a rather naïve view of the policy process.

Few proponents of heavier taxes on agriculture have actually been this naïve. Instead, they fall back on a second sort of explanation for the "inadequate" agricultural taxation they see characterizing most developing countries:

In many instances the hesitation to tax the agricultural sector is traceable to political factors, although administrative difficulties are generally cited as the explanation. *Either* the rural votes have to be safeguarded—a question of great significance in most democratic, underdeveloped countries in view of their massive rural sectors. *Or* the landed interests constitute an oligarchy powerful enough to block further taxation of the agricultural sector.[7]

Nicholas Kaldor prefers to emphasize only the political power of the wealthy in his explanation of the failure of the underdeveloped countries to tax agriculture adequately, although he agrees in downgrading the importance of the administrative obstacle to effective agricultural taxation.[8]

While there is certainly much merit in this view for some countries, attributing the widespread low level of direct taxation on agriculture entirely to a failure of political will is too simple. The administrative aspects of heavy agricultural land taxes, particularly those primarily intended to exert positive incentive effects, require more careful consideration than they have normally received from their proponents. The inevitable, severe administrative limitations in any developing country do in fact appear to constitute a formidable obstacle to the implementation of many of the more sophisticated recommendations, which explains in part the widespread absence of effective land taxes.

Feasibility Constraints on Tax Form

The crucial importance of the particular interweaving of political, economic, and administrative conditions that characterize each country in determining the feasibility of agricultural tax recommendations may be made clearer by looking at the likely fate of an "ideal" agricultural tax proposed by one of the leading writers in the field, Haskell Wald.

Wald's "ideal" tax plan for a mass land tax related to individual tax-paying capacity requires that all agricultural land be classified and assessed in terms of its presumptive net income. As he points out: "To achieve this, two types of soil classifications are necessary: (1) in terms of inherent soil characteristics (i.e. scientific soil mapping to determine the 'soil profile'), and (2) in terms of economic use capabilities, as determined by potential water supply, climate, exposure to sunshine, topography, availability of farm implements, etc. Each delineated land area should be assigned a rating in accordance with its potential net income under average growing conditions and proper management, with appropriate allowances for distance from trading centers and other market factors."[9]

The informational requirements for this tax system to work properly are enormous, as are the administrative costs. What is not at all clear, however, is how sensitive the results of the system will be to imperfect information. If, as is all too likely, they are sensitive, the introduction of such a system into any country will likely lead to considerable bargaining, graft, compromises, and nonachievement of theoretical standards. The unreality of postulating the existence of this information as a prerequisite thus speaks for itself. Indeed, as Wald himself noted, in what must be one of the more striking understatements in the literature on development finance: "The requirements for its successful implementation in all its phases are doubtless prohibitive for many countries. . . ."[10] Nevertheless, he suggested that this approach provides an appropriate target at which to aim.

The logic of this position may seem irrefutable. It has, however, frequently been refuted by the fact that, in virtually every country in which grandiose plans of this sort have been proposed, they have failed to come to fruition. This uniform failure suggests that something is wrong with the proposed solution. And so it appears to be. For, if a country were capable of even attempting on a large scale the sorts of things Wald proposes, it would no longer be an underdeveloped country. And, if it were not underdeveloped, it would presumably not need to rely on heavy agricultural taxation and on indirect and backdoor attempts at effective income taxation through "personalized" land taxes. In short, the basic problem with Wald's proposed reform of the agricultural land tax to achieve better its fiscal ends of revenue and equity is the same as that with many similar proposed reforms to achieve nonfiscal ends—that is, it really assumes away many of the problems which it was allegedly designed to solve.

Writers who favor the extensive use of agricultural taxation for nonfiscal purposes occasionally recognize, usually with a note of surprise, that the many good things for which the legislation was enacted never seem to materialize. But their analysis of the reasons for this repeated failure, many instances of which have been noted in earlier chapters, leaves much to be desired. One recent author, for example, attributes it to the difficulty producers have in understanding the incentive effects of tax structure and to the generally negative attitude most people have toward taxes–an attitude fostered by the "complexity, incoherence and lack of stability in the tax formulas which are passed" and by the inadequacy of the tax education program. When the taxes fail, as they usually do, "the failure may be attributed not to the tax itself but rather to the legal formulas adopted to carry out this particular law, which established, for example, exceedingly low rates or legal formulas which are too complicated, and which normally go hand-in-hand with a high percentage of tax evasion."[11] The problem with this approach is that it completely ignores the political economy of taxation.

It is true, for example, that one reason why no incentive uses of agricultural taxes appear to have worked is that the legislation has almost always been poorly laid out and inadequately based on facts. As has already been suggested, another important reason is that the necessary precise information on soils and their capacity to produce income simply does not exist in most countries. Even more important, however, such proposals as a rule have no political backing. These points are related. Advocates of nonfiscal uses of agricultural taxation usually focus on the first point and dispose of the second by saying one needs this information anyway to design an adequate agricultural development plan or an efficient agrarian reform; they simply ignore the third.

The administrative difficulty cannot be so easily disposed of. It may not be as hard to get a rough idea of the necessary information as has sometimes been claimed by opponents of any effective taxation of agriculture, but it will always be rough and, therefore, it will be hard to use harshly on an individual basis, even if the political environment permitted. Levying heavy progressive taxes on only large farmers, for example, as is sometimes suggested, would certainly reduce the size of the administrative task, but at the same time it would place very heavy weight upon the "objectivity" and nonarguability of the tax base. The level of taxation thus constrains its feasible form.

Furthermore, the assumption apparent not only in this argument but in a great deal of the literature favoring the nonfiscal use of agricultural taxation—that the state not only can but must have the requisite detailed information—can bear little weight. The additional argument that now-advanced countries have gotten along with wretched assessment systems so perhaps a good informational base is not crucial simply ignores the points that these countries have never tried to place much nonfiscal weight on their agricultural tax systems and, more important, they have never had to place so much fiscal weight on agriculture as many less developed countries, pressed by time and circumstance, now feel they must. Finally, as noted in Chapter 12, it seems unlikely that it will be efficient to employ scarce administrative resources in administratively subtle schemes to avoid direct political conflict.

Considering further the political aspect, it is curious that the many writers who have proposed major tax changes largely on the grounds of their allegedly beneficial effects on economic incentives never appear to recognize the peculiar political setting that would have to prevail for such proposals to be both feasible and effective. The common argument that heavier taxes on the potential output of agricultural land will induce landowners either to use land more productively or to get out of the landowning business and sell to someone who will do so rests, for example, on two quite implausible assumptions. The first is that the government can administer the complex tax envisaged (that is, it has all the relevant data, and can effectively assess and enforce the correct tax levy), and the second is that the only option facing landowners is to pay or sell. The implausibility of the first has been discussed. The second has received less attention. Landowners do have a third option: they can protest, or, in Hirschman's terminology, exercise the "voice" instead of the "exit" option.[12]

A possible interpretation of the failure to levy heavy taxes on agriculture in some countries is thus that landowners are able to utilize effectively the voice option, which probably costs less and is more readily available than the exit option on which the conventional argument depends so heavily. Exercised at an early stage, the voice option kills off such tax proposals before they are enacted. In other instances, the vocal role may be more crucial when it is time to implement penalty tax legislation already enacted. Chile, Brazil, Colombia, and many other Latin American countries offer examples. The most effective way to block reform legislation may often be to set up a body (or pass a law) charged with the reform task but so crippled by its organization or structure that it can do nothing.

Linking Taxes and Expenditures

This stress on the importance of political as well as economic means of avoiding tax pressure is not meant simply to deplore the former and praise the latter. Rather, it adds considerable weight to economic arguments adduced earlier for strategic investments in the agricultural sector as essential ingredients of development policy in many situations. The point now is different from the common argument, which is also sound, that in order to impose a tax successfully in most developing countries one must first demonstrate a good reason for spending the tax proceeds, preferably one which can be shown to benefit in some moderately direct way the prospective taxpayers. Properly designed earmarking and benefit-financing are perhaps even more useful and essential with respect to agricultural taxation than elsewhere.[13]

In particular, the potentially important role of effective betterment taxes and user charges demands much closer attention to these devices in the rural sectors of most developing countries than has been usual in the past. As a recent study noted, "There is probably no other place in Middle Eastern agriculture where an institutional innovation, at a low cash outlay, would pay off better in terms of increased agricultural production, than in some system of irrigation water charges which would be technically and administratively practical and would provide a tangible and significant incentive to the farmer to apply water in reasonable amounts."[14]

Consideration of the role of voice in shaping the outcome of tax policy suggests an extra virtue for policies linking taxes and expenditures: such policies may help to split opposition to the new tax measures, making their introduction more feasible. It seems much less likely that attempts to demonstrate "unused taxable capacity" and the relative sectoral tax burden of agriculture will help much in this respect, since landed interests (or just plain farmers) can unite in protest at attempts to justify additional taxation by this approach. Another point is that many government policies in developing countries favor the more prosperous farmers, so that, unless special efforts are made to tax away some of these benefits, existing inequalities will be accentuated.

STRATEGY AND TACTICS OF TAX CHANGE

Both the political and administrative constraints are crucial in shaping the feasible level and, especially, the structure of agricultural tax policy. In many countries, these considerations (and past experience) would appear to urge relatively simple taxes on agricultural land, supplemented by as many benefit taxes and user charges as possible and backed up by careful research on the appropriate level of the net intersectoral flow of resources in the country in question. Attempts to go beyond this simple prescription and to resolve all of man's ills with gimmick-ridden personalized taxes on potential agricultural income not only are unlikely to come to pass; they may also tend to block more feasible measures, which may sometimes be more, rather than less, drastic.

The most serious problem with most schemes for reforming agricultural taxation is that they are too perfect. Complexity may be a virtue rather than a vice—for example, when it is needed to cope with a complex economic situation or when it leapfrogs over problems— and perfection is presumably a desirable, though unattainable, quality. But attempts to achieve perfection through complexity seldom work. They paint so vivid a picture of the complicated problems that might be encountered that few political decision makers are willing to consider them seriously. And generally the politicians are right, for the only way they can cope in a difficult and changing world is to do what must be done next and not to worry too much about all the possible consequences of their actions.

Furthermore, we do not know what the "perfect" agricultural tax system is for any particular country; nor, if we did, would it be likely that it should be imposed all at once in a comprehensive all-or-nothing program. Rational, calculating man just does not work this way.

Those concerned with improving agricultural tax policy might be better advised to devote their efforts to the task of getting a small, sound basis upon which to build a better world piece by piece.

This argument for gradual and piecemeal adjustment of the agricultural tax system from where it now is to where it "should" be for any particular country at a particular point in time is fraught with technical and philosophic difficulties.[15] Any political system can absorb only so much policy change at any one time without serious risk. This is particularly true with respect to tax reform, which by its nature draws few supporters but has many opponents. Those whose tax burdens are lightened by the reform will take it as merely a delayed and inadequate recognition of their special circumstances, while those whose burdens are increased can never be persuaded that the increase is justified.

Major changes in tax systems usually take place after acute crises such as wars, depressions, or revolutions. All-or-nothing alternatives make strategic sense only when one either expects or hopes for radical change in the values of government. Whether a holistic or a piecemeal approach is more advisable as a tactical matter depends on the prevailing circumstances. Sometimes a more radical approach may make a less drastic, even though still radical, approach more acceptable than it otherwise would be. But as a rule it would appear that dramatic breaks with the existing system are more likely to generate conflict than to produce immediately acceptable solutions. Although in some situations conflict may be needed to precipitate desirable change, its more immediate result is usually to kill proposals for change. Attempts to achieve indirectly goals such as land reform that have been rejected directly are equally unlikely to get anywhere, as the previous chapter suggests.

There are also good theoretical reasons to support a continued piecemeal approach to tax reform. One such reason is the effort involved in obtaining information and reaching a decision. Given man's finite intelligence, it is reasonable to expect that, by considering only a part of the system at one time, we can reach more satisfactory decisions because the dimensions of the problem are more within the limits of our ability to communicate and absorb information.[16] Rationality is generally aided by the division of problems into manageable parts, so long as the relevant ramifications of changes throughout the economic and social system are adequately taken into account.

Furthermore, in practice, policy making is almost invariably a gradual, continuous process rather than a single, complete resolution of an important issue. A sequential process has several important advantages: it gives our limited intelligence a reasonable chance to consider the effects of particular measures; it provides the opportunity to take remedial action if something does not work out quite the way we expected it to; it allows incorporation into later measures of feedback from the affected constituency. Policy is, therefore, focused mainly on correcting perceived wrongs rather than on the more controversial and difficult task of establishing future norms. Policy can also be adjusted to accommodate shifting conditions and objectives.

This sequential approach to policy, far from being inherently deficient compared to the holistic, comprehensive approach favored by most would-be reformers, may actually improve our chances of making good policy decisions in the face of the constantly changing interdependent complexity of social and economic realities. As Charles Lindblom has put it, "analytical methods cannot be restricted to tidy scholarly procedures. The piecemealing, remedial incrementalist or satisficer may not look like an heroic figure. He is nevertheless a shrewd, resourceful problem-solver who is wrestling bravely with a universe he is wise enough to know is too big for him."[17] Unless, therefore, one has a very great deal of faith in the wisdom and foresight of any conceivable person or group, the piecemeal approach is not only the necessary tactical approach to implementing even large changes, but it is also, despite its untidiness, usually the only way we have to be even partly sure the changes we implement will be the "right" ones.

In the present context, this line of reasoning again supports the earlier stress on the importance of initiating and fostering the acceptable (for example, simple, low-rate land taxes associated with some tangible benefit to at least some prospective taxpayers), rather than the perfect. It is quite possible, however, that in particular countries objective analysis of the situation may suggest drastic land redistribution, which usually means a revolution of some sort, as the only way to achieve professed social and economic goals.

Edmundo Flores, for example, has argued that most underdeveloped countries in Latin America will have to foot the developmental bill from the agricultural sector alone. He cites the Mexican case as his model of the kind of land reform needed: "For capital formation

THE DESIGN OF AGRICULTURAL LAND TAXES

purposes, agriculture was subject to a steady drain. The peasants tolerated the ensuing forced austerity because it came from the same government that was giving them free land and was engaged in unprecedented efforts to build dams, highways, and schools."[18]

Three points seem crucial in this argument: taxes were linked with desired expenditures, and with wealth redistribution, in the popular mind; expenditures were aimed at increasing agricultural productivity; and, finally, the needed "taxation" was carried out by the crudest kind of tax system—a capital levy on a few landlords called "land reform," which in turn rested on political revolution. In short, this argument generally supports rather than weakens previous suggestions on linking taxes and expenditures and the need to direct expenditures in perceptible part toward agriculture, thus, simplifying administration, and providing the necessary political basis for any tax effort.

Even if Flores is right that this is the only way for a poor country to develop without foreign capital, there would seem to be nothing to gain (and perhaps something to lose—time) by attempting to achieve revolutionary aims through reformist measures such as land taxes. Indirect policies assume too much stupidity on the part of the landowning segment of the polity and an equally unwarranted capability on the administrative segment to stand much chance of success.

People, and governments, do not, as a rule, think comprehensively. They do not write down all the possible ends in which they may conceivably be interested, then list all the imaginable policy instruments at their disposal, and, finally, choose, on the basis of consideration of this comprehensive policy matrix and a social welfare function somehow derived, the optimal policy mix. Instead, the normal process of policy making, whether by individuals or governments, is incremental, sequential, and piecemeal. Furthermore, as has been argued, this messy process of "muddling through," which exhibits elaborate concern for side effects and second-order consequences, is not only the way in which we actually make decisions, but it may also be the best way in which, for the most part, to operate in this complex and ever-changing world, given our finite intelligence.

To rely on "muddle" alone is, nevertheless, neither a satisfactory nor a necessary way to design policy. A more systematic and comprehensive approach to policy making has considerable virtue even in a world in which policies are, as a rule, ultimately made for the most part in a piecemeal, incremental fashion. The consideration of a comprehensive policy matrix of the sort sketched in Chapter 2 has, for example, the virtue of setting out a conceptual framework within which information on the linkages between policy instruments and targets may be classified, so that policy makers can economically scan the array of possible instrument-goal combinations and select the policy most relevant to the specific circumstances at hand.

A comprehensive ordering along these lines may not only serve as a basis for classifying what is known but also, by pointing out what is not known, as a guide to the search and information-acquiring activities that lie at the heart of any rational policy process in an uncertain, changing world. Even if, as is generally true in economics, our models of reality can deal only with a few variable factors and it must necessarily be assumed that other things remain unchanged, consideration of a more general framework is at the very least a useful way of reminding us of the myriad "other things" which in reality are likely to be changing and unequal.

The need for caution and humility in deriving firm predictions about social reality on the basis of manipulations of limited economic models comes naturally to those who have taken care to view the whole within which partial analysis functions. Unless some very general conceptual basis is made explicit, we are inevitably groping in the dark when we observe isolated aspects of reality (as is usual in economics). We neither know what we look for nor what we see except in relation to some conceptual framework. Conversely, of course, concepts which can never be related to observable reality in any way, shape, or form are empty. What is needed, therefore, is a simultaneous advance with respect to both our conceptualizations of social reality and our operational ability to perceive those concepts in some form.

CONCLUSION

The principal concern of this study has been to illustrate the wide and often conflicting range of objectives and instruments conceivably open to those concerned with agricultural tax policy. The conclusions are not particularly encouraging to those who believe in the general applicability of simple developmental models or in the possibilities of technical end runs around the political difficulties and administrative weaknesses hampering agricultural tax policy in all countries. To talk, for instance, of the optimal tax in a world characterized by continuous change is nonsense; a tax can be "optimal" only in relation to certain objectives and initial conditions, and the vast range of possibilities with respect to both makes the question unanswerable.

Economists are generally inclined by virtue of their training to look for patterns, to abstract, to simplify, and to disregard exceptions. This search for generalizations has characterized economic theory for many years. It is exemplified by conventionally accepted views on the role and effects of land taxes in developing countries. A principal theme in this book is that the answers produced by this process of reasoning cannot and should not be applied in a given situation without substantial further work. In fact, when it comes to policy application, theoretical reasoning produces not answers, but questions. If the theory is good, they will be good questions, but they will never be answers that can be applied holus-bolus to yield a solution that will work in a particular country with particular needs at a particular time.

One reason why the state of the art in the land tax area has not advanced much beyond the primitive stage of drawing conceivably tenable generalizations from reasoning of undeniably tenuous applicability in particular circumstances is that in no area is basic field research more difficult. Even the data manipulation carried out by the technically proficient in other areas of economic development is impossible when there are virtually no data. What we have, then, is an example *par excellence* of an important policy and research area in which there has been almost no research of any sort, so that policy is based on textbook generalizations.

In view of the highly indigenous character of agriculture and its vital importance for development, this state of affairs is especially regrettable. What passes for research in this field is all too often simply a restatement of the conventional wisdom. One intent of the present study is, by questioning the validity of relying on that wisdom as a guide to policy, to stimulate new efforts at the detailed case studies needed to advance beyond the platitude. As with so many questions crucial to the development process, however, few professional kudos are to be gained by the kind of research that is needed since it is inherently "institutional," not to mention time-consuming, in character.

Another lesson that is particularly clear with respect to agricultural land taxation—it also applies to most other taxes—is that transfers of tax technology from abroad need to be handled selectively and adapted carefully to different local conditions if they are to do much good. This does not mean that poor countries must use eighteenth-century techniques. They may actually use twenty-first-century techniques with highly beneficial results in some instances, as, for example, when current techniques in use in advanced countries are inefficient and expensive in terms of scarce resources, which is largely true in the case of property taxes. The introduction of a highly refined system, such as computerized routines for assessment, automatic adjustment for price-level changes, and billing, may be easier than tackling directly the basic problems of inadequate and inefficient tax administration. A detour through sophisticated technology may even be an essential prerequisite to getting the experience needed to resolve more basic problems. A value-added tax, for example, may lead to a more efficient customs and excise administration. Nevertheless, the general point remains true: in no area of taxation is transplanted technology less likely to flourish than in agricultural taxation because of the inherently indigenous nature of agriculture and the extent to which it is inextricably related to a nation's whole life style.

Yet another point on attempts to introduce technical innovations that has not received sufficient attention with respect to institutional innovations like new taxes is that concentration of effort is likely to yield better results than dispersal of effort. No country has unlimited means of adapting and administering tax innovations, and it would seem obvious that concentrating on one particular area of the country might provide both a better test of the worth of the innovation and also a firmer base for its later expansion to other areas, if desired. This potential virtue is, of course, one of the oldest arguments for local government and decentralization. It seldom appears to have been taken to heart because of the holistic approach of most innovators on the one hand and the distaste for legal (not actual) nonuniformity found in many developing countries on the other hand, usually coupled with a fear of centrifugal politics leading to the disintegration of the nation-state. As experience in many countries suggests, however, properly differentiated policies may in fact offset, not reinforce, political separatism.

The problems of taxing agricultural land are subtle and complex, varying from country to country. A tentative general approach that is quite different in tone from those usually offered in studies on this subject has been ventured: the road to heavier agricultural taxation in general, if desired, and to more effective agricultural land taxes in particular lies in a simple, even crude valuation technique and tax structure, coupled with appropriate expenditure policy, rather than in such panaceas as personalized taxes on presumptive agricultural income. In practice, relevant choices must be made between rules or institutions that generate different probability distributions of outcomes. What evidence there is seems to suggest that a simpler levy is more likely to result in acceptable and desirable results than a more complex one.

The approach to land taxation suggested for most poor countries is basically to focus on the objective of revenue at the expense of various complicated refinements that are intended to achieve desirable side effects on the allocation of resources within the agricultural sector or on the private distribution of incomes in rural areas. These other objectives are valid but less important in the general framework of most, though not all, developing countries. Attempts to achieve them are likely to confuse the main issue and make its attainment substantially more difficult. Conceptually, subtle political handling might enable reforms and revenue increases to be linked but the probability of success in this venture would seem low. In addition, the use of scarce administrative resources in subtle administrative schemes of this sort is probably wasteful, with perhaps a partial exception in some instances for special assessments or betterment levies. Agricultural taxes may indeed have profound nonfiscal effects which should be foreseen and taken advantage of, but the useful and realizable ones seem more likely to be macroeconomic (concerned with income distribution, foreign exchange, migration) than microeconomic (idle lands, specific crops, and so forth) in nature.

For any degree of effective land taxation, there must be some critical minimum of political support and administrative capability. Given these, the tax should be designed to produce the required revenue in a roughly acceptable ("equitable") fashion and with as few disincentive effects as possible. Ideally, the design will include features such as linkages to expenditures or local government, which will create support for the tax itself, as well as other features such as index adjustment, which will enable it to maintain its place so long as it is relevant for the objectives of the society. When the development of institutions permits and the concomitant development of society requires it, more advanced fiscal instruments like the income and wealth taxes may of course be applied to some extent in agriculture. Until that time, there seems no reason to detract from the main aims of land taxes by trying to convert them into a tool that can do all things for all men.

APPENDIX, BIBLIOGRAPHY, NOTES, INDEX

APPENDIX

PATTERNS OF AGRICULTURAL TAXATION: YIELD BY TYPE OF TAX
AS A PERCENTAGE OF TOTAL TAX RECEIPTS

Country	Year	Type of tax			
		Personal	Export	Land	Products
AFRICA					
Cameroon	1966	—	10	—	—
Central African Republic	1966	9	5	0	—
Chad	1969	9	10	0	—
Congo (Brazzaville)	1967	—	0	—	—
Dahomey	1969	2	4	0	—
Egypt	1968	—	2	8	—
Ethiopia	1968	—	9	8	—
Gabon	1966	2	—	0	—
Ghana	1968	—	17	—	—
Ivory Coast	1966	—	20	1	—
Kenya	1968	2	0	0	—
Liberia	1969	5	2	0	—
Malagasy Republic	1969	12	6	5	—
Malawi	1968	12	—	—	—
Mali	1962	21	2	—	—
Mauritania	1968	1	—	—	—
Morocco	1969	2	2	6	—
Niger	1968	34	7	—	—
Nigeria	1963	6	18	—	3
Senegal	1968	3	7	—	—

| Country | Year | Type of tax | | | |
		Personal	Export	Land	Products
Sierra Leone	1969	—	4	—	—
Somalia	1968	—	9	1	—
Sudan	1964	—	24	—	—
Tanzania	1965	3	16	—	2
Togo	1968	—	11	—	—
Tunisia	1968	1	4	4	—
Uganda	1964	14	41	—	—
Upper Volta	1968	15	1	1	—
Zaire (formerly Congo [Kinhasa])	1965	3	—	—	—
ASIA					
Afghanistan	1967	—	18	2	—
Burma	1963	—	8	3	—
Cambodia	1963	—	3	—	—
Ceylon (now Sri Lanka)	1968	—	15	3	—
China, People's Republic of	1959	—	—	16	—
China, Republic of (Taiwan)	1968	—	3	11	—
India	1969	1	2	5	—
Indonesia	1969	—	—	2	—
Iran	1968	—	2	1	—
Iraq	1968	0	0	1	0
Korea	1968	—	0	8	—
Malaysia	1967	—	9	—	—
Nepal	1968	—	6	18	—
Pakistan	1968	—	0	6	—
Philippines	1968	—	2	8	—
Thailand	1968	—	12	2	—
Turkey	1968	—	8	1	—
Vietnam	1962	—	—	5	—
LATIN AMERICA					
Argentina	1963	—	1	1	—
Bolivia	1964	—	0	0	—
Brazil	1968	—	—	1	—
Chile	1968	—	0	6	—
Colombia	1963	—	14	8	—
Costa Rica	1968	—	2	6	—
Dominican Republic	1962	—	2	0	—
Ecuador	1968	—	10	10	—
El Salvador	1963	—	13	2	—
Guatemala	1968	—	7	6	—
Guyana	1968	—	3	3	—
Haiti	1964	—	17	0	—
Honduras	1968	—	13	2	—
Jamaica	1968	—	—	8	—

Country	Year	Type of tax			
		Personal	Export	Land	Products
Mexico	1963	—	7	0	1
Nicaragua	1971	—	1	6	—
Panama	1962	—	1	4	—
Paraguay	1968	—	18	6	—
Peru	1964	—	5	0	—
Trinidad and Tobago	1968	—	—	7	—
Uruguay	1965	—	—	7	—
Venezuela	1968	—	0	0	—

NOTE: A dash signifies that no information is available; an entry of 0 means that the value is less than 0.5 percent. As noted in the text, these figures have been brought together from many different, and sometimes incompatible, sources so that the data are not strictly comparable. Some of the classifications of particular taxes are quite arbitrary. In most cases central government tax revenues only are included, except where the major taxes treated are subnational in nature. In some cases, the figures shown for certain taxes may refer to different years—or even in a few instances to geographically different countries—than those indicated; the year shown is the most recent year covered. The major problem in interpreting this table concerns the extent to which the taxes cited fall on agriculture. In some instances, special estimates have been made: where possible, these have been used here. In other instances, information on, for example, export taxes has been omitted where it was known most exports were non-agricultural. In many countries the figures shown under "land taxes" are really total taxes on property and may come primarily from urban real estate. Similarly, the African "personal" taxes may in some instances be paid mainly by urban workers. It is largely because of the difficulty of interpreting the sectoral impact of the usual national fiscal statistics that incomplete secondary sources have in some cases been used in preference, despite the availability of some primary data.

Sources: Among the major sources used for more than one country in this table are: Raja J. Chelliah, "Trends in Taxation in Developing Countries," *I.M.F. Staff Papers*, XVIII (July 1971), 270–271; Richard Goode, George E. Lent, and P. D. Ojha, "Role of Export Taxes in Developing Countries," *I.M.F. Staff Papers*, XIII (November 1966), 460; Edward A. Arowolo, "The Taxation of Low Incomes in African Countries," *I.M.F. Staff Papers*, XV (July 1968), 338; Japan Tax Association, *Proceedings of the Special Meeting of Japan Tax Association on Tax System and Administration in Asian Countries* (Tokyo, 1963); International Monetary Fund, *Surveys of African Economies* (4 vols., Washington, 1968–1971); United Nations, "Tax Potential and Economic Growth in the countries of the ECAFE Region," *Economic Bulletin for Asia and the Far East*, XVII (September 1966), 29–48. In a number of other instances, the data are taken from studies dealing with the particular country in question, as cited in the bibliography.

APPENDIX

BIBLIOGRAPHY

Books and Pamphlets

Adelman, I., and E. Thorbecke, eds. *The Theory and Design of Economic Development*. Baltimore: Johns Hopkins Press, 1966.

Agarwala, A. N., and S. P. Singh, eds. *Accelerating Investment in Developing Economies*. Bombay: Oxford University Press, 1969.

————. *The Economics of Underdevelopment*. Bombay: Oxford University Press, 1958.

Andrus, J. R., and A. F. Mohammed. *The Economy of Pakistan*. London: Oxford University Press, 1958.

Bairoch, Paul. *Agriculture and the Industrial Revolution* (Vol. III, chap. 8, The Fontana Economic History of Europe). London: Collins, 1969.

Balogh, Thomas. *The Economics of Poverty*. New York: Macmillan Company, 1966.

Bangs, Robert B. *Financing Economic Development*. Chicago: University of Chicago Press, 1968.

Bauer, P. T. *West African Trade*. Cambridge, Eng.: At the University Press, 1954.

Becker, Arthur P., ed. *Land and Building Taxes: Their Effect on Economic Development*. Madison: University of Wisconsin Press, 1969.

Behrman, Jere R. *Supply Response in Underdeveloped Agriculture: A Case Study of Four Major Annual Crops in Thailand, 1937–1963*. Amsterdam: North-Holland Publishing Company, 1968.

Bhagwati, Jagdish. *The Economics of Underdeveloped Countries*. New York: McGraw-Hill, 1966.

Bird, Richard M. *Taxation and Development: Lessons from Colombian Experience.* Cambridge, Mass.: Harvard University Press, 1970.

———— and Oliver Oldman, eds. *Readings on Taxation in Developing Countries*, rev. ed. Baltimore: Johns Hopkins Press, 1967; 1st ed., 1964.

Black, C. E. *The Dynamics of Modernization: A Study in Comparative History.* New York: Harper & Row, 1966.

Bottomley, Anthony. *Factor Pricing and Economic Growth in Underdeveloped Rural Areas.* London: Crosby Lockwood & Son, Ltd., 1971.

Break, George F., and Ralph Turvey. *Studies in Greek Taxation.* Center of Planning and Economic Research, Monograph Series 11. Athens: the Center, 1964.

Buchanan, James M. *The Demand and Supply of Public Goods.* Chicago: Rand McNally, 1968.

Cheung, Steven N. S. *The Theory of Share Tenancy.* Chicago: University of Chicago Press, 1969.

Clark, Colin, and Margaret Haswell. *The Economics of Subsistence Agriculture*, 4th ed. London: Macmillan, St. Martin's Press, 1970.

Clawson, Marion, Hans H. Landsberg, and Lyle T. Alexander. *The Agricultural Potential of the Middle East.* New York: American Elsevier Publishing Company, Inc., 1971.

Currie, Lauchlin. *Accelerating Development.* New York: McGraw-Hill, 1966.

Cutt, James. *Taxation and Economic Development in India.* New York: Frederick A. Praeger, Publishers, 1969.

Diaz-Alejandro, Carlos F. *Essays on the Economic History of the Argentine Republic.* New Haven, Conn.: Yale University Press, 1970.

Due, John F. *Indirect Taxation in Developing Economies.* Baltimore: Johns Hopkins Press, 1970.

————. *Taxation and Economic Development in Tropical Africa.* Cambridge, Mass.: M.I.T. Press, 1963.

Dumont, René. *Types of Rural Economy.* London: Methuen and Co., Ltd., 1957.

Ecklund, George N. *Financing The Chinese Government Budget, Mainland China, 1950–1959.* Chicago: Aldine Publishing Company, 1966.

Eckstein, Solomon. *El marco macroeconómico del problema agrario mexicano.* México: Centro de Investigaciones Agrarias, 1968.

Eicher, Carl K. *Research on Agricultural Development in Five English-Speaking Countries in West Africa.* New York: Agricultural Development Council, Inc., 1970.

Fei, J. C. H., and Gustav Ranis. *Development of the Labor Surplus Economy.* Homewood, Ill.: Richard D. Irwin, Inc., 1964.

Firth, Raymond, and B. S. Yamey, eds. *Capital, Saving and Credit in Peasant Societies.* Chicago: Aldine Publishing Company, 1969.

Flores, Edmundo. *Tratado de economía agrícola.* México: Fondo de Cultura Económica, 1961.

————. *Vieja revolución, nuevos problemas.* México: Siglo XXI Editores, 1970.

Franco, Alberto, et al. *Tributaçâo progressiva: possibilidades e limitaçôes segundo a legíslacào agraria brasileira.* Bogotá: Instituto Interamericano de Ciencias Agrícolas, Centro Interamericano de Reforma Agraria, 1966.

Frankel, Francine R. *India's Green Revolution: Economic Gains and Political Costs.* Princeton, N.J.: Princeton University Press, 1971.

Gaffney, Mason, ed. *Extractive Resources and Taxation.* Madison: University of Wisconsin Press, 1967.

Gandhi, Ved P. *Tax Burden on Indian Agriculture.* Cambridge, Mass.: Law School of Harvard University, 1966.

Gimeno Sanz, José M. *La tributación agropecuaria,* 2 vols. Santiago: Oficina de Planificación Agrícola, Ministerio de Agricultura, 1970.

———. *Sugerencias para el diseño de una nueua política tributaria para el sector agropecuario.* Santiago: Oficina de Planificación Agrícola, 1971.

Gutelman, Michel. *Réforme et mystification agraires en Amérique Latine. Le cas du Mexique.* Paris: Maspero, 1971.

Harriss, George L., et al. *Iraq: Its People, Its Society, Its Culture.* New Haven, Conn.: HRAF Press, 1958.

Harvard Law School International Program in Taxation. *Taxation in Brazil.* Boston: Little, Brown, 1959.

———. *Taxation in Colombia.* Chicago: Commerce Clearing House, Inc., 1964.

———. *Taxation in India.* Boston: Little, Brown, 1960.

———. *Taxation in Italy.* Chicago: Commerce Clearing House, Inc., 1964.

———. *Taxation in Mexico.* Boston: Little, Brown, 1957.

Hayami, Yujiro, and Vernon W. Ruttan. *Agricultural Development: An International Perspective.* Baltimore: Johns Hopkins Press, 1971.

Helleiner, G. K. *Peasant Agriculture, Government, and Economic Growth in Nigeria.* Homewood, Ill.: Richard D. Irwin, Inc., 1967.

Hendry, James B. *The Small World of Khanh Hau.* Chicago: Aldine Publishing Company, 1964.

Heyer, Judith, Dunstan Ireri, and Jon Moris. *Rural Development in Kenya.* Nairobi: East African Publishing House, 1971.

Hicks, J. R., and U. K. Hicks. *Report on Finance and Taxation in Jamaica.* Kingston, Jamaica: Government Printer, 1955.

Hicks, Ursula K. *Development Finance.* Oxford, Eng.: Clarendon Press, 1965.

———. *Development from Below.* Oxford, Eng.: Clarendon Press, 1961.

Higgins, Benjamin. *Economic Development,* rev. ed. New York: W. W. Norton & Company, Inc., 1968.

Hinrichs, Harley H. *A General Theory of Tax Structure Change During Economic Development.* Cambridge, Mass.: Law School of Harvard University, 1966.

———, Raj Krishna, and Richard J. Ward, eds. *Fiscal Incentives to Promote Agricultural Development.* Forthcoming.

Hirschman, Albert O. *Exit, Voice and Loyalty.* Cambridge, Mass.: Harvard University Press, 1970.

———. *Journeys toward Progress: Studies of Economic Policy-Making in Latin America.* New York: Twentieth Century Fund, 1963.

———. *The Strategy of Economic Development.* New Haven, Conn.: Yale University Press, 1958.

Holland, Daniel M., ed. *The Assessment of Land Value*. Madison: University of Wisconsin Press, 1970.

House, Peter W. *Opposing Views on Taxation of Land Near Cities*. Washington, D.C.: U.S. Dept. of Agriculture, Economic Research Service, 1968.

Hunter, Guy. *Modernizing Peasant Societies: A Comparative Study in Asia and Africa*. New York: Oxford University Press, 1969.

Instituto de Economía. *La tributación agrícola en Chile, 1940–1958*. Santiago: University of Chile, 1960.

International Association of Assessing Officers. *Farm Land Assessment Practices in the United States*. Chicago: the Association, 1969.

Ishikawa, Shigeru. *Economic Development in Asian Perspective*. Tokyo: Kinokuniya Bookstore Co., Ltd., 1967.

Jarach, Dino. *El impuesto a la renta normal potencial de la tierra*. Cuaderno de Finanzas Públicas, 5, Programa Conjunto de Tributación. Washington, D.C.: Pan-American Union, n.d.

Japan Tax Association. *Proceedings of the Special Meeting of Japan Tax Association on Tax System and Administration in Asian Countries*. Tokyo: the Association, 1963.

Joint Tax Program, Organization of American States, Inter-American Development Bank, Economic Commission for Latin America. *Fiscal Policy for Economic Growth in Latin America*. Baltimore: Johns Hopkins Press, 1965.

Jones, E. L., and S. J. Woolf, eds. *Agrarian Change and Economic Development: The Historical Problems*. London: Methuen & Co., Ltd., 1969.

Joshi, T. M., N. Anjanaiah, and S. V. Bhende. *Studies in the Taxation of Agricultural Land and Income in India*. London: Asia Publishing House, 1968.

Kaldor, Nicholas. *Essays on Economic Policy*, 2 vols. London: Duckworth, 1964.

Keynes, J. M. *The General Theory of Employment, Interest and Money*. New York: Harcourt, Brace, and Company, 1936.

Kuznets, Simon. *Modern Economic Growth*. New Haven, Conn.: Yale University Press, 1966.

Land Reform. Madison: University of Wisconsin Land Tenure Center, 1963.

Lee, Eugene C. *Local Taxation in Tanzania*. Dar Es Salaam: Institute of Public Administration, University College, 1966.

Leff, Nathaniel H. *Economic Policy-Making and Development in Brazil, 1947–1964*. New York: John Wiley & Sons, Inc., 1969.

Levin, Jonathan V. *The Export Economies: Their Pattern of Development in Historical Perspective*. Cambridge, Mass.: Harvard University Press, 1960.

Levy, Marion J., Jr. *Modernization and the Structure of Societies*. Princeton, N.J.: Princeton University Press, 1966.

Lewis, Stephen R., Jr. *Economic Policy and Industrial Growth in Pakistan*. London: George Allen and Unwin, Ltd., 1969.

Lewis, W. Arthur. *Development Planning*. London: George Allen and Unwin, Ltd., 1965.

——. *The Theory of Economic Growth*. Homewood, Ill.: Richard D. Irwin, Inc., 1955.

Lindblom, Charles E. *The Policy-Making Process*. Englewood Cliffs, N.J.: Prentice-Hall, 1969.

Lipsky, George A., et al. *Ethiopia: Its People, Its Society, Its Culture*. New Haven, Conn.: HRAF Press, 1962.

Lockwood, William W., ed. *The State and Economic Enterprise in Japan: Essays in the Political Economy of Growth*. Princeton, N.J.: Princeton University Press, 1965.

Ludwig, Armin K., and Harry W. Taylor. *Brazil's New Agrarian Reform: An Evaluation of Its Property Classification and Tax Systems*. New York: Frederick A. Praeger, Publishers, 1969.

MacBean, Alasdair I. *Export Instability and Economic Development*. Cambridge, Mass.: Harvard University Press, 1966.

McClelland, David. *The Achieving Society*. New York: Free Press, 1967.

MacKay, Angus N. *Appraisal Notes for the Assessor*. Toronto: Department of Municipal Affairs, 1968.

Malinowski, Bronislaw. *Magic, Science and Religion*. New York: Doubleday Anchor Books, 1948.

Mathew, E. T. *Agricultural Taxation and Economic Development in India*. London: Asia Publishing House, 1968.

Meier, Gerald M. *Leading Issues in Development Economics*, 2nd ed. New York: Oxford University Press, 1970.

Mellor, John W. *The Economics of Agricultural Development*. Ithaca, N.Y.: Cornell University Press, 1966.

Murray, J. F. N. *Report to the Government of Jamaica on Valuation, Land Taxation and Rating*. Kingston, Jamaica: Government Printer, 1957.

Musgrave, Richard A. *Fiscal Systems*. New Haven, Conn.: Yale University Press, 1969.

————. *Revenue Policy for Korea's Economic Development*. Seoul: Nathan Economic Advisory Group, 1965.

———— and Malcolm Gillis, eds. *Fiscal Reform for Colombia*. Cambridge, Mass.: International Tax Program, Harvard Law School, 1971.

Myrdal, Gunnar. *Asian Drama: An Inquiry into the Poverty of Nations*, 3 vols. New York: Pantheon Books, 1969.

Nair, Kusum. *The Lonely Furrow: Farming in the United States, Japan and India*. Ann Arbor: University of Michigan Press, 1969.

Nakamura, James I. *Agricultural Production and the Economic Development of Japan 1873–1922*. Princeton, N.J.: Princeton University Press, 1966.

Netzer, Dick. *Economics of the Property Tax*. Washington, D.C.: Brookings Institution, 1966.

Nurkse, Ragnar. *Problems of Capital Formation in Underdeveloped Countries*. New York: Oxford University Press, 1953.

Ohkawa, Kazushi, Bruce F. Johnston, and Hiromitsu Kaneda, eds. *Agriculture and Economic Growth: Japan's Experience*. Tokyo: University of Tokyo Press, 1969.

Oldman, Oliver, et al. *Financing Urban Development in Mexico City*. Cambridge, Mass.: Harvard University Press, 1967.

Pathak, M. T., and A. S. Patel. *Agricultural Taxation in Gujarat*. New York: Asia Publishing House, 1970.

Popper, Karl R. *The Poverty of Historicism*. London: Routledge & Kegan Paul, 1957.

Posada F., Antonio J., and Jeanne de Posada. *CVC: Un reto al subdesarrollo y al tradicionalismo*. Bogotá: Ediciones Tercer Mundo, 1966.

Rao, C. H. Hanumantha. *Taxation of Agricultural Land in Andhra Pradesh*. London: Asia Publishing House, 1966.

Regmi, Mahesh C. *Land Tenure and Taxation in Nepal*, 4 vols. Berkeley: Institute of International Studies, University of California, 1963–1967.

Reynolds, Clark W. *The Mexican Economy*. New Haven, Conn.: Yale University Press, 1970.

Rivlin, Alice M. *Systematic Thinking for Social Action*. Washington, D.C., Brookings Institution, 1971.

Sahota, G. S. *Indian Tax Structure and Economic Development*. Bombay: Asia Publishing House, 1961.

Seligman, Edwin R. A. *Essays in Taxation*, 10th ed. New York: Macmillan Company, 1931; reprinted by Augustus M. Kelley, Publishers, New York, 1969.

————. *The Shifting and Incidence of Taxation*, 5th ed. New York: Columbia University Press, 1927; reprinted by Augustus M. Kelley, Publishers, New York, 1969.

Shoup, Carl S. *Public Finance*. Chicago: Aldine Publishing Company, 1969.

————. *Ricardo on Taxation*. New York: Columbia University Press, 1960.

————, C. Lowell Harriss, and William S. Vickrey. *The Fiscal System of the Federal District of Venezuela*. Baltimore: Garamond Press, 1960.

———— et al. *The Tax System of Liberia*. New York: Columbia University Press, 1970.

Simon, Herbert. *Administrative Behavior*, 2nd. ed. New York: Free Press, 1957.

Simons, Henry C. *Personal Income Taxation*. Chicago: University of Chicago Press, 1938.

Smith, Thomas C. *The Agrarian Origins of Modern Japan*. Stanford, Calif.: Stanford University Press, 1959.

Snodgrass, Donald R. *Ceylon: An Export Economy in Transition*. Homewood, Ill.: Richard D. Irwin, Inc., 1966.

Solís, Leopoldo. *La realidad económica mexicana*. México: Siglo XXI Editores, 1970.

Southworth, Herman M., and Bruce F. Johnston, eds. *Agricultural Development and Economic Growth*. Ithaca, N.Y.: Cornell University Press, 1967.

Stokes, Eric. *The English Utilitarians and India*. Oxford. Eng.: Clarendon Press, 1959.

Stolper, Wolfgang F. *Planning without Facts*. Cambridge, Mass.: Harvard University Press, 1966.

Streeten, Paul, and Michael Lipton, eds. *The Crisis of Indian Planning*. London: Oxford University Press, 1968.

Tait, A. A. *The Taxation of Personal Wealth*. Urbana: University of Illinois Press, 1967.

Takahashi, Masao. *Modern Japanese Economy since 1868*. Tokyo: Japan Cultural Society, 1968.

BIBLIOGRAPHY

Tax Institute of America. *Tax Incentives.* Lexington, Mass.: Heath Lexington Books, 1971.

Taylor, Milton. *Local Government Finance in Vietnam.* Vietnam Working Paper No. 1. New York: Development and Resources Corporation, 1969.

———. *The Taxation of Real Property in Vietnam.* Saigon: Michigan State University Viet-nam Advisory Group, 1959.

——— et al. *Estudio Fiscal del Peru.* Washington, D.C.: Pan-American Union, 1969.

——— et al. *Fiscal Survey of Colombia.* Baltimore: Johns Hopkins Press for the Joint Tax Program, 1965.

——— et al. *Fiscal Survey of Panama.* Baltimore: Johns Hopkins Press for the Joint Tax Program, 1964.

Thiesenhusen, William C., and Marion B. Brown. *Survey of the Alliance for Progress: Problems of Agriculture.* A study prepared at the request of the Subcommittee on American Republics Affairs of the Committee on Foreign Relations, U.S. Senate. Washington, D.C.: Government Printing Office, 1967.

Thorbecke, Erik, ed. *The Role of Agriculture in Economic Development.* New York: Columbia University Press, 1969.

Tripathy, R. N. *Fiscal Policy and Economic Development in India.* Calcutta: World Press, 1958.

———. *Public Finance in Underdeveloped Countries.* Calcutta: The World Press Private, Ltd., 1964.

Ullrich, Kurt, and Ricardo Lagos. *Agricultura y tributación.* Santiago: Instituto de Economía, University of Chile, 1965.

Vera, Luis. *Agricultural Land Inventory Techniques: Experience of the OAS/Chile Aerophotogrammetric Project.* Washington, D.C.: Pan-American Union, 1964.

Wald, Haskell P. *The Taxation of Agricultural Land in Underdeveloped Economies.* Cambridge, Mass.: Harvard University Press, 1959.

——— and Joseph N. Froomkin, eds. *Papers and Proceedings of the Conference on Agricultural Taxation and Economic Development.* Cambridge, Mass.: International Program in Taxation, Harvard Law School, 1954.

Warriner, Doreen. *Land Reform in Principle and Practice.* Oxford, Eng.: Clarendon Press, 1969.

Watkin, Virginia. *Taxes and Tax Harmonization in Central America.* Cambridge, Mass.: International Tax Program, Harvard Law School, 1967.

Woodruff, Archibald M., James R. Brown, and Sein Lin, eds. *International Seminar on Land Taxation, Land Tenure, and Land Reform in Developing Countries.* West Hartford, Conn.: John C. Lincoln Institute, University of Hartford, 1967.

Articles and Periodicals

Aaron, Henry. "Some Criticisms of Tax Burden Indices," *National Tax Journal,* XVIII (March 1965), 313–316.

Amatong, Juanita D. "Taxation of Capital Gains in Developing Countries," *I.M.F. Staff Papers,* XV (July 1968), 344–384.

Arowolo, Edward A. "The Taxation of Low Incomes in African Countries," *I.M.F. Staff Papers*, XV (July 1968), 322–341.

Azzini, Juan Eduardo, and Hugo A. De Marco. "The Tax System of Uruguay," *Public Finance/Finances Publiques*, II (No. 2, 1956), 112–129.

Baer, Werner. "Import Substitution Industrialization in Latin America: Experiences and Interpretations," *Latin American Research Review*, (February 1972), 95–122.

———— and Isaac Kerstenetsky. "The Brazilian Economy in the Sixties," in Riordan Roett, ed. *Brazil in the Sixties*. Nashville, Tenn.: Vanderbilt University Press, 1972.

Bank of London and South America Review, monthly.

Bardhan, P. K., and T. N. Srinivasan. "Cropsharing Tenancy in Agriculture: a Theoretical and Empirical Analysis," *American Economic Review*, LXI (March 1971), 48–64.

Barranclough, Solon L. "Agrarian Reform in Latin America: Actual Situation and Problems," *Land Reform, Land Settlement and Cooperatives* (No. 2, 1969), pp. 1–21.

————. "Agricultural Policy and Land Reform," *Journal of Political Economy*, LXXVIII (No. 4, July–August, suppl., 1970), 906–947.

Beasley, W. G. "Feudal Revenue in Japan at the Time of Meiji Restoration," *Journal of Asian Studies*, XIX (May 1960), 255–272.

Berry, R. Albert. "Presumptive Income Tax on Agricultural Land: The Case of Colombia," *National Tax Journal*, XXV (June 1972), 169–182.

Bertrand, Trent J. "Rural Taxation in Thailand," *Pacific Affairs*, MXLII (Summer 1969), 178–188.

Bird, Richard M. "A National Tax on the Unimproved Value of Land: The Australian Experience, 1910–1952," *National Tax Journal*, XIII (December 1960), 386–392.

————. "A Note on 'Tax Sacrifice' Comparisons," *National Tax Journal*, XVII (September 1964), 303–308.

————. "The Case for Taxing Personal Wealth," in *Report of Proceedings of 23rd Tax Conference*. Toronto: Canadian Tax Foundation, 1972, pp. 6–24.

————. "Coffee Tax Policy in Colombia," *Inter-American Economic Affairs*, XXII (Summer 1968), 75–86.

————. "Crecimiento de la población y desarrollo económico," *Desarrollo Económico* (Buenos Aires), I (July–September 1961), 17–41.

————. "Income Distribution and Tax Policy in Colombia," *Economic Development and Cultural Change*, XVIII (July 1970), 519–535.

————. "Income Distribution, Economic Growth, and Tax Policy," in *Proceedings of the Sixty-First Annual Conference of the National Tax Association*. Columbus, Ohio, 1968, pp. 146–152.

————. "Optimal Tax Policy for a Developing Country: The Case of Colombia," *Finanzarchiv* (N.F.), XXIX (No. 1, February 1970), 30–53.

————. "Stamp Tax Reform in Colombia," *Bulletin for International Fiscal Documentation*, XXI (June 1967), 247–255.

————. "The Tax Kaleidoscope: Perspectives on Tax Reform in Canada," *Canadian Tax Journal*, XVIII (September–October 1970), 444–473.

BIBLIOGRAPHY

————. "Wagner's 'Law' of Expanding State Activity," *Public Finance/Finances Publiques*, XXVI (No. 1, 1971), 1–24.

———— and D. G. Hartle, "The Design of Governments," in R. M. Bird and J. G. Head, eds. *Modern Fiscal Issues: Essays in Honour of Carl S. Shoup*. Toronto: University of Toronto Press, 1972.

Bose, Swadesh, and Edwin H. Clark. "Some Basic Considerations on Agricultural Mechanization in West Pakistan," *Pakistan Development Review*, IX (Autumn 1969), 273–308.

Buse, Reuben C. "Some Comments on Government Policy in Underdeveloped Countries," *Land Tenure Center Newsletter* (No. 29, March–August 1969), pp. 11–13.

Chelliah, Raja J. "Trends in Taxation in Developing Countries," *I.M.F. Staff Papers*, XVIII (July 1971), 254–327.

Choo, Hakchung J. "On the Empirical Relevancy of the Ranis-Fei Model of Economic Development: Comment," *American Economic Review*, LXI (September 1971), 695–703.

Clark, Ronald J. "Problems and Conflicts over Land Ownership in Bolivia," *Inter-American Economic Affairs*, XXII (No. 4, Spring 1969), 3–18.

Davis, L. Harlan. "Property Tax Administration in Rural Local Governments of Colombia," *Land Economics*, XLVI (May 1970), 146–152.

Domike, Arthur. "Tax Policy and Land Tenure in Argentina," *Land Reform* (No. 2, 1964), pp. 23–37.

Dore, R. P. "Agricultural Improvement in Japan 1870–1900," *Economic Development and Cultural Change*, IX (October 1960), 69–91.

Dorner, Peter. "A Comment on Professor Buse's Statement on Policy," *Land Tenure Center Newsletter* (No. 29, March–August 1969), pp. 13–14.

————, Marion Brown, and Don Kanel. "Land Tenure and Reform: Issues in Latin American Development," *Land Tenure Center Newsletter* (No. 29, March–August 1969), pp. 1–10.

Dosser, Douglas. "Tax Incidence and Growth," *Economic Journal*, LXXI (September 1961), 572–591.

The Economist (London), weekly.

Edminister, Robert. "Mexico," in Adamantios Pepelasis, Leon Mears, and Irma Adelman. *Economic Development*. New York: Harper & Brothers, Publishers, 1961, pp. 326–365.

Eicher, Carl, et al. "Employment Generation in African Agriculture," *Development Digest*, IX (January 1971), 77–87.

Elkan, Walter. "Central and Local Taxes on Africans in Uganda," *Public Finance/Finances Publiques*, XIII (1958), 312–320.

Fei, J. C. H., and Gustav Ranis. "Agrarianism, Dualism, and Economic Development," in Irma Adelman and Erik Thorbecke, eds. *The Theory and Design of Economic Development*. Baltimore: Johns Hopkins Press, 1966, pp. 3–41.

———— and Gustav Ranis. "On the Empirical Relevancy of the Ranis-Fei Model of Economic Development: Reply," *American Economic Review*, LXI (September 1971), 704–708.

Felstenhausen, Herman. "Economic Knowledge, Participation and Farmer Decision Making in a Developed and an Under-developed Country,"

International Journal of Agrarian Affairs, V (No. 4, July 1968), 263–281.

―――. "Planning Problems in Improving Colombian Roads and Highways," *Land Economics,* XLVII (February 1971), 1–13.

"Final Report on the Land Tax Administration Seminar (Panama, 1970)," *CIAT Newsletter,* IV (No. 2, October 1971), 1–18.

Flores, Edmundo. "Issues of Land Reform," *Journal of Political Economy,* LXXVIII (July–August, suppl., 1970).

―――. "The Significance of Land-Use Changes in the Economic Development of Mexico," *Land Economics,* XXXV (1959), 115–124.

French, Jerome T., and Princeton N. Lyman. "Social and Political Implications of the New Cereal Varieties," *Development Digest,* VII (No. 4, October 1969), 111–118.

Gaffney, Mason. "The Property Tax is a Progressive Tax," in *Proceedings of the 64th Annual Conference in Taxation.* Columbus, Ohio: National Tax Association, 1972, pp. 408–426.

Gandhi, Ved. "Agricultural Taxation Policy: Search for a Direction," *Artha-Vikas,* July 1969, pp. 3–49.

Gold, Ronald B., and Edward Foster. "Measuring Equity in the Taxation of Agricultural Land: A Case Study of Nepal," *Land Economics,* XLVIII (August 1972), 277–280.

Goode, Richard, George E. Lent, and P. D. Ohja. "Role of Export Taxes in Developing Countries," *I.M.F. Staff Papers,* XIII (November 1966), 453–503.

Gotsch, Carl H. "Technical Change and the Distribution of Income in Rural Areas," *American Journal of Agricultural Economics,* LV (May 1972), 326–341.

Groves, Harold M., and M. C. Madhaven. "Agricultural Taxation and India's Third Five Year Plan," *Land Economics,* XXXVIII (February 1962), 56–64.

Grunig, James E. "Economic Decision Making and Entrepreneurship among Colombian Latifundistas," *Inter-American Economic Affairs,* XXIII (No. 1, 1969), 21–46.

Harris, John R., and Michael P. Todaro. "Migration, Unemployment and Development: A Two-Sector Analysis," *American Economic Review,* LX (March 1970), 126–142.

Hayami, Yujiro, and V. W. Ruttan. "Agricultural Productivity Differences Among Countries," *American Economic Review,* LX (December 1970), 895–911.

―――― and V. W. Ruttan. "Factor Prices and Technical Change in Agricultural Development: The United States and Japan, 1880–1960," *Journal of Political Economy,* LXXVIII (September-October 1970), 1115–1141.

―――― and Saburo Yamada. "Technological Progress in Agriculture," in Lawrence Klein and Kazushi Ohkawa, eds. *Economic Growth: The Japanese Experience since the Meiji Era.* Homewood, Ill.: Richard D. Irwin, Inc., 1968, pp. 135–157.

Helleiner, G. K. "Agricultural Export Pricing Strategy in Tanzania," *East African Journal of Rural Development,* I (No. 1, 1969), 1–17.

BIBLIOGRAPHY

————. "The Fiscal Role of the Marketing Boards in Nigerian Economic Development, 1947–61," *Economic Journal,* LXXIV (1964), 582–605.

Hicks, J. R. "Unimproved Value Rating—the Case of East Africa," in *Essays in World Economics.* Oxford, Eng.: at the Clarendon Press, 1959, pp. 236–244.

Hinrichs, Harley H. "Certainty as Criterion: Taxation of Foreign Investment in Afghanistan," *National Tax Journal,* XV (June 1962), 139–154.

Hirschman, Albert O. "The Political Economy of Import-Substituting Industrialization in Latin America," *Quarterly Journal of Economics,* LXXXII (February 1968), 1–32.

Holland, Daniel M., and William N. Vaughn. "An Evaluation of Self-Assessment under Property Tax," in Arthur D. Lynn, Jr. *The Property Tax and Its Administration.* Madison: University of Wisconsin Press, 1969, pp. 79–118.

House, Peter W. "Assessment of Farmland in the Rural Urban Fringe," *Agricultural Finance Review,* XXII (September 1960).

Hymer, Stephen, and Stephen Resnick. "A Model of An Agrarian Economy with Nonagricultural Activities," *American Economic Review,* LIX (September 1969), 493–506.

Ike, Nobutaka. "Taxation and Landownership in the Westernization of Japan," *Journal of Economic History,* VII (November 1947), 160–182.

Inter-American Center of Tax Administrators (CIAT). *Newsletter,* monthly.

Johnson, Erwin H. "Land Tax and its Impact on Use and Ownership in Rural Japan," *Economic Development and Cultural Change,* XIX (No. 1, October 1970), 49–70.

Johnson, Glenn L. "Factor Markets and Economic Development," in W. W. McPherson, ed. *Economic Development of Tropical Agriculture.* Gainesville: University of Florida Press, 1968, pp. 93–111.

Johnston, Bruce F. "Agricultural Productivity and Economic Development in Japan," *Journal of Political Economy,* LIX (December 1951), 498–513.

————. "Agriculture and Structural Transformation in Developing Countries: A Survey of Research," *Journal of Economic Literature,* VIII (June 1970), 369–404.

———— and John Cownie. "The Seed-Fertilizer Revolution and Labor Force Absorption," *American Economic Review,* LIX (September 1969), 569–582.

———— and John W. Mellor. "The Role of Agriculture in Economic Development," *American Economic Review,* LI (September 1961), 566–593.

Junguito, Roberto. "Estudio del impuesto de renta presuntiva al sector agropecuario," *Revista del Banco de la República* (Bogotá), XLIV (October 1971), 1701–1723.

Junta de Planificación Económica. "El sistema impositivo de la Provincia de Buenos Aires," *Revista de Desarrollo Económico,* I (October–December 1958), 129–200.

Kanel, Don. "Size of Farm and Economic Development," *Indian Journal of Agricultural Economics*, XXII (No. 2, April–June 1967), 26–44.

Kimura, Motokazu. "Fiscal Policy and Industrialization in Japan, 1868–1895," in International Economic Association. *Economic Development with Special Reference to East Asia*. New York: Macmillan, 1964, pp. 273–286.

Land Tenure Center Newsletter (University of Wisconsin Land Tenure Center), quarterly.

Lele, Uma. "Agricultural Price Policy," *Economic and Political Weekly*, IV (No. 35, August 30, 1969), 1–11.

Lent, George E. "The Taxation of Land Value," *I.M.F. Staff Papers*, XIII (March 1967), 89–123.

Lewis, W. Arthur. "Economic Development with Unlimited Supplies of Labour," in A. N. Agarwala and S. P. Singh, eds. *The Economics of Underdevelopment*. Bombay: Oxford University Press, 1958, pp. 400–449.

————. "Planning Public Expenditure," in Max Millikan, ed. *National Economic Planning*. New York: Columbia University Press, 1967, pp. 201–227.

Lindauer, John, and Sarjit Singh. "Effects of the Punjab Land Tax," *National Tax Journal*, XIX (December 1966), 427–433.

Lipton, Michael. "A Game against Nature: Strategies of Security," *Development Digest*, VII (No. 2, April 1969), 18–21.

Little, I. M. D. "Tax Policy and the Third Plan," in P. N. Rosenstein-Rodan, ed. *Pricing and Fiscal Policies*. London: George Allen and Unwin, Ltd., 1964, pp. 30–76.

Lotz, Jorgen R., and Elliott R. Morss. "Measuring 'Tax Effort' in Developing Countries," *I.M.F. Staff Papers*, XIV (November 1967), 478–497.

Mieszkowski, Peter. "The Property Tax: Excise or Profits Tax?" *Journal of Public Economics*, I (March 1972), 73–96.

Mitra, Ashok. "Tax Burden for Indian Agriculture," in Ralph Braibanti and Joseph J. Spengler, eds., *Administration and Economic Development in India*. Durham, N.C.: Duke University Press, 1963, pp. 281–303.

Morag, Amotz. "Some Economic Aspects of Two Administrative Methods of Estimating Taxable Income," *National Tax Journal*, X (June 1957), 176–185.

Moral–Lopez, Pedro. "Tax Legislation as an Instrument to Assist in Achieving the Economic and Social Objectives of Land Reform," *Land Reform, Land Settlement and Co-operatives* (No. 2, 1965), pp. 2–12.

Morgan, D. J. "Land Valuation and Land Taxation in Jamaica," *Public Finance/Finances Publiques*, XII (No. 3, 1957), 232–238.

Navarrete, Ifigenia M. de. "Agricultural and Land Taxation," in Alan T. Peacock and Gerald Hauser, eds. *Government Finance and Economic Development*. Paris: Organisation for Economic Cooperation and Development, 1965, pp. 195–210.

Nyerere, Julius. "Education for Self-Reliance," *Africa Report* (No. 6, June 1967), reprinted in *Development Digest*, VIII (No. 4, October 1970), 3–13.

BIBLIOGRAPHY

Ohkawa, Kazushi, and Henry Rosovsky. "The Role of Agriculture in Modern Japanese Economic Development," *Economic Development and Cultural Change*, IX, Part II (October 1960), 43–68.

Oldman, Oliver. "Controlling Income Tax Evasion," in Joint Tax Program, *Problems of Tax Administration in Latin America*. Baltimore: Johns Hopkins Press, 1965, pp. 296–344.

———. "Tax Reform in El Salvador," *Inter-American Bar Review*, VI (July–December 1964), 379–420.

Osterhoudt, Frank. "Land Titles in Northeast Brazil: The Use of Aerial Photography," *Land Economics*, XLI (November 1965), 387–392.

Oweis, J. S. "The Impact of Land Reform on Egyptian Agriculture: 1952–1965," *Intermountain Economic Review*, II (Spring 1971), 45–72.

Owen, Wyn F. "The Double Developmental Squeeze on Agriculture," *American Economic Review*, LVI (March 1966), 43–70.

Pepper, H. W. T. "Taxation of Betterment and Capital Gains with Special Reference to Developing Countries," *Bulletin for International Fiscal Documentation*, XXI (No. 4, April 1967), 151–172.

Prest, Alan R. "The Role of Labour Taxes and Subsidies in Promoting Employment in Developing Countries," *International Labour Review*, CIII (No. 4, April 1971), 315–332.

Quindry, Kenneth E., and Billy D. Cook. "Humanization of the Property Tax for Low Income Households," *National Tax Journal*, XXII (September 1969), 357–367.

Ranis, Gustav. "The Financing of Japanese Economic Development," *Economic History Review*, XI (April 1959), 440–454.

Raup, Philip M. "The Contribution of Land Reforms to Economic Development: An Analytical Framework," *Economic Development and Cultural Change*, XII (October 1963), 1–21.

Rosovsky, Henry. "Rumbles in the Ricefields: Professor Nakamura vs. the Official Statistics," *Journal of Asian Studies*, XXVII (February 1968), 347–360.

Sanchez Cárdenas, Américo. "La reforma agraria en Ecuador: una prioridad desatendida," *Comercio Exterior*, XX (No. 5, May 1970), 400–404.

Sazama, Gerald W. "Land Taxes—Prerequisites and Obstacles: Bolivia," *National Tax Journal*, XXIII (September 1970), 315–324.

Schebeck, Emmerich M. "Fiscal Intervention and Employment in Agriculture," in *Fiscal Measures for Employment Promotion in Developing Countries* (Geneva: International Labour Office, 1972).

Schwab, Peter. "The Tax System of Ethiopia," *American Journal of Economics and Sociology*, XXIX (January 1970), 77–88.

Schwartz, Hugh H. "The Argentine Experience with Industrial Credit and Protection Incentives, 1943–1958," *Yale Economic Essays* (Fall 1968), pp. 261–327.

Shetty, N. S. "Agricultural Innovations: Leaders and Laggards," *Economic and Political Weekly* (August 17, 1968); reprinted in *Development Digest*, VII (No. 2, April 1969), 11–17.

Shoup, Carl S. "Production from Consumption," *Public Finance/Finances Publiques*, XX (Nos. 1–2, 1965), 173–201.

BIBLIOGRAPHY

314

Smith, R. Stafford. "Property Tax Capitalization in San Francisco," *National Tax Journal*, XXIII (June 1970), 177–193.

——— and Theodore M. Smith. "The Political Economy of Regional and Urban Revenue Policy in Indonesia," *Asian Survey*, XI (August 1971), 761–786.

Smith, T. C. "The Land Tax in the Tokugawa Period," *Journal of Asian Studies*, XVIII (November 1958), 3–19.

Solís, Leopoldo. "Mexican Economic Policy in the Post-War Period: The Views of Mexican Economists," *American Economic Review*, LXI (June 1971, suppl.), 2–67.

Sternberg, M. J. "The Economic Impact of the Latifundista," *Land Reform, Land Settlement and Cooperatives* (No. 2, 1970), pp. 21–34.

Stewart, Charles T., Jr. "Land Reform as Fiscal Policy for Agrarian Nations," *Social Research*, XXXII (1965), 98–109.

Stewart, Frances, and Paul Streeten. "Conflicts between Output and Employment Objectives in Developing Countries," *Oxford Economic Papers*, N.S., XXIII (July 1971), 145–168.

Strasma, John. "Financiamiento de la reforma agraria en el Peru," *El Trimestre Económico*, XXXII (July-September 1965), 484–500.

———. "Market-Enforced Self-Assessment for Real Estate Taxes," *Bulletin for International Fiscal Documentation*, XIX (1965), 353–363, 397–414.

Tanabe, Noboru. "The Taxation of Net Wealth," *I.M.F. Staff Papers*, XIV (March 1967), 124–168.

Tannenbaum, Frank. "Toward an Appreciation of Latin America," in *The United States and Latin America*. New York: The American Assembly, Columbia University, December 1959, pp. 5–57.

Thiesenhusen, William C. "Technological Change and Income Distribution in Latin American Agriculture," *Land Tenure Center Newsletter* (No. 33, February-July 1971), pp. 13–17.

Thome, Joseph R. "Title Problems in Rural Areas of Colombia: A Colonization Example," *Inter-American Economic Affairs*, XIV (No. 3, Winter 1965), 81–97.

———. "Water Regulation and Land Use: A Colombian Example," *Development Digest*, V (No. 3, October 1967), 39–44.

Todaro, Michael P. "A Model of Labor Migration and Urban Unemployment in Less Developed Countries," *American Economic Review*, LIX (March 1969), 138–148.

Trestrail, Richard W. "Forests and the Property Tax—Unsound Accepted Theory," *National Tax Journal*, XXII (September 1969), 347–356.

United Nations. "Tax Potential and Economic Growth in the Countries of the ECAFE Region," *Economic Bulletin for Asia and the Far East*, XVII (September 1966), 29–48.

———. "Taxation and Development of Agriculture in Underdeveloped Countries, with special reference to Asia and the Far East," *Economic Bulletin for Asia and the Far East*, IX (June 1958), 2–16.

Usher, Dan. "Income as a Means of Productivity: Alternative Comparisons of Agricultural and Non-Agricultural Productivity in Thailand," *Economica*, XXXIII (November 1966), 1430–1441.

BIBLIOGRAPHY

315

Van Roy, Edward "The Pursuit of Growth and Stability through Taxation of Agricultural Exports: Thailand's Experience," *Public Finance/Finances Publiques*, XXIII (No. 3, 1968), 294–313.

Wang, Yeh-Chien. "The Fiscal Importance of the Land Tax During the Ch'ing Period," *Journal of Asian Studies*, XXX (August 1971), 829–842.

Ward, Richard J. "Where to Now? The Future for Research and the Possibilities for Fiscal Innovating in Development Policy," in *Proceedings of the Sixty-Second Annual Conference on Taxation*. Columbus, Ohio: National Tax Association, 1970, pp. 691–704.

Wellisz, Stanislaw, and associates. "Resource Allocation in Traditional Agriculture: A Study of Andhra Pradesh," *Journal of Political Economy*, LXXVIII (August 1970), 655–684.

Wharton, Clifton R. "Risk, Uncertainty, and the Subsistence Farmer," *Development Digest*, VII (No. 2, April 1969), 3–10.

———. "The Green Revolution: Cornucopia or Pandora's Box?", *Foreign Affairs*, XLVII (April 1969), 464–476.

Wionzcek, Miguel S. "Incomplete Formal Planning: Mexico," in Everett S. Hagen, ed. *Planning Economic Development*. Homewood, Ill.: Richard D. Irwin, Inc., 1963, pp. 150–182.

Woodruff, A. M., and L. L. Ecker-Raus. "Property Taxes and Land-Use Patterns in Australia and New Zealand," *The Tax Executive*, XVIII (October 1965), 16–63.

PUBLIC DOCUMENTS

Agency for International Development. *Spring Review of Land Reform*, 12 vols. Washington, D.C.: Department of State, 1970.

———. *Spring Review of Land Reform: Findings and Implications for A.I.D.* Washington, D.C.: Department of State, 1970.

Argentina. *Boletín Oficial*. No. 21,600, January 13, 1969.

Chile, Ministerio de Agricultura, Oficina de Planificación Agrícola. *Plan de Desarrollo Agropecuario 1965–1980*. Santiago, 1968.

Foreign Tax Assistance Staff, Internal Revenue Service. *Report on Tax Administration in Costa Rica*. USAID, San José, 1967.

India. *Report of the Taxation Enquiry Commission*, 3 vols. Delhi: Manager of Publications, 1955.

Inter-American Committee for Agricultural Development. *Inventory of Information Basic to the Planning of Agricultural Development in Latin America: Regional Report*. Washington, D.C.: Pan-American Union, 1965.

International Labour Office. *Towards Full Employment: A Programme for Colombia*. Geneva, 1970.

International Monetary Fund. *Surveys of African Economies*, 4 vols. Washington, D.C., 1968–1971.

Joint Legislative-Executive Tax Commission. *Annual Report*. Manila, annual.

———. *Local Government Finance*. Manila, 1962.

———. *Summary of the Second Survey on Local Government Finance*. Manila, 1970.

————. *The Tax Monthly*, monthly.

Joint Tax Program. *Tax Systems of Latin America: Costa Rica.* Washington, D.C.: Pan-American Union, 1966.

————. *Tax Systems of Latin America: Guatemala.* Washington, D.C.: Pan-American Union, 1966.

————. *Tax Systems of Latin America: Honduras.* Washington, D.C.: Pan-American Union, 1967.

New Zealand Valuation Department. *A Critical Study of the Unimproved Value of Land.* Research Paper 68–1; Wellington, N.Z., 1968.

————. *"Land Value" and Rating Incidence.* Research Paper 68-5; Wellington, N.Z., 1968.

Ontario, Department of Municipal Affairs, Assessment Standards Branch. *Multivariate Analysis and Residential Property Valuation in Ontario.* Toronto, 1970.

Programa Conjunto de Tributación. *Estudio sobre Política Fiscal en Argentina* (Versión preliminar), 7 vols. Buenos Aires: Consejo Nacional de Desarrollo, 1967.

————. *Sistemas Tributarios de América Latina: Uruguay.* Washington, D.C.: Pan-American Union, 1967.

Social Progress Trust Fund, Inter-American Development Bank. *Socio-Economic Progress in Latin America: Report.* Washington, D.C., annual.

United Nations. *Manual of Land Tax Administration.* New York: Department of Economic and Social Affairs, 1968.

————. *Progress in Land Reform, Third Report.* New York, 1962.

————. *Progress in Land Reform, Fourth Report.* New York, 1966.

————. "Report of the Seminar on Cadastre," Addis Ababa, 1970 E/CN. 14/500, E/CN. 14/CART/278.

————. "Site Value Taxation in Developing Countries," United Nations-CIAT Seminar on Land Tax Administration, Panama City, September 2–9, 1971, ESA/FF/AC.6/1.

————, Comisión Económica para América Latina. *La política tributaria y el desarrollo económico en América Central.* New York, 1957.

————, Department of Economic and Social Affairs. Papers presented at meeting of the Expert Group on Tax Reform Planning, September 8–14, 1970.

Uruguay, Ministerio de Ganadería y Agricultura. *Estudio económico y social de agricultura en el Uruguay.* Montevideo, 1967.

Unpublished Material

Alsagaban, Abdulaal. "The Tax System in Iraq," United Nations Department of Economic Affairs, Studies on Tax Reform Planning (ESA/ECOSOC/LI/Misc. 2/Add.5), New York, 1971.

Babbitt, Bruce E. "Self-Assessment as a Means of Real Property Evaluation," unpub. paper, Harvard Law School, 1965.

Bolivia. "Proyecto de ley Impuesto unico al sector agropecuario," Versión aprobada en la Primera Conferencia Económica de Campesinos (mimeo; 1968).

Boscoli, Altamiro. "Agrarian Reform and Land Taxation in Brazil," unpub. paper, International Tax Program, Harvard Law School, 1964.

Brause Berreta, Alberto. "Uruguay: An Experience with the Tax on Potential Agricultural Income," unpub. paper, International Tax Program, Harvard Law School, 1969.

Buchon Rivas, Alfredo. "Rural Land Taxation in Bolivia," unpub. paper, International Tax Program, Harvard Law School, 1966.

Bulutoglu, Kenan. "Incentive and Welfare Effects of Tax Structure Change: The Case of Turkey," paper presented to Seminar on Fiscal Incentives to Promote Agricultural Development, Istanbul, Turkey, November 1968.

CIAT Executive Secretariat. "The Real Property Tax at the National Level in the CIAT Member Countries," Fifth Technical Seminar, Inter-American Center of Tax Administrators, No. V–ST/1.0–I, September 1971.

Cruz, Ernesto. "Competitive Self-Assessment: An Exercise in Rational Tax Design," unpub. paper, Harvard Law School, 1965.

Davis, L. Harlan. "Economics of the Property Tax in Rural Areas of Colombia," University of Wisconsin Land Tenure Center, Research Paper No. 25, 1967.

Edel, Mathew D. "The Colombian Community Action Program: An Economic Evaluation," unpub. study, Cambridge, Mass., 1968.

Eichbaum, William M. "Retroussons nous Manches: Agriculture and Fiscal Policy In the Democratic Republic of the Congo," unpub. paper, Harvard Law School, 1966.

Eklund, Per. "An Analysis of Capital Flows Between the Agricultural and Nonagricultural Sectors of West Pakistan," International Bank for Reconstruction and Development, Economics Department Working Paper No. 41, 1969.

———. "Taxation and Earmarking in Developing Countries," International Bank for Reconstruction and Development, Economics Department Working Paper No. 43, 1969.

Espinosa, Aristides, and Miguel Angel Pangrazzio. "Los organismos perceptores de impuestos y su relación con la economía agropecuaria del Paraguay," paper presented at Seminario Internacional sobre Tributación Agrícola, Santiago, Chile, November 1963.

Ferreira, Santoa E. "Regimen tributario uruguayo de sector agropecuario," paper presented to Seminario Internacional sobre Tributación Agrícola, Santiago, Chile, November 1963.

Gandhi, Ved P. "Taxes, Subsidies, and Agricultural Production (India)," paper presented to Seminar on Fiscal Incentives to Promote Agricultural Development, Istanbul, Turkey, November 1968.

Gimeno S., José "Taxation: Some Considerations Concerning Its Importance in the Economic Development of the Agricultural Sector," unpub. paper, Santiago, Chile, 1970.

Grether, David, and Peter Mieszkowski. "Determinants of Real Estate Values," unpub. paper, 1971.

Hinrichs, Harley H. "Tax Reform," Agency for International Development, Washington, 1970.

Holland, Daniel M. "Agricultural Taxation: New Possibilities for an Old

Device," paper presented to Seminar on Fiscal Inventives to Promote Agricultural Development, Istanbul, Turkey, November 1968.

Huth, William P. "Traditional Institutions and Land Tenure as Related to Agricultural Development among the Ibo of Eastern Nigeria," University of Wisconsin Land Tenure Center, Research Paper No. 6, August 1969.

Islam, Nurul. "The Tax System in Pakistan," United Nations Department of Economic Affairs, Studies in Tax Reform Planning (ESA/ECOSOC/ LI/Misc. 2/Add. 6) July 1971.

Joint Legislative-Executive Tax Commission. "Tax on Idle Lands" (mimeo; Manila, 1968).

Juran, M. Lionel. "Agricultural Organization, Administration, and Taxation under the Viet Mihn, 1949–51," unpub. paper, Harvard Law School, 1968.

Kalmanoff, George. "The Coffee Economy of Colombia, " International Bank for Reconstruction and Development, Economics Department Working Paper No. 15, May 1968.

Khan, Mohamad, and Edward R. Kittrell. "Land Inventory and Cadastral Survey: Revenues and Incentive Repercussions in Afghanistan," paper presented to Seminar on Fiscal Incentives to Promote Agricultural Development, Istanbul, Turkey, November 1968.

Khandker, R. H. "Distribution of Tax Burden in Pakistan" (mimeo; Dacca, November 1964).

Kher, S. P. "Betterment Taxes: A Case Study in Mysore and Maharastra," paper presented to the Seminar on Fiscal Incentives to Promote Agricultural Development, Istanbul, Turkey, November 1968.

Lent, George E. "Taxation of Agricultural Income in Developing Countries," unpub. paper, Washington, D.C., 1972.

Lewis, Stephen R., Jr. "Taxation and Growth in the Dual Economy: An Evaluation of Tax Devices in Underdeveloped Economies," unpub. diss., Stanford University, June 1963.

Maddison, Angus. "Social Development of Pakistan," paper presented to Conference of Development Advisory Service, Dubrovnik, June 1970.

Mengot, Ako Defang. "Financing Primary Education from Local Education Rates in West Cameroon," unpub. diss., Harvard Graduate School of Education, 1971.

Mohandes, Abootaleb. "Taxation of Income from Agricultural Activities in Iran," unpub. paper, International Tax Program, Harvard Law School, 1969.

Mohmand, Fahil Rahim, Richard F. Saunders, and Edward R. Kittrell. "Supply Responses to Price Changes: Two Afghanistan Cases—Cotton and Karakul," paper presented to Seminar on Fiscal Incentives to Promote Agricultural Development, Istanbul, Turkey, November 1968.

Morgan, Cecil. "Report on Taxation of Guatemalan Agriculture," U.S. Department of State, International Cooperation Administration, USOM/Guatemala, Airgram, November 23, 1960.

———. "Property Taxation in Central America," Department of State, Agency for International Development, Regional Office, Central America and Panama Affairs, November 1967.

Nepal, Ministry of Agriculture. "Mobilizing Rural Capital through Compulsory Savings: The Nepal Case," paper presented to International Seminar on Fiscal Incentives to Promote Agricultural Development, Istanbul, Turkey, November 1968.

Olatunbosun, Dupe. "Nigerian Governments' Policies Affecting Investment in Agriculture," CSNRD 16, Consortium for the Study of Nigerian Rural Development in collaboration with the Nigerian Institute of Social and Economic Research, July 1968.

Oldman, Oliver, and Daniel M. Holland. "Measuring Tax Evasion," unpub. paper, Harvard Law School and The Sloan School of Management, Massachusetts Institute of Technology, 1971.

Pistono Alvarez, José-Luis, et al. "Proyecto de Ley: Impuesto Unico a los Bienes Raices Agrícolas," Ministerio de Agricultura (Chile), Consejo Superior de Fomento Agropecuario (mimeo; 1964).

Please, Stanley. "Aspects of Agricultural Tax Policy in India and Pakistan," paper presented to Seminar on Fiscal Incentives to Promote Agricultural Development, Istanbul, Turkey, November 1968.

————. "Capital Flows and Income Transfers within and between Nations to Sustain the Agricultural Revolution," paper presented to Conference on International Agricultural Development, Bellagio, Italy, April 1969.

Sahota, G. S. "The Distribution of the Tax Burden in Brazil," unpub. study, Rio de Janeiro, 1968.

Saylor, R. G. "A Study of Obstacles to Investment in Oil Palm and Rubber Plantations," CSNRD 15, Consortium for the Study of Nigerian Rural Development, August 1968.

Sazama, Gerald W. "Agricultural Land Taxation in Chile," unpub. paper, 1970.

————. "Analisis Económico del Proyecto de Impuesto Unico para el Sector Agrícola," Informe al Gobierno de Bolivia y a la A.I.D., August 1968.

———— and L. Harlan Davis. "Land Taxation and Land Reform," unpub. paper, 1969.

Schebeck, Emmerich M. "An Analysis of Capital Flows between the Agricultural and Non-Agricultural Sectors of India," International Bank for Reconstruction and Development, Economics Department Working Paper No. 42, June 1969.

Schultz, T. W. "Production Opportunities in Asian Agriculture: An Economist's Agenda," Agriculture Economics Paper No. 68:12, Department of Economics, University of Chicago, July 1968.

Sherman, Frederick E. "Agricultural Taxation in Nigeria: The Produce Marketing Boards," unpub. paper, Harvard Law School, April 1968.

Strasma, John D. "Tax Reform in Bolivia, 1961," Report to the International Co-operation Administration, September 1961.

————. "Tributación de la agricultura," Paper presented to Seminario Internacional sobre Tributación Agrícola, Santiago, Chile, November 1963.

Taylor, Milton C. "Tax Policies for the Economic Development of Panama," unpub. paper, 1968.

Thomas, John W. "Rural Public Works and East Pakistan's Development,"

Economic Development Report No. 112, Development Advisory Service, Harvard University, 1968.

Torretti, Carlos, et al. "La tributación sobre la propiedad territorial como instrumento auxiliar de la política social y económica," paper presented to Seminario Internacional sobre Tributación Agrícola, Santiago, Chile, November 1963.

Tostes, Sergio, "The Agrarian Question in Brazil: Taxation Techniques," unpub. paper, International Tax Program, Harvard Law School, 1969.

Yucelik, Mustafa Zuhtu. "Taxation of Agricultural Incomes and Economic Development in Turkey," unpub. paper, International Tax Program, Harvard Law School, 1968.

Yulug, Mustafa. "Some Remarks on the Agricultural Taxation in Developing Countries," unpub. paper, International Tax Program, Harvard Law School, 1969 (based on his book *Azgelismis Ulkelerde Tarimin Vergilendirilmes.* [Ankara, 1968]).

NOTES

PART ONE. AGRICULTURE, DEVELOPMENT, AND TAXES

CHAPTER 1. THE CASE FOR TAXING AGRICULTURE

1. This point is stressed, for example, in Simon Kuznets, *Modern Economic Growth* (New Haven, Conn.: Yale University Press, 1966), pp. 113–127. Considerable supporting evidence for the proposition that the agricultural sector will secularly decline in the course of development is also marshaled in Bruce F. Johnston, "Agriculture and Structural Transformation in Developing Countries: A Survey of Research," *Journal of Economic Literature*, VIII (June 1970), 369–373.

2. Wyn F. Owen, "The Double Developmental Squeeze on Agriculture," *American Economic Review*, LVI (March 1966), 43–70.

3. Gerald M. Meier, *Leading Issues in Development Economics* (2nd ed., New York: Oxford University Press, 1970), pp. 198–199. Similar views have often been expressed by other influential authors: see, for example, Haskell P. Wald, "Reform of Agricultural Taxation to Promote Economic Development in Latin America," in Joint Tax Program, *Fiscal Policy for Economic Growth in Latin America* (Baltimore: Johns Hopkins Press, 1965), p. 329, and Nicholas Kaldor, "The Role of Taxation in Economic Development," in *ibid.*, p. 75.

4. The many public policies other than taxation which may be used, intentionally or unintentionally, to alter the internal terms of trade between agriculture and industry—credit policy, subsidies and other ex-

penditure policies, protective policy, price controls, etc.—are not treated except in passing in the present study. Nor is much attention devoted to the use of indirect taxes in tapping the agricultural sector. The resulting emphasis throughout on the role played by the direct taxation of agriculture is inevitably exaggerated but cannot be avoided, given that this is the main subject of the book.

Further useful discussion of other public policies affecting agriculture may be found in Stephen R. Lewis, Jr., "Agricultural Taxation in a Developing Economy," in Herman M. Southworth and Bruce F. Johnston, eds., *Agricultural Development and Economic Growth* (Ithaca, N.Y.: Cornell University Press, 1967), pp. 453–492; and in Stanley Please, "Capital Flows and Income Transfers within and between Nations to Sustain the Agricultural Revolution," paper presented to Seminar on International Agricultural Development, Bellagio, Italy, April 1969.

5. This aspect is stressed, for example, by R. F. Kahn, "The Pace of Development," in *The Challenge of Development* (Jerusalem, 1958), reprinted in A. N. Agarwala and S. P. Singh, eds., *Accelerating Investment in Developing Economies* (Bombay: Oxford University Press, 1969), p. 102; and Benjamin Higgins, *Economic Development* (rev. ed., New York: W. W. Norton & Company, Inc., 1968), p. 521.

6. W. Arthur Lewis, *The Theory of Economic Growth* (Homewood, Ill.: Richard D. Irwin, Inc., 1955), p. 231. Lewis' views on the importance of tapping the agricultural sector for substantial revenue have apparently not changed much since this passage was written. See his *Development Planning* (London: George Allen and Unwin, Ltd., 1965), pp. 115–130.

7. In addition to the citations in note 3, above, see, for representative instances, E. T. Mathew, *Agricultural Taxation and Economic Development in India* (London: Asia Publishing House, 1968), pp. 4–5; R. N. Tripathy, *Public Finance in Under-Developed Countries* (Calcutta: World Press Private, Ltd., 1965), pp. 112–116; Robert B. Bangs, *Financing Economic Development* (Chicago: University of Chicago Press, 1968), pp. 127–128; Milton C. Taylor et al., *Fiscal Survey of Colombia* (Baltimore: Johns Hopkins Press, 1965), pp. 107, 129; Ursula K. Hicks, *Development from Below* (Oxford, Eng.: Clarendon Press, 1961), pp. 321–322; and Lewis, "Agricultural Taxation in a Developing Economy," in Southworth and Johnston, eds., *Agricultural Development*, p. 460.

8. Wald, "Reform of Agricultural Taxation," in Joint Tax Program, *Fiscal Policy for Growth*, pp. 326, 329–330. See also Ved P. Gandhi, *Tax Burden on Indian Agriculture* (Cambridge, Mass.: Law School of Harvard University, 1966), and Mathew, *Agricultural Taxation*, chaps. 3–4, for other "equity" arguments.

9. Extended argument along the lines of this paragraph with respect to Colombia may be found in Richard M. Bird, *Taxation and Development: Lessons from Colombian Experience* (Cambridge, Mass.: Harvard University Press, 1970), chaps. 1–2, and "Optimal Tax Policy for a Developing Country: The Case of Colombia," *Finanzarchiv* (N.F.), XXIX (No. 1, February 1970), 30–53. The argument is generalized in Bird, "Income Distribution, Economic Growth, and Tax Policy," *Proceedings of the Sixty-First Annual Conference of the National Tax Association* (Columbus, Ohio, 1968), pp. 146–152.

10. Johnston, "Agriculture and Structural Transformation," p. 374; emphasis added.

11. See W. Arthur Lewis, "Economic Development with Unlimited Supplies of Labour," *The Manchester School*, May 1954, reprinted in A. N. Agarwala and S. P. Singh, eds., *The Economics of Underdevelopment* (Bombay: Oxford University Press, 1958), pp. 400–449; Ragnar Nurkse, *Problems of Capital Formation in Underdeveloped Countries* (New York: Oxford University Press, 1953).

12. See J. C. H. Fei and G. Ranis, *Development of the Labor Surplus Economy* (Homewood, Ill.: Richard D. Irwin, Inc., 1964), and, especially, Fei and Ranis, "Agrarianism, Dualism, and Economic Development," in I. Adelman and E. Thorbecke, eds., *The Theory and Design of Economic Development* (Baltimore: Johns Hopkins Press, 1966), pp. 3–41, and "Agriculture in the Open Economy," in Erik Thorbecke, ed., *The Role of Agriculture in Economic Development* (New York: Columbia University Press, 1969), pp. 129–164.
Many additional references to the literature, and some necessary qualifications to the brief summary possible here, may be found in Johnston's recent review article (cited in note 1, above), as well as in John W. Mellor, "Toward a Theory of Agricultural Development," in Southworth and Johnston, eds., *Agricultural Development*, pp. 21–60.

13. Fei and Ranis, "Agrarianism, Dualism, and Economic Development," in Adelman and Thorbecke, eds., *Theory and Design*, p. 24. A similar assumed asymmetry in the production functions of the agricultural and industrial sectors is crucial to the model proposed in Bruce F. Johnston and John W. Mellor, "The Role of Agriculture in Economic Development," *American Economic Review*, LI (September 1961), 570, as well as to the Lewis model (cited in note 11) and most other two-sector models.

14. Lewis, "Agricultural Taxation in a Developing Economy," in Southworth and Johnston, eds., *Agricultural Development*, p. 460.

15. It should be noted, however, that Fei and Ranis themselves stressed the "connectedness" between the agricultural and industrial sectors which facilitates the direct channeling of rural savings into decentralized rural industries. The role of agricultural land taxation in their model is thus not to transfer resources to industry directly but rather to finance the formation of social capital. As is so often true, the originators of a model appear more aware of its limited policy implications than some of their followers.

16. See Fei and Ranis, "Agrarianism, Dualism, and Economic Development," in Adelman and Thorbecke, eds., *Theory and Design*, pp. 38–39; Johnston and Mellor, "The Role of Agriculture," pp. 470–471. The lessons of the Japanese experience are seen, in Chapter 6 below, to be rather different than most writers on agricultural taxation appear to think.

17. Nicholas Kaldor, "The Role of Taxation in Economic Development," in Joint Tax Program, *Fiscal Policy for Growth*, p. 75 (different emphasis in original); cf. Mathew, *Agricultural Taxation and Economic Development*, p. 107, and Haskell P. Wald, *Taxation of Agricultural Land in Underdeveloped Economies* (Cambridge, Mass.: Harvard University Press, 1959), p. 130.

18. Gandhi, *Tax Burden,* p. 171—where (again!) Japan is the cited example of this process. Gandhi's analysis of this problem is more careful than this quotation suggests, but it is, of course, itself closely related to the peculiar conditions of India, as is that of Mathew, *Agricultural Taxation,* pp. 97–98, who reaches a similiar conclusion. The Indian experience is discussed at greater length in Chapter 6, below.

19. E. R. A. Seligman, *The Shifting and Incidence of Taxation* (5th ed., New York: Columbia University Press, 1927; reprinted 1969 by Augustus M. Kelley, Publishers, New York), pp. 5–8.

20. Gandhi, *Tax Burden,* pp. 163–164.

21. *Ibid.,* pp. 12–13, provides a particularly clear example of the approach, but it also underlies many other recommendations in this field, for example, Wald's (see the reference cited in note 8, above).

22. See Gandhi, *Tax Burden,* chaps. 3–4; also his "Agricultural Taxation Policy—Search for a Direction," *Artha-Vikas* (July 1969), pp. 3–49; R. H. Khandker, "Distribution of Tax Burden in Pakistan," unpub. study, Dacca, 1964; G. S. Sahota, "The Distribution of the Tax Burden in Brazil," unpub. study, Rio de Janeiro, 1968.

23. For a detailed critique of such models in a different sphere, see R. M. Bird, "Wagner's 'Law' of Expanding State Activity," *Public Finance,* XXVI (No. 1, 1971), 1–24.

24. Cf. J. M. Keynes, *The General Theory of Employment, Interest and Money* (New York: Harcourt, Brace, and Company, 1936), p. 383.

CHAPTER 2. THE ROLE OF AGRICULTURAL TAXATION
IN DEVELOPING COUNTRIES

1. Wald, *Taxation of Agricultural Land,* pp. 206–207, suggests such personalization of land taxes. Some have suggested the opposite sort of "personalization," i.e., discriminatory taxation of children (see references in Gunnar Myrdal, *Asian Drama* [3 vols.; New York: Pantheon Books, 1969], II, 1502n.). But these suggestions have been adopted nowhere; nor do they seem likely to be in the near future.

2. For further discussion of these and other interactions between economic and population growth, see R. M. Bird, "Crecimiento de la población y desarrollo económico," *Desarrollo Económico* (Buenos Aires), I (July-September 1961), 17–42.

3. See the interesting model of M. P. Todaro, "A Model of Labor Migration and Urban Unemployment in Less Developed Countries," *American Economic Review,* LIX (March 1969), 138–148; also John R. Harris and Michael P. Todaro, "Migration, Unemployment and Development: A Two-Sector Analysis," *ibid.,* LX (March 1970), 126–142.

4. Trent J. Bertrand, "Rural Taxation in Thailand," *Pacific Affairs,* XII (Summer 1969), 178–188.

5. See Todaro, "A Model of Labor Migration," p. 147n.; Harris and Todaro, "Migration, Unemployment and Development," p. 138.

6. See, for example, Wald, *Taxation of Agricultural Land,* p. 94.

7. Solon L. Barranclough, "Agricultural Policy and Land Reform," *Journal of Political Economy,* LXXVIII (No. 4, July–August, suppl., 1970), 934; Marion Clawson, Hans H. Landsberg, and Lyle T. Alexander, *The*

Agricultural Potential of the Middle East (New York: American Elsevier Publishing Company, Inc., 1971), p. 7.

8. Dino Jarach, *El impuesto a la renta normal potencial de la tierra* (Cuaderno de Finanzas Públicas, 5, Programa Conjunto de Tributación; Washington, D.C.: Pan-American Union, n.d.), p. 1.

9. See, for example, International Labour Office, *Towards Full Employment: A Programme for Colombia* (Geneva, 1970), chaps. 1, 4, 7; see also the discussion in Chapter 9, below.

10. Johnston and Mellor, "The Role of Agriculture in Economic Development," p. 590.

11. Impressive empirical documentation of this point has, for example, recently been assembled for India by Stanislaw Wellisz and associates, "Resource Allocation in Traditional Agriculture: A Study of Andhra Pradesh," *Journal of Political Economy*, LXXVIII (August 1970), 655–684.

12. Johnston, "Agriculture and Structural Transformation," p. 392.

13. Myrdal, *Asian Drama*, II, 1294.

14. See Gandhi, *Tax Burden*, pp. 151–153.

15. T. W. Schultz, "Production Opportunities in Asian Agriculture: An Economist's Agenda," Agriculture Economics Paper No. 68:12, Department of Economics, University of Chicago, July 1968.

A subtle discussion of the many complex issues involved in discerning and measuring saving and investment in more primitive agricultural communities may be found in Raymond Firth and B. S. Yamey, eds., *Capital, Saving and Credit in Peasant Societies* (Chicago: Aldine Publishing Company, 1969). In general, this discussion confirms that peasants act on the whole "economically" so that their behavior can be analyzed in quite conventional ways—although of course the conventions within which they "economize" vary widely among societies.

16. Stephen Hymer and Stephen Resnick, "A Model of an Agrarian Economy with Nonagricultural Activities," *American Economic Review*, LIX (September 1969), 493–506.

17. For instance, Guy Hunter, *Modernizing Peasant Societies* (New York: Oxford University Press, 1969), pp. 150–54.

18. Bruce F. Johnston and John Cownie, "The Seed-Fertilizer Revolution and Labor Force Absorption," *American Economic Review*, LIX (September 1969), 579.

19. Owen, "The Double Developmental Squeeze on Agriculture," p. 61.

20. Johnston and Mellor, "The Role of Agriculture in Economic Development," p. 572. Note that, a decade later, these same two authors would not make so categorical a statement: see the previous references to their respective recent review articles.

21. See Hunter, *Modernizing Peasant Societies*, pp. 10–11.

22. Julius Nyereye, "Education for Self-Reliance," *Africa Report* (No. 6, June 1967), reprinted in *Development Digest*, VIII, (No. 4, October 1970), 5.

23. Peter Dorner, Marion Brown, and Don Kanel, "Land Tenure and Reform: Issues in Latin American Development," *Land Tenure Center Newsletter*, (No. 29, March-August 1969), p. 10.

24. Cf. the discussion between Reuben C. Buse and Peter Dorner, *ibid.*, pp. 14–15.

25. See Johnston, "Agriculture and Structural Transformation," p. 383; Shigeru Ishikawa, *Economic Development in Asian Perspective* (Tokyo: Kinokuniya Bookstore Co., Ltd., 1967), chap. 4.

26. Yujiro Hayami and V. W. Ruttan, "Agricultural Productivity Differences among Countries," *American Economic Review*, LX (December 1970), 908.

27. For discussion of instances where increased consumption may increase productivity, see Carl S. Shoup, "Production from Consumption," *Public Finance*, XX (Nos. 1–2, 1965), 173–206.

28. See Carl K. Eicher, *Research on Agricultural Development in Five English-Speaking Countries in West Africa* (New York: Agricultural Development Council, Inc., 1970), pp. 19–29, for a summary of the relevant research.

29. Lauchlin Currie, *Accelerating Development* (New York: McGraw-Hill, 1966), pp. 25–27, 45, 200; Bird, *Taxation and Development*, p. 17.

30. See Mellor, "Toward a Theory of Agricultural Development," in Southworth and Johnston, eds., *Agricultural Development*, pp. 35–36; also Hymer and Resnick, "A Model of An Agrarian Economy."

31. An early recognition of the importance of this point may, however, be found in Johnston and Mellor, "The Role of Agriculture in Economic Development," p. 575.

32. See Bird, *Taxation and Development*, chap. 2, for a brief discussion of the upsetting effects of swings in foreign trade (however caused) on Colombia's development in the 1960's.

33. See the evidence summarized by Raj Krishna, "Agricultural Price Policy and Economic Development," in Southworth and Johnston, eds., *Agricultural Development*, chap. 13; and Eicher, *Research on Agricultural Development*.

34. See Clifton R. Wharton, Jr., "The Green Revolution: Cornucopia or Pandora's Box?", *Foreign Affairs*, XLVII (April 1969), 464–476; Johnston and Cownie, "The Seed-Fertilizer Revolution," pp. 569–582; Johnston, "Agricultural and Structural Transformation," pp. 379–380.

35. Johnston and Cownie, "The Seed-Fertilizer Revolution," p. 580.

36. Agency for International Development, *Spring Review of Land Reform: Findings and Implications for A.I.D.* (Washington, D.C.: Department of State, 1970).

37. *The Economist* (April 4, 1970), p. 39.

38. Cf. Johnston, "Agriculture and Structural Transformation," pp. 380, 394.

39. Barranclough, "Agricultural Policy and Land Reform," p. 935; Clawson, Landsberg, and Alexander, *The Agricultural Potential of the Middle East*, p. 141.

40. Cf. Carl Eicher et al., "Employment Generation in African Agriculture," *Development Digest*, IX (No. 1, January 1971), 77–87; Emmerich M. Schebeck, "Fiscal Intervention and Employment in Agriculture," in *Fiscal Measures for Employment Promotion in Developing Countries* (Geneva: International Labour Office, 1972).

41. Hayami and Ruttan, "Agricultural Productivity Differences"; also Yujiro Hayami and Vernon W. Ruttan, *Agricultural Development: An International Perspective* (Baltimore: Johns Hopkins Press, 1971).

42. For an interesting catalog of possible implications of the new agricultural innovations for tax policy, see Richard J. Ward, "Where to Now? The Future for Research and the Possibilities for Fiscal Innovating in Development Policy," *Proceedings of the Sixty-Second Annual Conference on Taxation* (Columbus, Ohio: National Tax Association, 1970), pp. 691–704.

PART TWO. TAXING AGRICULTURE: A SURVEY

CHAPTER 3. A QUANTITATIVE OVERVIEW

1. For further discussion of the data problems involved in putting together tables such as these, see Wald, *Taxation of Agricultural Land*, pp. 60–62. There has been little, if any, improvement in the situation since Wald wrote. Incidentally, it should be noted that taxes on the goods purchased by the agricultural sector are left out of account in these tables, as in this book.

2. Richard Goode, George E. Lent, and P. D. Ojha, "Role of Export Taxes in Developing Countries," *I. M. F. Staff Papers*, XIII (November 1966), 459.

3. Chapter 4 discusses briefly the incidence of export taxes. A more extensive treatment of the incidence of land-based taxes may be found in Chapter 8.

4. For example, in Uganda exports constituted 29 percent of G.N.P. in 1963–1964; in the Sudan the corresponding figure was 19 percent, and in Tanzania 23 percent (for 1962–1963). The correspondence between the importance of exports and the importance of export taxes is not always this close, however, even in Africa: Nigeria, for example, collected 18 percent of taxes from exports which constituted only 12 percent of G.N.P. in 1962–1963, while Ghana in the same year collected only 6 percent compared to an export ratio of 20 percent (Goode, Lent, and Ojha, "Role of Export Taxes," p. 460).

5. In Ethiopia, for example, taxes came to only 8 percent of G.N.P. in the 1964–1966 period; in Paraguay (1963–1965) to 10 percent; and in Niger (1964–1965) to 14 percent (Jorgen R. Lotz and Elliott R. Morss, "Measuring 'Tax Effort' in Developing Countries," *I.M.F. Staff Papers*, XIV (November 1967), 492–493).

6. The special cases of forest taxation and of the taxation of mineral extraction are also not treated here in view of their highly specialized nature. A thorough study of these questions in the context of developing countries is badly needed. For some useful discussion of general policy issues in the taxation of forests, fisheries, mining, oil and gas, see Mason Gaffney, ed., *Extractive Resources and Taxation* (Madison: University of Wisconsin Press, 1967).

7. See Harley H. Hinrichs, *A General Theory of Tax Structure Change During Economic Development* (Cambridge, Mass.: Law School of Harvard University, 1966); also Richard A. Musgrave, *Fiscal Systems* (New Haven, Conn.: Yale University Press, 1969), chaps. 5–6, and sources cited there.

8. United Nations, "Taxation and Development of Agriculture in Underdeveloped Countries, with special reference to Asia and the Far East," *Economic Bulletin For Asia and the Far East,* IX (June 1958), 9.

9. G. K. Helleiner, "The Fiscal Role of the Marketing Boards in Nigerian Economic Development, 1947–61," *Economic Journal,* LXXIV (1964), 582–605; Jonathan V. Levin, *The Export Economies: Their Pattern of Development in Historical Perspective* (Cambridge, Mass.: Harvard University Press, 1960), chap. 5 (on Burma's rice-marketing board).

10. Exports constituted only 4 percent of G.D.P. in India in 1962–1963 and only 6 percent of G.N.P. in Mexico in 1963 (Goode, Lent, and Ojha, "Role of Export Taxes," p. 460).

11. For some figures on the percentage of population engaged in agricultural occupations in different countries, see Higgins, *Economic Development,* p. 18. The proportion is over 90 percent in some African countries, around 70 percent in India and Indonesia, over 50 percent in most other Asian and a number of Latin American countries, but probably less in Argentina, Uruguay, and (by now) Chile than in such European countries as France and Italy.

12. Wald, *Taxation of Agricultural Land,* p. 68.

CHAPTER 4. DIRECT TAXES ON AGRICULTURE

1. This account is based on Levin, *The Export Economies,* chap. 5. The Burmese land tax, which produced 30 percent of government revenues in 1938–1939, was levied in theory at a rate of 25 percent of the value of "normal" gross production less the "normal" cost of cultivation, with the tax base being determined by surveys every twenty years and the tax due being fixed until the next survey. It closely resembled the Indian land tax described in Chapter 6, below.

2. Levin, *The Export Economies,* p. 262.

3. G. K. Helleiner, *Peasant Agriculture, Government, and Economic Growth in Nigeria* (Homewood, Ill.: Richard D. Irwin, Inc., 1967), p. 157.

4. Edward Van Roy, "The Pursuit of Growth and Stability through Taxation of Agricultural Exports: Thailand's Experience," *Public Finance/Finances Publiques,* XXIII (No. 3, 1968), 294–313.

5. Goode, Lent, and Ojha, "Role of Export Taxes," p. 500.

6. Ifigenia M. de Navarrete, "Agricultural and Land Taxation," in Alan T. Peacock and Gerald Hauser, eds., *Government Finance and Economic Development* (Paris: Organisation for Economic Co-operation and Development, 1965), p. 201.

7. Joint Legislative-Executive Tax Commission, *12th Annual Report 1970* (Manila, 1971), pp. 25–26.

8. G. K. Helleiner, "Agricultural Export Pricing Strategy in Tanzania," *East African Journal of Rural Development,* I (No. 1, 1969), 1-17. Helleiner calculates (p. 13) that the taxes collected from Tanzanian agriculture in 1966–1967 through export duties, development levies on exported commodities, produce cesses imposed by local authorities, and marketing board surpluses amounted to only 4 percent of net value for cotton but 26 percent for robusta coffee, and 17 percent for the higher-valued arabica.

9. For examples, see Levin, *The Export Economies,* chap. 5 (Burma);

Helleiner, "The Fiscal Role of the Marketing Boards," pp. 582–605 (Nigeria); and Bird, *Taxation and Development,* pp. 211–218 (Colombia).

10. Lewis, "Agricultural Taxation in a Developing Economy," in South-worth and Johnston, eds., *Agricultural Development,* pp. 477–478.

11. Hugh H. Schwartz, "The Argentine Experience with Industrial Credit and Protection Incentives, 1943–1958," *Yale Economic Essays* (Fall 1968), pp. 261–327; Stephen R. Lewis, Jr., *Economic Policy and Industrial Growth in Pakistan* (London: George Allen and Unwin, Ltd., 1969).

12. Bird, *Taxation and Development,* pp. 211–218.

13. Nathaniel H. Leff, *Economic Policy-Making and Development in Brazil, 1947–1964* (New York: John Wiley & Sons, Inc., 1969), pp. 24, 190.

14. This account is largely based on Van Roy, "The Pursuit of Growth," pp. 295–313; and Bertrand, "Rural Taxation in Thailand," pp. 178–188.

15. Oliver Oldman, "Tax Reform in El Salvador," *Inter-American Bar Review,* VI (July–December 1964), 405. This study recommended the replacement of the exemption system by a provision for credit, as in Guatemala, and the extension of the integrated export income tax system to other agricultural products. These recommendations were not accepted, however.

16. If all producing countries imposed similar taxes and acted together, the result would, of course, be different in the short run: in one sense, it is precisely this which has been the object of some international commodity agreements, though they have proved no easier to manage than any other cartel arrangement.

17. Goode, Lent, and Ojha, "Role of Export Taxes," p. 465.

18. Van Roy, "The Pursuit of Growth," p. 299, and sources cited there.

19. See the studies cited by Goode, Lent, and Ojha, "Role of Export Taxes," p. 465.

20. Levin, *The Export Economies,* p. 241; Frederick E. Sherman, "Agricultural Taxation in Nigeria: The Produce Marketing Boards," Harvard Law Library (typewritten MS., April 1968), p. 41.

21. Goode, Lent, and Ojha, "Role of Export Taxes," pp. 467–470, review a large body of evidence from three continents to this effect. See also Jere R. Behrman, *Supply Response in Underdeveloped Agriculture* (Amsterdam: North-Holland Publishing Company, 1968) for an especially thorough recent study of Thailand.

22. Dupe Olatunbosun, "Nigerian Governments' Policies Affecting Investment in Agriculture," CSNRD 16, Consortium for the Study of Nigerian Rural Development in Collaboration with the Nigerian Institute of Social and Economic Research (mimeo; July 1968), Appendix VII.

23. R. G. Saylor, "A Study of Obstacles to Investment in Oil Palm and Rubber Plantations," CSNRD 15, Consortium for the Study of Nigerian Rural Development (mimeo; August 1968), p. 77.

24. See Glenn L. Johnson, "Factor Markets and Economic Development," in W. W. McPherson, ed., *Economic Development of Tropical Agriculture* (Gainesville: University of Florida Press, 1968), pp. 97, 108; and Carl K. Eicher, *Research on Agricultural Development,* for further references to other recent studies. The evidence is thus increasingly in support of P. T. Bauer's early arguments along these lines: see, for ex-

ample, the debate reprinted in Richard M. Bird and Oliver Oldman, eds., *Readings on Taxation in Developing Countries* (rev. ed., Baltimore: Johns Hopkins Press, 1967), pp. 355–382.

25. Schwartz, "The Argentine Experience," pp. 266, 299.

26. Bird, *Taxation and Development*, pp. 35–39.

27. Donald R. Snodgrass, *Ceylon: An Export Economy in Transition* (Homewood, Ill.: Richard D. Irwin, Inc., 1966), chap. 7.

28. *Bank of London and South America Review*, V (No. 50, February 1971), p. 112.

29. Helleiner, "Agricultural Export Pricing Strategy in Tanzania," provides one of the few examples of this approach.

30. George Kalmanoff, "The Coffee Economy of Colombia," International Bank for Reconstruction and Development, Economics Department Working Paper No. 15 (mimeo, May 1968), p. 118.

31. Eugene C. Lee, *Local Taxation in Tanzania* (Dar Es Salaam: Institute of Public Administration, University College, 1966), p. 41. The word "cess" is sometimes also used, as in Pakistan, to refer to certain land taxes.

32. Navarrete, "Agricultural and Land Taxation," in Peacock and Hauser, eds., *Government Finance*, p. 200. Similar internal customs controls are maintained for excise tax purposes in other countries, e.g., in Colombia with respect to alcoholic beverages.

33. George F. Break and Ralph Turvey, *Studies in Greek Taxation*, Center of Planning and Economic Research, Monograph Series 11, (Athens: the Center, 1964), pp. 57–58. The social insurance agency for agriculture receives further support from a special poll tax on landless laborers and an area-based land tax on farmers.

34. Aristides Espinosa and Miguel Angel Pangrazzio, "Los organismos perceptores de impuestos y su relación con la economía agropecuaria del Paraguay," paper presented at Seminario Internacional sobre Tributación Agrícola, Santiago, Chile (mimeo; November 1963), p. 4.

35. The conventional case for the exemption of unprocessed food from sales taxes is presented by John F. Due, *Indirect Taxation in Developing Economies* (Baltimore: Johns Hopkins Press, 1970), pp. 145–46.

36. The tithe is described briefly in Wald, *Taxation of Agricultural Land*, pp. 30–33, where its present-day survival in the form of the *zakat* (or poor tax) in some Islamic countries, notably Saudi Arabia, is also noted. The important Ethiopian "tithe" referred to below is really a land tax and is treated as such in the present account.

37. The following account is based on Kenan Bulutoglu, "Incentive and Welfare Effects of Tax Structure Change: The Case of Turkey," paper presented to Seminar on Fiscal Incentives to Promote Agricultural Development, Istanbul, Turkey (mimeo; November 1968).

38. George L. Harriss et al., *Iraq: Its People, Its Society, Its Culture* (New Haven, Conn.: HRAF Press, 1958), pp. 187, 320.

39. Abdulaal Alsagaban, "The Tax System in Iraq," United Nations Department of Economic Affairs, Studies in Tax Reform Planning (mimeo; 1970).

40. "Under Ottoman rule (1534–1917) the peasantry reached a state of destitution. Taxes on agricultural produce reached extraordinarily un-

realistic heights. The methods of tax collection encouraged bribery and corruption, impoverished the fellahin while they enriched the wealthy landlords, and retarded agricultural development" Harriss et al., *Iraq*, p. 183).

41. Thomas Balogh, *The Economics of Poverty* (New York: Macmillan Company, 1966), p. 66. Until the 1920's such labor taxes were common in the United States for purposes of local road and bridge maintenance: commutation of the tax into cash was regarded as antisocial.

42. Gandhi, *Tax Burden*, pp. 220–222.

43. John W. Thomas, "Rural Public Works and East Pakistan's Development," Economic Development Report No. 112, Development Advisory Service, Harvard University, 1968; Matthew D. Edel, "The Colombian Community Action Program: An Economic Evaluation," unpub. study, Cambridge, Mass., 1968.

44. Bulutoglu, "Incentive and Welfare Effects," pp. 17–23.

45. Ronald J. Clark, "Land Reform in Bolivia," in Agency for International Development, *Spring Review of Land Reform*, Vol. VI (Washington, D.C.: Department of State, 1970), p. 80.

46. The best recent discussion of these taxes is Arowolo, "The Taxation of Low Incomes in African Countries," pp. 322–341. Useful earlier accounts may be found in John F. Due, *Taxation and Economic Development in Tropical Africa* (Cambridge, Mass.: M.I.T. Press, 1963), chap. 5, and Hicks, *Development from Below*, pp. 340–345.

47. Due, *Taxation and Economic Development*, p. 61.

48. This outline is based on Arowolo, "The Taxation of Low Incomes," pp. 332–335.

49. This discussion follows William M. Eichbaum, "Retroussons nous Manches: Agriculture and Fiscal Policy in the Democratic Republic of the Congo," paper submitted to Seminar on Tax Reform in Developing Countries, Harvard Law School (typewritten; May 1966).

50. Carl S. Shoup et al., *The Tax System of Liberia* (New York: Columbia University Press, 1970), p. 89.

51. C. M. Elliott, "Agriculture and Economic Development in Africa: Theory and Experience 1880–1914," in E. L. Jones and S. J. Woolf, eds., *Agrarian Change and Economic Development* (London: Methuen & Co., Ltd., 1969), pp. 134–135.

52. Walter Elkan, "Central and Local Taxes on Africans in Uganda," *Public Finance/Finances Publiques*, XIII (1958), 312–317.

53. Due, *Taxation and Economic Development*, pp. 75–76; Hicks, *Development from Below*, pp. 340–341.

54. International Monetary Fund, *Surveys of African Economies* (Washington, D.C., 1969), II, 250.

55. The tax riots of 1955 in Sierra Leone point up the apparent importance of local benefits (there were none) and decent administration (sadly lacking) if the personal tax—or any other levy—is to make much headway in subsistence agriculture (Hicks, *Development from Below*, pp. 200–201).

56. Richard Goode, "Reconstruction of Foreign Tax Systems," in Bird and Oldman, eds., *Readings on Taxation*, pp. 122–124.

57. See Oliver Oldman and Daniel Holland, "Measuring Tax Evasion,"

unpub. paper, Harvard Law School and Sloan School of Management, M.I.T., 1971.

58. Richard A. Musgrave and Malcolm Gillis, *Fiscal Reform for Colombia* (Cambridge, Mass.: Harvard Law School International Tax Program, 1971), pp. 388, 414.

59. Harvard Law School International Tax Program, *Taxation in Italy* (Chicago: Commerce Clearing House, Inc., 1964), pp. 500–501.

60. For an outline of all these systems, see George E. Lent, "Taxation of Agricultural Income in Developing Countries," unpub. paper, Washington, D.C., 1972.

61. George N. Ecklund, *Financing The Chinese Government Budget, Mainland China, 1950–1959* (Chicago: Aldine Publishing Company, 1966), describes the Chinese system in detail. See also Wald, *The Taxation of Agricultural Land*, p. 33.

62. M. Lionel Juran, "Agricultural Organization, Administration, and Taxation under the Viet Mihn, 1949–51," unpub. paper, Harvard Law School, 1968, p. 97.

63. Lent, "Taxation of Agricultural Income."

64. For historical references, see Hinrichs, *A General Theory*, pp. 83–91, and Edwin R. A. Seligman, *Essays in Taxation* (10th ed. 1931; reprinted by Augustus M. Kelley, Publishers, New York, 1969), chaps. 1–2.

65. Bulutoglu, "Incentive and Welfare Effects," p. 9. He goes on to quote a statement by the Turkish Minister of Finance in 1961 to the effect that "the erosion of the tax base had reached such a degree that the tax collector preferred to pay the tax of a whole village out of his own pocket rather than going to remote villages to collect the taxes."

66. Carl S. Shoup et al., *The Tax System of Liberia*, pp. 57, 91.

67. Peter Schwab, "The Tax System of Ethiopia," *American Journal of Economics and Sociology*, XXIX (January 1970), 77–88. Schwab is extremely critical of the Ethiopian land tax, as are George A. Lipsky et al. in *Ethiopia: Its People, Its Society, Its Culture* (New Haven, Conn.: HRAF Press, 1962), p. 293. An even more motley collection of ancient land taxes is levied in neighboring Sudan.

68. See the exhaustive discussion in Mahesh C. Regmi, *Land Tenure and Taxation in Nepal* (4 vols., Berkeley: Institute of International Studies, University of California, 1963–1967), esp. Vol. I, chaps. 5 and 10. In recent years the tenurial situation has been simplified by land reform.

69. For a brief historical summary, see Joseph N. Froomkin, "Structure and Taxation of Agriculture in China," in Haskell P. Wald and Joseph N. Froomkin, eds., *Papers and Proceedings of the Conference on Agricultural Taxation and Economic Development* (Cambridge, Mass.: International Program in Taxation, Harvard Law School, 1954), pp. 416–420; also Yeh-Chien Wang, "The Fiscal Importance of the Land Tax During the Ch'ing Period," *Journal of Asian Studies*, XXX (August 1971), 829–842. A more modern parallel that may have had some influence was the Soviet experience of levying a heavy tax in kind via compulsory deliveries: see F. D. Holzman, in Bird and Oldman, eds., *Readings on Taxation* (1964 ed.), pp. 83–84.

70. Shih-ko Shen, "Land Taxation as Related to the Land Reform Program in Taiwan," in Archibald M. Woodruff, James R. Brown, and Sein

Lin, eds., *International Seminar on Land Taxation, Land Tenure and Land Reform in Developing Countries* (W. Hartford, Conn.: John C. Lincoln Institute, University of Hartford, 1967), pp. 334–338.

71. R. A. Musgrave, *Revenue Policy for Korea's Economic Development* (Seoul: Nathan Economic Advisory Group, 1965), p. 73. In 1953, this so-called "land income tax" took 11 percent of the rice harvest and was the largest single source of government revenue in Korea, according to Haskell P. Wald, "The Recent Experience of the Republic of Korea with Tax Collections in Kind," in Wald and Froomkin, eds., *Agricultural Taxation and Economic Development*, p. 429. By 1964, the yield of the land tax was down to less than 2 percent of the value added in agriculture (Musgrave, *Revenue Policy*, p. 77).

72. Bertrand, "Rural Taxation in Thailand," pp. 178–179.

73. Joint Legislative-Executive Tax Commission, *Summary of the Second Survey on Local Government Finance* (Manila, 1970), p. 1.

74. Joint Legislative-Executive Tax Commission, *Twelfth Annual Report 1970* (Manila, 1971), pp. 19–20.

75. George E. Lent, "The Taxation of Land Value," *I.M.F. Staff Papers*, XIII (March 1967), 106–108.

76. Juanita D. Amatong, "Taxation of Capital Gains in Developing Countries," *I.M.F. Staff Papers*, XV (July 1968), 344–384.

77. Cecil Morgan, "Report on Taxation of Guatemalan Agriculture," U.S. Department of State, International Cooperation Administration, USOM/Guatemala (Airgram, November 23, 1960).

78. Break and Turvey, *Studies in Greek Taxation*, pp. 22, 51–53.

79. *Ibid.*, pp. 222–231. Break and Turvey analyze the Greek transfer tax in detail and conclude that it did tend to have noticeable effects in urban areas. Similar comments on the lower transfer taxes in Mexico and Colombia may be found in Oliver Oldman et al., *Financing Urban Development in Mexico City* (Cambridge, Mass.: Harvard University Press, 1967), pp. 133–134, and Richard M. Bird, "Stamp Tax Reform in Colombia," *Bulletin for International Fiscal Documentation*, XXI (June 1967), 253–254.

80. Stanley Please, "Aspects of Agricultural Tax Policy in India and Pakistan," p. 12.

81. Ricardo's *Principles of Political Economy and Taxation*, quoted in Break and Turvey, *Studies in Greek Taxation*, p. 231.

82. Seligman, *Essays in Taxation*, p. 33.

CHAPTER 5. LAND TAXES IN LATIN AMERICA

1. In Colombia locations with populations of over 1,500 are considered "urban"; in Mexico, the figure is 2,500; in Chile and Uruguay the classification depends on the presence of certain "urban characteristics," and so on; see Inter-American Committee for Agricultural Development (ICAD), *Inventory of Information Basic to the Planning of Agricultural Development in Latin America: Regional Report* (Washington, D.C.: Pan-American Union, 1965), p. 51. Similar ambiguities attach to the concept of "workforce in agriculture."

2. See the ICAD data summarized in Barranclough, "Agricultural Policy and Land Reform," p. 936.

3. *Ibid.*, p. 907.

4. M. J. Sternberg, "The Economic Impact of the Latifundista," *Land Reform, Land Settlement and Cooperatives* (No. 2, 1970), pp. 24–25.

5. On Chile, see *ibid.* and Nicholas Kaldor, "Economic Problems of Chile," in *Essays on Economic Policy* (2 vols., London: Duckworth, 1964), II, 242–267; on Colombia, see R. M. Bird, "Income Distribution and Tax Policy in Colombia," *Economic Development and Cultural Change*, XVIII (July 1970), 519–535.

6. For a vivid description of the traditional hacienda, see Frank Tannenbaum, "Toward an Appreciation of Latin America," in *The United States and Latin America* (New York: The American Assembly, Columbia University, December 1959), pp. 29–38.

7. The Colombian land tax is discussed at length in Bird, *Taxation and Development*, pp. 155–165.

8. Milton C. Taylor et al., *Fiscal Survey of Panama* (Baltimore: Johns Hopkins Press for the Joint Tax Program, 1964), p. 79.

9. *Ibid.*, p. 63.

10. *Ibid.*, pp. 72–74.

11. Cecil Morgan, "Property Taxation in Central America," Department of State, Agency for International Development, Regional Office, Central America and Panama Affairs, November 1967, p. 8.

12. Wolfram Drewes, "The Cadaster," in A.I.D., *Spring Review of Land Reform*, Vol. XI, p. 17, notes that "without doubt, Panama's cadaster is one of the most comprehensive fiscal cadasters; and when titling is initiated, it will also be one of the first countries in the world where the survey accuracy is adequate to serve as the basis to a legal cadaster as well."

13. Morgan, "Property Taxation in Central America," p. 8.

14. Foreign Tax Assistance Staff, Internal Revenue Service, *Report on Tax Administration in Costa Rica* (USAID, San José, 1967), pp. 5, 13.

15. An earlier tax on "idle" lands at rates of 2 to 4 mills on assessed values produced the total sum of $300 in 1952–1953 (United Nations, Comisión Económica para América Latina, *La Política Tributaria y el Desarrollo Económico en América Central* (New York, 1957), p. 75).

16. Joint Tax Program, *Tax Systems of Latin America: Guatemala* (Washington, D.C.: Pan-American Union, 1966), p. 27.

17. Antonio Gayoso, "Land Reform in Guatemala," in A.I.D., *Spring Review of Land Reform*, Vol. VII, p. 40.

18. Aristides Espinosa and Miguel Angel Pangrazzio, "Los organismos perceptores de impuestos y su relación con la economía agropecuaria del Paraguay."

19. Doreen Warriner, *Land Reform in Principle and Practice* (Oxford, Eng.: Clarendon Press, 1969), pp. 241–248.

20. Ronald J. Clark, "Land Reform in Bolivia," in A.I.D., *Spring Review of Land Reform*, Vol. VI. That rural living standards are higher, especially in the northern highlands, is attested by both dietary changes and the greatly increased ownership of factory-made goods such as sewing machines and radios.

21. "I think of land reform as a primitive, rather brutal measure of income redistribution. In a more modern country you resort to income taxes for income redistribution; in countries like Bolivia you resort to land

reform" (Edmundo Flores in *Land Reform*, University of Wisconsin Land Tenure Center [Madison, 1963], p. 4).

22. Richard Goode, "Reconstruction of Foreign Tax Systems," in Bird and Oldman, eds., *Readings on Taxation*, p. 130. The mission also proposed that assessed values be adjusted annually on the basis of an index of current property values prepared by the Ministry of Finance. More unusually, they also proposed that small parcels *not* be exempted, on the grounds that pieces of land unable to bear a minimum tax are probably not suitable for private ownership.

23. Alfredo Buchón Rivas, "Rural Land Taxation in Bolivia," paper submitted to Harvard Law School International Tax Program, March 1966, p. 6.

24. It is hardly a coincidence that Goode's well-known six stringent conditions for the successful use of income taxes in developing countries were based on his early experience in Bolivia (see Chapter 4, above).

25. Gerald W. Sazama, "Land Taxes—Prerequisites and Obstacles: Bolivia," *National Tax Journal*, XXIII (September 1970), 315–324.

26. John D. Strasma, "Tax Reform in Bolivia, 1961," report to the International Co-operation Administration (mimeo; September 1961). In the paper cited above, Buchón proposed a scheme much like the 1961 proposal, except that land taxes were to be deducted rather than credited against income taxes. He estimated the yield of this tax at around 10 percent of tax revenues (Buchón Rivas, "Rural Land Taxation," p. 33).

27. Social Progress Trust Fund, *1963 Report*, p. 153.

28. This account is based on Sazama, "Land Taxes," *National Tax Journal*, and on Gerald W. Sazama, "Analisis Económico del Proyecto de Impuesto Unico para el Sector Agrícola," Informe al Gobierno de Bolivia y a la A.I.D. (duplicated; August 1968).

29. See Wald, "Reform of Agricultural Taxation," in Joint Tax Program, *Fiscal Policy*, pp. 331–332.

30. Clark, "Land Reform in Bolivia," pp. 75–76.

31. Sazama, "Land Taxes," p. 319. Sazama argues convincingly that most peasants already have sufficient cash income to pay the tax.

32. This account is based mainly on Ministerio de Ganadería y Agricultura, *Estudio Económico y Social de Agricultura en el Uruguay*, Vol. I (Montevideo, 1967), 568–641.

33. *Ibid.*, p. 595.

34. Henry C. Simons, *Personal Income Taxation* (Chicago: University of Chicago Press, 1938), p. 219.

35. Juan Eduardo Azzini and Hugo A. De Marco, "The Tax System of Uruguay," *Public Finance*, II (No. 2, 1956), 112–129.

36. Programa Conjunto de Tributación, *Sistemas Tributarios de América Latina: Uruguay* (Washington, D.C.: Pan-American Union, 1967).

37. In addition to the studies by the Joint Tax Program and the Ministry of Agriculture cited above, this account draws on Alberto Brause Berreta, "Uruguay: An Experience with the Tax on Potential Agricultural Income," paper submitted to International Tax Program, Harvard Law School, April 1969, as well as private correspondence with Edward Foster, George Lent, and José Gimeno, and the texts of Laws 13,636 and 13,695.

38. Brause Berreta, "Uruguay," pp. 98–99. Less than half of the taxes collected from agriculture go to general revenues, however: in addition to

the taxes for local governments and social security noted above, a large proportion of the proceeds of the export taxes are earmarked for agricultural development and food subsidies.

39. A full outline of the reasoning underlying the 1964 proposal may be found in Jarach, *El Impuesto a la Renta Normal Potencial de la Tierra*. See also Programa Conjunto de Tributación, *Estudio sobre Política Fiscal en Argentina* (versión preliminar) (7 vols., Buenos Aires: Consejo Nacional de Desarrollo, 1967), VII, 123.

40. Harvard Law School International Program in Taxation, *Taxation in Brazil* (Boston: Little, Brown, 1959), p. 65.

41. See Sergio Tostes, "The Agrarian Question in Brazil: Taxation Techniques," paper submitted to International Tax Program, Harvard Law School, April 1969, and Armin K. Ludwig and Harry W. Taylor, *Brazil's New Agrarian Reform: An Evaluation of Its Property Classification and Tax Systems* (New York: Frederick A. Praeger, Publishers, 1969).

42. A similar conclusion is suggested by a study of two municipalities in São Paulo—one with a progressive tax seven times heavier than the proportional tax in the other (Alberto Franco et al., *Tributação Progressiva: Possibilidades e Limitações segundo a Legislacão Agraria Brasileira* [Bogotá: Instituto Interamericano de Ciencias Agrícolas, Centro Interamericano de Reforma Agraria, 1966]).

43. Land values were estimated to rise 40 percent faster than the cost of living and 60 percent faster than agricultural prices in the period from 1940 to 1958 (Instituto de Economía, *La Tributación Agrícola en Chile, 1940–1958* [Santiago: Universidad de Chile, 1960], p. 25). The value of irrigated land rose substantially faster than that of nonirrigated land, which suggests that different adjustment indexes should be employed.

44. José M. Gimeno Sanz, *La Tributación Agropecuaria* (Santiago: Oficina de Planificación Agrícola, Ministerio de Agricultura, 1970), I, 28.

45. John Strasma, "Property Taxation in Chile," in Arthur P. Becker, ed., *Land and Building Taxes* (Madison: University of Wisconsin Press, 1969), p. 193.

46. A United Nations mission in 1949–1950 had proposed that such an annual adjustment be introduced, based on either the average increase in newly assessed values or on an index of sales values (Wald, *The Taxation of Agricultural Land*, pp. 204–205).

47. Farms were appraised in terms of tables of values per hectare for 12 qualities of land in each township, the values of individual properties being calculated on the basis of indices of potential-use capacity, location, and distance to markets and quality of access roads, utilizing a computer. No appeals were permitted against these valuations, which, despite the adjustments, really amounted to approximate market values for agricultural purposes. Luis Vera, *Agricultural Land Inventory Techniques: Experience of the OAS/Chile Aereophotogrammetric Project* (Washington, D.C.: Pan-American Union, 1964).

48. Gerald W. Sazama and L. Harlan Davis, "Land Taxation and Land Reform," unpub. paper, 1969.

49. José-Luis Pistono Alvarez et al., "Proyecto de Ley: Impuesto Unico a los Bienes Raices Agrícolas," Ministerio de Agricultura (Chile), Consejo Superior de Fomento Agropecuario (mimeo.; 1964).

50. Ministerio de Agricultura (Chile), Oficina de Planificación Agrícola, *Plan de Desarrollo Agropecuario 1965–1980* (Santiago, 1968), chap. 12, sec. D; Gimeno, *La Tributación Agropecuaria.*

51. Wald, *Taxation of Agricultural Land,* pp. 206–207.

52. José Gimeno Sanz, *Sugerencias para el diseño de una nueva política tributaria para el sector agropecuario* (Santiago: Oficina de Planificación Agrícola, 1971).

53. Gerald W. Sazama, "Agricultural Land Taxation in Chile," unpub. paper, 1970.

54. This account is largely based on Daniel M. Holland, "A Study of Land Taxation in Jamaica," in Becker, ed., *Land and Building Taxes,* pp. 239–286, and Wilfred S. Chang, "Recent Experience of Establishing Land Value Taxation in Jamaica," in Woodruff, Brown, and Lin, eds., *International Seminar on Land Taxation,* pp. 210–238.

55. J. F. N. Murray, *Report to the Government of Jamaica on Valuation, Land Taxation and Rating* (Kingston, Jamaica: Government Printer, 1957). The doubts on the desirability of a shift to the unimproved basis expressed in the well-known Hicks report of around the same time (J. R. and U. K. Hicks, *Report on Finance and Taxation in Jamaica* (Kingston, Jamaica: Government Printer, 1955) have little application to rural areas.

56. See A. M. Woodruff and L. L. Ecker-Racz, "Property Taxes and Land-Use Patterns in Australia and New Zealand," *The Tax Executive,* XXVIII (October 1965), 16–63.

57. Chang, "Recent Experience of Establishing Land Value Taxation in Jamaica," in Woodruff, Brown, and Lin, eds., *International Seminar,* p. 227.

58. Holland, "A Study of Land Taxation in Jamaica," in Becker, ed., *Land and Building Taxes,* pp. 276–277.

59. Similar doubts have been expressed on the earlier Australian experience with progressive unimproved value taxes: see R. M. Bird, "A National Tax on the Unimproved Value of Land: The Australian Experience, 1910–1952," *National Tax Journal,* XIII (December 1960), 386–392.

60. United Nations Secretariat, "Site Value Taxation in Developing Countries," United Nations-CIAT Seminar on Land Tax Administration, Panama City, Panama, September 2–9, 1971, ESA/FF/AC.6/1.

61. Holland, "A Study of Land Taxation in Jamaica," in Becker, ed., *Land and Building Taxes,* pp. 250–51.

CHAPTER 6. LESSONS FROM HISTORY

1. James I. Nakamura, *Agricultural Production and the Economic Development of Japan 1873–1922* (Princeton, N.J.: Princeton University Press, 1966), pp. 140–141. This account is a fair summary of the views put forward in such well-known and frequently cited papers as Kazuski Ohkawa and Henry Rosovsky, "The Role of Agriculture in Modern Japanese Economic Development," *Economic Development and Cultural Change,* IX, Part II (October 1960), 43–68; Gustav Ranis, "The Financing of Japanese Economic Development," *Economic History Review,* XI (April 1959), 440–454; and Bruce F. Johnston, "Agricultural Productivity and Economic Development in Japan," *Journal of Political Economy,* LIX (De-

cember 1951), 498–513, as well as in subsequent works by these and other authors.

2. Harry T. Oshima, "Meiji Fiscal Policy and Agricultural Progress," in William W. Lockwood, ed., *The State and Economic Enterprise in Japan: Essays in the Political Economy of Growth* (Princeton, N.J.: Princeton University Press, 1965), p. 353.

3. Fei and Ranis, "Agrarianism, Dualism, and Economic Development," in Adelman and Thorbecke, eds., *Theory and Design*, p. 39, stress the latter transfer mechanism: "the Japanese government's role, using the famous land tax, was undoubtedly of considerable importance in financing social and economic overheads in the early Meiji period. But it was really the flow of private voluntary savings through a large number of small hands which was responsible—increasingly throughout the nineteenth century—for financing of the prodigious Japanese industrialization effort. It was, in fact, mainly the medium-sized landlord, with one foot in the agricultural and one in the industrial sector, reacting to the intersectoral terms of trade and the changing relative returns to investments of his time and ingenuity, who propelled the dualistic system forward." In contrast, Ohkawa and Rosovsky emphasize the role of the land tax (see "A Century of Japanese Economic Growth," in Lockwood, ed., *The State and Economic Enterprise in Japan*, p. 70), as do Johnston and Mellor ("The Role of Agriculture in Economic Development," p. 578), and the well-known FAO study (reprinted in Bird and Oldman, eds., *Readings on Taxation*, p. 485).

4. E. Sydney Crawcour, "The Tokugawa Heritage," in Lockwood, ed., *The State and Economic Enterprise in Japan*, p. 44.

5. The main sources for this account are W. G. Beasley, "Feudal Revenue in Japan at the Time of the Meiji Restoration," *Journal of Asian Studies*, XIX (May 1960), 255–272; and T. C. Smith, "The Land Tax in the Tokugawa Period," *Journal of Asian Studies*, XVIII (November 1958), 3–19.

6. Thomas C. Smith, *The Agrarian Origins of Modern Japan* (Stanford, Calif.: Stanford University Press, 1959), pp. 181–182, suggests some of the probable difficulties with this assessment process in feudal Japan.

7. Nakamura, *Agricultural Production*, pp. 178–181, outlines the complex nature of the system at the time of the Meiji reform of 1873.

8. Tokugawa Iyeyasu, founder of the Shogun line, when asked how much should be left to the peasants for their own support, reportedly replied that they should be left with an amount such that "they can neither live nor die" (Marion J. Levy, Jr., *Modernization and the Structure of Societies* (Princeton, N.J.: Princeton University Press, 1966), p. 801).

9. "High as the rate of tax on land was, however, it did not represent an increase over the Tokugawa period. Already at the end of that period the take from agriculture by the warrior class was immense, and the Meiji government merely redirected it into new channels" (Smith, *Agrarian Origins*, p. 211).

10. Nakamura, *Agricultural Production*, p. 184.

11. Nobutaka Ike, "Taxation and Landownership in the Westernization of Japan," *Journal of Economic History*, VII (November 1947), 164. Nakamura, *Agricultural Production*, p. 188, summarizes the formula as

$V = (R - C)/(i + t + t^1)$, where V = capitalized value, R = value of gross output, C = cost of seeds and fertilizer, t = rate of national land tax, t^1 = local surtax rate, and i = prevailing interest rate. Nakamura's Appendix A (pp. 182–196) describes the valuation procedure in the Meiji period in detail.

12. Motokazu Kimura, "Fiscal Policy and Industrialization in Japan, 1868–1895," in International Economic Association, *Economic Development with Special Reference to East Asia* (New York: Macmillan, 1964), p. 281.

13. On the question of understatement, see the persuasive account in Nakamura, *Agricultural Production*, chaps. 2–4. His estimates of the degree of evasion may be questioned, but to anyone with experience in land tax administration anywhere his general argument has the clear ring of truth.

14. See Ishikawa, *Economic Development in Asian Perspective*, pp. 318–320.

15. Oshima, "Meiji Fiscal Policy," in Lockwood, ed., *The State and Economic Enterprise*, pp. 372–380.

16. Nakamura, *Agricultural Production*, chaps. 5–6.

17. Oshima, "Meiji Fiscal Policy," in Lockwood, ed., *The State and Economic Enterprise*, p. 354.

18. See note 3, above; also Nakamura, *Agricultural Production*, pp. 155–169.

19. Henry Rosovsky, "Rumbles in the Ricefields; Professor Nakamura vs. the Official Statistics," *Journal of Asian Studies*, XXVII (February 1968), 347–360.

20. "The frequency of disputes, uprisings and riots, the rise in unpaid taxes and land confiscated in lieu of tax payments, the increase in debts and mortgage foreclosures, and the rapid rise in the amount of tenanted land . . . were clear signs of the difficulties experienced by the majority of agriculturists in the period" (Oshima, "Meiji Fiscal Policy," in Lockwood, ed., *The State and Economic Enterprise*, p. 364).

21. Ishikawa, *Economic Development in Asian Perspective*, p. 347. Nakamura shares this view; Rosovsky and Ohkawa do not. The list on both sides could be extended.

22. Some evidence along these lines is presented by Smith, *Agrarian Origins*, and by Yujiro Hayami and Saburo Yamada, "Technological Progress in Agriculture," in Lawrence Klein and Kazushi Ohkawa, eds., *Economic Growth: The Japanese Experience since the Meiji Era* (Homewood, Ill.: Richard D. Irwin, Inc., 1968), pp. 135–157.

23. David S. Landes, "Japan and Europe: Contrasts in Industrialization," in Lockwood, ed., *The State and Economic Enterprise*, p. 169.

24. *Ibid.*, p. 167.

25. Ishikawa, *Economic Development in Asian Perspective*, p. 322.

26. Yujiro Hayami and V. W. Ruttan, "Factor Prices and Technical Change in Agricultural Development: The United States and Japan, 1880–1960," *Journal of Political Economy*, LXXVIII (September–October 1970), 1115.

27. An exhaustive discussion of India's failure in this regard on many counts may be found in Myrdal's monumental *Asian Drama,* although

his emphasis on the "soft state" overstresses the ability of *any* leadership, no matter how "hard" and modernizing in intent, to impose Japanese (or Chinese?) habits on Indian (or Latin American?) institutions.

28. Johnston and Cownie, "The Seed-Fertilizer Revolution," pp. 573–574.

29. Clawson, Landsberg, and Alexander, *The Agricultural Potential of the Middle East*, p. 143.

30. For corroborative detail, see Higgins, *Economic Development*, pp. 635–653; Miguel S. Wionzcek, "Incomplete Formal Planning: Mexico," in Everett S. Hagen, ed., *Planning Economic Development* (Homewood, Ill.: Richard D. Irwin, Inc., 1963), pp. 150–182.

31. See Edmundo Flores, *Vieja Revolución, nuevos problemas* (Mexico: Siglo XXI Editores, 1970), chaps. 5–6.

32. Except for Venezuela (which has a very small agricultural sector) in recent years; see data in Colin Clark and Margaret Haswell, *The Economics of Subsistence Agriculture* (4th ed., London: Macmillan, St. Martin's Press, 1970), p. 86.

33. The *ejido* is a system of landholding by villages introduced in Mexico following the Revolution. Although some ejidos operate in a cooperative fashion, most are run by individual farmers who are, however, constitutionally prohibited from selling or renting their ejidal lands. Although apparently often vitiated by illegal practices, this prohibition may have restrained rural outmigration.

34. Aron J. Aizenstat, "Structure and Taxation of Agriculture in Mexico," in Wald and Froomkin, eds., *Agricultural Taxation and Economic Development*, pp. 305–321; Navarrete, "Agricultural and Land Taxation," in Peacock and Hauser, eds., *Government Finance*, pp. 195–210. In the early 1950's there were reportedly over 200 different taxes levied on rural real property in Mexico, all at very low rates (Harvard Law School International Program in Taxation, *Taxation in Mexico* [Boston: Little, Brown, 1957], p. 67).

35. Navarrete, "Agricultural and Land Taxation," in Peacock and Hauser, eds., *Government Finance*, p. 200.

36. *Ibid.;* estimate for 1947 based on Aizenstat, "Structure and Taxation of Agriculture in Mexico," in Wald and Froomkin, eds., *Agricultural Taxation.*

37. Although there is substantial controversy on the extent of the intersectoral flow of resources in Mexico, there appears to be general agreement that there has been no noticeable transfer out of agriculture through the fiscal system: see Leopoldo Solís, *La realidad económica mexicana* (Mexico: Siglo XXI Editores, 1970), p. 182.

38. This account follows Edmundo Flores, "The Significance of Land-Use Changes in the Economic Development of Mexico," *Land Economics,* XXXV (1959), 115–124 and Clark W. Reynolds, *The Mexican Economy* (New Haven, Conn.: Yale University Press, 1970), chaps. 3, 4, and 7.

39. Edmundo Flores, "Issues of Land Reform," *Journal of Political Economy,* LXXVIII (July–August, suppl., 1970), 904.

40. Reynolds, *The Mexican Economy*, p. 144. For arguments suggesting a substantial transfer through the terms of trade and other means, see Solomon Eckstein, *El marco macroeconómico del problema agrario mex-*

icano (Mexico: Centro de Investigaciones Agrarios, 1968) and Michel Gutelman, *Réforme et mystification agraires en Amérique latine* (Paris: Maspero, 1971).

41. Edmundo Flores, *Tratado de Economía Agrícola* (Mexico: Fondo de Cultura Económica, 1961), pp. 211–212.

42. Robert Edminster, "Mexico," in Adamantios Pepelasis, Leon Mears, and Irma Adelman, *Economic Development* (New York: Harper & Brothers, Publishers, 1961), p. 346.

43. Inter-American Committee on Agricultural Development, *Inventory*, pp. 118–119.

44. Reynolds, *The Mexican Economy*, p. 154.

45. Folke Dovring, "Land Reform in Mexico," in A.I.D., *Spring Review of Land Reform*, Vol. VII.

46. Reynolds, *The Mexican Economy*, p. 159.

47. Flores, *Vieja Revolución*, chaps. 4–5. An alternative view suggests that, even if Mexico has now reached the limits of import substitution, its middle and lower middle classes are now large enough to provide an expanding local market without needing to alleviate the still widespread rural poverty (Raymond Carr, "Mexican Agrarian Reform, 1910–1960," in Jones and Woolf, eds., *Agrarian Change and Economic Development*, pp. 165–166).

48. John Sheahan, book review (of Solís work cited in n. 37, above), *Journal of Economic Literature*, IX (June 1971), 497. See also the discussion of the Lewis model in Chapter 1, above.

49. This outline follows T. M. Joshi, N. Anjanaiah, and S. V. Bhende, *Studies in the Taxation of Agricultural Land and Income in India* (London: Asia Publishing House, 1968), pp. 2–8.

50. By 1830 Mill had become the executive head of the India House. Mill's ideas and influence are thoroughly documented in Eric Stokes, *The English Utilitarians and India* (Oxford, Eng.: Clarendon Press, 1959), pp. 81–139. An excellent exposition of Ricardian tax theory with respect to agriculture is Carl S. Shoup, *Ricardo on Taxation* (New York: Columbia University Press, 1960), chaps. 4–7.

51. Quoted in Shoup, *Ricardo on Taxation*, p. 82. Ricardo mistakenly considered this "the Asiatic mode."

52. This summary, which omits many significant details and variations, is largely based on Stokes, *The English Utilitarians*, chap. 2; and Joshi et al., *Studies*, pp. 8–15.

53. John H. Lindauer and Sarjit Singh ("Effects of the Punjab Land Tax," *National Tax Journal*, XIX [December 1966], 427–433) carry this point to an extreme, however, when they argue that the Indian land tax has so often exceeded the economic rent of the land that it has driven many landowners into indebtedness and loss of their land. Historically, there is indeed some evidence that this was true in the nineteenth century, but to conclude, as they do (p. 433), that "the land tax remains intact today throughout India and other Asian countries. Thus, the effects described above are probably continuing at the present time" is beyond belief. The reasoning in this paper is extremely questionable. No mention is made of population increase as a main cause of fractionalization, for example, and no account is taken of the dramatic decline in land revenue

as a proportion of output in recent decades. The conclusion they draw therefore seems completely unwarranted.

54. Harvard Law School, International Program in Taxation, *Taxation in India* (Boston: Little, Brown, 1960), pp. 90–91. For detailed studies of two states, see Mahesh T. Pathak and Arun S. Patel, *Agricultural Taxation in Gujarat* (New York: Asia Publishing House, 1970), and C. H. Hanumantha Rao, *Taxation of Agricultural Land in Andhra Pradesh* (London: Asia Publishing House, 1966).

55. Stokes, *The English Utilitarians*, pp. 96–97.

56. *Ibid.*, pp. 99–100.

57. Joshi et al., *Studies*, p. 13.

58. Wald, *Taxation of Agricultural Land*, pp. 19–21, sketches events up to the land reforms of the early 1950's. See also Joshi et al., *Studies*, chaps. 1–3.

59. India, *Report of the Taxation Enquiry Commission* (3 vols., Delhi: Manager of Publications, 1955), III, 216.

60. R. N. Tripathy, *Fiscal Policy and Economic Development in India* (Calcutta: World Press, 1958), p. 106; Harold M. Groves and M. C. Madhaven, "Agricultural Taxation and India's Third Five Year Plan," *Land Economics*, XXXVIII (February 1962), 58.

61. In general terms the agricultural tax system in Pakistan is very similar to that in India, since in both countries the system was established before partition took place in 1947: see J. R. Andrus and A. F. Mohammed, *The Economy of Pakistan* (London: Oxford University Press, 1958), chap. 19; also Nurul Islam, "The Tax System in Pakistan," United Nations Department of Economic Affairs, Studies in Tax Reform Planning (mimeo; 1971). As noted elsewhere, Burma and Nepal also fall largely within the same family.

62. Lindauer and Singh, "Effects of the Punjab Land Tax."

63. Andrus and Mohammed, *The Economy of Pakistan*, p. 342. James Cutt (*Taxation and Economic Development in India* [New York: Frederick A. Praeger, 1969], chap. 5) proposed that the tax yield be made elastic by five-year reassessments of rated regional production and by annual adjustments for price changes.

64. Raj Krishna in a talk at the 1968 Istanbul Seminar on Fiscal Incentives to Promote Agricultural Development.

65. Walter C. Neale, "Land Reform in Uttar Pradesh, India," A.I.D., *Spring Review of Land Reform* Vol. I, 47.

66. See the discussion in M. L. Dantwala, "Agricultural Taxation and Land Reform in India," in Woodruff, Brown, and Lin, eds., *International Seminar on Land Taxation*, pp. 287–297.

67. Ved P. Gandhi, "Taxes, Subsidies, and Agricultural Production (India)," paper presented to Seminar on Fiscal Incentives to Promote Agricultural Development, Istanbul, Turkey, November 1968.

68. See, for example, Ashok Mitra, "Tax Burden for Indian Agriculture," in Ralph Braibanti and Joseph J. Spengler, eds., *Administration and Economic Development in India* (Durham, N.C.: Duke University Press, 1963), pp. 297–298.

69. Gandhi, *Tax Burden*, pp. 223–224.

70. Stanley Please, "Aspects of Agricultural Tax Policy in India and

Pakistan," paper presented to Seminar on Fiscal Incentives to Promote Agricultural Development, Istanbul, Turkey, November 1968.

71. Gandhi, "Taxes, Subsidies, and Agricultural Production." Emmerich M. Schebeck, "An Analysis of Capital Flows between the Agricultural and Non-Agricultural Sectors of India"; International Bank for Reconstruction and Development, Economics Department Working Paper No. 42 (mimeo; June 1969), argues, however, that there may have been a net *total* outflow from agriculture as a result of the savings patterns of large private farmers.

72. For example, among those cited above, Joshi, the Taxation Enquiry Commission, Groves and Madhaven, Mitra, and Gandhi all put forth reform schemes.

73. Mathew, *Agricultural Taxation*, p. 145.

74. On the political underpinnings of recent Indian agricultural policy, see Paul Streeten and Michael Lipton, eds., *The Crisis of Indian Planning* (London: Oxford University Press, 1968), chap. 4.

75. E. L. Jones and S. J. Woolf, "The Historical Role of Agrarian Change in Economic Development," in Jones and Woolf, eds., *Agrarian Change and Economic Development*, p. 2.

76. R. Zangheri, "The Historical Relationship between Agricultural and Economic Development in Italy," in Jones and Woolf, eds., *Agrarian Change and Economic Development*, pp. 28–29.

77. Jones and Woolf, "The Historical Role of Agrarian Change," pp. 4–12. For a cross-sectional analysis pointing in the same direction, see Hayami and Ruttan, "Agricultural Productivity Differences Among Countries," pp. 895–911.

78. R. P. Dore, "Agricultural Improvement in Japan 1870–1900," *Economic Development and Cultural Change*, IX (October 1960), 69–91, documents this for Japan.

79. Bruce F. Johnston, "The Japanese 'Model' of Agricultural Development: Its Relevance to Developing Nations," in Kazushi Ohkawa, Bruce F. Johnston, and Hiromitsu Kaneda, eds. *Agriculture and Economic Growth: Japan's Experience* (Tokyo: University of Tokyo Press, 1969), pp. 58–102.

80. C. E. Black, *The Dynamics of Modernization* (New York: Harper & Row, 1966), p. 159.

PART THREE. ANALYSIS OF AGRICULTURAL LAND TAXES

CHAPTER 7. CLASSIFICATION OF LAND TAXES

1. Much of the material in this chapter is adapted from Wald, *Taxation of Agricultural Land*, chap. 1.

2. Ronald B. Gold and Edward Foster, "Measuring Equity in the Taxation of Agricultural Land: A Case Study of Nepal," *Land Economics*, XLVIII (August 1972), 277–280. (The actual classification system used in Nepal is fairly complicated, but its most important feature is the distinction between dry and wet land.)

3. Carl S. Shoup, C. Lowell Harriss, and William S. Vickrey, *The Fiscal System of the Federal District of Venezuela* (Baltimore: Garamond Press, 1960), p. 62.

4. S. P. Kher, "Betterment Taxes: A Case Study in Mysore and Maharastra," paper presented to the Seminar on Fiscal Incentives to Promote Agricultural Development, Istanbul, Turkey, November 1968.

5. The tax base would not, of course, include income produced outside the agricultural sector, such as income from securities, urban real estate, or trading activities, unless the tax were part of a general income tax and not a land tax.

6. Amotz Morag, "Some Economic Aspects of Two Administrative Methods of Estimating Taxable Income," *National Tax Journal*, X (June 1957), 180.

7. A very critical view of the use of the rental basis for property taxation in an urban area is taken on these grounds in Oliver Oldman et al., *Financing Urban Development in Mexico City*, pp. 85–87.

8. Net rental income must be distinguished from the cultivator's net income, which includes the value of the cultivator's own labor and a return on his productive capital; if he also is the owner of the land, his net income includes net rental income as well. Selling value rests upon a rental, not an income, concept.

9. Obviously, this statement does not apply to the common case in which rental value is calculated by assuming a rate of return on capital value, or to the opposite case of capital value being computed as a multiple of rental value.

10. For some cogent doubts on the conventional treatment of tree crops, minerals, etc., see Richard W. Trestrail, "Forests and the Property Tax— Unsound Accepted Theory," *National Tax Journal*, XXII (September 1969), 347–356, and Gaffney, ed., *Extractive Resources and Taxation.*

11. See, for example, Wald, *Taxation of Agricultural Land*, p. 27 (also his "Taxation of Agriculture in Developing Countries," in Agarwala and Singh, eds., *Accelerating Investment*, p. 464); also Hicks, *Public Finance*, p. 175.

12. A lengthy list of special incentive and penalty land taxes may be found in Pedro Moral-Lopez, "Tax Legislation as an Instrument to Assist in Achieving the Economic and Social Objectives of Land Reform," *Land Reform, Land Settlement, and Co-operatives* (No. 2, 1965), pp. 2–12.

13. This justification for special land taxation is examined very critically in Wald, *Taxation of Agricultural Land*, chap. 4.

14. Dick Netzer, *Economics of the Property Tax* (Washington, D.C.: Brookings Institution, 1966), pp. 212–213.

15. This account is based on William G. Rhoads and Richard M. Bird, "The Valorization Tax in Colombia: An Example for Other Developing Countries?" in Becker, ed., *Land and Building Taxes*, pp. 201–238.

16. For example, Herman Felstenhausen, "Planning Problems in Improving Colombian Roads and Highways," *Land Economics*, XLVII (February 1971), 1–13, proposes financing rural roads by benefit taxes. Similarly, another recent author suggested not only that special assessments be used to recover the costs of irrigation works, but that lands "not willing to receive irrigation" be penalized by high property taxes (Joseph Thome,

"Water Regulation and Land Use: A Colombian Example," *Development Digest,* V [No. 3, October 1967], 39–44).

17. The project and the attempts to finance it by valorization are described in detail in Antonio J. Posada F. and Jeanne de Posada, *CVC: Un Reto al Subdesarrollo y al Tradicionalismo* (Bogotá: Ediciones Tercer Mundo, 1966), pp. 189–190.

18. See, for example, the evidence for Thailand (highways) in Behrman, *Supply Response in Underdeveloped Agriculture,* pp. 57–58, and for Pakistan (roads, drainage) in Thomas, "Rural Public Works," pp. 57, 68.

19. Although the potential use of special assessments in the rural areas of developing countries is discussed briefly in Wald, *Taxation of Agricultural Land,* pp. 221–223, his appraisal is overly negative because of the restrictive form of tax he assumes.

CHAPTER 8. SHIFTING AND INCIDENCE

1. Much of the discussion in this chapter is adapted from Wald, *Taxation of Agricultural Land,* chap. 5.

2. René Dumont, *Types of Rural Economy* (London: Methuen and Co., Ltd., 1957), pp. 1–2.

3. Anthony Bottomley, *Factor Pricing and Economic Growth in Underdeveloped Rural Areas* (London: Crosby Lockwood & Son, Ltd., 1971), chap. 6.

4. Bottomley, *Factor Pricing,* chap. 5.

5. Uma Lele, "Agricultural Price Policy," *Economic and Political Weekly,* IV (No. 35, August 30, 1969), 1–11.

6. Philip M. Raup, "The Contribution of Land Reforms to Economic Development: An Analytical Framework," *Economic Development and Cultural Change,* XII (October 1963), 1–21.

7. Peter Mieszkowski, "The Property Tax: An Excise Tax or A Profits Tax?", *Journal of Public Economics,* I (March 1972), 73–96.

8. See, for example, R. Stafford Smith, "Property Tax Capitalization in San Francisco," *National Tax Journal,* XXIII (June 1970), 177–193, and studies cited there (which all refer to the United States and mostly to urban areas).

9. J. D. Strasma, "Tributación de la agricultura," paper presented to Seminario Internacional sobre Tributación Agrícola, Santiago, Chile, November 1963.

10. For a fuller analysis along these lines, see Daniel M. Holland, "A Study of Land Taxation in Jamaica," in Becker, ed., *Land and Building Taxes,* pp. 279–280.

11. R. Albert Berry, "Presumptive Income Tax on Agricultural Land: The Case of Colombia," *National Tax Journal,* XXV (June 1972), 169–182.

12. See Bottomley, *Factor Pricing,* chaps. 2–3 (wages) and 9–15 (interest rates).

13. See, for example, Myrdal, *Asian Drama,* pp. 1065, 1326.

14. Michael Lipton, "Strategy for Agriculture: Urban Bias and Rural Planning," in Paul Streeten and Michael Lipton, eds., *The Crisis of Indian Planning* (London: Oxford University Press, 1968), p. 125.

15. Steven N. S. Cheung, *The Theory of Share Tenancy* (Chicago: University of Chicago Press, 1969). For a critique of some of the basic assump-

tions of Cheung's argument, see P. K. Bardhan and T. N. Srinivasan, "Cropsharing Tenancy in Agriculture: A Theoretical and Empirical Analysis," *American Economic Review*, LXI (March 1971), 48–64.

16. Bottomley, *Factor Pricing*, chap. 16.

CHAPTER 9. ECONOMIC EFFECTS OF LAND TAXATION

1. Myrdal, *Asian Drama*, p. 102.

2. John W. Mellor, *The Economics of Agricultural Development* (Ithaca, N.Y.: Cornell University Press, 1966), pp. 245–247.

3. Hunter, *Modernizing Peasant Societies*, p. 52.

4. As Bronislaw Malinowski, *Magic, Science and Religion* (New York: Doubleday Anchor Books, 1948), p. 29, points out, in addition to the well-known set of natural conditions affecting agriculture in the Trobriand Islands, "there is the domain of the inaccountable and adverse influences, as well as the great unearned increment of fortunate coincidence. The first conditions are coped with by knowledge and work, the second by magic."

5. Hunter, *Modernizing Peasant Societies*, p. 137.

6. Portions of this section, as well as some other passages in this chapter, are adapted from Wald, *Taxation of Agricultural Land*, chap. 8.

7. Although forest taxation is not treated explicitly in this study, it should be noted that there would seem no reason to treat forested land any differently from any other land use from the point of view of property taxation. In fact, rather than being specially penalized by an annual tax because it takes twelve to fifteen years more to produce salable timber, as is often claimed, forest owners are in a way uniquely favored by being able to choose the time and size of harvest—and they can also sell before harvesting if they choose to do so. Investing in forests is thus no different from any other form of agricultural investment and requires no special tax treatment unless, perhaps, one places considerable weight on the possible externalities produced by reforestation with respect to erosion. See Trestrail, "Forests and the Property Tax."

8. See Michael Lipton, "A Game against Nature: Strategies of Security," *Development Digest*, VII (No. 2, April 1969), 18–21, and Clifton R. Wharton, "Risk, Uncertainty, and the Subsistence Farmer," *ibid.*, pp. 3–10.

9. Raj Krishna, "Agricultural Price Policy and Economic Development," in Southworth and Johnston, eds., *Agricultural Development*, pp. 497–540.

10. See Behrman, *Supply Response in Underdeveloped Agriculture*, for an elaborate econometric study of Thailand, together with a summary of other relevant work.

11. Myrdal, *Asian Drama*, pp. 2140, 2158.

12. Lele, "Agricultural Price Policy."

13. Helleiner, "Agricultural Export Pricing Strategy in Tanzania."

14. The following argument is adapted from Rhoads and Bird, "The Valorization Tax in Colombia," in Becker, ed., *Land and Building Taxes*.

15. Bottomley, *Factor Pricing*, chaps. 2–3.

16. C. M. Elliott, "Agricultural and Economic Development in Africa: Theory and Experience 1880–1914," in Jones and Woolf, eds., *Agrarian Change and Economic Development*, p. 131.

17. For a valuable discussion of the appropriate way of organizing goods with different degrees of "publicness," see James M. Buchanan, *The De-*

mand and Supply of Public Goods (Chicago: Rand McNally, 1968), chap. 9; also R. M. Bird and D. G. Hartle, "The Design of Governments," in Bird and J. G. Head, eds., *Modern Fiscal Issues* (Toronto: University of Toronto Press, 1972), pp. 45–62.

18. Alan R. Prest, "The Role of Labour Taxes and Subsidies in Promoting Employment in Developing Countries," *International Labour Review*, CIII (No. 4, April 1971), 315–332.

19. Bird, *Taxation and Development*, chap. 4.

20. Swadesh Bose and Edwin H. Clark, "Some Basic Considerations on Agricultural Mechanization in West Pakistan," *Pakistan Development Review*, IX (Autumn 1969), 273–308.

21. The general arguments on this point in Bird, "Income Redistribution, Economic Growth, and Tax Policy," are germane here.

22. Berry, "Presumptive Income Tax on Agricultural Land."

23. Hunter, *Modernizing Peasant Agriculture*, p. 94.

24. See, for example, N. S. Shetty, "Agricultural Innovations: Leaders and Laggards," *Economic and Political Weekly* (August 17, 1968); reprinted in *Development Digest*, VII (No. 2, April 1969), 11–17.

25. Don Kanel, "Size of Farm and Economic Development," *Indian Journal of Agricultural Economics*, XXII (No. 2, April–June 1967), 26–44.

26. This concept is elaborated in Douglas Dosser, "Tax Incidence and Growth," *Economic Journal*, LXXI (September 1961), 572–591.

27. Unless there is a "Giffen effect" so that a rise in the price of the basic food items actually increases the amount spent on them.

CHAPTER 10. EQUITY ASPECTS OF TAXING LAND

1. Gandhi, *Tax Burden*, p. vii.

2. Sahota, "The Distribution of the Tax Burden in Brazil."

3. See especially Gandhi, *Tax Burden*; also Mathew, *Agricultural Taxation and Economic Development in India*.

4. Carl S. Shoup, *Public Finance* (Chicago: Aldine Publishing Company, 1969), chap. 1.

5. Mathew, *Agricultural Taxation*, p. 49.

6. Gandhi, "Taxes, Subsidies, and Agricultural Production"; the general policy implications of these later, more refined results are similar to those in Gandhi's earlier study. The depressed agricultural terms of trade owing to Indian trade and exchange rate policies were not, however, taken into account in these estimates.

7. See R. M. Bird, "A Note on 'Tax Sacrifice' Comparisons," *National Tax Journal*, XVII (September 1964), 303–308, and Henry Aaron, "Some Criticisms of Tax Burden Indices," *ibid.*, XVIII (September 1965), 313–316.

8. An extensive appraisal of equity aspects of land taxation may be found in Wald, *Taxation of Agricultural Land*, chap. 5. Although some portions of his text have been adapted for use in this chapter, it should be noted that the present argument does not agree with his emphasis on personalizing the land tax so as to make it coincide as closely as possible with each taxpayer's ability to pay.

9. See Richard M. Bird, "The Case for Taxing Personal Wealth," *Report*

of Proceedings of 23rd Tax Conference (Toronto: Canadian Tax Foundation, 1972), pp. 6–24.

10. Gold and Foster, "Measuring Equity in the Taxation of Agricultural Land."

11. Seligman, *Essays in Taxation*, p. 11.

12. See G. S. Sahota, *Indian Tax Structure and Economic Development* (Bombay: Asia Publishing House, 1961), pp. 12, 19.

13. Angus Maddison, "Social Development of Pakistan," paper presented to Conference of Development Advisory Service, Dubrovnik, June 1970, p. 23.

14. José Gimeno Sanz, "Taxation: Some Considerations Concerning Its Importance in the Economic Development of the Agricultural Sector," unpub. paper, Santiago, Chile, 1970, pp. 5–9.

15. See, for example, Tax Institute of America, *Tax Incentives* (Lexington, Mass.: Heath Lexington Books, 1971).

16. Chang, "Recent Experience of Establishing Land Value Taxation in Jamaica," in Woodruff, Brown and Lin, eds., *International Seminar*, p. 223.

17. Wald, "Taxation of Agriculture in Developing Countries," in Agarwala and Singh, eds., *Accelerating Development*, p. 468.

18. It is of course not possible in the case of low-income countries to offset the regressivity of the property tax by credits against income tax, as has been done in some parts of North America for certain taxpayers (see Kenneth E. Quindry and Billy D. Cook, "Humanization of the Property Tax for Low Income Households," *National Tax Journal*, XXII (September 1969), 357–367). Exemption is thus the only path open, despite its problems.

19. Joshi et al., *Studies*, p. 198; somewhat similar proposals are common in the literature: e.g., I. M. D. Little, "Tax Policy and the Third Plan," in P. N. Rosenstein-Rodan, ed., *Pricing and Fiscal Policies* (London: George Allen and Unwin, 1964), pp. 37–38; Mellor, *Economics of Agricultural Development*, p. 89; Taylor et al., *Fiscal Survey of Panama*, p. 79, etc. A more skeptical view may be found in Gandhi, *Tax Burden*, pp. 207–211. See also Chapter 11, below.

20. Joshi et al., *Studies*, p. 207.

21. Regmi, *Land Tenure*, I, 172.

22. Mason Gaffney, "The Property Tax is a Progressive Tax," in *Proceedings of the 64th Annual Conference on Taxation* (Columbus, Ohio: National Tax Association, 1972), pp. 408–426.

23. See Harley H. Hinrichs, "Certainty as Criterion: Taxation of Foreign Investment in Afghanistan," *National Tax Journal*, XV (June 1962), 139–154.

CHAPTER 11. LAND TAX ADMINISTRATION

1. See Stanley S. Surrey, "Tax Administration in Underdeveloped Countries," in Bird and Oldman, eds., *Readings on Taxation*, pp. 497–527; also Wald, *Taxation of Agricultural Land*, chap. 9.

2. See, for example, United Nations, "Report of the Seminar on Cadastre," Addis Ababa, 1970, E/CN.14/500, E/CN.14/CART/278; and "Final Report on the Land Tax Administration Seminar (Panama, 1970)," *CIAT Newsletter*, IV (No. 2, October 1971), pp. 1–18.

3. The following discussion is adapted from Wald, *Taxation of Agricultural Land*, pp. 47–50.

4. United Nations, *Manual of Land Tax Administration* (New York: Department of Economic and Social Affairs, United Nations, 1968), p. 12.

5. For a more detailed discussion, see the excellent report by Vera, *Agricultural Land Inventory Techniques;* also Frank Osterhoudt, "Land Titles in Northeast Brazil: The Use of Aerial Photography," *Land Economics*, XLI (November 1965), 387–392; and Drewes, "The Cadaster," in AID, *Spring Review of Land Reform*, Vol. XI.

6. A useful summary of AID-financed cadastral surveys has been compiled by Harley H. Hinrichs, "Tax Reform," Agency for International Development, Washington, 1970.

7. United Nations, *Manual*, pp. 108–109.

8. For this reason, Wald, *Taxation of Agricultural Land*, p. 56, makes a cogent argument for the use of the word "notional" instead of "presumptive," but the latter usage is now so firmly embedded in tax literature that it is employed here. (The next few paragraphs of the text are adapted from Wald, *ibid.*, pp. 56–59).

9. I.R.C. *v.* Crossman (1937), A.C.26 at p. 69, cited in A. A. Tait, *The Taxation of Personal Wealth* (Urbana: University of Illinois Press, 1967), pp. 158–159.

10. An excellent example is offered by Angus N. MacKay, *Appraisal Notes for the Assessor* (Toronto: Department of Municipal Affairs, 1968), which strongly stresses the desirability of the "most probable selling price" standard, *except* in the case of rural land for which values are to be estimated on the basis of 15 soil types and 4 to 5 gradations of 6 physical characteristics (topography, erosion, stoniness, drainage, depth to bedrock, and susceptibility to flooding).

11. Jarach, *El impuesto a la renta normal potencial de la tierra*, pp. 26–30. This proposal is almost identical to a tax proposed in Argentina in 1964 (see Chapter 5). See also the proposal for India outlined in Chapter 10.

12. R. P. Dore, "Sociological Aspects of Land Valuation and Land Reform," in: Woodruff, Brown, and Lin, eds., *International Seminar on Land Taxation*, p. 561.

13. See, especially, Musgrave and Gillis, *Fiscal Reform for Colombia*, p. 391; Gimeno Sanz, *La tributación agropecuaria*, chap. 14, notes a similar phenomenon in Chile.

14. For a rationale along these lines, see John M. Copes, "Reckoning with Imperfections in the Land Market," in Daniel M. Holland, ed., *The Assessment of Land Value* (Madison: University of Wisconsin Press, 1971), p. 67.

15. Many states and provinces provide preferential tax assessment for such properties in one form or another: see International Association of Assessing Officers, *Farmland Assessment Practices in the United States* (Chicago, 1969), and Peter W. House, *Opposing Views on Taxation of Land near Cities* (Washington, D.C.: U.S. Department of Agriculture, Economic Research Service, 1968).

16. In Becker, ed., *Land and Building Taxes*, pp. 180–181.

17. David Grether and Peter Mieszkowski, "Determinants of Real Estate

Values" (Multilith, 1971); also Ontario Department of Municipal Affairs, Assessment Standards Branch, *Multivariate Analysis and Residential Property Valuation in Ontario* (Toronto, 1970).

18. United Nations, *Manual*, chap. 11.

19. New Zealand Valuation Department, *A Critical Study of the Unimproved Value of Land* (Research Paper 68-1; Wellington, N.Z., 1968), esp. pp. 67–68.

20. New Zealand Valuation Department. *"Land Value" and Rating Incidence* (Research Paper 68-5; Wellington, N.Z., 1968), p. 5.

21. A. O. Hirschman, *Journeys Toward Progress* (New York: Twentieth Century Fund, 1963), p. 124.

22. A. C. Harberger, "Issues of Tax Reform for Latin America," in Joint Tax Program, *Fiscal Policy for Economic Growth*, p. 120; John Strasma, "Market Enforced Self-Assessment for Real Estate Taxes," *Bulletin for International Fiscal Documentation*, XIX (1965), 353–363, 397–414.

23. Musgrave and Gillis, *Fiscal Reform for Colombia*, p. 411: "In 1966, only 868 of 1.9 million rural parcels were valued on a self-assessment basis, several years after a limited program of self-assessment was initiated."

24. D. M. Holland and W. N. Vaughn, "An Evaluation of Self-Assessment under Property Tax," in A. D. Lynn, Jr., *The Property Tax and Its Administration* (Madison: University of Wisconsin Press, 1969), p. 112.

25. *Ibid.*, p. 113.

26. Shoup, *Public Finance*, p. 434.

27. This discussion is adapted from Wald, *Taxation of Agricultural Land*, pp. 167–174.

28. Cf. Shoup, *Public Finance*, pp. 431–434.

29. For some suggestive discussion of the design of penalty structures, see Oliver Oldman, "Controlling Income Tax Evasion," in Joint Tax Program, *Problems of Tax Administration in Latin America* (Baltimore: Johns Hopkins Press, 1965), pp. 316–343.

30. L. Harlan Davis, "Economics of the Property Tax in Rural Areas of Colombia," University of Wisconsin Land Tenure Center, Research Paper No. 25, 1967, pp. 113–114. The United Nations, *Manual*, p. 41, suggests a penalty of 1 percent per month is generally severe enough: the clear inadequacy of this deterrent to delinquency in many circumstances illustrates again the difficulty of laying down specific rules.

31. Bird, *Taxation and Development*, p. 163.

32. This section is adapted from Wald, *Taxation of Agricultural Land*, pp. 154–159.

33. The Korean experience is described in Haskell P. Wald, "The Recent Experience of the Republic of Korea with Tax Collections in Kind," in Wald and Froomkin, eds., *Agricultural Taxation*, pp. 424–431.

34. Lele, "Agricultural Price Policy," p. 1. Sahota, *Indian Tax Structure and Economic Development*, pp. 54–56, Mellor, *The Economics of Agricultural Development*, p. 90, and Cutt, *Taxation and Economic Development*, pp. 261–262, have all urged more use of in-kind collections in India, though Gandhi, *Tax Burden*, pp. 211–212 is skeptical of this idea.

35. This was reportedly one reason for the decline of in-kind collection in Nepal (Regmi, *Land Tenure*, I, chap. v.).

36. Albert Hirschman, *The Strategy of Economic Development* (New Haven, Conn.: Yale University Press, 1958), pp. 144–146, points out that more structured processes, even though more capital-intensive, reduce the latitude for poor performance and may therefore be justified. In the case of land tax administration, for example, computerized billing procedures might be justified in this fashion even in countries with widespread clerical unemployment.

37. Gold and Foster, "Measuring Equity in the Taxation of Agricultural Land."

PART FOUR. TAXING AGRICULTURAL LAND: AN APPRAISAL

CHAPTER 12. LAND REFORM AND LOCAL GOVERNMENT

1. Myrdal, *Asian Drama*, p. 1367.

2. Cf. Bird, "Income Redistribution, Economic Growth, and Tax Policy."

3. William C. Thiesenhusen and Marion B. Brown, *Survey of the Alliance for Progress: Problems of Agriculture.* A study prepared at the request of the Subcommittee on American Republics Affairs of the Committee on Foreign Relations, U.S. Senate (Washington, D.C.: Government Printing Office, 1967), p. 15.

4. Bottomley, *Factor Pricing and Economic Growth*, chap. 18.

5. Jerome T. French and Princeton N. Lyman, "Emerging Problems: Social and Political Implications of the New Cereal Varieties," *Development Digest*, VII (No. 4, October 1969), pp. 111–118.

6. Peter Dorner, Marion Brown, and Don Kanel, "Land Tenure and Reform," p. 10. Similar views are put forward in many other Land Tenure Center publications.

7. Erven J. Long, "Summing up of Preceding Sessions," in A.I.D., *Spring Review of Land Reform: Findings and Implications for A.I.D.*, No. AID-5D-LR. 70-13, p. 20.

8. Hunter, *Modernizing Peasant Societies*, p. 152.

9. Hirschman, *Journeys Toward Progress*, pp. 121–127.

10. Hunter, *Modernizing Peasant Societies*, p. 180.

11. Doreen Warriner, *Land Reform in Principle and Practice*, illustrates the truth of this statement through extended case studies in different parts of the world, as do many of the studies included in the A.I.D. *Spring Review of Land Reform*.

12. See the extended summary of the relevant legislation in United Nations, *Progress in Land Reform, Fourth Report* (New York, 1966), pp. 7–17.

13. Warriner, *Land Reform in Principle and Practice*, p. 232. Miss Warriner argues elsewhere that another problem with land reform in Latin America is simple ignorance. In her rather strongly worded terms: "What the arrogantly sophisticated educated class seems to need most, if politicians and officials are to be equal to their functions, is advanced education in the agricultural sciences. Again and again, in interviews with revolutionaries and officials, one was reminded that they do not even know that there is such a thing as good farming, because they have never seen it." (*Ibid.*, p. 372).

14. Dumont, *Types of Rural Economy*, for example, cites Italy, Spain, and Morocco in this connection.

15. Américo Sanchez Cardenas, "La reforma agraria en Ecuador: una prioridad desatendida," *Comercio Exterior*, XX (No. 5, May 1970), 400–404.

16. Charles T. Stewart, Jr., "Land Reform as Fiscal Policy for Agrarian Nations," *Social Research*, XXXII (1965), 98–109.

17. Tait, *Taxation of Personal Wealth*, chap. 6, argues that such levies raise substantial problems of equity and practicality, but his criticisms seem considerably less cogent in the circumstances of poor agrarian countries in which there is a sharp dichotomy between the landed wealthy and the landless or virtually landless peasant.

18. United Nations, *Progress in Land Reform, Fourth Report*, p. 159.

19. Raup, "The Contribution of Land Reforms to Agricultural Development."

20. John Strasma, "Financiamiento de la reforma agraria en el Peru," *El Trimestre Económico*, XXXII (July–September 1965), 484–500.

21. This paragraph draws on papers by James R. Brown, "World Land Reform Conference," pp. 87–122, and Yitzchak Abt, "Institutional Approach to Agrarian Programs and Related Tax Problems," pp. 524–555, in Woodruff, Brown, and Lin, eds., *International Seminar on Land Taxation*, as well as the Third and Fourth U.N. reports on land reform.

22. Mellor, *The Economics of Agricultural Development*, pp. 86–88, 393.

23. Myrdal, *Asian Drama*, p. 876.

24. *Ibid.*, p. 859.

25. Edel, "The Colombian Community Action Program: An Economic Evaluation."

26. See Herman Felstenhausen, "Economic Knowledge, Participation and Farmer Decision Making in a Developed and an Under-developed Country," *International Journal of Agrarian Affairs*, V (No. 4, July 1968), 263–281; also see David McClelland, *The Achieving Society* (New York: Free Press, 1967), pp. 431–437.

27. Persuasive general argument along similar lines may be found in W. Arthur Lewis, "Planning Public Expenditure," in Max F. Millikan, ed., *National Economic Planning* (New York: Columbia University Press, 1967), pp. 201–227. See also Wolfgang F. Stolper, *Planning without Facts* (Cambridge, Mass.: Harvard University Press, 1966), p. 12. Stolper (like Edel) also stresses the advantage of special local knowledge in coping with local needs and problems.

28. The efforts of the Joint-Legislative Executive Tax Commission in the Philippines to introduce "tax education" at very low levels in the school system constitute a commendable response along these lines.

29. For a more extended argument along these lines, focusing on urban areas, see Bird, *Taxation and Development*, Chap. 5.

30. R. Stafford Smith and Theodore M. Smith, "The Political Economy of Regional and Urban Revenue Policy in Indonesia," *Asian Survey*, XI (August 1971), 761–786.

1. Carlos F. Diaz Alejandro, *Essays on the Economic History of the Argentine Republic* (New Haven, Conn.: Yale University Press, 1970), chap. 6.

2. Bird, *Taxation and Development*, pp. 124–131; see also Chapter 9, above.

3. See the evidence for Brazil cited in Werner Baer and Isaac Kerstenetzky, "The Brazilian Economy in the Sixties," in Riordan Roett, ed., *Brazil in the Sixties* (Nashville, Tenn.: Vanderbilt University, 1972).

4. See the cogent doubts in Werner Baer, "Import Substitution Industrialization in Latin America: Experiences and Interpretations," *Latin American Research Review* (February 1972), 107–108.

5. Almost none of the questions raised twenty years ago at the Harvard Conference on Agricultural Taxation and Economic Development have yet been answered; for example, see Wald and Froomkin, eds., *Agricultural Taxation and Economic Development*, pp. 31–56, for an impressive list of problems requiring research. A very similar list was recently put forth by Ward, "Where to Now? The Future for Research and the Possibilities for Fiscal Innovating in Development Policy."

6. Johnston and Mellor, "The Role of Agriculture," p. 579. Gandhi, *Tax Burden*, p. 8, appears to consider this an important factor even in India, where all these issues have been explicitly discussed for years.

7. Jagdish Bhagwati, *The Economics of Underdeveloped Countries* (New York: McGraw-Hill, 1966), p. 78; emphasis in original.

8. Kaldor, *Essays on Economic Policy*, I, xviii; also his "Will Underdeveloped Countries Learn to Tax?" *ibid.*, pp. 262–265.

9. Wald, "Taxation of Agriculture in Developing Countries," in Agarwala and Singh, eds., *Accelerating Investment*, pp. 168–169. Another example of the administrative demands of taxes of this variety may be found in Chapter 11, above.

10. Wald, "Taxation of Agriculture in Developing Countries," in Agarwala and Singh, eds., *Accelerating Investment*, p. 169.

11. José Gimeno Sanz, "Taxation," pp. 13–15. See also Gimeno Sanz, *La tributación agropecuaria.*

12. See Albert O. Hirschman, *Exit, Voice and Loyalty* (Cambridge, Mass.: Harvard University Press, 1970).

13. See, for example, the discussion in Chapter 12, above, and in Bird, *Taxation and Development*, chap. 5; also Per Eklund, "Taxation and Earmarking in Developing Countries," IBRD Economics Department Working Paper No. 43, April 1969.

14. Clawson, Landsberg, and Alexander, *The Agricultural Potential of the Middle East*, p. 108.

15. Some of which are explored in my "Optimal Tax Policy," and, in a very different context, in my "The Tax Kaleidoscope: Perspectives on Tax Reform in Canada," *Canadian Tax Journal*, XVIII (September–October 1970), 444–473.

16. See Charles E. Lindblom, *The Policy-Making Process* (Englewood Cliffs, N.J.: Prentice-Hall, 1969). See also Herbert Simon, *Administrative Behavior* (2nd ed., New York: Free Press, 1957) for similar ideas in a different context. A general philosophical argument against holistic plan-

ning of reforms may be found in K. R. Popper, *The Poverty of Historicism* (London: Routledge & Kegan Paul, 1957).

17. Lindblom, *The Policy-Making Process*, p. 27.

18. See Edmundo Flores, "Issues of Land Reform," p. 904. See also the discussion of the Mexican case in Chapter 6.

INDEX

Absentees, taxes on, 95, 96, 221

Administration: of export tax, 47; of marketing tax, 53, 233–234, 248, 250; of tithe, 53–54; favors large farms, 198, 239, 266; of land taxes, 223–255; cost, 246–248. *See also* Aerial survey; Appeals; Appraisal; Cadastre; Centralization; Evasion; In rem taxes; Local assessment committees; Self-assessment; Size coefficient; Tax farming

Aerial survey, 103, 107, 147, 228, 229, 249

Afghanistan, 50, 69

Agricultural income tax, 39, 54, 135. *See also* Income tax; Presumptive taxation

Agricultural pricing strategy, 51

Agricultural surplus, taxation, 3–4, 7–8, 9–10. *See also* Capital transfer; Food supply; Intersectoral resource flow; Labor supply; Marketed surplus; Migration

Annual value tax, 150–152, 153, 154, 232, 233. *See also* Capital value tax; Rental value concept

Antiquity, land tax in, 67

Appeals, 87, 245–246

Appraisal, 230, 233, 241. *See also* Cadastre; Standard assessments; Yardstick farms

Area-based land tax, 145–147; in Liberia, 68; in Nepal, 69; in Bolivia, 92, 93–94; in Uruguay, 96; in India, 131, 133; effects, 146, 147, 188, 210; classified, 146-147, 222, 224, 229, 232; administration, 146–147,

226, 232, 233, 234, 247

Argentina, 49, 100, 276

Assessment, *see* Appraisal; Cadastre

Australia, 106, 241

Benefit taxation, 57, 146, 162, 192, 286. *See also* Community development; Earmarking; Expenditures; Special assessments

Betterment levy, 67, 136. *See also* Special assessments

Bogotá, 158

Bolivia, 57, 73, 89–94

Brazil, 45, 100–101, 207

Britain, 121; influence on India, 129–132

Burma, 43, 48, 243, 329n

Cadastre, 86, 102, 104, 107, 225–231; in Turkey, 68; in Ethiopia, 69; in Taiwan, 70; in Panama, 85–86, 228, 335n12; in Uruguay, 97, 98, 99; in Brazil, 101; in Chile, 103, 104, 228, 337n47; in Jamaica, 106, 107; in Japan, 114, 117; in India, 132. *See also* Aerial survey; Index adjustment; Urban fringe land; Yardstick farms

Cameroon, 62

Capital gains tax, 72–73, 92, 157, 240. *See also* Transfer taxes

Capital levy, 67, 265, 353n17; in Mexico, 125, 127, 298

Capital transfer, 4, 5–6, 7–8, 19–22. *See also* Agricultural surplus

Capital value tax, 152–156, 222, 224, 247. *See also* Annual value tax;

356

Innovation, tax effects on, 177–178, 184–186, 187, 189, 196. *See also* Risk-taking

Inputs, agricultural, 74, 185–186

Integration, of different taxes, 92, 93, 99, 349n18

Intersectoral equity, 5, 11. *See also* Equity; Tax burden

Intersectoral resource flow, 7–8, 120, 123, 124–126, 136–137, 139, 169. *See also* Agricultural surplus; Capital transfer; Food supply; Labor supply; Tax burden

Investment, tax effects on, 169, 197. *See also* Effects of taxes; Incentives

Invisible improvements, 106, 242–243. *See also* Improvements; Site value tax

Iran, 39, 64

Iraq, 54, 217

Ishikawa, Shigeru, 120

Israel, 72

Istihlak, 54

Italy, 65, 139

Jamaica, 106–109, 218

Japan: as common example, 8, 25, 40, 75; the Meiji experience, 112, 113–122, 141, 200, 201, 339n3, 340n13

Johnston, Bruce F., 6, 17

Joshi, T. M., 218–220

Kaldor, Nicholas, 9, 282

Keynes, J. M., 12

Kind, taxation in, 35, 66, 70, 115, 116, 117, 251–254. *See also* Labor tax

Korea, 35, 70–71, 253, 334n71

Labor supply, tax effects on, 15–17, 193–195. *See also* Migration; Population

Labor tax, 55–57, 332n41. *See also* Poll tax

Land income tax, 35, 65–66. *See also* Income tax; Tithe

Land prices, tax effects on, 10, 172–174, 205, 266

Land redistribution, tax effects on, 10, 11

Land reform, 20–21, 81, 199–200, 259–262, 352n13; and land taxes, 10, 105, 173, 262–267; in Bolivia, 90–94; in Mexico, 124–128 passim; in India, 133, 135

Land revenue, *see* India, land taxes

Land tenure, *see* Communal land ten-

ure; Land reform; Titles, land

Land value increment tax, 67, 72, 157. *See also* Special assessments

Land value tax, *see* Site value tax

Landes, David, 120

Landlords, 163–164. *See also* Incidence

Latifundia, 80–81, 180, 264. *See also* Concentration, land

Latin America, 77–81. *See also* individual countries

Lewis, Stephen, 7

Lewis, W. Arthur, 4, 7, 128, 323n6

Liberia, 68

Lindholm, Charles, 289

Liquidity effect of taxes, 119, 192. *See also* Effects of taxes; Incentives

Livestock tax, 52, 69. *See also* Cattle tax

Local assessment committees, 62, 66, 227, 230, 251, 254, 353n27. *See also* Centralization

Local government, 58, 60, 61, 62, 267–272, 293, 294

Local taxes, 52, 53, 70–71, 96, 108–109, 124, 147, 186, 206, 251

Location, as value factor, 238

Mahalawari system, 131

Malawi, 58

Market, agriculture as, 22

Market value, as tax base, 152, 153, 154, 233, 234, 236–237, 350n10. *See also* Capital value tax

Marketed surplus, tax effects on, 8–9, 55, 170, 189–190, 202. *See also* Agricultural surplus

Marketing boards, 39, 43, 44–45, 48, 50

Marketing tax, 36, 37, 39, 52–55, 170, 188, 190, 202, 273; administration of, 53, 233–234, 248, 250

Medellín, 161–162

Meiji model, *see* Japan

Mellor, John, 17, 267

Mexico, 44, 52, 90, 97, 124–129, 289, 341n34; as model, 112, 200, 122–123, 127–128. *See also* Dualistic agriculture; Green Revolution

Migration, 6–17, 19, 78, 196, 205. *See also* Labor supply; Population

Mill, James, 130

Minimum land value, as tax base, 85. *See also* Area-based land tax

Models, critique of, 11–14, 25. *See also* Dualistic model; Fei-Ranis model; Harrod-Domar model

Turkey, 68; in Panama, 84–85, 228; in Bolivia, 91; in Brazil, 101; in Chile, 103; in Japan, 118; in Colombia, 243–244, 351n23

Seligman, E. R. A., 10, 74

Sharecropping, 177–178. *See also* Tithe

Sheahan, John, 128

Shifting cultivation, 39

Shifting of land taxes: intrasectoral, 163–164, 171–179; intersectoral, 165–171

Shoup, Carl, 245

Sierra Leone, 332n55

Simons, Henry, 97

Sind, 134

Site value tax, 96, 103, 106–107, 109, 155, 191–192, 203, 241–243. *See also* Improvements

Size coefficient, 239, 266

Slack, 7, 8–10, 18

Sliding scale: export tax, 43, 44; land tax, 134

Sociological framework, 194, 195, 237. *See also* Incentives, response to

Spain, 217

Special assessments, 74, 157–162, 183, 191–193, 238, 286, 345n16, 346n19

Squatters, 86. *See also* Titles, land

Stamp tax, 73

Standard assessments, 65, 66. *See also* Cadastre; Yardstick farms

Strasma, John, 243

Substitution effect, 194. *See also* Effects of taxes; Incentives

Sudan, 54, 333n67

Taiwan, 35, 70, 122

Tanzania, 20, 44, 50, 52, 63, 189, 329n8

Tax burden: studies, 11, 32, 207–209, 280, 287; in Bolivia, 92, 94; in Uruguay, 98; in Chile, 102; in Japan, 115, 116, 119; in Mexico, 123, 124; in India, 136–137; in Tanzania, 329n8

Tax consciousness, 67, 93–94, 225, 269, 270, 353n28

Tax design, 25–28, 41. *See also* Policy matrix

Tax farming, 53–54, 86, 129. *See also* Zamindars

Tax reform, 267, 286, 288

Tax riots, 116, 117, 332n55, 340n20

Taxable capacity, 11, 207, 208

Technique, choice of, *see* Factor mix; Innovation

Tenants, 98, 163–164. *See also* Incidence

Thailand, 16, 33, 43, 46–48, 71, 187

Tithe, 53–54, 148, 177–178, 183, 186, 198, 202, 234, 331n36; in Turkey, 67, 68; in Ethiopia, 69; in Japan, 115, 118; in India, 131

Titles, land, 85, 86, 91, 92, 93, 213. *See also* Administration; Cadastre; Communal land tenure; In rem tax

Tokugawa land tax, *see* Japan

Transfer taxes, 67, 70, 72–74, 97, 221. *See also* Capital gains tax

Turkey, 53–54, 56–57, 67–68

Uganda, 62–63

Unearned increment, 130, 156, 157. *See also* Special assessments

Unexploited land, *see* Idle lands tax

Unimproved value, 242–243. *See also* Site value tax

United Nations, 91, 105, 106, 229

United States, 25, 254

Unutilized resources, *see* Slack

Urban fringe land, 108, 154, 232, 240–241

Uruguay, 94–100, 151, 215–217

Valorization tax, 158–162. *See also* Special assessments

Valuation of land, 106, 231–246. *See also* Market value

Vietnam, North, 66

Village tax, *see* Collective assessment

Wage rates, 175–176, 193–194

Wald, Haskell P., 5, 41, 93, 105, 145, 209, 218, 283–284

Water, as value factor, 238. *See also* Special assessments

Wealth tax, 67, 155, 209–210. *See also* Capital levy; Net wealth tax

Woodruff, Archibald, 241

World Bank, 106

Yardstick farms, 65, 149, 229, 230, 232. *See also* Cadastre

Yugoslavia, 217

Zaire, 61

Zakat, 331n36. *See also* Tithe

Zambia, 57–58

Zamindars, 129, 130, 135